THE
Automobile

FIVE–VIEW PHOTOGRAPHS · **250** CLASSIC CARS

General Editor: Craig Cheetham

amber
BOOKS

First published in 2007 by
Amber Books Ltd
Bradley's Close
74–77 White Lion Street
London N1 9PF
United Kingdom
www.amberbooks.co.uk

Reprinted in 2008

ISBN 978-1-905704-65-1

Printed and bound in Thailand

10 9 8 7 6 5 4 3 2

THE Automobile

CONTENTS

INTRODUCTION

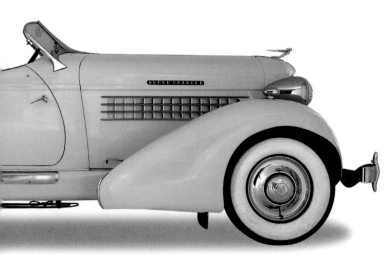

Auburn **SPEEDSTER**

Alfa **ROMEO 8C 2300**

Many great inventions arose from the industrial revolution, but one has had more of a social and economic impact than any other. That invention is the automobile – a machine that started life as a substitute for the humble horse, yet quickly became a symbol of emancipation for the masses. It offered the freedom to travel across land, in whichever direction you wanted, at your own timetable – a freedom that we take for granted today, yet which transformed the lives of many throughout the twentieth century.

This book celebrates the vehicles that changed the world. From the cars created by the pioneers of the global auto industry, to the latest and greatest performance models which have become icons of our generation, this book gets under the skin of the world's finest motor cars. These pages feature cars from all eras, including machines from the early days of motoring, such as the Ford Model T and Willys Knight, through the excesses of the pre-depression era, when Hollywood dictated a new breed of super sedan. Vehicles as excessive as the Duesenberg SJ, Auburn Speedster and Mercedes 540K, marvellously beautiful, frighteningly expensive and reserved for stars and moguls.

The story continues through the 1940s and 1950s, when car design evolved at such a pace that it was possible to identify a car's country of origin from its style. America had fins, the U.K. had curves, and Italy was then, as it is now, the automotive styling capital of the world, with a series of top companies providing

Plymouth **HEMI 'CUDA**

Vector W8-M12

designs for names as romantic as Ferrari, Maserati and Lamborghini.

As the Fifties gave way to the Sixties, a whole new style emerged. Cleaner, squarer and less elaborate, the Sixties was nonetheless a decade of great technological advances. As well as being the era of the incredible breed that was the muscle car, the decade saw the first use of features such as anti-lock brakes, fuel injection and engine management systems – all of which we take for granted today.

But it's not just older cars that fire the emotions. Even in the fuel-starved Seventies there were some fabulous, classic designs, the Eighties saw the birth of the supercar, and even in more recent times there have been some truly inspirational designs.

This book celebrates all of these, from early legends such as the Rolls-Royce Silver Ghost and Bugatti Royale, to some of the world's best-loved classics like the original Mini, or the Chevy Corvette.

What's more, the five-view photography in this book allows you to see each of these all-time greats from every angle to appreciate the intricacies and details of their design. Backed up by detailed technical specifications and essential details on the mechanics and styling of each car, this book takes you on a journey through motoring, allowing you to feel the character of 250 of the world's most inspirational motor cars. Enjoy the ride!

Saab 99 TURBO

Renault SPORT SPIDER

AC ACECA 🇬🇧

AC is undoubtedly one of the great British sports car names and the Aceca's all-around quality balanced the company's reputation. It boasted a design and build quality of great integrity.

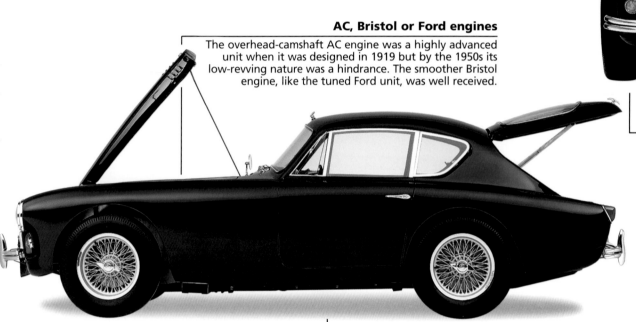

AC, Bristol or Ford engines
The overhead-camshaft AC engine was a highly advanced unit when it was designed in 1919 but by the 1950s its low-revving nature was a hindrance. The smoother Bristol engine, like the tuned Ford unit, was well received.

Simple but effective chassis
Tojeiro's chassis is a very simple twin-tube affair, combining light weight with clever suspension. It efficiency and simple design made it ideal for competition use

Wooden frame
The bodywork is made of aluminum panels but underneath it lies a complex framework composed partly of steel tubes and partly of ash—strong but light.

Practical cabin
Unlike the basic roadster form of the Ace, the Aceca was designed to be a practical GT car. As such, it has a large luggage platform behind the seats that can be accessed from inside the cabin or the tailgate.

Italian-inspired styling

For the Aceca, AC closely examined the Touring body on the Ferrari 195 coupe. Most pundits recognized the Aceca as superbly proportioned and correctly styled.

All-independent suspension

The Ace/Aceca was the first British sports car to gain independent suspension on all four wheels. Its handling is much superior to that of rivals with rigid rear-axles.

Dunlop wire wheels

Elegant and classically sporty Dunlop center-lock wire wheels are standard. Their generous diameter (at 16 inches) is typical of the time.

Specifications
1955 AC Aceca

ENGINE

Type: In-line six-cylinder

Construction: Aluminum cylinder block and head

Valve gear: Two valves per cylinder operated by a single chain-driven overhead camshaft

Bore and stroke: 2.56 in. x 3.94 in.

Displacement: 1,991 cc

Compression ratio: 8.0:1

Induction system: Three SU carburetors

Maximum power: 90 bhp at 4,500 rpm

Maximum torque: 110 lb-ft at 2,500 rpm

Top speed: 104 mph

0–60 mph: 9.4 sec.

TRANSMISSION

Four-speed manual

BODY/CHASSIS

Separate chassis with aluminum two-door coupe body

SPECIAL FEATURES

While the Ace roadster has a flat windshield, the Aceca benefits from curved glass.

The Aceca's rear tailgate enhances GT practicality considerably.

RUNNING GEAR

Steering: Cam gear

Front suspension: Dual wishbones with transverse leaf spring and telescopic shock absorbers

Rear suspension: Dual wishbones with transverse leaf spring and telescopic shock absorbers

Brakes: Drums (front and rear)

Wheels: Wire, 16-in. dia.

Tires: 5.50 x 16 in.

DIMENSIONS

Length: 153.5 in. **Width:** 61.0 in.

Height: 52.0 in. **Wheelbase:** 90.0 in.

Track: 50.0 in. (front and rear)

Weight: 2,156 lbs.

AC **COBRA 289**

The AC Cobra is the most legendary U.S. sports car ever manufactured. American muscle combined with a lightweight British sports car body to produce a fast machine. On the track it was almost unbeatable.

Ford V8

Ford agreed to supply Carroll Shelby with its V8 engines for use in the Cobra. Cast into the aluminum valve covers were 'Cobra' and 'Powered by Ford.' The 289 small-block engine produced a very healthy 271 bhp but was light enough not to upset the handling.

Manual transmission

Mated to the Ford V8 engine was a Borg-Warner four-speed manual transmission. A Salisbury final drive and limited-slip differential were also standard.

Sports body

The only body option offered for the Cobra was an open sports style shell with a removable soft-top. The coupe option of the earlier Aceca was not carried over.

AC chassis

John Tojeiro and John Cooper had built various racing chassis in the early 1950s and the design was adapted to sit under the AC Ace. With surprisingly little modification, this large-diameter twin-tube ladder frame was carried over for the Cobra.

Disc brakes

While the old Ace was equipped with drum brakes, the extra performance of the V8 engine led to the sensible fitment of four-wheel disc brakes.

Wire wheels

72-spoke wire wheels with knock off hubs were standard on all 289 Cobras.

Specifications

1963 Shelby Cobra 289

ENGINE

Type: V8

Construction: Cast-iron cylinder block and cylinder heads

Valve gear: Two valves per cylinder operated by single camshaft with pushrods and rockers

Bore and stroke: 4.00 in. x 2.87 in.

Displacement: 289 c.i.

Compression ratio: 10.5:1

Induction system: Single Holley four-barrel carburetor

Maximum power: 271 bhp at 5,750 rpm

Max torque: 285 lb-ft at 4,500 rpm

Top speed: 140 mph

0–60 mph: 5.5 sec

TRANSMISSION
Four-speed close ratio manual

BODY/CHASSIS
Separate chassis with two-door body in aluminum

SPECIAL FEATURES

The soft-top has a slightly clumsy look to it when up.

The discrete badge just above the cooling vent is the only real clue to the Ford engine.

RUNNING GEAR

Steering: Rack-and-pinion

Front suspension: Wishbones with transverse leaf spring and shocks

Rear suspension: Wishbones with transverse leaf spring and shocks

Brakes: Discs (front and rear)

Wheels: Wire 15-in. dia.

Tires: 6.5 x 15 or 6.7 x 15

DIMENSIONS

Length: 151.5 in.	**Width:** 63.0 in.
Height: 48.0 in.	**Wheelbase:** 90.0 in.

Track: 51.5 in. (front), 52.5 in. (rear)

Weight: 2,020 lbs.

Alfa ROMEO 6C 1750

There are some ordinary, even dull-looking 1750s, but the convertibles by Zagato, Touring, and Castagna are among the most perfectly styled and proportioned sports cars ever made.

Supercharger

The 1750's twin-cam layout guarantees power, but for real performance Alfa added a Roots-type supercharger. This is driven off the crankshaft at the front of the engine.

Separate chassis

There was much more development in engines than in the chassis in the 1930s, so the 1750's basic boxed-section chassis is little changed from that found on the earlier 1500.

Twin-cam engine

This 1.75-liter, in-line six is the engine that really started Alfa's great twin-cam reputation.

Four-speed transmission

All 1750s have a four-speed transmission mounted in line with the engine. Early cars have crash boxes, but from the sixth series cars of 1933, there is synchromesh on third and fourth gears.

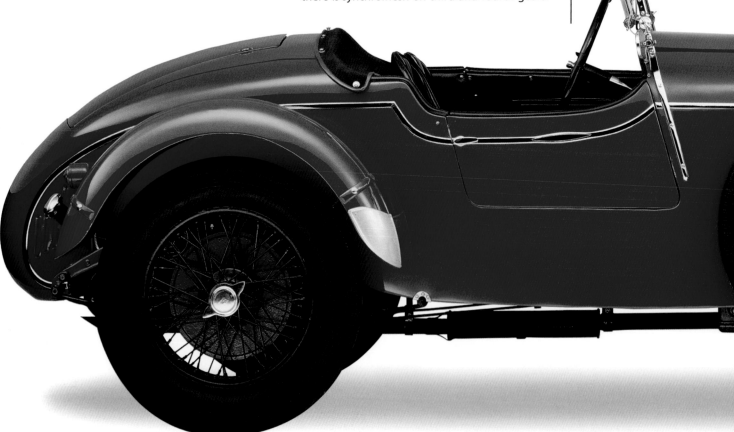

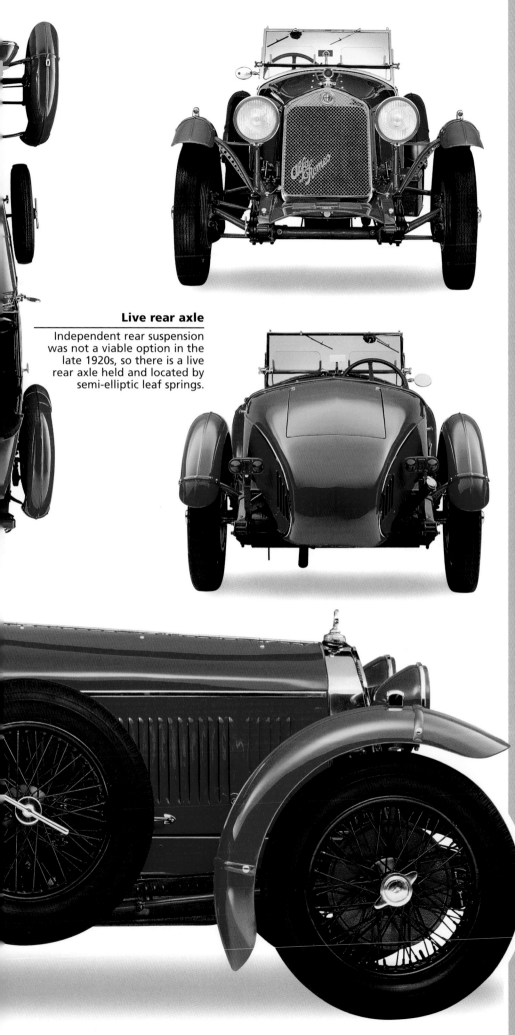

Live rear axle

Independent rear suspension was not a viable option in the late 1920s, so there is a live rear axle held and located by semi-elliptic leaf springs.

Specifications
1932 Alfa Romeo 6C 1750 Super Sport

ENGINE

Type: In-line six cylinder

Construction: Cast-iron block and head, with alloy crankcase and sump

Valve gear: Two valves per cylinder operated by double gear-driven overhead camshafts via adjustable tappets

Bore and stroke: 2.56 in. x 3.46 in.

Displacement: 1,752 cc

Compression ratio: 5.0:1

Induction system: Single Memini carburetor with mechanical Roots-type supercharger

Maximum power: 85 bhp at 4,500 rpm

Maximum torque: N/A

Top speed: 95 mph

0–60 mph: 14.0 sec.

TRANSMISSION

Four-speed manual

BODY/CHASSIS

Separate steel channel-section chassis frame with choice of coachbuilt bodywork

SPECIAL FEATURES

A rumble seat is used to carry additional passengers.

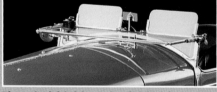

The windshield can be folded forward for competition use.

RUNNING GEAR

Steering: Worm-and-wheel

Front suspension: Beam axle with semi-elliptic leaf springs and adjustable friction shock absorbers

Rear suspension: Live axle with torque tube, semi-elliptic leaf springs, and adjustable friction shock absorbers

Brakes: Finned alloy drums, 12.6-in. dia.

Wheels: Rudge Whitworth center fixing knock-on/off wire spoke, 18-in. dia.

Tires: 5.00 x 18

DIMENSIONS

Length: 156.0 in. **Width:** 65.0 in.

Height: 55.6 in. **Wheelbase:** 108.0 in.

Track: 54.3 in. (front and rear)

Weight: 2,072 lbs.

Alfa ROMEO 8C 2300

The 8C 2300 was a masterpiece by one of Alfa Romeo's greatest designers, Vittorio Jano. In the early 1930s there was nothing to match its supercharged performance on Europe's great road races.

Twin-cam engine

The Alfa needed a long hood to house the alloy straight-eight engine with its two gear-driven overhead camshafts, which gave an excellent 142 bhp at 5,200 rpm.

Cutaway doors

Doors on cars such as the Alfa were cut away because drivers needed the room for their elbows when steering and higher doors would have got in the way in such narrow cockpits.

Hood straps

The hood has conventional latches but many of the roads on which the Alfas raced were rough and bumpy and straps avoided the chance of the hood flying open at high speed.

Knock-on wheels

Punctures were common in the Alfa's day and the wire wheels were designed to be changed very quickly. The big center nut could be knocked on or off quickly with a soft hammer to release the wheel.

Tool box

The battery box on one side was mirrored by the tool box on the other. Tools were a must as cars of this era needed constant maintenance and adjustment.

Quick release fuel filler

Quick release fuel caps were used so race mechanics could flip them open immediately and pour fuel in from large drums.

Fold-flat windshield

For racing the windshield could be folded flat, slightly reducing the frontal area of the car and thus increasing its speed.

Battery box

Because the eight-cylinder engine takes up all the under-hood space, the battery is mounted in a separate box behind the driver's door.

Four-speed transmission

Even in the 1930s Alfas had four-speed transmissions while more ordinary cars had just three. There was no synchromesh, however, so the driver had to be skilled in matching engine revs to gear shifts.

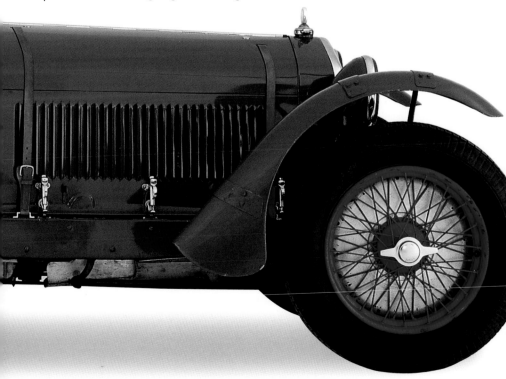

Specifications
1932 Alfa Romeo 8C 2300

ENGINE

Type: In-line eight cylinder
Construction: Alloy block and head with cast-iron liners
Valve gear: Two valves per cylinder operated by two gear-driven overhead cams
Bore and stroke: 2.56 in. x 3.33 in.
Displacement: 2,336 cc
Compression ratio: 5.75:1
Induction system: Single Memini updraft carburetor with Roots-type supercharger
Maximum power: 142 bhp at 5,200 rpm
Maximum torque: Not quoted
Top speed: 106 mph
0–60 mph: 9.4 sec.

TRANSMISSION

Four-speed manual

BODY/CHASSIS

Ladder frame chassis is three lengths and choice of coach-built bodywork

SPECIAL FEATURES

Much of the Alfa's power comes from the Roots-type supercharger which, like the overhead cams, is driven by the crankshaft.

Alfa's finned-alloy brakes fill the wheel rim and were very effective for their day.

RUNNING GEAR

Steering: Worm-and-wheel
Front suspension: Solid beam axle with semi-elliptic leaf springs and single friction shocks
Rear suspension: Live axle with semi-elliptic leaf springs and two friction shocks per side
  Brakes: Drums, 15.5 in. dia. (front and rear), rod operated
  Wheels: Wire spoke, 19-in. dia.
  Tires: 5.5 in. x 19 in.

DIMENSIONS*

Length: 156 in.   **Width:** 65 in.
Wheelbase: 107.9 in.   **Height:** 44.2 in.
Track: 54 in. (front and rear)
Weight: 2,464 lbs.
*Vary according to body fitted, Figures for short chassis model

Alfa Romeo SPIDER

There's always been a convertible Spider sports car in Alfa's model line, but this was the first front-wheel drive model, launched in 1995. Alfa managed the change perfectly—the new car delivered all the enthusiast could expect.

Strut front suspension

Sports cars like Alfas traditionally had double wishbone front suspension, but the Spider shows the same results can be achieved with simpler struts.

Tiny convertible top

The upswept rear lines of the Spider mean the convertible top is actually very small.

Transverse engine

The Spider is the first Alfa sports car to have the engine mounted transversely.

Twin-spark

Naturally, the Alfa has a twin-cam engine with two spark plugs for each cylinder, an approach Alfa used in some of its racing cars in the 1960s.

Anti-lock brakes

ABS is standard and works in conjunction with four-wheel disc brakes. Larger Brembo units are fitted to the more powerful and heavier V6 version of the mechanically similar GTV.

Leather trimmed

The Alfa is a luxury convertible as well as a sports car, and the interior and seats are leather trimmed.

Rigid top cover

The Spider's looks would have been spoiled with an untidy top staked behind the seats, so it's hidden away under a rigid panel.

Rear light strip

Like the Fiat Coupe, the Spider has a high rear end, but the rear light strip right across the back of the car minimizes the effect.

Multi-link rear suspension

The Spider's multi-link system gives precise wheel control, good handling and a good ride.

Specifications
1997 Alfa Romeo Spider

ENGINE

Type: In-line four cylinder
Construction: Iron block, alloy head
Valve gear: Four valves per cylinder operated by twin overhead camshafts
Bore and stroke: 3.27 in. x 3.58 in.
Displacement: 1,970 cc
Compression ratio: 9.5:1
Induction system: Electronic fuel injection
Maximum power: 150 bhp at 6,200 rpm
Maximum torque: 137 lb-ft at 4,000 rpm

TRANSMISSION

Five-speed manual

BODY/CHASSIS

Unitary steel construction with two-door, two-seat convertible body

SPECIAL FEATURES

Sculpted Alfa Romeo grill is a styling feature that first appeared on the series-topping 164 sedan.

The four small headlights are actually a styling trick. There are two large lights shining through four small holes.

RUNNING GEAR

Steering: Rack-and-pinion
Front suspension: MacPherson struts with lower wishbones and anti-roll bar
Rear suspension: Multi-link with coil springs, telescopic shocks and anti-roll bar
Brakes: Vented discs front, solid discs rear, 10.1 in. dia. (front), 9.5 in. dia. (rear)
Wheels: Alloy 6 in. x 15 in.
Tires: 195/760 ZR15

DIMENSIONS

Length: 168.7 in.   **Width:** 70 in.
Height: 51.7 in.   **Wheelbase:** 100 in.
Track: 59 in. (front), 159.3 in. (rear)
Weight: 3,021 lbs.

Allard J2

The J2 was conceived after Sydney Allard visited the U.S. and saw the benefits of an American V8 engine combined with a lightweight chassis.

Split-axle suspension

To produce an independently sprung set up, Allard chopped a Ford beam axle in half and located each piece by long radius arms.

Stark style

The interior is spartan, with driver protection limited to a small aero windshield.

Three-speed transmission

The transmission is taken straight from the Mercury. The sheer torque from the V8 engine in such a light frame makes extra ratios completely redundant.

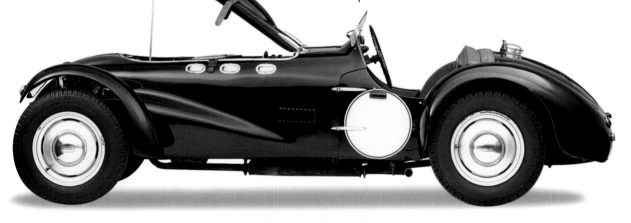

Ford-based rear end

To reduce unsprung weight a de Dion type rear suspension, with a quick-change center section, is used. Radius arms and a bronze block provides location.

Classic dashboard

The engine-turned aluminum dash follows the contours of the 'double-bubble' cowl. The fascia contains a 5-inch speedometer and tachometer, oil and temperature gauge, fuel gauge and a fuel switch.

American V8

The standard J2 engine is a sidevalve Mercury V8, but for more power an overhead-valve Cadillac or Chrysler V8 was commonly installed.

Specifications
1952 Allard J2

ENGINE
Type: V8

Construction: Cast-iron cylinder block and heads

Valve gear: Two valves per cylinder operated by single camshaft via pushrods and rockers

Bore and stroke: 3.81 in. x 3.62 in.

Displacement: 4,375 cc

Compression ratio: 7.5:1

Induction system: Twin carburetors

Maximum power: 140 bhp at 4,000 rpm

Maximum torque: 225 lb-ft at 2,500 rpm

Top speed: 110 mph

0–60 mph: 8.0 sec.

TRANSMISSION
Three-speed manual

BODY/CHASSIS
Separate chassis with two-door aluminum sports body

SPECIAL FEATURES

The shape of the grill is distinctively Allard, and is a feature of all models.

Six functional ventiports on either side of the hood allow hot air to escape from the cramped engine compartment.

RUNNING GEAR
Steering: Marles recirculating ball

Front suspension: Split Ford axle with radius arms, coil springs and shock absorbers

Rear suspension: De Dion tube with radius arms and coil springs

Brakes: Drums (front and rear)

Wheels: Wires, 16-in. dia.

Tires: 6.00 x 16 in.

DIMENSIONS
Length: 148.0 in.   **Width:** 63.0 in.

Height: 44.5 in.   **Wheelbase:** 100.0 in.

Track: 56.0 in. (front), 52.0 in. (rear)

Weight: 2,072 lbs.

Alvis **TD21**

The elegant look of the TD21 was all thanks to the Swiss coachbuilder Hermann Graber, who had been building his own design on an Alvis chassis since the early 1950s.

Recirculating-ball steering

You might expect a car of the Alvis' class to have rack-and-pinion steering, but it used an unassisted recirculating-ball system. By 1965, the car could be ordered with ZF power steering.

In-line six-cylinder

Alvis steadily increased the power of its conventional in-line six-cylinder all-iron engine from just 90 bhp in 1950. By the time the TD21 was made, the output had risen to 115 bhp, thanks to a higher compression and twin carburetors.

Separate chassis

There is nothing particularly complicated about the Alvis chassis; it is a conventional ladder-type frame with crossmembers. Because the car had a separate chassis, it was easier to make a convertible version.

Wooden frame

Until 1963, Alvis still used a lot of wooden framing in the old-fashioned way to make the bodies. The windshield pillars are made of solid ash, as are the door posts and the door frames.

Alloy bodywork

The Alvis bodies were coachbuilt and very labor intensive. They are made from a mixture of aluminum and steel. The trunk and hood are alloy, and the first TD21s had steel doors. For the Mk II, they were changed to alloy frames and skins.

Live axle
The conventional live rear axle is sprung by semi-elliptic leaf springs.

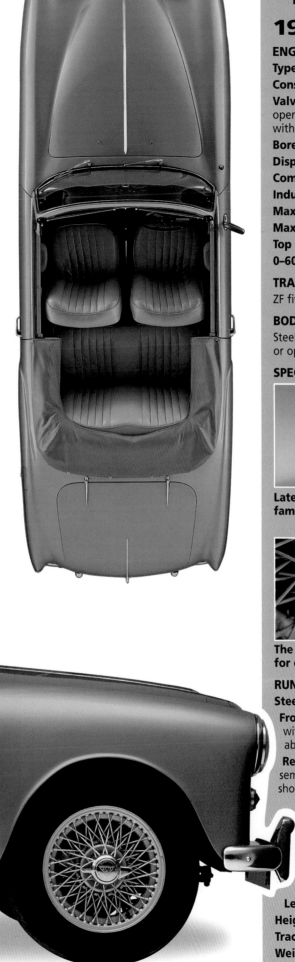

Specifications
1962 Alvis TD21

ENGINE
Type: In-line straight six-cylinder

Construction: Cast-iron block and head

Valve gear: Two valves per cylinder operated by a block-mounted camshaft with pushrods and rockers

Bore and stroke: 3.31 in. x 3.54 in.

Displacement: 2,993 cc

Compression ratio: 8.5:1

Induction system: Twin SU carburetors

Maximum power: 115 bhp at 4,000 rpm

Maximum torque: 152 lb-ft at 2,500 rpm

Top speed: 106 mph

0–60 mph: 13.5 sec.

TRANSMISSION
ZF five-speed manual

BODY/CHASSIS
Steel chassis with four-seater closed or open body

SPECIAL FEATURES

Late model TD21s were bodied by famous coachbuilders Park Ward.

The chrome wire wheels are knock-on for easy wheel changes.

RUNNING GEAR
Steering: Recirculating ball

Front suspension: Double wishbones with coil springs, telescopic shock absorbers and anti-roll bar

Rear suspension: Live axle with semi-elliptic leaf springs and telescopic shock absorbers

Brakes: Dunlop discs, 11.5-in. dia. (front), 11.0-in. dia. (rear)

Wheels: Wire spoke, 4.5 x 15 in.

Tires: Dunlop RS5 crossply, 600 x 15 in.

DIMENSIONS
Length: 189.0 in.   **Width:** 66.0 in.

Height: 58.0 in.   **Wheelbase:** 111.5 in.

Track: 54.5 in. (front and rear)

Weight: 3,360 lbs.

AMC **AMX**

By shortening the Javelin, AMC produced a cheap all-American two-seater sports coupe. Just 19,134 AMXs were built, making it a highly desirable muscle car today.

Bulging hood

A popular and sporty option on the AMX was the performance hood complete with dual air scoops. In 1968 the hood bulge was only decorative, but in 1970 the 'Go' package included a fully functional ram air system.

Sporty rear styling

The rear end is styled to give the car a smooth side profile but a ridged-out appearance from behind.

Chrome sills

With AMC's move toward flashier styling, the AMX featured chrome-plated sill covers. Later, these sills gained mock vents, mimicking a side-mounted exhaust.

Short wheelbase

Riding on a 97-inch wheelbase, the AMX is 12 inches shorter than the Javelin. This is even shorter than the Corvette, and qualified the AMX as one of the most compact American cars on the market at the time.

Two-seat interior

Shortening the bodyshell of the 2+2 Javelin means the AMX has room for just two passengers sitting on bucket seats, although there is a large space behind the seats for extra luggage.

Racing paintwork

The typical paint scheme for the AMX in its first two years was twin racing stripes running down the center. Late 1970 models lose the hood stripes but have side stripes instead.

V8 power

Emphasizing its sporty role, the AMX was only ever sold with V8 engines. It was the only AMC at the time not to be offered with a straight-six engine as standard.

Specifications
1968 AMC AMX

ENGINE
Type: V8

Construction: Cast-iron block and cylinder heads

Valve gear: Two valves per cylinder operated by a single camshaft, pushrods and rockers

Bore and stroke: 4.16 in. x 3.57 in.

Displacement: 390 c.i.

Compression ratio: 10.2:1

Induction system: Single four-barrel carburetor

Maximum power: 315 bhp at 4,600 rpm

Maximum torque: 425 lb-ft at 3,200 rpm

TRANSMISSION
Three-speed automatic or four-speed manual

BODY/CHASSIS
Integral with two-door steel coupe body

SPECIAL FEATURES

AMX meant something special after AMC showed a stunning mid-engined sports car with the AMX badge.

The 390-cubic inch V8 was AMC's biggest engine in the late 1960s.

RUNNING GEAR
Steering: Recirculating ball

Front suspension: Wishbones with coil springs and shocks

Rear suspension: Rigid axle with leaf springs and shocks

Brakes: Drums (front and rear)

Wheels: Steel, 14-in. dia.

Tires: E70 x 14 in.

DIMENSIONS
Length: 177 in.   **Width:** 71.5 in.

Height: 51.7 in.   **Wheelbase:** 97 in.

Track: 58.8 in. (front), 57 in. (rear)

Weight: 3,400 lbs.

Amilcar **C6**

Six-cylinder Amilcars are among the rarest of pre-war classics. A mere 40 or so Amilcar C6s were assembled by the small, Paris-based manufacturer.

Beam front axle

Independent front suspension had no place in sports or racing cars in the 1920s. The customary system, as on the C6, was a beam axle joining both wheels. In the Amilcar's case the axle is underslung, with the ends cranked to keep the ride height as low as possible.

Twin-cam engine

The Amilcar C6 is powered by a tiny, 1,094-cc engine but despite the unit's size it has six cylinders. It was an advanced design with twin-overhead camshafts and hemispherical combustion chambers.

Twin-rotor supercharger

The six-cylinder engine's power is achieved with the use of a twin-rotor, Roots-type supercharger mounted at the front of the engine bay. Maximum boost is 12 psi, and the compression ratio low at 6.6:1.

Drum brakes

Large drum brakes were fitted to all four wheels. Although hydraulic brakes had been developed by this time, the Amilcar's drums were cable operated.

Front-mounted oil tank

In order to keep the overall height of the engine low, it is dry sumped and the oil is kept in a separate tank mounted between the front leaf springs.

arter-elliptic leaf springs

e all cars of its era, the C6 features a live rear axle, but tead of using the more usual semi-elliptic leaf springs it ocated and sprung by quarter-elliptic leaf springs, the ds of which are mounted outboard of the body.

Specifications
1928 Amilcar C6

ENGINE

Type: In-line six-cylinder

Construction: Cast-iron block and head

Valve gear: Two valves per cylinder operated by twin overhead camshafts

Bore and stroke: 2.20 in. x 2.91 in.

Displacement: 1,094 cc

Compression ratio: 6.6:1

Induction system: Single Solex carburetor with twin-rotor Roots-type supercharger

Maximum power: 83 bhp at 6,000 rpm

Maximum torque: Not quoted

Top speed: 105 mph

0–60 mph: 11.9 sec.

TRANSMISSION

Four-speed manual

BODY/CHASSIS

Steel ladder-type chassis with an aluminum two-seater open racing-type body

SPECIAL FEATURES

The Amilcar supercharger is driven off the end of the crankshaft.

The seven-bearing crankshaft is a superb piece of machining.

RUNNING GEAR

Steering: Worm-and-sector

Front suspension: Underslung beam axle with semi-elliptic leaf springs and Hartford friction shock absorbers

Rear suspension: Live axle with quarter-elliptic leaf springs and Hartford friction shock absorbers

Brakes: Drums (front and rear)

Wheels: Knock-off wire, 27-in. dia.

Tires: Dunlop, 4.40 x 27 in.

DIMENSIONS

Length: 133.9 in.   **Width:** 50.4 in.

Height: 37.0 in.   **Wheelbase:** 74.0 in.

Track: 44.3 in. (front and rear)

Weight: 1,567 lbs.

Aston Martin **C-TYPE**

The bold styling with its exaggerated long rear fenders and tail contrasted with a large, blunt nose to produce a shape that many thought looked very unbalanced. Its visual impact was undeniable when it appeared, however.

Four-cylinder engine

Designed to be revved hard and for long periods, the 2-liter, overhead-cam four was made as strong as possible despite having just three main bearings. The crankshaft was nitrided to give the hardest, most wear-resistant finish, and there was a mechanical drive to the generator. A four-branch exhaust manifold allowed the engine to breathe easier.

Steel superstructure

On top of the traditional chassis frame, Aston Martin erected small square-section steel tube framework. This served the same purpose as the old-fashioned wooden ash frame used by English coachbuilders, but was stronger and helped overall stiffness.

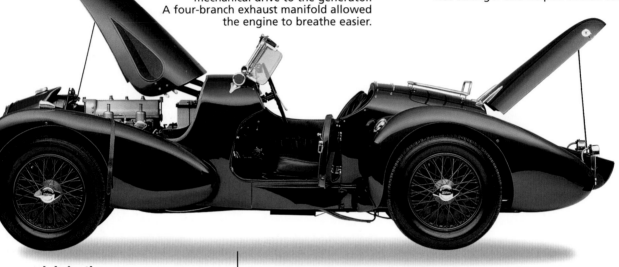

Dry-sump lubrication

To prevent oil starvation during racing the engine had dry-sump lubrication. All the oil is held in a separate tank and pumped to and from the engine. The oil tank is mounted at the front of the car and doubles as an oil cooler.

Wind deflectors

One interesting feature is the dual-purpose windshield. When the main windshield is raised, the smaller windows also double as side deflectors.

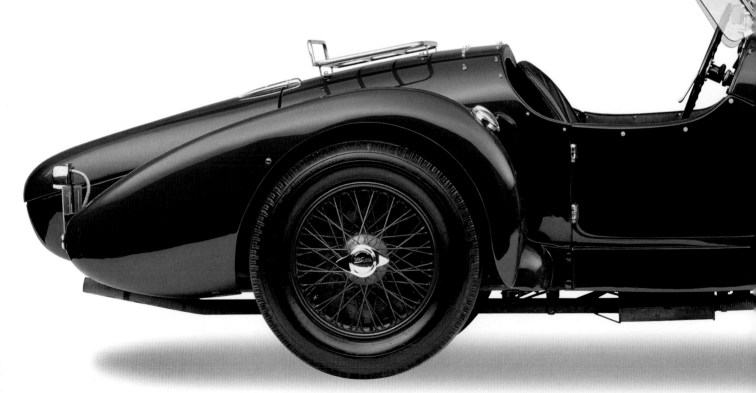

Streamlined front

Part of the reason for the very advanced-looking alloy bodywork over the tubular-steel frame was to make what was basically an old car look modern. Another reason was aircraft-style aerodynamics.

Specifications

1939 Aston Martin C-Type

ENGINE

Type: Inline four-cylinder

Construction: Cast-iron block and head

Valve gear: Two valves per cylinder operated by a single chain-driven overhead camshaft

Bore and stroke: 3.07 in. x 4.02 in.

Displacement: 1,950 cc

Compression ratio: 8.25:1

Induction system: Two SU carburetors

Maximum power: 110 bhp at 5,500 rpm

Maximum torque: Not quoted

Top speed: 97 mph

0–60 mph: 15.4 sec.

TRANSMISSION

Four-speed manual

BODY/CHASSIS

Separate underslung ladder-type frame with steel superstructure and alloy two-seater convertible body

SPECIAL FEATURES

Dual carburetors help add a few extra bhp on the track.

The four-speed transmission did not feature synchromesh, requiring the driver to double declutch.

RUNNING GEAR

Steering: Cam-and-peg

Front suspension: Beam axle with semi-elliptic leaf springs and friction shock absorbers

Rear suspension: Live axle with semi-elliptic leaf springs and friction shock absorbers

Brakes: Ribbed drums, 14-in. dia.

Wheels: Knock-on/off center-fixing wire spoke, 18-in. dia.

Tires: 5.25 x 18

DIMENSIONS

Length: 168.0 in.   **Width:** 64.0 in.

Height: 55.0 in.   **Wheelbase:** 102.0 in.

Track: 54.5 in. (front and rear)

Weight: 2,567 lbs.

Aston Martin **DB4** 🇬🇧

The DB4 to DB6 series is perhaps the most famous to roll off Aston Martin's Newport Pagnell production line. The classic Touring styling lasted for more than 12 years and still looks great today.

All-new engine

Unlike the previous model—the Aston Martin DB Mk III—which used the old Lagonda twin-cam engine, the DB4 had a completely new engine. The twin-overhead-camshaft straight six displaces 3.7 liters and produces 240 bhp in standard form and 302 bhp in the DB4 GT.

Short wheelbase

The wheelbase of the GT model is 5 inches shorter than that of the standard DB4. This makes the car lighter and more nimble.

Limited-slip differential

The live rear axle features a Salisbury Powr-lok limited-slip differential to help put all the power onto the road.

Superleggera construction

Styling house Touring was renowned for its use of Superleggera construction, which gives the DB4 a light but rigid bodyshell.

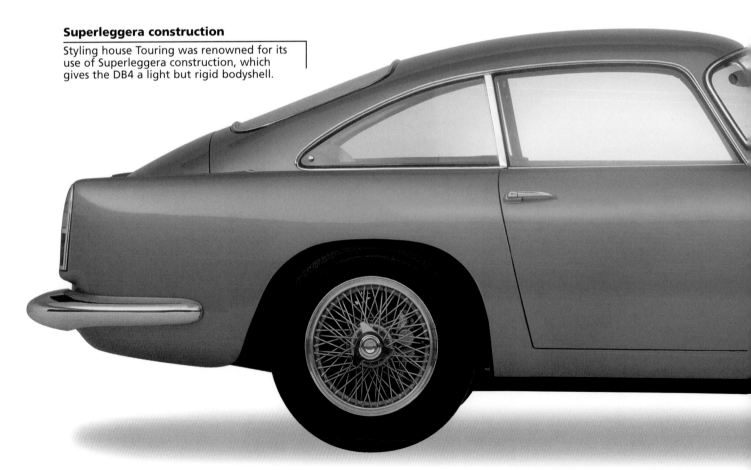

Italian styling

The DB4 was styled by Italian styling house Touring of Milan. This styling lasted, with subtle tweaks, until the demise of the DB6 in 1970.

Strong steel chassis

The DB4 uses a pressed-steel chassis with strong welded box sections. It was introduced for the DB4 and is completely different from the chassis of the DB Mk III.

Specifications

1962 Aston Martin DB4 GT

ENGINE

Type: In-line six-cylinder

Construction: Cast-iron block and head

Valve gear: Two valves per cylinder operated by twin overhead camshafts

Bore and stroke: 3.62 in. x 3.62 in.

Displacement: 3,670 cc

Compression ratio: 9.0:1

Induction system: Three twin-choke Weber carburetors

Maximum power: 302 bhp at 6,000 rpm

Maximum torque: 240 lb-ft at 5,000 rpm

Top speed: 149 mph

0–60 mph: 6.4 sec.

TRANSMISSION

Four-speed manual

BODY/CHASSIS

Steel chassis with alloy over steel tube two-door coupe body

SPECIAL FEATURES

Unlike the standard cars, the DB4 GT has faired-in headlights. A small number of Vantage-engined DB4s also feature these lights.

Hot air from the engine bay exits through vents in the fenders.

RUNNING GEAR

Steering: Rack-and-pinion

Front suspension: Double wishbones with coil springs, telescopic shock absorbers and anti-roll bar

Rear suspension: Live axle with coil springs, radius arms, Watt linkage and lever-arm shock absorbers

Brakes: Discs (front and rear)

Wheels: Wire, 16-in. dia.

Tires: 6.00 x 16 in.

DIMENSIONS

Length: 179.0 in.   **Width:** 55.5 in.

Height: 51.0 in.   **Wheelbase:** 93.0 in.

Track: 54.4 in. (front), 54.5 in. (rear)

Weight: 2,800 lbs.

Aston **MARTIN DB6**

With its graceful lines, elegant interior, and sophisticated mechanicals, the DB6 lived up to the Aston Martin reputation of providing expensive upper-class Grand Touring cars.

Alloy engine

The Tadek-Marek-designed straight-six is made of light alloy. It features removable wet liners and wet sump lubrication. All engines have triple carburetors except for the Vantage powerplant which has twin-choke Webers.

Four-wheel disc brakes

To stop more than 3,000 lbs. from speeds approaching 150 mph, disc brakes are necessary. They are substantial and are clearly visible through the chromed wire wheels.

Kamm tail

While the DB6's rear end styling may lack the purity of line of the original DB4/DB5 design by Touring of Milan, it certainly helps aerodynamics. The raised rear lip forms a spoiler and halves the aerodynamic lift on the rear end, thereby boosting high-speed stability.

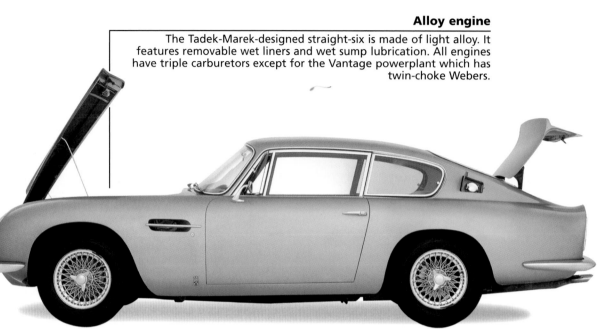

Choice of body styles

The most popular body style is the fastback sedan, of which 1,567 were made between 1965 and 1970. The desirable Volante convertible is much rarer—only 215 were built.

Luxurious interior

The interior is of the highest quality. Wall-to-wall carpeting, rich leather upholstery, multiple gauges and a racing-style wood/metal sandwich steering wheel are just some of its features.

Specifications

1965 Aston Martin DB6 Vantage

ENGINE

Type: In-line six-cylinder

Construction: Aluminum block and head

Valve gear: Two valves per cylinder operated by double overhead camshafts

Bore and stroke: 3.77 in. x 3.62 in.

Displacement: 3,995 cc

Compression ratio: 8.9:1

Induction system: Three twin-choke Weber carburetors

Maximum power: 325 bhp at 5,750 rpm

Maximum torque: 290 lb-ft at 4,500rpm

Top speed: 150 mph

0–60 mph: 6.7 sec.

TRANSMISSION

Five-speed manual or three-speed automatic

BODY/CHASSIS

Integral steel chassis with two-door aluminum coupe or convertible body

SPECIAL FEATURES

The wire wheels are held on by central spinners which have to be knocked off using a special mallet.

The vents in the front fenders are still a current feature on new Aston Martins.

RUNNING GEAR

Steering: Rack-and-pinion

Front suspension: Double wishbones with coil springs, telescopic shocks and anti-roll bar

Rear suspension: Live axle with radius arms, Watt linkage, telescopic shocks and coil springs

Brakes: Discs (front and rear)

Wheels: Spoked, 15-in. dia.

Tires: 6.70 x 15 in.

DIMENSIONS

Length: 182 in.　　**Width:** 66 in.

Height: 52 in.　　**Wheelbase:** 101.8 in.

Track: 54 in. (front), 53.5 in. (rear)

Weight: 3,418 lbs.

Aston MARTIN DBS

Just right for the era, the DBS is a heavy and muscular beast. It is also a beautifully hand-crafted machine with a very high degree of luxury and a quality of finish that can easily be compared with Rolls-Royce.

Luxurious interior

The cabin is a picture of traditional Aston craftsmanship. The sumptuous leather seats are superb, and there are lots of nice touches, such as a wood-rimmed steering wheel, seven round gauges housed in an oval instrument panel, standard air conditioning, power windows and a radio.

Quad-cam V8

Despite the first versions of the DBS that used a six-cylinder engine, the car was designed for V8 power. The 5.3-liter V8—raced in a Lola T70—was designed by Tadek Marek.

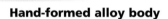

Hand-formed alloy body

Like all Aston Martins, each body was lovingly hand-formed in aluminum by highly skilled craftsmen. Some parts were formed in steel.

Block-like aerodynamics

The styling may have been muscular and brawny but the shape is nowhere near as slippery through the air as the previous DB6. Early tests indicated a drag coefficient figure between 0.42 and 0.47 for the DBS, compared with 0.36 for the DB6.

disc brakes

The DBS was launched with solid disc brakes on all four wheels. For the V8 model, these had to be uprated and vented.

William Towns styling

The DBS was the first Aston designed by young British designer William Towns, who had worked with General Motors and Rootes. He was open in admitting influence from contemporary GM styling.

Specifications
1971 Aston Martin DBS V8

ENGINE
Type: V8

Construction: Aluminum block and heads

Valve gear: Two valves per cylinder operated by twin overhead camshafts per bank

Bore and stroke: 3.94 in. x 3.35 in.

Displacement: 5,340 cc

Compression ratio: 9.0:1

Induction system: Bosch fuel injection

Maximum power: 320 bhp at 5,000 rpm

Maximum torque: 360 lb-ft at 4,000 rpm

Top speed: 160 mph

0–60 mph: 5.9 sec.

TRANSMISSION
Five-speed manual

BODY/CHASSIS
Unitary monocoque construction with aluminum and steel two-door coupe body

SPECIAL FEATURES

Aston's hallmark side air intake first emerged in the late 1950s.

The DBS features dual exhaust pipes— one pipe on each side exits through the rear valance panel.

RUNNING GEAR
Steering: Rack-and-pinion

Front suspension: Wishbones with coil springs, shock absorbers and anti-roll bar

Rear suspension: De Dion axle with parallel radius arms, Watt linkage, coil springs and shock absorbers

Brakes: Vented discs (front and rear)

Wheels: Alloy, 15-in. dia.

Tires: GR70 VR15

DIMENSIONS
Length: 180.5 in.   **Width:** 72.0 in.

Height: 52.3 in.   **Wheelbase:** 102.8 in.

Track: 59.0 in. (front and rear)

Weight: 3,800 lbs.

Aston Martin ZAGATO

Zagato had the reputation of styling cars unlike any other. Here it went for a short car with tall wheels and a blunt aggressive look which radiated power, performance and exclusivity.

V8 engine

At the time the Zagato had the most powerful version of the aluminum Aston Martin quad-cam V8 engine. Revisions to the camshaft, cylinder head ports and carburetors helped to increase power to 432 bhp from its 5.3 liters. This output was more impressive than the peak torque as the engine was tuned for outright power.

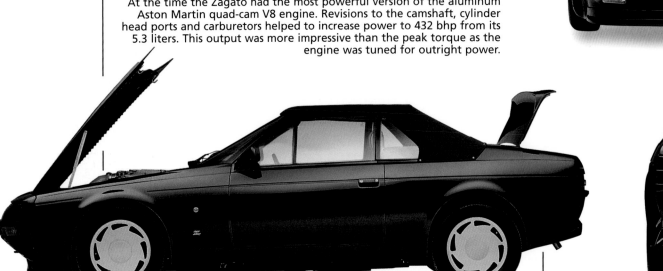

ZF transmission

Aston used the tough German ZF five-speed manual transmission. It featured a dog leg first gear with the rest of the gears in the normal 'H' pattern.

De Dion axle

De Dion axles were popular with Aston Martin. They served the purpose of keeping the rear wheels upright at all times with none of the camber changes.

Short rear overhang

Zagato made its design look more compact than the existing Vantage by chopping 12 inches from the rear, reducing the size of the trunk. Extra luggage could be placed behind the front seats.

Lancia seats

With Zagato in charge of all interior trim, it chose Lancia Delta S4 front seats. These were trimmed in top-quality leather like all Aston Martin seats.

Foam bumpers

One way in which Zagato lightened the Aston was by discarding the steel bumpers and designing deformable foam-filled replacements mounted on hydraulic rams.

In-board discs

In theory, with a de Dion axle the logical place to mount the brakes is inboard next to the final drive, and that's where Aston put them.

Alloy body

Zagato was the master craftsmen in aluminum bodywork and made all the panels for the car, mounted on a modified form of the existing folded and welded sheet-metal substructure. All the panels were formed over a full-size wooden template.

Specifications

1987 Aston Martin Zagato

ENGINE

Type: V8

Construction: Alloy block and heads

Valve gear: Two valves per cylinder operated by four chain-driven overhead camshafts

Bore and stroke: 3.93 in. x 3.35 in.

Displacement: 5,340 cc

Compression ratio: 10.2:1

Induction system: Four downdraft Weber IDF carburetors

Maximum power: 432 bhp at 6,200 rpm

Maximum torque: 395 lb-ft at 5,100 rpm

Top speed: 183 mph

0–60 mph: 4.8 sec

TRANSMISSION

TorqueFlite 727 five-speed automatic

BODY/CHASSIS

Steel substructure with alloy two-door coupe body

SPECIAL FEATURES

Volantes are distinguished from Zagato coupes by their headlight covers.

With its shortened tail and convertible top, the Volante's trunk space is limited.

RUNNING GEAR

Steering: Rack-and-pinion

Front suspension: Double wishbones with coil springs, Koni shock absorbers and anti-roll bar

Rear suspension: Rigid de Dion axle with trailing arms, Watt linkage, coil springs and Koni shock absorbers

Brakes: Vented discs, 11.5-in. dia. (front), 10.4-in. dia. (rear)

Wheels: Alloy, 8 x 16 in.

Tires: Goodyear Eagle, 255/50 VR16

DIMENSIONS

Length: 173.5 in.   **Width:** 73.5 in.

Height: 51.1 in.   **Wheelbase:** 103.2 in.

Track: 60.1 in. (front), 60.8 in. (rear)

Weight: 3,630 lbs.

Auburn SPEEDSTER

Auburn's famous designer Gordon Buehrig wanted the Speedster to appear to be the fastest car on the road. He succeeded, using features like the low V windshield, sloping grill and flowing wing-line to give a streamlined look to the car.

Teardrop headlights

The Auburn's styling is supposed to suggest speed. The streamlined lights, with bulging convex lenses, help achieve this impression.

Supercharged engine

The Auburn's mechanically driven supercharger runs at six times engine-speed and helps the Lycoming engine generate 150 bhp—35 bhp more than without the supercharger.

Top cover

The Auburn's top folds away neatly under this rigid cover to maintain the car's sleek lines.

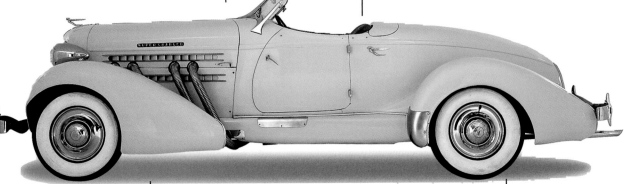

Flexible exhaust headers

Each of the four flexible exhaust headers serve two cylinders. The conventional rigid pipes are hidden under the flexible tubes.

Dual-ratio rear axle

The driver could switch from a low- to a high- axle ratio, and with a three-speed transmission that gave six gears overall. In high-ratio top gear, the Speedster's engine rotated at only 2,250 rpm at 60 mph.

Winged mascots

Each of the side 'flying lady' mascots was made by slicing the radiator mascot in two.

Luggage hatch

A carriage key opens this hatch. The compartment is just large enough to take a set of golf clubs, a feature much appreciated by the typical playboy Speedster owner.

Hydraulic lever-arm shocks

Before telescopic shocks were introduced, cars like the Auburn used hydraulic lever arms to replace the previous friction shocks.

Drum brakes

All the cars in the 1930s had drum brakes, but the Auburn's hydraulically-operated drums were more modern than most.

Boat-tail design

From above, the description is obvious. The style was popular in the 1920s and '30s and here it is mirrored in in its rearend styling.

Specifications
1935 Auburn Speedster 851

ENGINE

Type: In-line eight
Construction: Cast-iron block and light alloy cylinder head
Valve gear: Side-valve with two valves per cylinder and single block-mounted camshaft
Bore and stroke: 3.06 in. x 4.75 in.
Displacement: 280 c.i.
Compression ratio: 6.5:1
Induction system: Single downdraft Stromberg carburetor with Schwitzer-Cummins supercharger
Maximum power: 150 bhp at 4,000 rpm
Top speed: 108 mph
0–50 mph: 10.0 sec.

TRANSMISSION

Three-speed manual with dual-ratio rear axle

BODY/CHASSIS

Steel two-door, two-seat speedster body with steel box-section ladder-type chassis rails

SPECIAL FEATURES

Each Speedster has a signed plaque guaranteeing it has been tested to more than 100 mph.

Mechanically-driven supercharger is used to boost power.

RUNNING GEAR

Steering: Worm-and-peg
Front suspension: Solid axle with semi-elliptic leaf springs and Delco hydraulic shock absorbers
Rear suspension: Live axle with semi-elliptic leaf springs and Delco hydraulic shock absorbers
Brakes: Four-wheel Lockheed drums, hydraulically operated with Bendix vacuum booster
Wheels: Pressed steel or wire spoke, 6.5 in. x 15 in.
Tires: Crossply 6.5 in. x 16 in.

DIMENSIONS

Length: 194.4 in.   **Width:** 71.5 in.
Height: 56.5 in.   **Wheelbase:** 127 in.
Track: 59 in. (front), 62 in. (rear)
Weight: 3,753 lbs.

Audi 100 S COUPE

Luckily for Audi, the appeal of its 100 S, four-cylinder Coupe was enhanced because, by chance, its styling had a very close resemblance to the more exotic and expensive Aston Martin DBS supercar.

Rear-mounted battery
To help minimize the Coupe's excessive front-heavy weight distribution, Audi mounted the battery below the rear seat rather than in the engine bay.

Slant four-cylinder
To enable the engine to fit easily under the low hood, Audi tilted the engine at a 45-degree angle with the carburetor and its large air intake near the center of the hood.

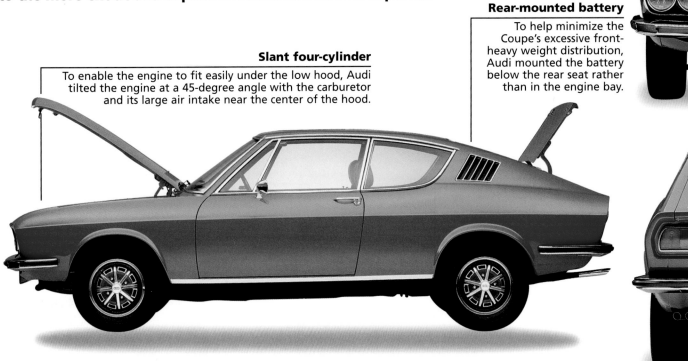

Rear drum brakes
Another effect of having such a front-heavy design is that the Coupe can easily get away with rear-mounted drum brakes at the back. At a mere 7.9 inches in diameter, they are quite small.

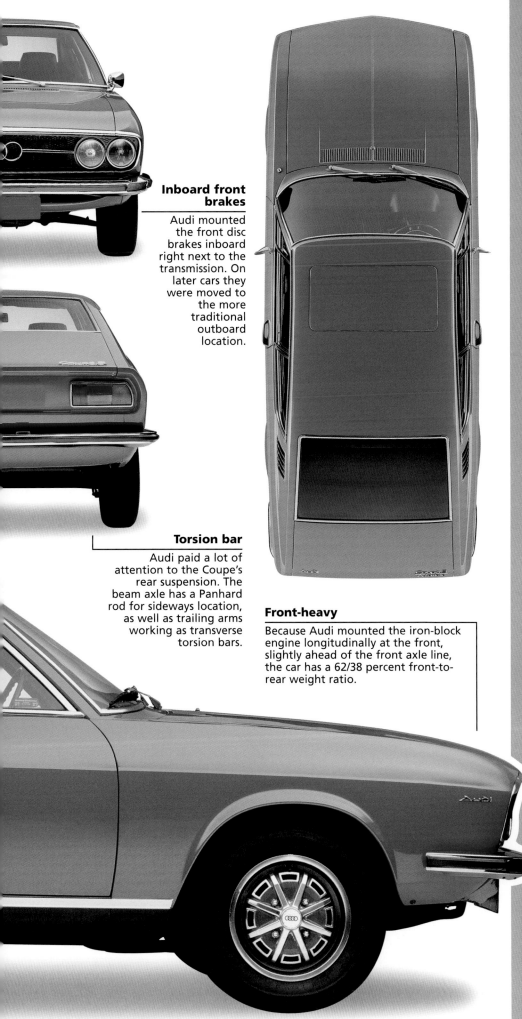

Inboard front brakes

Audi mounted the front disc brakes inboard right next to the transmission. On later cars they were moved to the more traditional outboard location.

Torsion bar

Audi paid a lot of attention to the Coupe's rear suspension. The beam axle has a Panhard rod for sideways location, as well as trailing arms working as transverse torsion bars.

Front-heavy

Because Audi mounted the iron-block engine longitudinally at the front, slightly ahead of the front axle line, the car has a 62/38 percent front-to-rear weight ratio.

Specifications
1971 Audi 100 S Coupe

ENGINE
Type: Inline four-cylinder
Construction: Cast-iron block and alloy head
Valve gear: Two valves per cylinder operated by a single block-mounted camshaft via pushrods and rockers
Bore and stroke: 3.31 in. x 3.32 in.
Displacement: 1,871 cc
Compression ratio: 10.2:1
Induction system: Single Solex carburetor
Maximum power: 112 bhp at 5,600 rpm
Maximum torque: 118 lb-ft at 3,500 rpm
Top speed: 112 mph
0–60 mph: 10.9 sec.

TRANSMISSION
Three-speed automatic

BODY/CHASSIS
Unitary monocoque construction with steel two-door 2+2 coupe body

SPECIAL FEATURES

The grills behind the rear side windows keep the cabin well ventilated.

The Coupe's three-speed automatic transmission was advanced for its time.

RUNNING GEAR
Steering: Rack-and-pinion
Front suspension: Double wishbones with coil springs, telescopic shock absorbers and anti-roll bar
Rear suspension: Beam axle with trailing arms, Panhard rod, torsion bars, telescopic shock absorbers and anti-roll bar
Brakes: Vented discs, 11.0-in. dia. (front), drums, 7.9-in. dia. (rear)
Wheels: Pressed steel disc, 5 x 14 in.
Tires: 185/70 HR14

DIMENSIONS
Length: 175.8 in.   **Width:** 68.8 in.
Height: 52.5 in.   **Wheelbase:** 101.0 in.
Track: 56.5 in. (front), 56.8 in. (rear)
Weight: 2,410 lbs.

Audi **RS2**

Speedier and more capable than the legendary short-wheelbase Quattro Sport, the RS2 is the fastest car Audi has made. The Porsche effect is evident everywhere.

Sports interior

Audi did not forget about upgrading the cabin on its wicked wagon. Black-on-white gauges, Recaro seats and Kevlar or wood trim were added to the normal-issue Audi 80 interior. Standard equipment on the RS2 includes a power roof, power windows, CD changer and air conditioning.

Six-speed transmission

To make the most of its awesome power, Audi specified a six-speed manual transmission tweaked by Porsche. Its ratios are chosen to keep the power band around 3,000 rpm.

Porsche wheels

The elegance of the five-spoke alloy wheels should come as no surprise, as they were taken straight from the Porsche 911. They are fitted with ultra-low-profile Dunlop tires.

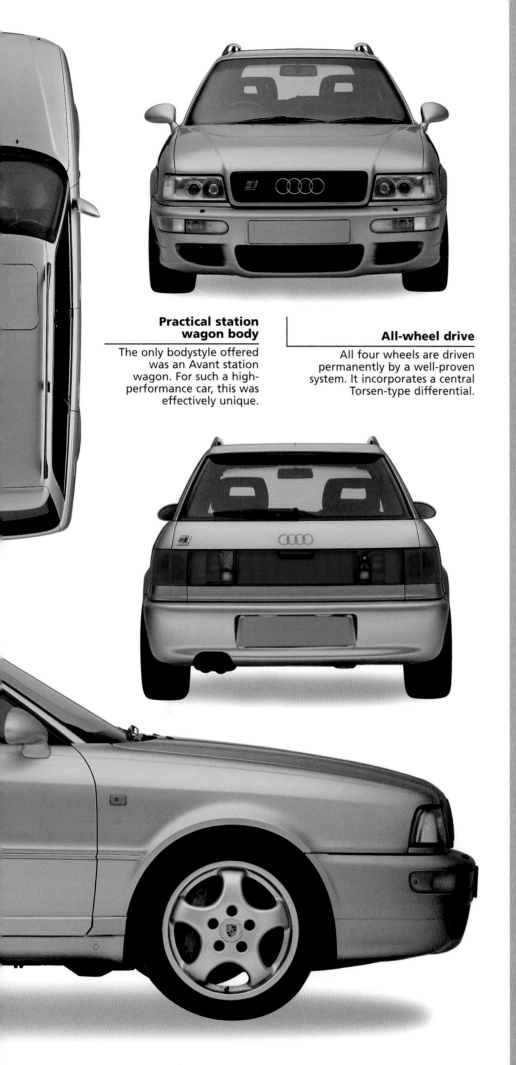

Practical station wagon body

The only bodystyle offered was an Avant station wagon. For such a high-performance car, this was effectively unique.

All-wheel drive

All four wheels are driven permanently by a well-proven system. It incorporates a central Torsen-type differential.

Specifications
1994 Audi RS2

ENGINE
Type: Inline five-cylinder

Construction: Cast-iron block and aluminum head

Valve gear: Four valves per cylinder operated by twin overhead camshafts

Bore and stroke: 3.19 in. x 3.40 in.

Displacement: 2,226 cc

Compression ratio: 9.0:1

Induction system: Sequential fuel injection

Maximum power: 315 bhp at 6,500 rpm

Maximum torque: 302 lb-ft at 3,000 rpm

Top speed: 158 mph

0–60 mph: 4.8 sec

TRANSMISSION
Six-speed manual

BODY/CHASSIS
Unitary monocoque construction with steel five-door station wagon body

SPECIAL FEATURES

The rear lights extend around onto the tailgate.

The larger, red brake calipers come from the Porsche parts bin and are from the 968 model.

RUNNING GEAR
Steering: Rack-and-pinion

Front suspension: Struts with coil springs, shock absorbers and anti-roll bar

Rear suspension: Struts with torsion beam axle, coil springs, shock absorbers and anti-roll bar

Brakes: Vented discs (front and rear)

Wheels: Alloy, 17-in. dia.

Tires: 245/40 ZR17

DIMENSIONS
Length: 177.5 in.   **Width:** 66.7 in.

Height: 54.6 in.   **Wheelbase:** 100.4 in.

Track: 57.0 in. (front), 57.9 in. (rear)

Weight: 3,510 lbs.

Austin-Healey 3000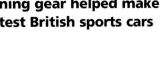

This hybrid designed by Donald Healey and incorporating Austin running gear helped make the 3000 one of the greatest British sports cars ever assembled.

Front disc brakes

Early Austin-Healeys were drum braked but from 1959 more effective servo-assisted discs were fitted at the front.

Austin engine

All the 'Big Healeys', as they were commonly known, use modified cast-iron Austin engines. They are uncomplicated overhead-valve designs, but are tuneable and very strong.

Knock-on wire wheels

Traditional knock-on center-lock wire wheels are the usual fitment on the Austin-Healey, although bolt-on steel disc wheels were available.

In-house styling

Donald Healey relied on his own company to style the original Healey 100, and much of that style lived on in the 3000.

Poor ground clearance

Austin-Healeys are notorious for their poor ground clearance and the exhaust system is particularly vulnerable. This was a great problem for the rally cars and one reason why clearance was improved in 1964.

Two-seaters and 2+2s

From 1962 the two-seater option was deleted and all the 3000 MkII and MkIII models were 2+2s, so occasional passengers could be squeezed in.

Live rear axle

Donald Healey did not want the expense and complication of independent rear suspension and used a live axle. At one time there was a Panhard rod but that was discarded after 1964 and radius arms were fitted.

Cam-and-peg steering

Although the smaller Austin-Healey Sprite uses rack-and-pinion steering, the 3000 has a less precise cam-and-peg system because it was easier to accommodate with the big six-cylinder engine.

Underslung chassis

The chassis was designed for a low, sleek look with the rear axle mounted above the chassis rails.

Specifications
1964 Austin-Healey 3000 MkIII

ENGINE

Type: In-line six cylinder
Construction: Cast-iron block and head
Valve gear: Two in-line valves per cylinder operated by single block-mounted camshaft, pushrods and rockers
Bore and stroke: 3.26 in. x 3.50 in.
Displacement: 2,912 cc
Compression ratio: 9.0:1
Induction system: Two SU carburetors
Maximum power: 148 bhp at 5,250 rpm
Maximum torque: 165 lb-ft at 3,500 rpm

TRANSMISSION

Four-speed manual with overdrive on third and fourth gear

BODY/CHASSIS

X-braced ladder-frame chassis with steel 2+2 convertible body

SPECIAL FEATURES

The left-exiting exhaust on this car indicates that this is a left-hand-drive model. Around 90 percent of 3000s were exported.

The big six-cylinder engine generates a lot of heat and the competition cars have large vents behind the front wheels to help cooling.

RUNNING GEAR

Steering: Cam-and-peg
Front suspension: Double wishbones, coil springs, lever arm shocks and anti-roll bar
Rear suspension: Live axle with semi-elliptic leaf springs, lever arm shocks and radius arms
Brakes: Discs (front), drums (rear)
Wheels: Knock-on center-lock wire spoke 4.5 in. x 15 in.
Tires: Crossply 5.9 in. x 15 in.

DIMENSIONS

Length: 157.5 in.   **Width:** 60.5 in.
Wheelbase: 92 in.   **Height:** 50 in.
Track: 48.8 in. (front), 50 in. (rear)
Weight: 2,549 lbs.

Austin Healey 100M

One of the most famous and perfect sports car shapes ever created was produced in-house by the small Healey Motor Company, with no input from any of the world's great stylists.

Alloy bodywork

For a simple car the bodywork is very complex, with a main understructure of a substantial front bulkhead, rear bulkhead and inner fenders. The outer panels are mounted on this and are all-alloy in the 100S to save weight.

Tuned engine

The cylinder head of the standard Austin engine is poor, with restricted breathing and inlet and exhaust ports on the same side. The 100M features a higher compression ratio and the 100S had a completely new head, with individual ports and different cam timing.

Underslung chassis

One reason all the big Healeys sit so low is that the chassis rails actually run under the live axle at the rear. This is in total contrast to most designs where the chassis rails kick up at the back to clear the axle.

Two-tone bodywork

The contour of the body lent itself to a two-tone paint scheme. The natural body line started from the top of the front fender and ran the length of the car through the rear wheel well to the rear bumper.

Distinctive grill
The 100 and the 100M have this distinctive curved triangular grill. The 100S uses a different oval grill like that used on the later Austin-Healey 3000.

Separate chassis
The chassis consists of two main box-section longitudinal rails with 'X' cross braces near the center of the car, a single crossmember at the rear and a bigger, stronger crossmember at the front. Outriggers are fitted to carry the inner sills.

Specifications
1955 Austin-Healey 100M

ENGINE
Type: In-line four

Construction: Cast-iron block and cylinder head

Valve gear: Two valves per cylinder operated by single block-mounted camshafts via pushrods and rockers

Bore and stroke: 3.44 in. x 4.37 in.

Displacement: 2,660 cc

Compression ratio: 8.1:1

Induction system: Twin SU carburetors

Maximum power: 110 bhp at 4,500 rpm

Maximum torque: 143 lb-ft at 2,000 rpm

Top speed: 110 mph

0–60 mph: 9.6 sec.

TRANSMISSION
Four-speed manual; optional overdrive

BODY/CHASSIS
Separate chassis with alloy and steel two-seater roadster body

SPECIAL FEATURES

Powerful headlights are a must on a sports car.

The 100M has a leather hood-retaining strap that wasn't fitted to standard 100s.

RUNNING GEAR
Steering: Cam-and-peg

Front suspension: Double wishbones with coil springs, lever-arm shock absorbers and anti-roll bar

Rear suspension: Live axle with leaf springs, lever-arm shock absorbers and Panhard rod

Brakes: Drums (front and rear)

Wheels: 72-spoke wires, 4 x 15 in.

Tires: Crossply, 5.90-15

DIMENSIONS
Length: 147.5 in. **Width:** 60.5 in.

Height: 47.0 in. **Wheelbase:** 90.0 in.

Track: 49.0 in. (front), 50.8 in. (rear)

Weight: 2,385 lbs.

Austin SEVEN

This Austin Seven Special looks a world apart from the day-to-day sedans and tourers. Its minimal, doorless, two-seater sports racing bodywork is designed to be as light as possible to make the most of the performance.

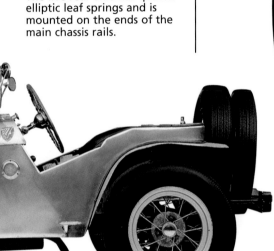

Sidevalve engine

When the 747-cc inline sidevalve four was reengineered in 1936, it was given a third main bearing. At the same time, the head was redesigned to give more efficient combustion and power.

Live rear axle

The live rear axle has quarter-elliptic leaf springs and is mounted on the ends of the main chassis rails.

Gravity-feed tank

Early Austin Seven engines had their fuel fed to them by a gas tank, located under the scuttle and behind the engine. From there, gravity alone shifted the fuel to the single Zenith updraft carburetor. The tank was moved to the rear late in the car's life.

Three-speed transmission

Initially, only a three-speed transmission was offered. More than 10 years later, the car was given a four-speed that was soon improved with synchromesh.

Worm-and-sector steering

The Seven requires little effort to steer through the worm-and-sector system, as the car is so light and runs on very narrow, high-pressure tires.

Wire wheels

The Seven could get by with such spindly wire wheels because the tire size is narrow, the car is light, and the performance, both in acceleration and braking, is so low. Wheel size varied over time, with some cars having 15-inch rims and others having 19-inch rims.

Beam front axle

To keep the front suspension cheap and simple, it consists of a solid beam, which is suspended by a transverse semi-elliptic leaf spring above it. Location is provided by two radius arms running back from the hubs to a point behind the engine.

Specifications

1930 Austin Seven

ENGINE

Type: Inline four-cylinder

Construction: Cast-iron block and head

Valve gear: Two inline sidevalves per cylinder operated by a single block-mounted camshaft

Bore and stroke: 2.24 in. x 3.04 in.

Displacement: 747 cc

Compression ratio: 4.8:1

Induction system: Single Zenith updraft carburetor

Maximum power: 12 bhp at 2,600 rpm

Maximum torque: Not quoted

Top speed: 66 mph

0–60 mph: Not quoted

TRANSMISSION

Three-speed manual

BODY/CHASSIS

Separate steel chassis with wood, fabric and steel bodywork

SPECIAL FEATURES

This Special features twin carburetors in place of the single Zenith.

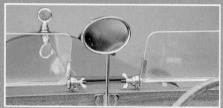

Twin aero screens are the only protection for driver and passenger.

RUNNING GEAR

Steering: Worm-and-sector

Front suspension: Beam axle with transverse semi-elliptic leaf spring, radius arms and friction shock absorbers

Rear suspension: Live axle with torque tube, quarter-elliptic leaf springs, radius arms and friction shock absorbers

Brakes: Drums (front and rear)

Wheels: Wire spoke

Tires: Beaded edge

DIMENSIONS

Length: 106.0 in. **Width:** 46.0 in.

Height: 55.2 in. **Wheelbase:** 75.0 in.

Track: 40.0 in. (front and rear)

Weight: 952 lbs.

Bentley **MK VI**

The MKVI may have looked staid and upright, but it was at the helm of a postwar British motor industry renaissance. The MKVI was more about comfortable transportation and prestige than about speed.

Steel bodywork

While a chassis-only version of the MKVI was listed, for the first time ever Bentley fitted its own bodywork (built by the Pressed Steel Company).

Tiny trunk

The major criticism of the MKVI was its tiny luggage area, accessed by a drop-down trunk lid. The deficiency was not rectified until the 1952 R-Type, which had an extended trunk with a lift-up lid

Hydraulic brakes

Bentley was at the forefront of technology in 1946, when it fitted a hydraulic servo for its braking system. However, it operates only on the front drums; the rear ones have a mechanical linkage.

Manual transmission

The MKVI was only ever offered with four-speed manual transmission, unlike later models, which were also available with automatic. Righthand-drive cars had a floor-mounted lever, but lefthand-drive cars for export had a column shift.

Chassis lubrication

A centralized system of chassis lubrication means easier maintenance. Stepping on a pedal delivers lubricant to the steering and suspension systems. There is also a side jacking system.

Specifications
Bentley MKVI

ENGINE

Type: Inline six-cylinder

Construction: Cast-iron block and aluminum head

Valve gear: Two valves per cylinder, one overhead/one side, operated by a single camshaft with pushrods and rockers

Bore and stroke: 3.56 in. x 4.57 in.

Displacement: 4,257 cc

Compression ratio: 6.4:1

Induction system: Twin SU carburetors

Maximum power: Not quoted

Maximum torque: Not quoted

Top speed: 94 mph

0–60 mph: 15.2 sec.

TRANSMISSION

Four-speed manual

BODY/CHASSIS

Separate chassis with steel four-door sedan body

SPECIAL FEATURES

Most British home market MKVIs had floor-mounted shifters on the right of the steering wheel. Export cars came with column shift.

Picnic tables were quaint features that could be folded out from the backs of the front seats.

RUNNING GEAR

Steering: Cam-and-roller

Front suspension: Wishbones with coil springs, shock absorbers and anti-roll bar

Rear suspension: Live axle with semi-elliptic leaf springs and shock absorbers

Brakes: Drums (front and rear)

Wheels: Steel, 16-in. dia.

Tires: 6.50 x 16

DIMENSIONS

Length: 192.0 in. **Width:** 70.0 in.

Height: 68.0 in.

Wheelbase: 120.0 in.

Track: 56.0 in. (front), 58.5 in. (rear)

Weight: 4,075 lbs.

Bentley 4½ LITRE

When W. O. Bentley wanted more power from his cars he made the engines bigger, moving up to 6½ and then 8.0 liters. Ironically the supercharged car he disapproved of so much has become the most famous.

Solid beam front axle

All of W. O. Bentley's cars had a solid beam axle located and sprung by two semi-elliptic leaf springs, along with friction shock absorbers.

Center lock wheels

Tire changes could be made quickly in the pits because the Rudge Whitworth wheels have a single knock-off center fixing, undone with a soft-faced hammer.

Worm-and-wheel steering

The Bentley has a worm-and-wheel. The driver's side wheel is linked to the steering mechanism and a bar from that wheel runs under the chassis to the other front wheel.

Fold-down windshield

Although the Bentley had the aerodynamics of a barn door, the windshield can be folded flat and the small aero-window erected to slightly improve the car's aerodynamics.

Massive brakes

It's heavy and fast, requiring 17-inch brakes that are ribbed for cooling. Although Duesenberg had pioneered hydraulic brakes, the Bentley's are cable operated.

Stone guards

The world's race tracks were neither as smooth nor stone-free as today's. To prevent damage Bentley used stone guards to protect the exposed carburetors next to the supercharger and the fuel tank at the rear.

External handbrake

There was no room inside the cockpit for the externally-mounted handbrake lever. Even the gearshifter isn't in the middle of the cockpit, but off to the driver's side.

No driver's door

With the side cutaway to allow the driver to move his elbows there was no need for a door.

Live rear axle

Like all its rivals of the era, the Bentley uses a simple live axle, located and sprung on two semi-elliptic leaf springs.

Specifications
1930 Bentley 4½ Litre supercharged

ENGINE

Type: In-line four cylinder
Construction: Cast-iron block and head
Valve gear: Four valves per cylinder operated by single gear-and shaft-driven overhead camshafts
Bore and stroke: 3.93 in. x 5.51 in.
Displacement: 4,398 cc
Compression ratio: 5.0:1
Induction system: Two SU carburetors with Amherst Villiers Roots-type supercharger
Maximum power: 175 bhp at 3,500 rpm
Maximum power (racing): 240 bhp at 2,400 rpm
Maximum torque: not quoted
Top speed: 125 mph
0–60 mph: Not quoted

TRANSMISSION

Four-speed manual

BODY/CHASSIS

Steel ladder frame with cross bracing, and open steel and fabric body

SPECIAL FEATURES

The Roots-type supercharger drives off the crankshaft. Two lobes are rotated, drawing air and fuel through the carburetors, compressing it and forcing it through the intake manifold and into the engine.

Bentley used four-valve technology as early as 1919, and continued it in the 4½ Litre's engine.

RUNNING GEAR

Steering: Worm-and-wheel
Front suspension: Solid beam axle with leaf springs and shocks
Rear suspension: Live axle with semi-elliptic leaf springs and shocks
Brakes: Four-wheel drums
Wheels: Rudge Whitworth 6 in. x 20in.
Tires: Dunlop crossply, 6 in. x 20 in.

DIMENSIONS

Length: 172.5 in.   **Width:** 68.5 in.
Height: 63 in.   **Wheelbase:** 130 in.
Track: 54.49 in. (front and rear)
Weight: 4,235 lbs.

Bentley 8-LITRE

The enormous engine was developed by Bentley because its customers would insist on fitting their cars with the largest and heaviest bodies available. Such was the power of the 8-Litre that weight did not matter.

Straight-six engine

The biggest Bentley engine was basically the same as that used for the Speed Six 6.6-liter engine, but with the bore increased to give 8 liters. That still made it a very long-stroke (4.33-inch x 5.51-inch) design, and the engine was very tall and narrow.

Twin spark ignition

In some very large combustion chambers, Bentley used a twin-spark ignition. The spark plugs were mounted horizontally below the valves on each side of the block. One set was fired by a magneto, the other set using a coil.

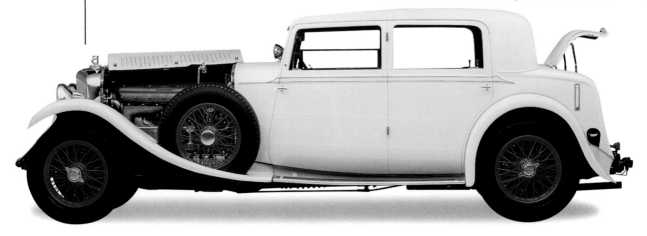

Coachbuilt bodywork

Bentley was more interested in supplying the chassis than a complete car. An 8-Litre customer would have his car bodied by any one of a number of great outside coachbuilders like Mulliner or Vanden Plas.

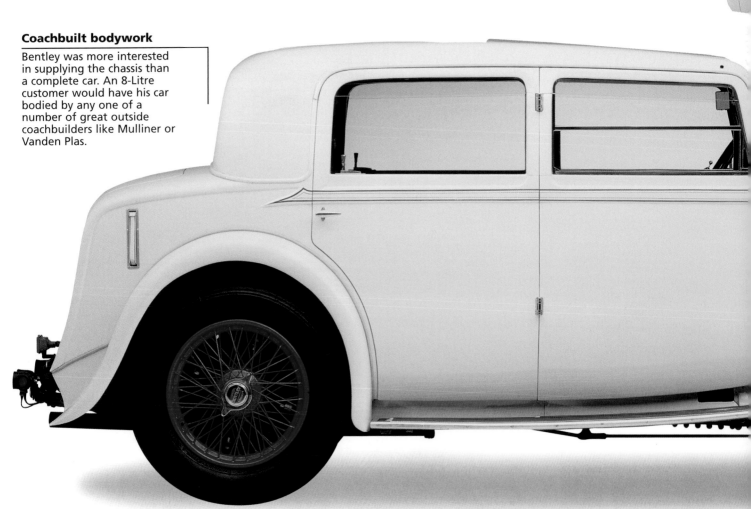

Solid front axle

Bentley was not interested in experiments with independent front suspension and stayed with a solid axle with a semi-elliptic leaf spring system along with adjustable friction-type shocks.

Drum brakes

One advantage of having tall wheels (21 inches) is for the enormous brake drums. They need to be big to stop the car. They have finned alloy casings and are operated with a rod.

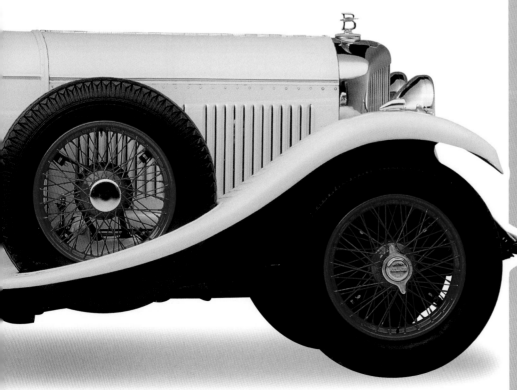

Specifications
1930 Bentley 8-Litre

ENGINE

Type: Inline six-cylinder
Construction: Integral cast-iron cylinder block and head with separate crankcase and sump
Valve gear: Four valves per cylinder operated by single overhead camshaft driven by three shafts and gears from the crankshaft
Bore and stroke: 4.33 in. x 5.51 in.
Displacement: 7,982 cc
Compression ratio: 5.3:1
Induction system: Two SU carburetors
Maximum power: 225 bhp at 3,500 rpm
Maximum torque: N/A
Top speed: 101 mph
0–60 mph: N/A

TRANSMISSION

Four-speed manual

BODY/CHASSIS

Separate steel channel-section chassis with two side members and tubular cross-members with choice of bodywork

SPECIAL FEATURES

Flip-out, semaphore-type turn signals are mounted on the sides of the trunk.

As on previous Bentleys, the parking brake and shifter are mounted on the right side.

RUNNING GEAR

Steering: Worm-and-wheel
Front suspension: Solid axle with semi-elliptic leaf springs and friction shocks
Rear suspension: Live axle with semi-elliptic leaf springs and friction shocks
Brakes: Finned drums (front and rear), servo-assisted
Wheels: Quick-release knock-on/off wire spoke, 21-in. dia.
Tires: Crossply 21-in. dia.

DIMENSIONS

Length: 200.5 in. **Width:** 69.4 in.
Height: 71.5 in. **Wheelbase:** 144.0 in.
Track: 55.9 in. (front and rear)
Weight: 5,390 lbs.

Bentley CONTINENTAL R

This was the world's most expensive car in 1952, and was also a strong contender as the world's fastest four-seater road car. This pinnacle of the touring car tradition was also one of the most handsome cars ever made.

Straight-six engine

The intake-over-exhaust straight-six engine could easily get the hefty Continental R moving along at more than 100 mph.

Choice of transmission

The four-speed manual transmission was a model of slick operation and has a higher final drive ratio for relaxed high-speed cruising. A four-speed automatic transmission was also available.

Classic Bentley grill

To distinguish Bentley from Rolls-Royce, the grill is very different. The profile is more rounded and the 'Flying Lady' mascot is replaced by Bentley's winged 'B.' In the interest of cutting frontal area, and hence drag, the height of the grill is reduced by 1.5 inches.

Comfortable suspension

To achieve the optimum ride quality, there is an independent coil-sprung wishbone front end and a semi-elliptic leaf-sprung rear axle.

Elegant coachwork

To true automotive enthusiasts, the Continental R remains one of the greatest all-time body designs. The aluminum body was hand-crafted by H.J. Mulliner.

Aerodynamic shape

The body was shaped by the wind, literally, as it was developed in the Rolls-Royce wind tunnel. The fastback shape certainly helped airflow, as did the curved windshield. An uncanny lack of wind noise was one important fringe benefit.

Sporty interior
The Continental has a wooden dashboard, deep-pile carpeting, front bucket seats and leather upholstery. The prominent tachometer's redline is set at 4,250 rpm.

Specifications

1952 Bentley Continental R

ENGINE
Type: In-line six-cylinder

Construction: Cast-iron block and aluminum head

Valve gear: Two valves per cylinder, (overhead inlet/side exhaust) operated by a single camshaft via pushrods and rockers

Bore and stroke: 3.62 in. x 4.50 in.

Displacement: 4,566 cc

Compression ratio: 7.0:1

Induction system: Two SU carburetors

Maximum power: Not quoted

Maximum torque: Not quoted

Top speed: 117 mph

0–60 mph: 13.5 sec.

TRANSMISSION
Four-speed manual

BODY/CHASSIS
Separate chassis with aluminum two-door coupe body

SPECIAL FEATURES

The high-quality engineering even extends to the alloy gas filler cap.

The lowered radiator grill carries the traditional Bentley winged 'B' mascot.

RUNNING GEAR
Steering: Cam-and-roller

Front suspension: Wishbones with coil springs and lever-arm shock absorbers

Rear suspension: Live axle with semi-elliptic leaf springs and adjustable telescopic shock absorbers

Brakes: Drums (front and rear)

Wheels: Steel, 16-in. dia.

Tires: 6.50 x 16

DIMENSIONS
Length: 206.4 in.   **Width:** 71.5 in.

Height: 63.0 in.   **Wheelbase:** 120.0 in.

Track: 56.7 in. (front), 58.5 in. (rear)

Weight: 3,543 lbs.

Bentley **TURBO R/T**

The Bentley Turbo R/T is an enormous car with a huge power output and almost excessive luxury. Unsurprisingly, it has an enormous price tag to match.

Turbo V8 engine

The naturally aspirated Rolls/Bentley V8 produces enough power, but to increase the output to 400 bhp the engine is now turbocharged. More important for performance is the increase in torque that turbocharging produces.

Electronic shocks

The key to the Bentley's great poise is its electronic shocks. Each shock is adjusted in microseconds to cope with the changes in road surface and speed or cornering forces.

Four-speed automatic

The four-speed automatic transmission has adaptive changes—it learns the driver's style whether relaxed or enthusiastic, and varies the shift points accordingly.

Alloy wheels

To carry the Bentley's great weight and handle the performance, the Turbo R/T needs large wheels and is fitted with handsome and wide five-spoke alloys.

Semi-trailing arm rear suspension

Semi-trailing arm rear suspension has been used on Rolls-Royces and Bentleys for many years. It's retained on the the Turbo R/T, but with much of the compliance engineered out.

Connolly leather interior
The interior is covered in Connolly leather, including the seats, steering wheel, gear selector, door panels and windshield pillars.

Specifications

1998 Bentley Turbo R/T

ENGINE

Type: V8

Construction: Alloy block and heads

Valve gear: Two valves per cylinder operated by single camshafts via pushrods

Bore and stroke: 4.09 in. x 3.89 in.

Displacement: 6,750 cc

Compression ratio: 8.0:1

Induction system: Zytec EMS3 controlled electronic fuel injection with Garrett T04B turbocharger

Maximum power: 400 bhp at 4,000 rpm

Maximum torque: 490 lb-ft at 2,000 rpm

Top speed: 152 mph

0–60 mph: 6.7 sec

TRANSMISSION

Four-speed automatic

BODY/CHASSIS

Monocoque four-door saloon

SPECIAL FEATURES

The sportier Bentleys have mesh radiator grills rather than the chrome ones used on Rolls-Royces.

Before tire technology caught up, the Turbo had to have an electronically-limited top speed.

RUNNING GEAR

Steering: Rack-and-pinion

Front suspension: Double wishbones with coil springs, electronically-controlled shocks and anti-roll bar

Rear suspension: Semi-trailing arms, coil springs, electronically-controlled shocks and anti-roll bar

Brakes: Vented discs (front), solid discs (rear); ABS standard

Wheels: Alloy, 8.5 x 18 in.

Tires: 265/45 ZR18

DIMENSIONS

Length: 212.4 in.   **Width:** 83.1 in.

Height: 58.5 in.   **Wheelbase:** 124.5 in.

Track: 61 in. (front and rear)

Weight: 5,450 lbs.

Bizzarrini **GT STRADA**

Evolved as the racing version of the Iso Grifo, the Strada's dramatic body, racing chassis and powerful engine made an intoxicating brew. For a while in the 1960s, Bizzarrini looked like a major force in the supercar stakes.

Corvette V8

The 327-cubic inch Corvette V8 engine was a logical choice for Bizzarrini, who had worked around this powerplant in the Iso Grifo (which he engineered). It was offered in near-standard specification.

Cast-alloy wheels

The evocative Campagnolo magnesium alloy wheels with knock-off center spinners look extremely purposeful. For competition use, it could be ordered with even wider rims (7 inches front and 9 inches rear).

Three fuel tanks

The GT Strada is a thirsty car, so to prevent constant fuel stops no less than three fuel tanks are fitted. There are two 7.5-gallon tanks in the rocker panels and a 20-gallon tank behind the seats, giving a total of 35 gallons.

Fiberglass bodywork

Apart from the earliest cars, which have aluminum bodywork built by Italian artisans, the bodywork is made of fiberglass. This keeps weight and costs down and makes manufacturing simpler. For competition use you could even specify thinner fiberglass body work with larger wheel openings.

Giugiaro design

The stunning shape was drawn up by a youthful Giorgetto Giugiaro while he was still working with Bertone. It was even more dramatic than the closely related Iso Grifo, also styled by Giugiaro. At just 44 inches high, it made a very strong impression.

Stripped-out cockpit

True to this car's racing roots, the cabin is not very luxurious. Two narrow bucket seats nestle between the wide sills and transmission tunnel, and the trim is minimal.

Specifications

1966 Bizzarrini GT Strada 5300

ENGINE

Type: V8

Construction: Cast-iron block and heads

Valve gear: Two valves per cylinder operated by a single camshaft with pushrods and rockers

Bore and stroke: 4.00 in. x 3.25 in.

Displacement: 327 c.i.

Compression ratio: 11.0:1

Induction system: Single Holley four-barrel carburetor

Maximum power: 365 bhp at 6,200 rpm

Maximum torque: 344 lb-ft at 4,000 rpm

Top speed: 165 mph

0–60 mph: 6.4 sec

TRANSMISSION

Four-speed manual

BODY/CHASSIS

Separate pressed-steel chassis with two-door coupe body

SPECIAL FEATURES

Ducts behind the front wheels carry hot air away from the cramped engine compartment.

The headlights are concealed behind plastic shrouds.

RUNNING GEAR

Steering: Recirculating ball

Front suspension: Wishbones with coil springs, shock absorbers and anti-roll bar

Rear suspension: De Dion axle with trailing arms, Watt linkage, coil springs and shock absorbers

Brakes: Discs (front and rear)

Wheels: Alloy, 15-in. dia.

Tires: Dunlop, 6.00 x 15 in. (front), 7.00 x 15 in. (rear)

DIMENSIONS

Length: 172.0 in.   **Width:** 68.0 in.

Height: 44.7 in.   **Wheelbase:** 96.5 in.

Track: 55.5 in. (front), 56.5 in. (rear)

Weight: 2,530 lbs.

BMW 2000 CS

Although it was obviously inspired by the look of the bigger Bertone-designed, V8-powered 3200 CS coupe, the 2000 CS was designed independently by BMW and was easily just as stylish and attractive.

MacPherson struts

In the 1960s, BMW decided MacPherson struts were the ideal way to suspend the front wheels and used them with lower wishbones and an anti-roll bar.

Four-cylinder engine

The inline, single overhead-cam, 2.0-liter, four-cylinder engine developed for the 2000 was an excellent and extremely strong design, which was used more effectively in the lighter 2002 models.

Pillarless design

One of the keys to the 2000 CS's good looks is the absence of a central door pillar. This helps give a longer, sleeker look.

Covered lights

In Europe, the 2000 CS was sold with its original headlight design of one round and one square light behind curved glass covers. But this arrangement was illegal in the U.S., where the car had two small headlights without glass coverings.

Specifications

1966 BMW 2000 CS

ENGINE

Type: Inline four-cylinder

Construction: Cast-iron block and alloy cylinder head

Valve gear: Two valves per cylinder operated by an overhead camshaft

Bore and stroke: 3.50 in. x 3.15 in.

Displacement: 1,990 cc

Compression ratio: 9.3:1

Induction system: Two Solex 40 PHH sidedraft carburetors

Maximum power: 135 bhp at 5,800 rpm

Maximum torque: 123 lb-ft at 3,600 rpm

Top speed: 115 mph

0–60 mph: 11.3 sec

TRANSMISSION

Four-speed manual

BODY/CHASSIS

Unitary monocoque construction with steel two-door coupe body

SPECIAL FEATURES

U.S.-market cars have exposed quad headlights with no glass covering.

The 2000 CS came with these standard steel wheels which suit the car's uncluttered and simple lines.

RUNNING GEAR

Steering: Worm-and-roller

Front suspension: MacPherson struts with lower wishbones, telescopic shock absorbers and anti-roll bar

Rear suspension: Semi-trailing arms with coil springs and telescopic shock absorbers

Brakes: Discs, 10.8-in. dia. (front), drums, 9.8-in. dia. (rear)

Wheels: Pressed steel discs, 14-in. dia.

Tires: 6.95 x 14

DIMENSIONS

Length: 178.3 in.   **Width:** 65.9 in.

Height: 53.5 in.   **Wheelbase:** 100.4 in.

Track: 52.4 in. (front), 54.3 in. (rear)

Weight: 2,630 lbs.

Four-speed transmission

With the four-speed manual, BMW had top gear as the conventional 1:1 ratio and geared the final-drive ratio to give 19.8 mph per thousand revs as the best compromise between outright performance and acceptable top-gear cruising. Buyers could opt for a ZF three-speed automatic instead.

BMW 2002 TURBO

In the mid-1970s no one cared that the 2002 Turbo had a problem with turbo lag. They were just delighted that BMW could produce a 2-liter car with 170 bhp and acceleration in Porsche's league.

Vented front brakes

To cope with its performance, the Turbo has vented disc brakes in the front, but it retains the 2002 tii's drums at the rear.

Four-cylinder engine

The four-cylinder engine in the 2002 could trace its ancestry back to the 1500. The same iron block was also used in the BMW turbo F1 engine, which at one stage produced more than 1000 bhp.

Square rear lights

The first 2002s had raised round tail lights, but when the Turbo was launched, BMW changed the design to these newer square lights.

KKK turbocharger

The KKK turbocharger that BMW used was large, by modern standards, and capable of producing tremendous power. But the inertia in its large rotors meant it was slow to start spinning when the throttle was pressed. Consequently, there was too much lag before the turbo began to make boost.

High-geared steering

To make the Turbo feel more responsive, it was given a higher ratio steering gear than the fuel-injected 2002 tii.

Front spoiler

The front spoiler reduces the amount of turbulent air flowing under the car which can hamper its performance.

Wider wheels

For the Turbo, BMW went up from the 5-inch wide steel wheels of the 2002 tii to 6-inch wide alloy rims, carrying wider 185/70 HR13 tires.

Lowered suspension

The 2002 was lowered to improve handling. With stiffer springs and shocks there was no danger of the wheels hitting the bodywork.

Specifications
1973 BMW 2002 Turbo

ENGINE
Type: In-line four cylinder
Construction: Cast-iron block and alloy cylinder head
Valve gear: Two inclined valves per cylinder operated by single chain-driven overhead cam
Bore and stroke: 3.50 in. x 3.14 in.
Displacement: 1,990 cc
Compression ratio: 6.9:1
Induction system: Kugelfischer fuel injection
Maximum power: 170 bhp at 5,800 rpm
Maximum torque: 177 lb-ft at 4,500 rpm
Top speed: 130 mph
0–60 mph: 7.6 sec

TRANSMISSION
Four- or five-speed manual

BODY/CHASSIS
Steel monocoque two-door sedan

SPECIAL FEATURES

When the driver you were following looked in his mirrors, the reversed badges on the front spoiler told him he was being caught by the Turbo.

Radical wheel arches are needed to cover the Turbo's wide tires.

RUNNING GEAR
Steering: ZF worm-and-roller
Front suspension: MacPherson struts and anti-roll bar
Rear suspension: Semi-trailing arms, coil springs, telescopic shocks and anti-roll bar
Brakes: Vented discs 10 in. dia. (front), drums 9 in. dia. (rear)
Wheels: Alloy, 6 in. x 13 in.
Tires: 185/70 HR13

DIMENSIONS
Length: 166.1 in.   **Width:** 63.8 in.
Height: 55 in.   **Wheelbase:** 98.4 in.
Track: 62.2 in. (front and rear)
Weight: 2,381 lbs.

BMW 328

The 328 was light, nimble and, with 80 bhp, powerful enough to form the basis of a successful competition car. It was also an excellent sports car.

Triple carburetors

The 328 has a high bodyline because the straight-six engine is fed by three downdraft Solex carburetors mounted above it. The 328's unique valve gear leaves no room for side-mounted carburetors.

Tubular-steel chassis

Built before monocoque construction became commonplace, the 328 uses a simple tubular-steel chassis. The two main longitudinal chassis members are wide-based at the rear and angled inward toward the front.

Rack-and-pinion steering

The 328 has very direct handling, partly due to the car's high-geared steering. The use of rack-and-pinion steering was very advanced for the 1930s.

Hemi-head straight-six

The 2.0-liter straight-six engine has only one block-mounted camshaft, but it still has hemispherical combustion chambers with inclined valves.

Excellent brakes

The 328 has hydraulically-operated drums all around. These are very effective and helped by the car's light weight.

ENGINE

Type: In-line six

Construction: Cast-iron block and aluminum alloy head

Valve gear: Two valves per cylinder operated by a single camshaft via pushrods and rockers; inlet valves operated directly, exhaust valves by cross-over pushrods

Bore and stroke: 2.6 in. x 3.8 in.

Displacement: 1,971 cc

Compression ratio: 7.5:1

Induction system: Three downdraft Solex carburetors

Maximum power: 80 bhp at 4,500 rpm

Maximum torque: 93 lb-ft at 4,000 rpm

Top speed: 103 mph

0–60 mph: 9.5 sec.

TRANSMISSION

Four-speed manual

BODY/CHASSIS

Tubular-steel ladder-type chassis with two-seater open sports body

SPECIAL FEATURES

The spare wheel is mounted on the trunk to give more luggage space.

These leather retaining straps hold the hood closed.

RUNNING GEAR

Steering: Rack-and-pinion

Front suspension: Independent with lower wishbones, transverse semi-elliptic leaf spring and lever-arm shocks

Rear suspension: Live axle with semi-elliptic leaf springs and lever-arm shocks

Brakes: Drums, 11-in. dia. (front and rear)

Wheels: Knock-on pressed-steel discs

Tires: Crossply, 5.25 x 16 in.

DIMENSIONS

Length: 153.5 in.   **Width:** 61 in.

Height: 49 in.   **Wheelbase:** 93 in.

Track: 45.5 in. (front), 48 in. (rear)

Weight: 1,638 lbs.

BMW 507

It is undoubtedly the elegant bodywork styled by Count Albrecht Goertz which gives the 507 its tremendous allure. It was an outstanding sports car in its day, and is a true classic today.

Aristocratic design

The faultless lines of the 507 were styled by Count Albrecht Goertz. He was approached by Max Hoffman, BMW's American sales representative, and submitted proposals for a sporty two-seater which were accepted, despite some resistance from BMW's board.

Rare V8 power

The technically advanced V8 engine was the mainstay of BMW's program in the late 1950s, providing all the torque and power its big luxury cars required.

Stylized kidney grill

The trademark upright split 'kidney' front grill—an unmistakable and universal BMW feature—at first appears to be absent from the 507. But Albrecht Goertz merely flattened the profile of the split grill so that it runs horizontally across the front of the car and, undoubtedly, suits this body design to perfection.

Close-ratio transmission

To suit its more sporting role, the four-speed manual transmission is fitted with a new cluster of close-set ratios for more spirited acceleration. The standard final drive ratio is 3.70:1, which is lower than other BMWs of the period, but an optional 3.42:1 or 3.90:1 differential was also available to suit a customer's driving style—sporty or touring.

Powerful brakes

The brakes are hydraulically-actuated servo-assisted. When launched, the 507 had four-wheel 11.2-inch drum brakes, but Alfin 10.5-inch front discs were installed on later cars. These were very advanced for the time and provide excellent stopping power.

Plenty of aluminum

To keep weight down, aluminum is used as much as possible. The bodywork and doors are handcrafted in alloy, as are the cylinder block and heads.

Specifications
1957 BMW 507

ENGINE

Type: V8

Construction: Light-alloy cylinder block and heads

Valve gear: Two overhead valves per cylinder operated by a single camshaft

Bore and stroke: 3.28 in. x 2.95 in.

Displacement: 3,168 cc

Compression ratio: 7.8:1

Induction system: Two twin-choke carburetors

Maximum power: 150 bhp at 5,000 rpm

Maximum torque: 174 lb-ft at 4,000 rpm

Top speed: 124 mph

0–60 mph: 8.8 sec.

TRANSMISSION

Four-speed manual

BODY/CHASSIS

Separate steel chassis with two-door aluminum convertible body

SPECIAL FEATURES

'Bullet' front marker lights show its American styling influence.

The highly distinctive side louvers have become a BMW hallmark; the current M Roadster has the same arrangement.

RUNNING GEAR

Steering: Pinion-and-sector

Front suspension: Upper and lower wishbones with torsion bars, and telescopic shock absorbers

Rear suspension: Live axle with torsion bars and Panhard rod, and telescopic shock absorbers

Brakes: Drums (front and rear); later front discs

Wheels: Steel, 16-in. dia.

Tires: 6.00H x 16 in. racing type

DIMENSIONS

Length: 173 in.   **Width:** 65 in.

Height: 49.5 in.   **Wheelbase:** 97.6 in.

Track: 56.9 in. (front), 56.1 in. (rear)

Weight: 2,840 lbs.

BMW **ISETTA**

The shape of the Isetta is extremely clever. Not only can two people fit inside easily, there is still room for a surprising amount of luggage. Also, the car is so short it can be parked nose-first curbside and in tiny spaces.

Single door

The key to the Isetta's design is that the whole front of the car swings out as a single door. The only drawback is the blindspots caused by the thickness of the front pillars.

Single-cylinder engine

The biggest engine used in the Isetta is BMW's 298-cc single-cylinder—an air-cooled overhead-valve design with an almost equal bore and stroke. Its output of 13 bhp sounds small, but at the time it was about the same output per liter as a conventional car.

Movable steering column

In the Isetta's rival, the Heinkel, the steering column is fixed, making entry and exit awkward. In the Isetta, a lower universal joint enables it to swing clear of the door and instrument panel, and it also acts as a convenient handle with which to pull the door closed.

Swinging arm suspension

Due to limited space, the front suspension uses Dubonnet-type swinging arms with integral coil spring/shock absorber units.

Single rear wheel

Although the early Isettas have four wheels, the design evolved into a three-wheeler, with a single chain-driven rear wheel on a swinging arm with a quarter elliptic leaf spring.

Specifications

1960 BMW Isetta 300

ENGINE

Type: BMW one-cylinder

Construction: Alloy block and head

Valve gear: Two valves operated by a single camshaft via pushrods and rockers

Bore and stroke: 2.83 in. x 2.87 in.

Displacement: 298 cc

Compression ratio: 6.8:1

Induction system: Single Bing carburetor

Maximum power: 13 bhp at 5,200 rpm

Maximum torque: Not quoted

Top speed: 55 mph

0-40 mph: 16.3 sec.

TRANSMISSION

Four-speed manual

BODY/CHASSIS

Separate tubular steel chassis with steel single-door body

SPECIAL FEATURES

A central fuel filler cap means the Isetta can be filled with ease from either side.

There was no shortage of imagination when it came to the design of details.

RUNNING GEAR

Steering: Worm-and-nut

Front suspension: Dubonnet swinging arms with enclosed coil spring/shock absorber units

Rear suspension: Single quarter elliptic leaf spring with telescopic shock absorber

Brakes: Drums (front and rear)

Wheels: Pressed steel disc, 10-in. dia.

Tires: 4.40-10

DIMENSIONS

Length: 90.0 in. **Width:** 54.3 in.

Height: 52.8 in. **Wheelbase:** 59.1 in.

Track: 47.2 in. (front)

Weight: 795 lbs.

BMW M1

It might not look as spectacular as its exotic Ferrari and Lamborghini rivals, but don't let that fool you. The M1 has one major advantage—it was designed as a real racing car.

Tubular steel chassis

Originally, it made sense to farm out the chassis construction to Lamborghini because they had far more experience than BMW in building tubular steel chassis. Eventually Marchesi of Modena made the chassis.

Fiberglass bodywork

All the M1 body panels are fiberglass and they are both riveted and bonded to the tubular steel frame. The body was produced by Italian company TIR (Transformazione Italiana Resina) to a very high standard.

Twin-cam straight-six

In street-legal form the BMW's six-cylinder, twin-cam engine produces 277 bhp from 3.5 liters.

Pirelli P7 tires

The low-profile Pirelli P7 tire was a huge advance in its day and the car's suspension was set up to suit the tire's characteristics.

Slatted engine cover

Hot air from the engine compartment escapes between these large slats. Rearward vision is very good for a mid-engined supercar, and a glass window behind the driver's head insulates the cockpit from the engine bay.

Air intakes

Slots just behind the nearside, rear window feed air to the engine's induction system. The matching slots on the other side are for engine bay ventilation.

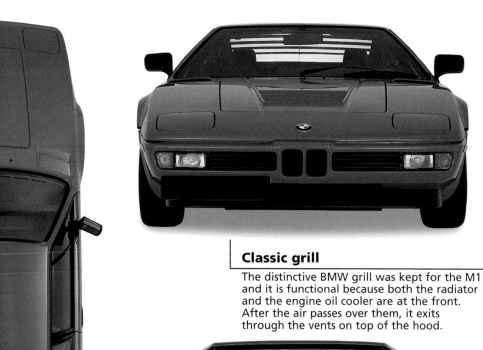

Classic grill

The distinctive BMW grill was kept for the M1 and it is functional because both the radiator and the engine oil cooler are at the front. After the air passes over them, it exits through the vents on top of the hood.

Servo brakes

Street-legal M1s have servo-assisted brakes but these were left off the racers, although the driver could adjust the brake balance between front and rear wheels.

Double-wishbone suspension

Most BMWs have some form of semi-trailing arm suspension at the rear but the M1 is different, with racing-type double wishbones in the front and rear.

Specifications
1980 BMW M1

ENGINE
Type: Straight-six twin cam
Construction: Cast-iron block and alloy head
Valve gear: Four valves per cylinder operated by two chain-driven overhead camshafts
Bore and stroke: 3.68 in. x 3.31 in.
Displacement: 3,453 cc
Compression ratio: 9.0:1
Induction system: Bosch-Kugelfischer mechanical fuel injection
Maximum power: 277 bhp at 6,500 rpm
Maximum torque: 239 lb-ft at 5,000 rpm

TRANSMISSION
ZF five-speed manual

BODY/CHASSIS
Fiberglass two-door, two-seat coupe body with tubular steel chassis

SPECIAL FEATURES

Rear screen louvers afforded reasonable rearward vision and helped to keep engine temperatures down.

Dated wheel with Pirelli P7s that are narrow by today's standards.

RUNNING GEAR
Steering: Rack-and-pinion
Front suspension: Double wishbones, coil springs, telescopic shocks and anti-roll bar
Rear suspension: Double wishbones, coil springs, telescopic shocks and anti-roll bar
Brakes: Vented discs front and rear
Wheels: Alloy, 7 in. x 16 in. (front), 8 in. x 16 in. (rear)
Tires: Pirelli P7, 205/55 VR16 (front), 225/50 VR16 (rear)

DIMENSIONS
Length: 171.7 in.   **Width:** 71.7 in.
Height: 44.9 in. **Wheelbase:** 100.8 in.
Track: 61 in. (front), 60.9 in. (rear)
Weight: 3,122 lbs.

BMW **M3**

Very few full four-seaters would come near the top of a list of performance cars. One car that would, however, is BMW's M3.

Six-speed transmission

To make the most of the power, the European M3 has a six-speed transmission, whereas the U.S. spec cars use a five speed.

321-bhp engine

The heart of the M3 is its incredible engine. The 24-valve, twin-cam straight-six produces 321 bhp at 7,400 rpm. Peak torque comes at a more down to earth 3,250 rpm thanks to variable valve timing.

Practical trunk

Unlike many cars in the same performance league, the M3 can carry more than just an overnight bag.

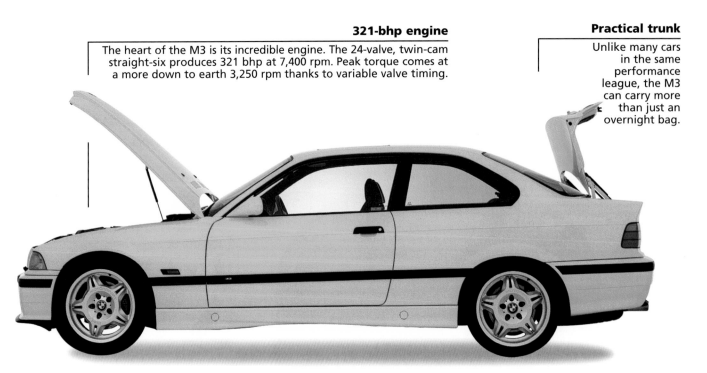

Different body styles

Although it was launched as a two-door coupe, the M3 is now also available as a practical four-door sedan or an eye-catching convertible.

Performance suspension

The 3 Series MacPherson strut front and multi-link rear suspension is uprated for use on the M3. It is regarded as one of the finest handling cars in its class.

Easily recognized

If you want subtle looks and decent performance, then buy the 328i. The M3 looks as fast as it goes thanks to a distinctive body kit.

Specifications

1996 BMW M3 Evolution*

ENGINE

Type: In-line six

Construction: Cast block and alloy head

Valve gear: Four valves per cylinder operated by twin overhead camshafts with VANOS variable valve timing

Bore and stroke: 3.4 in. x 3.58 in.

Displacement: 3,201 cc

Compression ratio: 11.3:1

Induction system: Electronic digital engine management system

Top speed: 140 mph

0–60 mph: 5.6 sec.

TRANSMISSION

Six-speed manual

BODY/CHASSIS

Steel monocoque two-door coupe

SPECIAL FEATURES

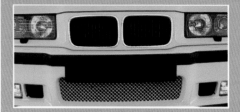

The M3 can be easily recognized by its deep chin spoiler.

Wide 17-inch alloy wheels and very low-profile tires help to sharpen the M3's handling.

RUNNING GEAR

Steering: Power-assisted rack-and-pinion

Front suspension: MacPherson struts with arc-shaped lower arms, coils springs, twin-tube shocks and anti-roll bar

Rear suspension: Independent system with coil springs, twin-tube shocks and anti-roll bar

Brakes: Vented discs, 12.4 in. dia. (front), 12.3 in. dia. (rear)

Wheels: Alloy, 17 x 7.5J (front), 17 x 8.5J (rear)

Tires: 225/45ZR-17 (front), 245/40ZR-17 (rear)

DIMENSIONS

Length: 174.5 in.   **Width:** 66.9 in.

Height: 53.7 in.   **Wheelbase:** 106.3 in.

Track: 56 in. (front), 56.6 in. (rear)

Weight: 3,352 lbs.

*Details apply to European-spec M3 Evolution.

Borgward ISABELLA

The Borgward Isabella remains one of the greatest unsung cars from Germany. Many of the qualities of the Isabella were adapted by BMW, so the Borgward has a right to be called the 1950s equivalent of today's BMW.

Elegant style

One German magazine said the Isabella coupe was perhaps the prettiest German car of the 1950s. Designed by Karl Deutsch of Cologne, it features an elegant body and shapely rear fenders.

Tough engine

The 1.5-liter, pushrod, four-cylinder engine is a model of quality and reliability. In postwar Germany, this quality was widely appreciated. The engine is also very capable, and in its day, had a lot of success in competition.

Column shift

The vast majority of Isabellas have a four-speed manual transmission with an H-pattern column shifter. For the final years of production, 1960-1961, an automatic was also offered as an option.

Near-perfect weight distribution

Part of the Isabella's handling prowess can be attributed to its perfect 50/50 weight distribution. Testers remarked on how adjustable the car was. Understeer and oversteer were virtually selectable.

Distinctive grill

Like all postwar Borgwards, the Isabella has a diamond-pattern badge in the middle of the grill. Horizontal bars emanate from both sides of the diamond.

Generous equipment

Befitting its image as a high-quality car, the Isabella is equipped with many luxury features. In TS form, these include deeply upholstered reclining seats, armrests, door pockets, clock, cigar lighter, multiple gauges and heater.

1958 Borgward Isabella TS

ENGINE

Type: Inline 4-cylinder

Construction: Cast-iron cylinder block and aluminum cylinder head

Valve gear: Two valves per cylinder operated by single camshaft with pushrods and rockers

Bore and stroke: 2.95 in. x 3.27 in.

Displacement: 1,493 cc

Compression ratio: 8.2:1

Induction system: Single Solex dual-throat carburetor

Maximum power: 82 bhp at 5,200 rpm

Maximum torque: 84 lb-ft at 3,000 rpm

Top speed: 93 mph

0–60 mph: 16.0 sec.

TRANSMISSION

Four-speed manual (or automatic from 1960)

BODY/CHASSIS

Steel unitary construction chassis with two-door sedan, wagon, coupe or convertible

SPECIAL FEATURES

A padded armrest is one of the features that gives the Isabella its charm.

TS models have side markerlights on the front fenders.

RUNNING GEAR

Steering: Worm-and-roller

Front suspension: Unequal-length double wishbones with coil springs and shock absorbers

Rear suspension: Swing axles with coil springs and shock absorbers

Brakes: Drums (front and rear)

Wheels: Steel, 13-in. dia.

Tires: 5.90 x 13

DIMENSIONS

Length: 173.0 in.   **Width:** 67.7 in.

Height: 53.2 in.   **Wheelbase:** 102.4 in.

Track: 52.8 in. (front), 53.5 in. (rear)

Weight: 2,320 lbs.

Boyd SMOOTHSTER

It took almost three years and an untold number of man hours to produce the Smoothster. This effort was rewarded in 1995 when it won the 'World's Most Beautiful Roadster' competition in Oakland.

Corvette engine

The 350-cubic inch LT1 engine from a 1992 Corvette was used in the Smoothster because it was a well-proven, reliable unit that fitted the dimensions of the engine bay and produced sufficient power.

Hardtop

Initially, the Smoothster was to have a folding roof. However, Hot Rods by Boyd decided to fit a Carson-style removable hardtop.

Big wheels

Originally, the Smoothster was built to run on 15- and 16-inch wheels. However, Boyd's Wheels developed some new 17- and 18-inch designs, and so the wells were opened up to fit the larger wheels and tires.

Hidden exhausts

To retain its sleek lines, the Smoothster's exhaust pipes are hidden under the running boards.

Art deco grill

The finely ribbed grill consists of 22 hand-formed bars which flow back into the bodywork, with the top rib forming a chrome belt line that runs down the trunk line at the rear.

Aluminum body

The unique aluminum body was formed over a wooden buck. In order to get a smoother appearance, the 1937 Ford has been sectioned, chopped and lowered to produce a fat-fendered look. The floor is made of steel for stiffness and reliability.

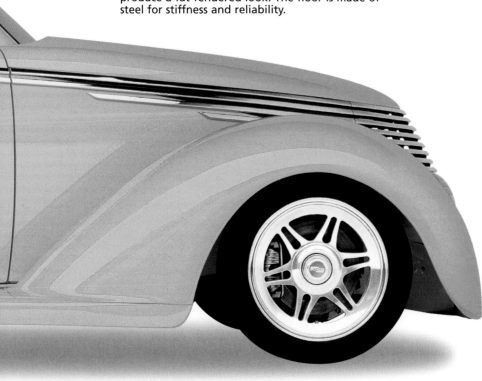

Specifications

1995 Boyd Smoothster

ENGINE

Type: V8

Construction: Cast-iron block and heads

Valve gear: Two valves per cylinder operated by a single chain-driven camshaft with pushrods

Bore and stroke: 4.00 in. x 3.48 in.

Displacement: 350 c.i.

Compression ratio: 10.25:1

Induction system: Multiport electronic fuel injection

Maximum power: 300 bhp at 5,000 rpm

Maximum torque: 330 lb-ft at 2,400 rpm

Top speed: 122 mph

0–60 mph: 6.0 sec.

TRANSMISSION

Three-speed automatic

BODY/CHASSIS

Aluminum roadster body and steel chassis

SPECIAL FEATURES

The Smoothster retains the 1937 Ford's rear-hinged 'suicide' doors.

Six-spoke tailpipes mimic the design of the alloy wheels.

RUNNING GEAR

Steering: Rack-and-pinion

Front suspension: A-arms with single transverse fiberglass leaf springs, telescopic shock absorbers, and anti-sway bar

Rear suspension: Independent with A-arms transverse fiberglass leaf spring, telescopic shock absorbers, and anti-sway bar

Brakes: Vented discs (front and rear)

Wheels: 16-in. dia. (front), 20-in. dia. (rear)

Tires: 205/45ZR-16 (front), 295/35ZR-18 (rear)

DIMENSIONS

Length: 164.0 in.   **Width:** 78.0 in.

Height: 56.0 in.   **Wheelbase:** 112.0 in.

Track: 63.0 in. (front and rear)

Weight: Not quoted

Bristol **407/411**

Bristols are unique: conservative in style, advanced in features, luxurious yet sporty in character and always more exclusive than Rolls-Royce. The V8 407 marked a new departure, but it still had top-notch quality.

V8 power

For the first time, Bristol used V8 engines in its 407 instead of straight sixes. The engine came from Chrysler in Canada and was modified by Bristol to extract greater power and make it more free-revving.

Four-wheel disc brakes

Disc brakes are necessary to stop the considerable bulk of the 407. Bristol specified substantial 11-inch Dunlop discs on all four wheels.

Pre-war chassis

The bulky separate chassis under the 407 dated from the prewar era, being a direct development of the BMW 326 chassis. Remarkably, this chassis is still in use in Bristol's current car, the Blenheim.

Luxurious cabin

The dashboard is fine walnut veneer, and there is full leather upholstery and rich carpeting. All the instruments (a total of seven) are grouped together in an easy-to-see cluster directly in front of the driver. The only option was an HMV radio and two speakers.

Ample interior space

Compared to most other sporty luxury cars of its era, the Bristol boasts plenty of space for four six-foot-tall passengers. Enormous armchair-like front seats can recline for comfort and have built-in headrests.

Aluminium bodywork

Aluminium was more abundant than steel in post-war Europe. Bristol was originally an airplane manufacturer and knew the benefits of aluminium: although it was more expensive than steel, it was lighter, easier to hand-form and entirely impervious to rust.

Aircraft-inspired nose

The 407 was the last Bristol to have this distinctive nose treatment, which is strongly reminiscent of airplanes. The front grille is set in to force cool air into the engine bay.

Specifications
1962 Bristol 407

ENGINE
Type: V8

Construction: Cast-iron block and heads

Valve gear: Two valves per cylinder operated by a single camshaft

Bore and stroke: 3.86 in. x 3.31 in.

Displacement: 313 c.i.

Compression ratio: 9.0:1

Induction system: Carter four-barrel carburetor

Maximum power: 250 bhp at 4400 rpm

Maximum torque: 340 lb-ft at 2800 rpm

Top speed: 122 mph

0–60 mph: 9.9 sec

TRANSMISSION
TorqueFlite three-speed automatic

BODY/CHASSIS
Separate chassis with aluminium two-door sedan body

SPECIAL FEATURES
Like Chryslers of the period, the 407 has push-button transmission controls.

RUNNING GEAR
Steering: Cam-and-roller

Front suspension: Unequal-length wishbones with coil springs, shock absorbers and anti-roll bar

Rear suspension: Live axle with Watt linkage, shock absorbers and longitudinal torsion bars

Brakes: Discs (front and rear)

Wheels: Steel discs, 16 in. dia.

Tyres: Dunlop, 6.00 x H16

DIMENSIONS
Length: 199.0 in.

Width: 68.0 in.

Height: 60.0 in.

Wheelbase: 114.0 in

Track: 53.0 in. (front), 54.5 in. (rear)

Weight: 13640 lbs.

Bugatti **EB110**

Despite the name, Bugatti was originally a French company. However, when it reformed in the 1990s, it was Italian-owned and the EB110 rivaled other Italian greats, the Ferrari F40 and Lamborghini Diablo.

Four-wheel drive

The Bugatti's 552 bhp is fed to all four wheels, although not in equal amounts: 63 percent of the drive goes to the rear and 37 percent to the front.

Six-speed transmission

To enable the driver to exploit all the power from the rev-happy V12, the EB110 has a six-speed close-ratio transmission mounted in front of the engine.

Four turbochargers

To avoid turbo lag at low engine speeds, the EB110 has no fewer than four small intercooled IHI turbos, two for each bank of cylinders.

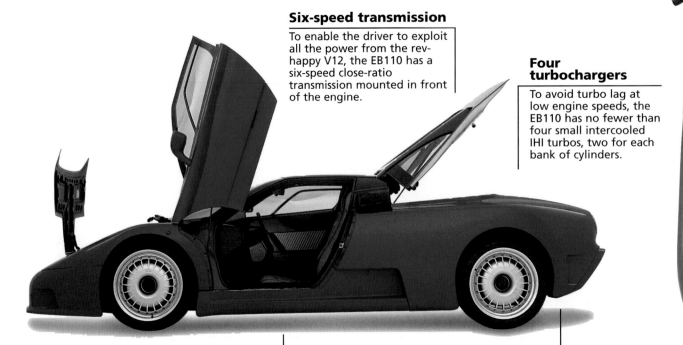

Carbon fiber chassis

Even before the advanced McLaren F1 appeared, the EB110 had a main structural "tub" or chassis made of carbon fiber, making it incredibly strong.

Special Michelin tires

Bugatti's close relationship with Michelin resulted in special ultra low-profile MXX3 tires for the EB110, fitted to alloy wheels inspired by those fitted to the pre-war Bugatti Royale.

Quad-cam V12

The EB110's 3.5-liter V12 revs to 8,200 rpm and produces as much power as the early Cosworth DFV Formula One engines.

Traditional Bugatti grill

Bugatti's horseshoe shaped radiator opening was retained for the EB110, to give it unmistakable links to Bugatti's past.

Anti-pollution devices

Four turbos are complemented by four catalytic convertors and an oil vapor collector to make the EB110 as eco-friendly as possible.

Twin rear shocks

To give the best wheel control, the EB110 uses two shocks on each side of the car's rear double wishbone suspension.

Alloy bodywork

To save weight, the body is made from lightweight aluminum alloy, usually painted traditional Bugatti blue, although some EB110s are silver.

Specifications
1993 Bugatti EB110

ENGINE

Type: V12, quad-cam

Construction: Light alloy block and heads with wet cylinder liners

Valve gear: Five valves per cylinder (three inlet, two exhaust) operated by four overhead camshafts

Bore and stroke: 3.3 in. x 2.2 in.

Displacement: 3,500 cc

Compression ratio: 7.5:1

Induction system: Bugatti multi-port fuel injection with four IHI turbos

Maximum power: 552 bhp at 8,000 rpm

Maximum torque: 450 lb-ft at 3,750 rpm

Top speed: 212 mph

0–60 mph: 3.5 sec

TRANSMISSION

Six-speed manual

BODY/CHASSIS

Alloy two-door, two-seat coupe with carbon fiber monocoque chassis

SPECIAL FEATURES

Like the Lamborghini Diablo, the EB110 has "butterfly" doors. On a car this wide, it would be almost impossible to open conventional doors in a standard size parking space or garage.

RUNNING GEAR

Steering: Rack-and-pinion

Front suspension: Twin wishbones, coil springs, telescopic shocks and anti-roll bar

Rear suspension: Twin wishbones, with twin coil spring/shock units per side

Brakes: Vented discs (front and rear), 12.7 in. with ABS

Wheels: Magnesium alloy 9 in. x 18 in. (front),12 in. x 18 in. (rear)

Tires: Michelin 245/40 (front) and 325/30 (rear)

DIMENSIONS

Length: 173.2 in.

Width: 76.4 in.

Wheelbase: 100.4 in.

Height: 44.3 in.

Track: 61 in. (front), 63.7 in. (rear)

Weight: 3,571 lbs.

Bugatti ROYALE

Designed to be simply the best car in the world, the Royale was also the biggest, with the largest engine ever seen in a production car. Unfortunately it was just too big and expensive to attract even the royalty for whom it was intended.

Straight-eight engine

With a huge displacement of 12,763 cc the Royale engine produced 275 bhp. The engine was later used to power high-speed railcars for French railroads.

Live rear axle

Normal practice for pre-war cars was a live axle and the Royale is the same. Unusually, however, it is carried on reversed quarter elliptic springs rather than semi-elliptics.

Beam front axle

The Royale's front axle is a hollow forging, with two square holes cast into it, allowing the springs to pass through them.

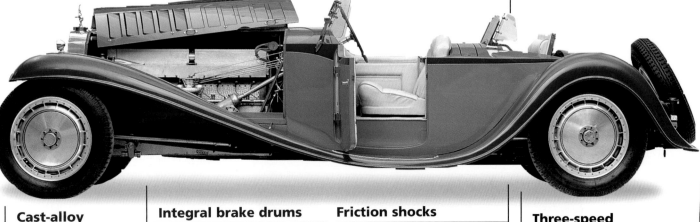

Cast-alloy wheels

Everything about the Royale is huge, including the wheels which, at a 36-inch diameter, were the largest ever fitted to a road car. The tires had to be specially made for the Royale by Michelin.

Integral brake drums

Like Bugatti's Type 35 racing car the Royale's brake drums are integral with the wheels so that removing a wheel gives instant access to the brake.

Friction shocks

The movement of the suspension was controlled by friction shocks in the days before hydraulic shocks were available.

Three-speed transaxle

The Royale's transmission is mounted at the back to offset the weight of the huge front engine. Only three gears were necessary.

Fold-away rumble seat

This model appears to be only a two-seater but two other passengers can be carried in the rumble seat. It even has its own windshield that can be raised.

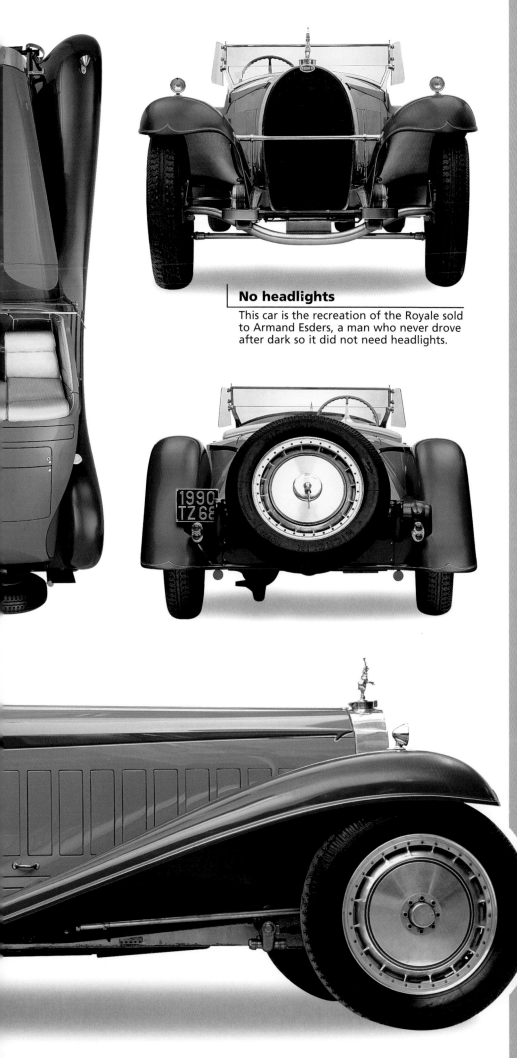

No headlights

This car is the recreation of the Royale sold to Armand Esders, a man who never drove after dark so it did not need headlights.

Specifications
1931 Bugatti Royale

ENGINE

Type: Straight-eight, overhead cam
Construction: Cast-iron monobloc with block and head cast as one
Valve gear: Three valves per cylinder (two intake, one exhaust) operated by single overhead camshaft
Bore and stroke: 4.92 in. x 5.11 in.
Displacement: 12,763 cc
Compression ratio: 6.0:1
Induction system: Single Bugatti-Schebler carburetor
Maximum power: 275 bhp at 3,000 rpm
Maximum torque: Not quoted
Top speed: 117 mph
0–60 mph: Not quoted

TRANSMISSION

Three-speed, rear-mounted transaxle

BODY/CHASSIS

Steel coachbuilt body made to order with X-braced, steel channel-section, ladder chassis

SPECIAL FEATURES

The simple fascia of the Esders roadster testifies to Bugatti's attention to quality.

The elephant mascot was designed by Ettore's sculptor brother, Rembrandt, and adopted by Ettore for the Royale.

RUNNING GEAR

Steering: Worm-and-sector
Front suspension: Solid axle with semi-elliptic leaf springs and friction shocks
Rear suspension: Live axle with reversed quarter elliptic leaf springs, additional 'helper' springs and friction shocks
Brakes: Drums front and rear, cable operated
Wheels: Alloy, 36-in. dia
Tires: Michelin 6.75 in. x 36 in.

DIMENSIONS

Length: 235 in.*   **Width:** 79 in.*
Height: 64 in.   **Wheelbase:** 170 in.
Track: 63 in. (front and rear)
Weight: up to 6,999 lbs.*
*varies according to model

Bugatti **TYPE 35**

There was a Type 35 to suit everyone, from the naturally-aspirated three-bearing Type 35A through to the cars that dominated Targa Florio and the supercharged Type 35B Grand Prix winner.

Roller-bearing engine

The Type 35's crankshaft runs in roller bearings instead of plain metal, and therefore does not require high-pressure lubrication.

Outside shifter and brake lever

Inside, space is at a premium and so the shifter actually projects through the side of the cockpit through a leather gaiter. The handbrake lever is also very long to generate sufficient leverage.

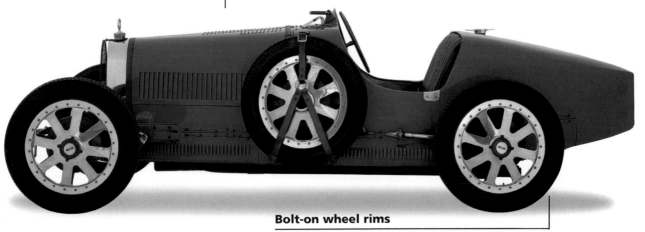

Bolt-on wheel rims

The distinctive bolt-on rims were designed to prevent punctured tires from separating from the rims—a common problem with 1920s racing cars.

Offset bodywork

Type 35s are two-seaters so they can carry a riding mechanic. The unfortunate passenger has little or no protection from the wind, whereas the driver has a cowl to deflect wind away from his face.

Hollow front axle

To save weight and for improved control, the axle is hollow. It is a complicated forging.

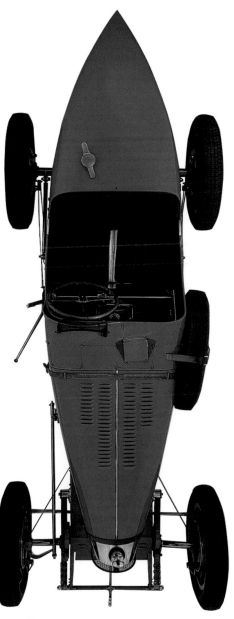

Integral wheel and brake

The wheel is integrated with the brake drum. This means that when the wheels are removed the brake linings can be easily inspected at the same time.

Specifications
1924 Bugatti Type 35

ENGINE

Type: In-line eight-cylinder
Construction: Cast-iron block and head with alloy crankcase
Valve gear: Three valves per cylinder (two inlet, one exhaust) operated by a shaft-driven overhead camshaft via rockers
Bore and stroke: 2.36 in. x 3.93 in.
Displacement: 2,262 cc
Compression ratio: Not quoted
Induction system: Zenith carburetor with crankshaft-driven supercharger
Maximum power: 130 bhp at 5,500 rpm
Maximum torque: Not quoted
Top speed: 125 mph
0–60 mph: 7.0 sec.

TRANSMISSION

Four-speed manual

BODY/CHASSIS

Tapered channel-section steel chassis with two-seat alloy body

SPECIAL FEATURES

The engine-turned dashboard has a full set of gauges— even a clock.

Bugatti persisted in using cable brakes so adjustment was vital.

RUNNING GEAR

Steering: Worm-and-wheel
Front suspension: Hollow axle with semi-elliptic leaf springs and friction shocks
Rear suspension: Live axle with reversed quarter elliptic leaf springs, forward radius rods and friction shocks
Brakes: Cable-operated drums (front and rear)
Wheels: Cast-alloy with integral drums
Tires: Crossply 4.95 x 28 in.

DIMENSIONS

Length: 145.1 in.   **Width:** 52 in.
Height: 42.9 in.   **Wheelbase:** 94.5 in.
Track: 45 in. (front), 47 in. (rear)
Weight: 1,654 lbs.

Bugatti **TYPE 57**

Regarded by many as one of the greatest sports cars ever produced, the Bugatti Type 57 could outhandle and outperform almost anything else on the road except, perhaps, the Alfa Romeo 8C 2900.

Monobloc engine design

To avoid blowing a head gasket, the engine block and head were cast in one unit. This made valve adjustment a very awkward affair.

Straight-eight twin-cam

By the time the Type 57 was launched, the traditional single overhead-cam, three-valves-per-cylinder Bugatti layout had been discarded in favor of a twin-cam arrangement, inspired by the engines of designer Harry Miller.

Live rear axle

All Bugattis had live rear axles and all featured reversed quarter-elliptic leaf springs, with the end of the spring attached to the rear crossmember.

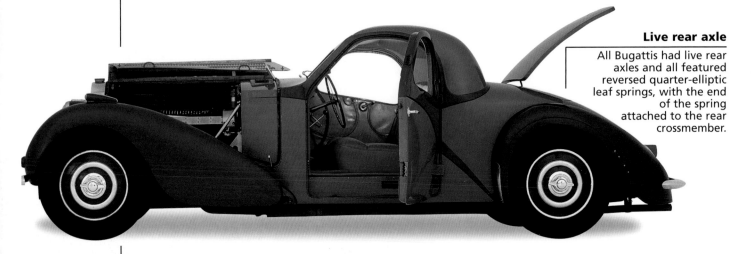

Four-speed transmission

Power is fed to the rear wheels with a four-speed transmission mounted in unit with the straight-eight engine (a Bugatti first). Fourth gear is a direct 1:1 ratio.

Coupe bodywork

The Type 57 was available with a variety of coachbuilt bodies. This Atalante coupe has a Bugatti body produced by its contracted coachbuilders, Gangloff.

Specifications
1937 Bugatti Type 57 Atalante

ENGINE

Type: In-line eight-cylinder

Construction: Alloy monobloc

Valve gear: Two valves per cylinder operated by twin gear-driven overhead camshafts with rocker arms

Bore and stroke: 2.83 in. x 3.94 in.

Displacement: 3,257 cc

Compression ratio: 6.0:1

Induction system: Single Zenith updraft carburetor

Maximum power: 140 bhp at 48 rpm

Maximum torque: Not quoted

Top speed: 120 mph

0–60 mph: 10.0 sec

TRANSMISSION

Four-speed manual

BODY/CHASSIS

Ladder-type steel chassis with two-door coupe body

SPECIAL FEATURES

A small hatch behind the door provides access to extra cargo.

A small split window was a common feature of late-1930s coupes.

RUNNING GEAR

Steering: Worm-and-wheel

Front suspension: Beam axle with semi-elliptic leaf springs and Hartford Telecontrol shock absorbers

Rear suspension: Live axle with reversed quarter-elliptic springs and Hartford Telecontrol shock absorbers

Brakes: Drums (front and rear)

Wheels: Knock-on steel discs, 18-in. dia.

Tires: Crossply, 5.5 x 18 in.

DIMENSIONS

Length: 159.0 in.   **Width:** 64.0 in.

Height: 52.0 in.   **Wheelbase:** 130.0 in.

Track: 53.1 in. (front and rear)

Weight: 2,127 lbs.

Side-opening hood

Access to both sides of the engine is made easier by a side-opening hood hinged in the middle, so that either engine cover can be raised.

Buick GSX

With its loud paintwork, spoilers, scoops and graphics, plus a monstrous 455 engine, the GSX is Buick's finest muscle car and comes complete with all the trimmings.

Front disc brakes

With so much performance just a stab of the throttle away, the GSX needs powerful brakes. It uses 11-inch diameter disc brakes at the front, but made do with finned drum brakes at the rear.

Awesome power

1970 marked the introduction of 455-cubic inch engines in GM intermediates. A standard Buick GS 455 churns out 350 bhp, but the optional Stage 1 produces 360 bhp due to a more aggressive cam and a higher compression ratio.

Transmissions

Three different transmissions were available: three- or four-speed manual, or a TurboHydramatic 400 automatic transmission with a Hurst gear shifter.

Suspension upgrades

The GSX has heavy-duty suspension and powered front disc brakes, plus uprated shock absorbers and stiffer springs for better handling.

Color availability

Introduced halfway through the model year, the 1970 GSX was available in only two colors: Apollo White or Saturn Yellow.

Chrome wheels

The GSX package included a handsome set of 7-in wide Magnum 500 chrome-plated steel wheels and Goodyear Polyglas GT series tires.

Restyled body

Some people criticized the 1968-1969 GS for looking out of proportion. For the 1970 model year, the Skylark received an attractive facelift and full rear wheel cut-outs.

Specifications
1970 Buick GSX

ENGINE
Type: V8

Construction: Cast-iron block and heads

Valve gear: Two valves per cylinder operated by pushrods and rockers

Bore and stroke: 4.33 in. x 3.9 in.

Displacement: 455 c.i.

Compression ratio: 10.5:1

Induction system: Rochester four-barrel Quadrajet carburetor

Maximum power: 360 bhp at 4,600 rpm

Maximum torque: 510 lb-ft at 2,800 rpm

TRANSMISSION
Four-speed close-ratio manual

BODY/CHASSIS
Steel coupe body on separate chassis

SPECIAL FEATURES

A hood-mounted tachometer came standard on all GSX models.

The rear spoiler and black accent stripes are some of the GSX's styling features.

RUNNING GEAR
Steering: Power-assisted recirculating ball

Front suspension: Independent wishbones with coil springs, telescopic shocks and heavy-duty roll bar

Rear suspension: Live axle fitted with 3.64:1 axle gears, heavy-duty coil springs, telescopic shocks and anti-roll bar

Brakes: Vented discs, 11-in. dia. (front), finned drums, 9.5-in. dia. (rear)

Wheels: Magnum 500, 7 x 15 in.

Tires: Goodyear Polyglas GT G60-15

DIMENSIONS
Length: 202 in.   **Width:** 75.9 in.

Height: 53 in.   **Wheelbase:** 112 in.

Track: 60.1 in. (front), 58.9 in. (rear)

Weight: 3,561 lbs.

Buick RIVIERA

Known as 'Phat Riv,' this particular car stands out thanks to its contrasting green paint, white vinyl top and interior. It is also unique in being a custom not normally associated with the street scene.

Big-block V8 engine

With gas selling for around 30 cents a gallon in 1969, a big-block V8 was mandatory in luxury cars like the Riviera. This one has a 430-cubic inch mill with 360 bhp and 475 lb-ft of torque. As expected, this car is exceedingly quick in a straight line.

Custom wheels and tires

No custom is complete without aftermarket wheels and tires. This one has a set of reverse-rim chrome-plated 15-inch steel wheels wearing period-looking modern BFGoodrich whitewall radials.

Smoothed body

A popular custom touch, which is still in vogue, is to smooth the body and remove as much chrome trim as possible. Consequently, this Riviera has had its door handles, trunk latch and trademark side spear chrome trim removed.

Body-on-frame construction

General Motors' larger cars of the 1960s have separate bodies and frames. This saved on production tooling costs, with new bodies being fitted on existing chassis. It also helps in tuning the chassis and suspension for a smooth ride.

Firm setup

The all-coil-sprung suspension is conventional for a car of this type and era, but the Riviera's setup is unusually firm and gives great stability.

Immaculate interior

One feature that really stands out on this car is the interior. The door panels, dashboard and seats have all been upholstered in white leather accentuated by green piping, highlighting the Riviera's luxury status.

Specifications

1969 Buick Riviera

ENGINE

Type: V8

Construction: Cast-iron block and heads

Valve gear: Two valves per cylinder operated by a single camshaft with pushrods and rockers

Bore and stroke: 4.19 in. x 3.90 in.

Displacement: 430 c.i.

Compression ratio: 10.25:1

Induction system: Rochester Quadrajet four-barrel carburetor

Maximum power: 360 bhp at 5,000 rpm

Maximum torque: 475 lb-ft at 3,200 rpm

Top speed: 125 mph

0–60 mph: 7.2 sec.

TRANSMISSION

GM TurboHydramatic three-speed automatic

BODY/CHASSIS

Separate steel chassis with steel two-door coupe body

SPECIAL FEATURES

Even the air cleaner has been color-coded to match the exterior.

A popular option on street customs is to french the radio antenna.

RUNNING GEAR

Steering: Recirculating ball

Front suspension: Unequal-length wishbones with coil springs, telescopic shock absorbers and anti-roll bar

Rear suspension: Live axle with coil springs, telescopic shock absorbers and anti-roll bar

Brakes: Discs (front), drums (rear)

Wheels: Steel, 6 x 15 in.

Tires: 175/60 R15

DIMENSIONS

Length: 211.6 in.   **Width:** 79.4 in.

Height: 52.7 in.   **Wheelbase:** 119.0 in.

Track: 63.5 in. (front), 63.0 in. (rear)

Weight: 4,199 lbs.

Buick ROADMASTER

For 1949, the Roadmaster's new flatter side styling and the first appearance of portholes in the front fenders were an instant hit. Buick sales increased by more than 100,000.

Straight-eight engine

The design of Buick's straight-eight engine dates back to 1931. Straight-eights were built for prestige and, although very smooth, had drawbacks, such as length and the very long crankshaft, which limited engine speeds.

Foot starter

To start the Roadmaster, the ignition is switched on and then, with the transmission in 'Park' or 'Neutral,' the throttle is pressed right to the floor, activating the starter button.

Dynaflow transmission

Buick was not the first to offer an automatic transmission but was the first to have a torque converter. It called its new transmission dynaflow. It is a much more sophisticated version of a fluid coupling, which magnifies the effect of the torque produced by the engine, so Drive is the only selection really needed.

Rear wheel covers

The 1949 Buicks, including the Roadmaster, were the last to have enclosed rear wheels. A removable panel allows the wheel to be changed.

Split windshield

The 1949 Roadmaster was one of the last Buicks to have a split windshield. Soon technology enabled curved, one-piece windshields to be produced.

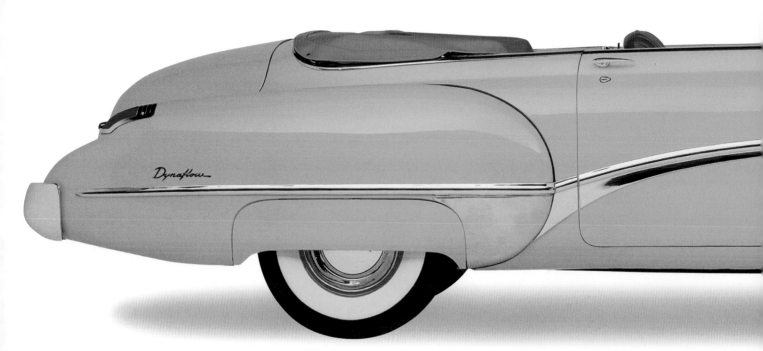

Recirculating-ball steering

The Roadmaster is a big and very heavy car, so the recirculating-ball steering needed more than five turns to go from lock to lock. This was improved with the power steering introduced in 1952. By 1954, there were 4.5 turns lock to lock, but the steering was still vague.

Drum brakes

Large, cast-iron drums give the Roadmaster good stopping power and can halt the car from 60 mph in 240 feet. Brake fade soon sets in if the car is driven hard.

A-arm front suspension

Coil-sprung double A-arm suspension and an anti-roll bar are used at the front to give the best possible ride.

Specification

1949 Buick Roadmaster

ENGINE
Type: In line eight-cylinder
Construction: Cast-iron block and head
Valve gear: Two valves per cylinder operated by a block-mounted camshaft.
Bore and stroke: 3.44 in. x 4.25 in.
Displacement: 320.2 c.i.
Compression ratio: 6.9:1
Induction system: One two-barrel Stromberg carburetor/ or carter carburetor
Maximum power: 150 bhp at 3,600 rpm
Maximum torque: 260 lb-ft at 2,400 rpm
Top speed: 100 mph
0–60 mph: 17.1 sec.

TRANSMISSION
Two-speed Dynaflow automatic with a torque converter

BODY/CHASSIS
Separate steel chassis with two-door convertible body

SPECIAL FEATURES

The Roadmaster has four portholes compared to the three of other Buicks.

The Dynaflow transmission was the first torque-converter automatic on a production car.

RUNNING GEAR
Steering: Recirculating-ball
Front suspension: Double A-arms with coil springs, telescopic shock absorbers and anti-roll bar
Rear suspension: Live axle with leaf springs, torque arm and telescopic shock absorbers
Brakes: Drums, 12-in. dia. (front and rear)
Wheels: Steel disc, 15-in. dia.
Tires: 8.20 x 15

DIMENSIONS
Length: 214.1 in. **Width:** 80.0 in.
Height: 63.2 in. **Wheelbase:** 126.0 in.
Track: 59.1 in. (front), 62.2 in. (rear)
Weight: 4,370 lbs.

Buick SKYLARK

Rare and exclusive, the Skylark was a short-lived image maker for General Motors' other premium division. It showed that the cars from Flint could compete with the best luxury automobiles that Lincoln had to offer.

Fireball power

A 200-bhp, 322-cubic inch version of Buick's famed 'Fireball' overhead-valve V8 powers the 1954 Skylark. This engine was stroked to 364 cubic inches in 1957 and remained as an option until 1967, in 401- and 425-cubic inch forms.

Changing chassis

When introduced in 1953, the Skylark rode a 121.5-inch Roadmaster chassis. For 1954, as a cost-saving measure, this was changed to the 122-inch Series 60 Century chassis.

Dynaflow

While some critics called it the Dynaslush, Buick's fully automatic Dynaflow transmission was, for the most part, well received. In 1953, an improved twin-turbine unit was introduced and proved more responsive. It was standard on all Skylarks.

Drum brakes

The Skylark used four-wheel drum brakes. A power brake booster was standard, but repeated firm applications on the pedal could result in fading.

Special touches

Skylarks have a number of distinguishing features, including the absence of fender vents, unique wheel well styling (flared at the rear), special front fenders and big chrome fins grafted on the rear quarter panels.

Specifications

1954 Buick Skylark

ENGINE

Type: V8

Construction: Cast-iron block and heads

Valve gear: Two valves per cylinder operated by a single V-mounted camshaft via pushrods and rockers

Bore and stroke: 4.00 in. x 3.20 in.

Displacement: 322 c.i.

Compression ratio: 8.5:1

Induction system: Carter four-barrel carburetor

Maximum power: 200 bhp at 4,100 rpm

Maximum torque: Not quoted

TRANSMISSION

Dynaflow two-speed automatic

BODY/CHASSIS

Separate steel chassis with two-door convertible body

SPECIAL FEATURES

Skylarks even have their own special steering wheel boss.

The stylish Kelsey-Hayes 15-inch wire wheels have knock off spinners.

RUNNING GEAR

Steering: Recirculating ball

Front suspension: Unequal-length wishbones with coil springs and telescopic shock absorbers.

Rear suspension: Live axle with semi-elliptic leaf springs and lever-arm shock absorbers

Brakes: Drums (front and rear)

Wheels: Kelsey-Hayes wire, 15-in. dia.

Tires: 6.70 x 15 in.

DIMENSIONS

Length: 206.3 in.   **Width:** 69.8 in.

Height: 55.8 in.   **Wheelbase:** 122.0 in.

Track: 59.0 in. (front and rear)

Weight: 4,260 lbs.

Luxurious interior

Power steering, brakes, four-way front bench seat and a power convertible top are all standard equipment. A Selectronic radio, which automatically searches for stations at the touch of a button, and 'Easy-Eye' tinted glass are also included.

Cadillac ELDORADO

Cadillac was the 'Standard of the World' back in the 1950s and theBrougham was the ultimate expression of luxury on wheels. At a staggering $13,075 in 1957, however, few could afford it.

Powerful V8

By 1957 the 1949 vintage Cadillac V8 had been stroked to 365 cubic inches and produced a muscular 325 bhp on Eldorados (300 bhp on other models). All Cadillacs got an extra 10 bhp for 1958.

Air suspension

A state-of-the-art feature, air suspension, was introduced on the Brougham. It basically consisted of a rubber diaphragm and piston at each wheel controlled by a central compressor. The system was not very reliable and many owners chose to replace it with coil springs.

Suicide doors

Another feature unique to the 1957-1958 Eldorado Brougham are the suicide doors. Those at the front open in the normal manner, but the back doors are hinged at the rear. This allows easy access for passengers and also means that the Brougham was a pillarless four-door sedan that allowed the elimination of the rear quarter windows.

Modest fins

Cadillac pioneered fins among domestic manufacturers as far back as 1948. In 1955 Eldorados gained tall blade-like items, and these were adopted for the Brougham when it was launched in 1958. Interestingly, although regular Cadillacs had fins of gigantic proportions for 1959, Broughams had fairly small fins with dagger-shaped taillight lenses.

Sumptuous interior

Eldorado Broughams were laden with luxury options inside, including power steering, brakes and windows, plus air-conditioning, electric memory seats and cruise control. Buyers also had the choice of 44 interior and exterior trim and color combinations.

Huge chrome grill

Broughams have a unique eggcrate mesh-pattern grill which is neater than those on other Cadillacs. Broughams were also the first to get quad headlights.

Smooth styling

Panoramic windshields were first seen on the limited production Eldorado convertible in 1953. By 1958 all Cadillacs had them. They offered good visibility, but were costly to replace and necessitated a front dog-leg A-pillar which could make entry into the car rather difficult.

Specifications

1957 Cadillac Eldorado Brougham

ENGINE

Type: V8

Construction: Cast-iron block and heads

Valve gear: Two valves per cylinder operated by a single camshaft via pushrods and rockers

Bore and stroke: 4.00 in. x 3.63 in.

Displacement: 365 c.i.

Compression ratio: 10.0:1

Induction system: Two four-barrel carburetors

Maximum power: 325 bhp at 4,800 rpm

Maximum torque: 435 lb-ft at 3,400 rpm

Top speed: 110 mph

0–60 mph: 11.4 sec.

TRANSMISSION

Three-speed automatic

BODY/CHASSIS

Separate chassis with two-door steel convertible body

SPECIAL FEATURES

A full-length stainless-steel roof was standard on 1957-1958 Broughams—a feature lifted virtually intact from the Eldorado show car of 1954.

A gold anodized air cleaner is mounted atop the 365-cubic inch V8.

RUNNING GEAR

Steering: Recirculating ball

Front suspension: Wishbones with airbags and shock absorbers

Rear suspension: Live axle with airbags and shock absorbers

Brakes: Drums (front and rear)

Wheels: Steel, 15-in. dia.

Tires: 8.0 x 15.0 in.

DIMENSIONS

Length: 216.3 in.   **Width:** 78.5 in.

Height: 55.5 in.   **Wheelbase:** 126.0 in.

Track: 61.0 in. (front and rear)

Weight: 5,315 lbs.

Cadillac 62/DEVILLE

The 1959 Cadillacs were at their most glamorous in convertible form, either as Series 62 models or the flagship Eldorado Biarritz. As one of the world's premier luxury cars of the late 1950s, they were almost unchallenged.

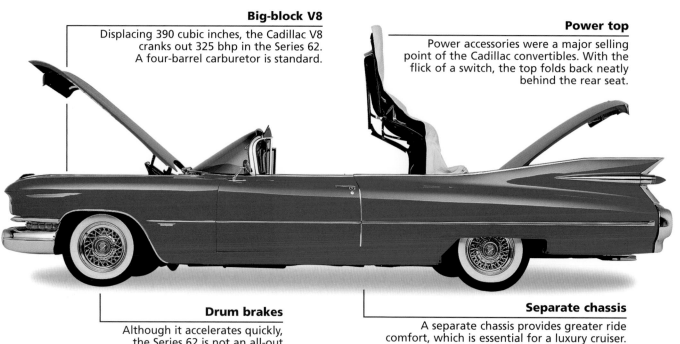

Big-block V8
Displacing 390 cubic inches, the Cadillac V8 cranks out 325 bhp in the Series 62. A four-barrel carburetor is standard.

Power top
Power accessories were a major selling point of the Cadillac convertibles. With the flick of a switch, the top folds back neatly behind the rear seat.

Drum brakes
Although it accelerates quickly, the Series 62 is not an all-out performer. Repeated heavy braking from high speed may cause the four-wheel drums to lock and quickly fade.

Separate chassis
A separate chassis provides greater ride comfort, which is essential for a luxury cruiser. The frame is X-braced for greater stiffness.

Mass-produced quality
For a mass-produced vehicle, the 1959 Cadillac was well put together. Only the finest quality materials were used during the manufacturing process.

Flamboyant styling
The 1959 Caddy was one of the last cars styled by the legendary Harley Earl and marked the end of an era.

utomatic headlights

adillac's 'Twilight Sentinel'
eadlights switch on automatically at
usk and also switch from high to
w beams for oncoming traffic.

Chromed bumper

In the 1950s, designers looked to
the space program for inspiration.
The 1959 Cadillac has a heavy,
full-width chromed rear bumper
with back-up lights built into the
center of its fins.

Specifications

1959 Cadillac Series 62

ENGINE

Type: V8

Construction: Cast-iron block and heads

Valve gear: Two valves per cylinder
operated by a single camshaft via pushrods
and rockers

Bore and stroke: 4.00 in. x 3.88 in.

Displacement: 390 c.i.

Compression ratio: 10.5:1

Induction system: Carter four-barrel
carburetor

Maximum power: 325 bhp at 4,800 rpm

Maximum torque: 435 lb-ft at 3,400 rpm

Top speed:, 110 mph

0–60 mph: 11.4 sec.

TRANSMISSION

GM TurboHydramatic automatic

BODY/CHASSIS

Steel body on steel X-frame chassis

SPECIAL FEATURES

By 1959, quad
headlights were in
fashion. For the
ultimate in excess,
all 1959 Cadillacs
have dual parking
lights in chrome
housings which
form the lower
part of the
bumper.

The most
recognizable
feature are the
fins—the tallest
ever on a
production car.
Huge chrome
bumpers further
accentuate its
advanced styling.

RUNNING GEAR

Steering: Recirculating ball

Front suspension: Wishbones with coil
springs and telescopic shock
absorbers

Rear suspension: Live axle with
coil springs and telescopic shock
absorbers

Brakes: Drums, 12-in. dia. (front
and rear)

Wheels: Steel discs, 15-in. dia.

Tires: 8.20-15

DIMENSIONS

Length: 224.8 in.   **Width:** 79.9 in.

Height: 55.9 in.   **Wheelbase:** 130.0 in.

Track: 61.0 in. (front), 60.2 in. (rear)

Weight: 4,885 lbs.

Checker **A11**

Although operated by cab companies in many different cities across the U.S., New York is considered the Checker's natural habitat. Big Apple cabs even had their own special NYC package.

V6 or V8

By 1980, when this cab left the factory, engine choices were 229-cubic inch V6s or V8s displacing 267 or 305 cubic inches. A diesel V8 was also listed on the order form.

Heavy-duty suspension

Traveling thousands of miles over cratered and broken pavement requires heavy-duty suspension. The Checker's proven setup of stiff coils and leaf springs is well up to the job.

Propan

Although most Checke run on gas, some hav been converted to u propane. These cars a identified by a fairin over the gas cap on th rear valanc

Spacious interior

Two different wheelbases were available (120 or 129 inches). The longer A11E version has rear-facing jump seats and can seat up to eight instead of six passengers.

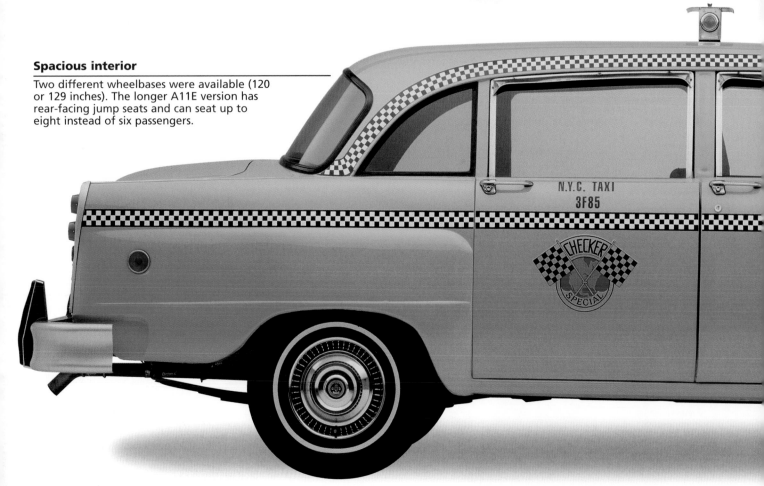

New York certified

Manhattan cabs are operated under the control of the NYC Taxi and Limousine Commission. Official cabs have yellow paint and a medallion number, which is assigned to each driver and marked on the roof, rear doors and license plates. A driver is not allowed to pick up fares in the Big Apple without it.

Bumper guards

Due to heavy traffic in New York, many cabs were fitted with bumper guards to keep wayward motorists at bay.

Specifications

1980 Checker A11

ENGINE

Type: V8

Construction: Cast-iron block and heads

Valve gear: Two valves per cylinder operated by pushrods and rockers

Bore and stroke: 3.74 in. x 3.48 in.

Displacement: 305 c.i.

Compression ratio: 8.6:1

Induction system: Rochester four-barrel carburetor

Maximum power: 155 bhp at 3,800 rpm

Maximum torque: 250 lb-ft at 2,400 rpm

TRANSMISSION

GM Turbohydramatic 350 three-speed automatic

BODY/CHASSIS

Steel-perimeter chassis with separate four-door sedan body

SPECIAL FEATURES

Cabs working 24 hour or night shifts were required to have a glass divider.

All official New York taxis have a medallion number on the roof sign.

RUNNING GEAR

Steering: Recirculating ball

Front suspension: Unequal-length wishbones with telescopic shock absorbers and anti-roll bar

Rear suspension: Live axle with semi-elliptic leaf springs and telescopic shock absorbers

Brakes: Discs (front), drums (rear)

Wheels: Pressed steel, 15-in. dia.

Tires: 155/70 R15

DIMENSIONS

Length: 201.0 in. **Width:** 79.5 in.

Height: 71.6 in. **Wheelbase:** 120.0 in.

Track: 64.6 in. (front and rear)

Weight: 3,830 lbs.

Chevrolet **BEL AIR**

Huge tires, an immaculate custom paint job, a wild interior, low aggressive stance and a powerful blown V8 engine installed in a classic American car—all the ingredients of a great hot rod.

Chromework
Although this car has been built as a high-performance vehicle, little has been done to reduce its weight. Even the heavy chrome bumpers are retained.

Blown engine
A B&M supercharger gives a huge boost to the power and torque outputs of this car's 350-cubic inch small-block Chevy V8 engine.

Custom interior
It looks just as good inside. The flame motif is carried through to the interior and even appears on the headlining and steering wheel.

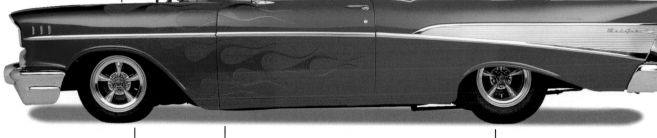

Alloy wheels
The popular American Racing Torq-Thrust five-spoke wheels are used. They are similar in style to racing wheels often used in the 1960s.

Lowered suspension
To lower the lines of the car and give it that road-hugging stance, the suspension has been lowered. Two-inch drop spindles and chopped coil springs lower the front, while custom semi-elliptic leaf springs, relocated on the chassis, ease down the rear end.

Huge rear tires
The Mickey Thompson tires added to the rear of the car are designed to give maximum traction off the line.

Smoothed hood and trunk
Both the hood and rear deck have been smoothed off and stripped of badges to give the car a much cleaner look.

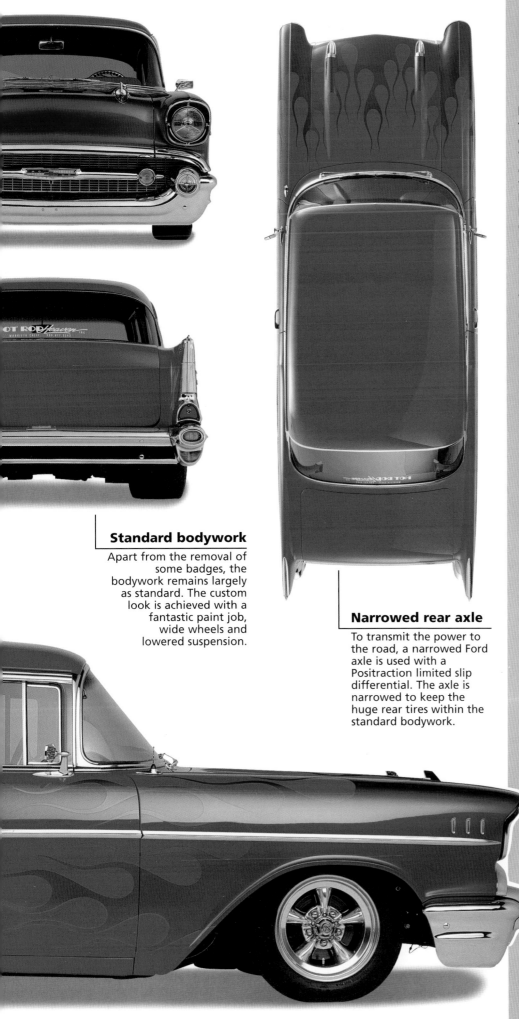

Standard bodywork

Apart from the removal of some badges, the bodywork remains largely as standard. The custom look is achieved with a fantastic paint job, wide wheels and lowered suspension.

Narrowed rear axle

To transmit the power to the road, a narrowed Ford axle is used with a Positraction limited slip differential. The axle is narrowed to keep the huge rear tires within the standard bodywork.

Specifications
1957 Modified Chevrolet Bel Air

ENGINE

Type: V8

Construction: Cast-iron block and heads

Valve gear: Single block-mounted camshaft operating two valves per cylinder via pushrods

Bore and stroke: 4 in. x 3.5 in.

Displacement: 350 c.i.

Compression ratio: 8.5:1

Induction system: B&M 4-71 mechanical supercharger with Holley four-barrel carb

Maximum power: 420 bhp at 5,400 rpm

Maximum torque: 435 lb-ft at 2,500 rpm

Top speed: 147 mph

0-60 mph: 3.9 sec.

TRANSMISSION

350 Turbo automatic

BODY/CHASSIS

Standard 1957 Bel Air steel body with smoothed hood and rear deck on steel perimeter chassis

SPECIAL FEATURES

To achieve its enormous power output, the hot 350-cubic inch V8 uses a B&M supercharger.

This car features outstanding chromework. The hidden gas filler cap is a typical feature for a car of the '50s.

RUNNING GEAR

Steering: Power-assisted recirculating ball

Front suspension: Fabricated tubular wishbones, 2-in. drop spindles, chopped coil springs, telescopic shock absorbers

Rear suspension: Custom semi-elliptic leaf springs, lowering blocks, traction bars and air shock absorbers

Brakes: Discs (front and rear)

Wheels: American Racing Torq-Thrust D, 7.5 in. x 15 in. (front), 11 in. x 15 in. (rear)

Tires: BF Goodrich 205/60-15 (front), Mickey Thompson Sportsman I N50/15

DIMENSIONS

Length: 200 in.   **Width:** 73.9 in.

Height: 46.9 in.   **Wheelbase:** 115 in.

Track: 58 in.(front), 58.8in. (rear)

Weight: 3,197 lbs.

Chevrolet **CAMARO Z28**

To compete in the prestigious Trans Am championship, the rules required that Chevrolet had to build 1,000 suitable cars ready for sale to the public to homologate the car for racing. The result was the Z28, a racing car for the road.

Coupe-only body style

You could not order the Z28 package with the convertible body because Chevrolet only needed to homologate the coupe for Trans Am racing.

Performance V8

Chevrolet originally rated the Z28's short-stroke V8 at 290 bhp. Some critics thought its potential was being deliberately underrated, and it could really produce something nearer to 350 bhp at well over 6,000 rpm.

Vented disc brakes

Z28s are heavy cars, so with the performance available they have to have vented front disc brakes. Even with the harder pads though, the Z28's braking isn't its strongest feature.

Close-ratio transmission

Standard Z28 transmission was an automatic but for $184 a Muncie four-speed manual was available that could also be ordered with close-ratio gears.

Harder brake linings

Although the Z28 carries rear drum brakes, just like stock Camaros, the linings are a harder compound to improve performance under sustained high-speed braking.

Rear spoiler

The rear spoiler is as much about adding just a touch of style to the rear of the Camaro as managing the airflow over the car to improve rear downforce.

Wide tires

The Z28 used Goodyear WideTread tires on relatively wide (for the time) seven-inch rims.

Stiffer rear springs

The one major suspension change was the switch to multi-leaf instead of the stock single-leaf rear springs which were 25 percent stiffer than standard. Despite this change, the front spring rates did not need to be altered at all.

Specifications
1968 Chevrolet Camaro Z28

ENGINE
Type: V8
Construction: Cast-iron block and heads
Valve gear: Two valves per cylinder operated by single block-mounted camshaft via pushrods and hydraulic lifters
Bore and stroke: 4.0 in. x 3.0 in.
Displacement: 302 c.i.
Compression ratio: 11.0:1
Induction system: Single four-barrel 800-cfm Holley carburetor
Maximum power: 290 bhp at 5,800 rpm
Maximum torque: 290 lb-ft at 4,200 rpm
Top speed: 123 mph
0-60 mph: 6.5 sec

TRANSMISSION
Three-speed automatic or four-speed manual

BODY/CHASSIS
Unitary steel construction with two-door coupe body

SPECIAL FEATURES

The 302-cubic inch engine was new for the Z28. It combined 327 block with a 283 crank to achieve a capacity of less than 305 cubic inches for SCCA racing.

This car has been fitted with a roll cage to comply with SCCA racing regulations.

RUNNING GEAR
Steering: Recirculating ball
Front suspension: Double wishbones with coil springs, telescopic shocks and anti-roll bar
Rear suspension: Live axle with multi-leaf semi-elliptic springs and telescopic shocks
Brakes: Front vented discs, 11 in. dia., and rear drums, 9 in. dia.
Wheels: Steel disc, 7 in. x 15 in.
Tires:: Goodyear WideTread E70-15

DIMENSIONS
Length: 184.7 in.   **Width:** 72.5 in.
Height: 51.4 in.   **Wheelbase:** 108 in.
Track: 59.6 in. (front), 59.5 in. (rear)
Weight: 3525 lbs.

Chevrolet **CAMARO PACE CAR**

Driven by 1960 Indy 500 winner Jim Rathmann at the Brickyard, the actual Pace Car was powered by a 375-bhp, 396-cubic inch big-block, but in the interests of driveability most of the replicas had small-block engines.

Pace Car package

To get a 1969 Camaro Pace Car, you had to check off the Regular Production Order (RPO) Z11 on the order form. This put you behind the wheel of a hot Camaro decorated with white paint and orange stripes on the hood and decklid. Pace Car decals for the doors were dealer-installed at the owner's request.

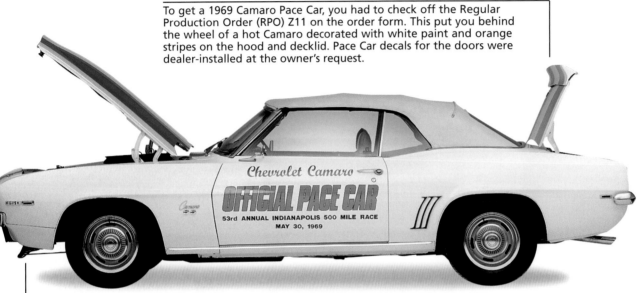

One-year wonder

Although they were based on the 1967-1968 cars, the 1969 Camaros received new sheet metal with sweeping fender lines.

RS/SS package

The price of $37 for the Z11 option was deceiving because you also had to order the SS package, Z/28 cowl induction hood and rear spoiler, plus the hidden headlight RS grill.

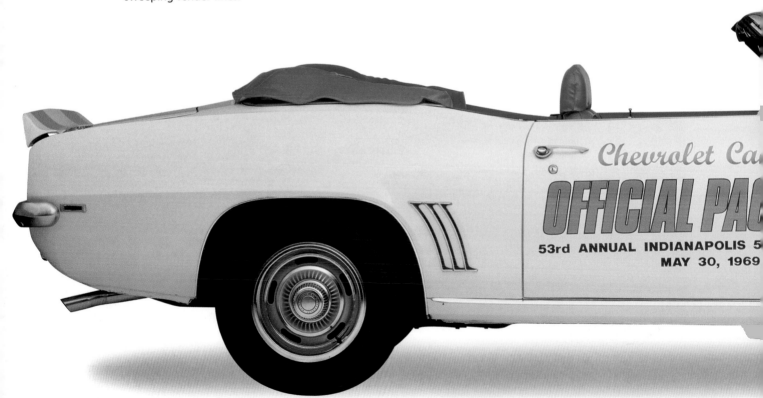

Automatic transmission

Two different automatic transmissions were available on the Pace Cars depending upon what engine the car was equipped with. Cars with the 350 V8 were equipped with a TH350, while ones with the big-block 396 used the TH400.

Posi-traction rear end

First-year Camaros came with single rear leaf springs, but severe axle tramp on the more powerful versions caused Chevrolet to fit multi-leaf springs in 1968. A Posi-traction, limited-slip differential also helped increase tire grip.

Specifications

1969 Chevrolet Camaro Pace Car

ENGINE

Type: V8

Construction: Cast-iron block and heads

Valve gear: Two valves per cylinder operated by a single V-mounted camshaft with pushrods and rockers

Bore and stroke: 4.00 in. x 3.48 in.

Displacement: 350 c.i.

Compression ratio: 10.25:1

Induction system: Rochester Quadrajet four-barrel carburetor

Maximum power: 300 bhp at 4,800 rpm

Maximum torque: 380 lb-ft at 3,200 rpm

TRANSMISSION

Turbo 350 automatic

BODY/CHASSIS

Steel unitary chassis with two-door convertible body

SPECIAL FEATURES

Convertibles were sold with pace car decals in the trunk ready to stick on.

The actual pace car used in the race was fitted with Chevy rally wheels like these.

RUNNING GEAR

Steering: Recirculating ball

Front suspension: Unequal length A-arms with coil springs, telescopic shock absorbers and anti-roll bar

Rear suspension: Live axle with semi-elliptic leaf springs and telescopic shock absorbers

Brakes: Discs (front), drums (rear)

Wheels: Steel Rally, 7.0 x 14 in.

Tires: Goodyear Polyglas, G-70 14

DIMENSIONS

Length: 186.0 in.   **Width:** 74.0 in.

Height: 51.0 in.   **Wheelbase:** 108.0 in.

Track: 59.6 in. (front) 59.5 in. (rear)

Weight: 3,395 lbs.

Chevrolet **CAMARO ZL1**

Most ZL-1s had plain bodies with skinny steel wheels—they didn't even have any badging to designate their model or engine size. This unique ZL-1 has the RS appearance package, vinyl top and 427 badging.

ZL2 cowl hood

All ZL-1s came with cowl induction hoods. It forced cool air into the engine from the high pressure area just below the windshield.

Expensive engine

You had to have a healthy bank account to be able to afford a ZL-1 Camaro. The engine's all-aluminum construction saved 160 lbs. over the cast-iron 427. Because it is virtually hand built, the engine alone cost $4,160—more than most cars of the period.

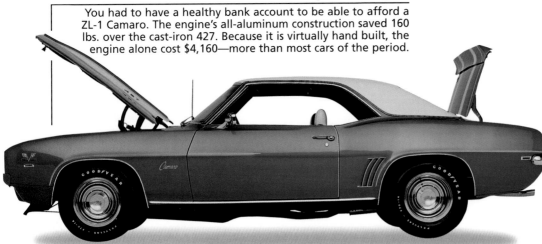

Better balance

Although it is a big-block unit, the ZL-1 engine weighs about 500 lbs. which is roughly the same as a 327, and so these special Camaros actually handle better than the stock SS 396™. However, these cars were designed for use in NHRA Super Stock drag racing events.

Standard exhaust system

ZL-1s left the factory with lots of mismatched parts because the owners were expected to do a lot of race development themselves. The stock exhaust manifolds restrict the flow of exhaust gases and were usually among the first items to be replaced.

The ZL-1 option package

All ZL-1s began life as SS 396s, but the engine and Super Sport™ option were deleted. Instead, the special cars received the ZL-1 option package which included the aluminum engine, F41 suspension, front discs and a cowl induction hood.

Heavy duty suspension components

All ZL-1s were equipped with the heavy duty F41 suspension and front disc brakes. To better handle the 450 lb-ft of torque from the powerful engines, ZL-1s were equipped with 12-bolt rear ends with 4.10 gears.

Performance transmission

Only two transmissions were strong enough to cope with the ZL-1 V8: the Muncie M-22 'Rock Crusher' four-speed or the equally stout TurboHydramatic 400 automatic.

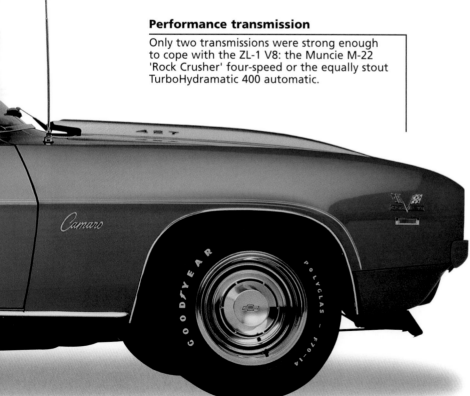

Specifications

1969 Chevrolet Camaro ZL-1

ENGINE

Type: V8

Construction: Aluminum block and cylinder heads

Valve gear: Two valves per cylinder operated by a single camshaft

Bore and stroke: 4.25 in. x 3.76 in.

Displacement: 427 c.i.

Compression ratio: 12.0:1

Induction system: Holley four-barrel carburetor

Maximum power: 430 bhp at 5,200 rpm

Maximum torque: 450 lb-ft at 4,400 rpm

Top speed: 125 mph

0–60 mph: 5.3 sec

TRANSMISSION

Muncie M-22 four-speed manual

BODY/CHASSIS

Unitary steel chassis with two-door hardtop coupe body

SPECIAL FEATURES

Each ZL-1 engine has a special sticker on the valve cover.

Most ZL-1s have exposed headlights, but this car has the RS package.

RUNNING GEAR

Steering: Recirculating ball

Front suspension: Double wishbones with coil springs, telescopic shock absorbers and anti-roll bar

Rear suspension: Live axle with semi-elliptic leaf springs and telescopic shock absorbers

Brakes: Discs (front), drums (rear)

Wheels: Steel, 6 x 15 in.

Tires: Goodyear Wide Tread GT, E70-15

DIMENSIONS

Length: 186.0 in.   **Width:** 74.0 in.

Height: 51.0 in.   **Wheelbase:** 108.0 in.

Track: 59.6 in. (front), 59.5 in. (rear)

Weight: 3,300 lbs.

Chevrolet CHEVELLE SS 454

The LS-6 Chevelle was one of the most powerful muscle cars ever produced. It combined Chevrolet's largest engine with its sporty midsize car to give outrageous results.

Body stripes

By 1970 style was every bit as important as performance, and SS Chevelles were available with twin stripes running over the hood and rear decklid.

LS-6 454-cubic inch V8

The biggest performance option in 1970 was the LS-6 engine. It produces 450 bhp at 5,600 rpm and 500 lb-ft of torque at 3,600 rpm. It has high compression pistons, rectangle port cylinder heads, and solid valve lifters. Few other muscle machines could rival the power of the LS-6.

M-22 'Rock crusher' transmission

With 500 lb-ft of torque, only two transmissions were strong enough to cope with the LS-6 engine. This one has a Muncie M22 'Rock crusher' four-speed. This stout unit has a 2.20:1 straight-cut first gear.

Magnum 500 wheels

Magnum 500 steel wheels were used on all 1970 Chevelle Super Sports. The Polyglas F70x14 could barely handle the engine's torque.

Hardtop body

While all LS-6 engines were supposed to be installed in hardtops only, it's rumored that a few found their way into convertibles.

Upgraded suspension

The SS package included the F41 suspension which has stiffer front springs to compensate for the weight of the big-block engine.

Cowl induction hood

A vacuum-controlled flap at the top of the hood draws air in from the high-pressure area at the base of the windshield to help the engine exploit its power. This is known as cowl induction.

Dual exhaust

A full-length 2.5-inch dual exhaust system enables the LS-6 to optimize the engine's performance.

Specifications
1970 Chevrolet Chevelle SS 454

ENGINE
Type: V8
Construction: Cast-iron block and heads
Valve gear: Two valves per cylinder operated by pushrods and rockers
Bore and stroke: 4.25 in. x 4.00 in.
Displacement: 454 c.i.
Compression ratio: 11.25:1
Induction system: Holley four-barrel carburetor and aluminum intake manifold
Maximum power: 450 bhp at 5,600 rpm
Maximum torque: 500 lb-ft at 3,600 rpm
Top speed: 125 mph
0-60 mph: 6.1 sec

TRANSMISSION
Manual four-speed, close-ratio M-22

BODY/CHASSIS
Steel body on separate steel chassis

SPECIAL FEATURES

All Chevelle Super Sports came with Magnum 500 steel wheels and Polyglas F70x14 tires in 1970.

These NASCAR-style tie down hood pins were a popular item and helped keep the hood from lifting at high speed.

RUNNING GEAR
Steering: Recirculating ball
Front suspension: Independent with wishbones, anti-roll bar, coil springs and telescopic shock absorbers
Rear suspension: Live axle with coil springs and telescopic shock absorbers
Brakes: Disc, 11-in. dia. (front), drum 9-in. dia. (rear)
Wheels: Magnum 500, 14-in. dia.
Tires: Polyglas F70x14

DIMENSIONS
Length: 189 in. **Width:** 70.2 in.
Height: 52.7 in. **Wheelbase:** 112 in.
Track: 56.8 in. (front), 56.9 in. (rear)
Weight: 4,000 lbs.

Chevrolet CORVAIR

The Corvair was a true cutting edge car, but Ralph Nader's book *Unsafe at Any Speed* tarnished its image. In fact, the Corvair was later vindicated by Congress, and today it has a reputation as an enthusiast's car.

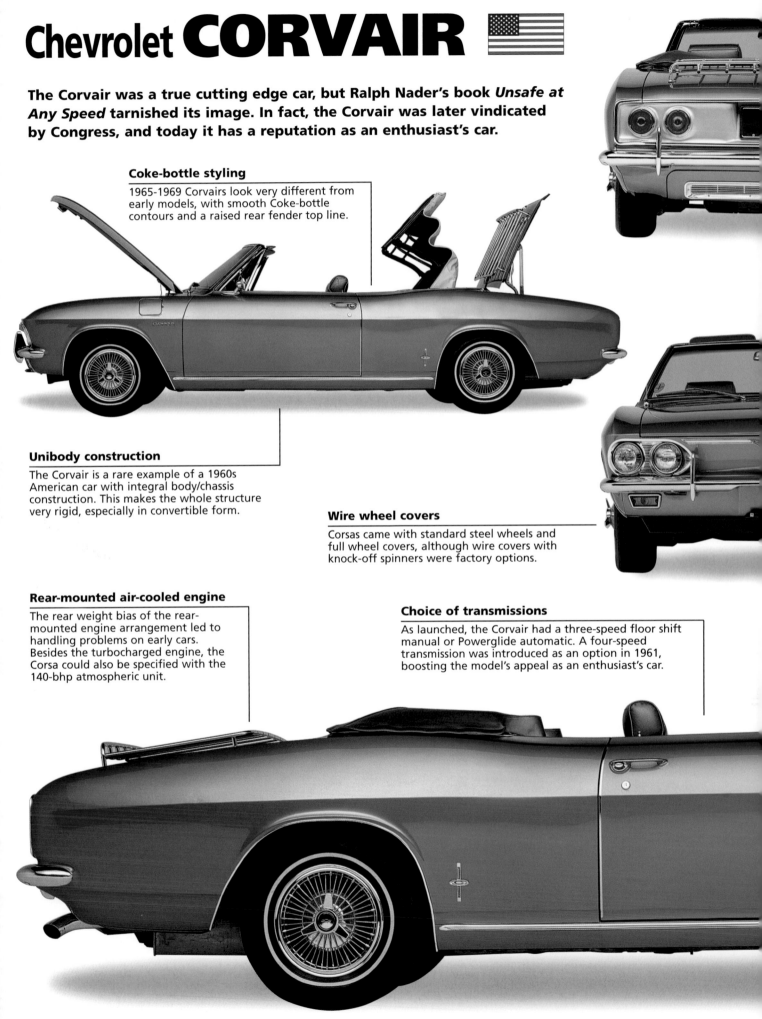

Coke-bottle styling

1965-1969 Corvairs look very different from early models, with smooth Coke-bottle contours and a raised rear fender top line.

Unibody construction

The Corvair is a rare example of a 1960s American car with integral body/chassis construction. This makes the whole structure very rigid, especially in convertible form.

Wire wheel covers

Corsas came with standard steel wheels and full wheel covers, although wire covers with knock-off spinners were factory options.

Rear-mounted air-cooled engine

The rear weight bias of the rear-mounted engine arrangement led to handling problems on early cars. Besides the turbocharged engine, the Corsa could also be specified with the 140-bhp atmospheric unit.

Choice of transmissions

As launched, the Corvair had a three-speed floor shift manual or Powerglide automatic. A four-speed transmission was introduced as an option in 1961, boosting the model's appeal as an enthusiast's car.

Revised suspension

For 1965, the Corvair received a revised rear suspension employing upper and lower control arms to better monitor wheel movement. Rods connect the lower arms to the main rear cross-member to absorb longitudinal forces.

Grill-less nose

Like the Beetle, the Corvair does not have a front grill. The headlights are set back in chrome bezels, which results in a striking and attractive appearance.

Specifications

1966 Chevrolet Corvair Corsa

ENGINE

Type: Horizontally-opposed six-cylinder

Construction: Aluminum block and heads

Valve gear: Two valves per cylinder operated by a single camshaft

Bore and stroke: 3.44 in. x 2.94 in.

Displacement: 164 c.i.

Compression ratio: 9.25:1

Induction system: Four carburetors

Maximum power: 180 bhp at 4,000 rpm

Maximum torque: 232 lb-ft at 3,200 rpm

TRANSMISSION

Three-speed manual, four-speed manual or optional two-speed automatic

BODY/CHASSIS

Integral chassis with two-door steel body

SPECIAL FEATURES

High-back buckets were a feature not too many people ordered on the Corsa.

The highest performance engine was the turbocharged flat six with 180 bhp.

RUNNING GEAR

Steering: Recirculating ball

Front suspension: Wishbones with coil springs, shock absorbers and anti-roll bar

Rear suspension: Multi-link with coil springs and shock absorbers

Brakes: Drums (front and rear)

Wheels: Steel, 13-in. dia.

Tires: 6.50 x 13

DIMENSIONS

Length: 183.3 in.   **Width:** 69.7 in.

Height: 51.3 in.   **Wheelbase:** 108.0 in.

Track: 55.0 in. (front), 57.2 in. (rear)

Weight: 2,720 lbs.

Chevrolet CORVETTE

Because of poor sales, GM almost gave up on the little sports car. In 1955 it got a husky V8 engine and the car was making the power it lacked. Luckily, sales picked up and the Corvette has been in Chevrolet's line up ever since.

Wishbone front suspension

The Corvette's double wishbone and coil spring front suspension was a modified version of the contemporary Chevrolet sedans, with different spring rates to suit the sports car.

Six-cylinder engine

The first Corvettes used a modified Chevrolet sedan engine. Tuning made it an effective sports car powerplant with 150 bhp.

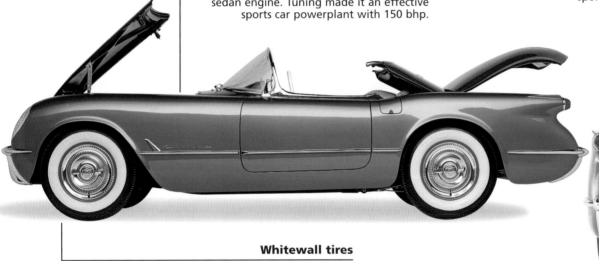

Whitewall tires

Whitewall tires were very fashionable in the 1950s. One advantage was that they broke up the high-sided look of the tall sidewalls.

Fiberglass body

Although there were a number of fiberglass-bodied specialty and kit cars around in the U.S. in the early 1950s General Motors was the first to make a regular production car out of the material. In production the fiberglass panels used were about half as thick as the prototype's.

Specifications

1954 Chevrolet Corvette

ENGINE

Type: Inline six cylinder

Construction: Cast iron block and head

Valve gear: Two valves per cylinder operated by single block-mounted camshaft via pushrods and solid valve lifters

Bore/stroke: 3.56 in. x 3.94 in.

Displacement: 235 c.i.

Compression ratio: 8.0:1

Induction system: Three Carter YH sidedraft carburetors

Maximum power: 150 bhp at 4,200 rpm

Maximum torque: 233 lb-ft at 2,400 rpm

TRANSMISSION

Two-speed Powerglide automatic

BODY/CHASSIS

X-braced steel chassis with fiberglass two-seater convertible body

SPECIAL FEATURES

The first Corvettes have very curvaceous rear ends with subdued fins and prominent taillights.

Stone guards over the front headlights were purely a styling feature and unnecessary on ordinary roads.

RUNNING GEAR

Steering: Worm-and-sector

Front suspension: Double wishbones with coil springs, telescopic shocks and anti-roll bar

Rear suspension: Live axle with semi-elliptic leaf springs and telescopic shocks

Brakes: Drums (front and rear), 11-in. dia.

Wheels: Steel disc, 15-in. dia.

Tires: Crossply 5.5 x 15

DIMENSIONS

Length: 167 in.   **Width:** 72.2 in.

Height: 51.3 in.   **Wheelbase:** 102 in.

Track: 57 in. (front), 59 in. (rear)

Weight: 2,851 lbs.

Two-speed transmission

Incredibly, the only available GM transmission which would take the power and torque of the modified engine was the two-speed Powerglide automatic. A three-speed manual became available for the 1955 model year cars.

Wrap-around windshield

The wrap-around style of windshield was popular in the early 1950s. Apart from looking great, it improved three-quarter vision compared with a conventional flat front glass with thick pillars.

Live rear axle

Because it was a limited-production car, the first Corvettes had to use many off-the-shelf Chevrolet components and the engineering had to be as simple as possible.

Chevrolet CORVETTE '56-'62

Style, power and performance. In the 1950s and early-1960s, the Corvette had it all. Despite its fiberglass body it was no lightweight but no one cared—it had power to burn.

Color schemes

In 1961, the Corvette was available in a choice of seven colors: Tuxedo Black, Ermine White, Roman Red, Sateen Silver, Jewel Blue, Fawn Beige and Honduras Maroon. For an extra $16, you could have the side cove highlighted in silver or white, an option deleted the next year.

Concealed hood

Unlike some of its European convertible rivals, the Corvette has a top which folds down completely to be hidden out of sight under a lockable cover.

Front vents

When the Corvette was widened for the 1958 model year, some of that extra width was taken up by vents behind the front bumper, there purely for styling.

Jaguar wheelbase

Chevrolet evaluated the Jaguar XK120 while developing the Corvette, but the only sign of any influence is that both cars have exactly the same wheelbase.

Limited slip differential

To stop the Corvette from spinning away its power on relatively narrow tires, the option of a Positraction limited slip differential was offered from 1957 on.

Power windows

From 1956 onward, Vettes were available with electrically-operated windows. In 1961, that option would have cost you just under $60.

'Duck tail' rear

The major styling change introduced for the 1961 model is this 'duck tail' rear, created by stylist Bill Mitchell and carried over into the '62 models.

Fiberglass body

Vettes have always been fiberglass and Chevrolet became better at producing it as the years passed. Early bodies were made from 46 different panels but that process had been streamlined by 1961.

Live rear axle

By 1961, the Corvette was only two years away from independent rear suspension. Until then it soldiered on with an old-fashioned live axle.

Specifications
1961 Chevrolet Corvette

ENGINE
Type: V8
Construction: Cast-iron block and heads
Valve gear: Two valves per cylinder operated by single block-mounted camshaft, pushrods and rockers
Bore and stroke: 3.87 in. x 2.99 in.
Displacement: 283 c.i.
Compression ratio: 11:1
Induction system: Rochester Ramjet mechanical fuel injection
Maximum power: 315 bhp at 6,200 rpm
Maximum torque: 295 lb-ft at 4,000 rpm
Top speed: 135 mph
0-60 mph: 6.1 sec.

TRANSMISSION
Four-speed manual

BODY/CHASSIS
X-braced ladder frame with fiberglass two-seat convertible body

SPECIAL FEATURES

All 1958-1962 Corvettes have a side cove, but the detail design and amount of chrome was changed every year.

From 1957 a Rochester Ramjet fuel injection option offered owners even more power to play with.

RUNNING GEAR
Steering: Worm-and-ball
Front suspension: Double wishbones with coil springs, telescopic shocks and anti-roll bar
Rear suspension: Live axle with semi-elliptic leaf springs and telescopic shocks
Brakes: Drums, 11 in. dia. (front and rear)
Wheels: Steel discs 6 in. x 17 in.
Tires: Crossply 6.70 in. x 16 in.

DIMENSIONS
Length: 177.5 in.   **Width:** 72.8 in.
Height: 52.4 in.   **Wheelbase:** 102 in.
Track: 57 in. (front), 59 in. (rear)
Weight: 2,905 lbs.

Chevrolet CORVETTE STING RAY

The Sting Ray was introduced in 1963, 10 years after the Corvette's first appearance. The engine is set well back in the frame, giving nearly 50/50 weight distribution and excellent handling for the day.

Fiberglass body

Like all Corvettes, the Sting Ray has a body made from a number of fiberglass panels mounted on a traditional separate frame.

Disc brakes all around

Vented discs with dual-pot calipers on each wheel were fitted from 1965. While old stocks lasted, buyers could opt for the discontinued drums to save money.

V8 engine

Apart from the very early models, all Corvettes are powered by V8 engines. There is a wide variety of displacements and states of tune. The 327-cubic inch engine in 350-bhp tune is typical.

Optional side exhausts

The Sting Ray's enormous options list included the Side Mount Exhaust System. The side pipes are covered with a perforated shield to prevent the driver or passengers from burning themselves. Side exhausts were chosen mainly for visual effect.

No trunk lid

To preserve the contour of the car, there is no trunk lid and access to the luggage compartment is from behind the seats.

Foldaway top

The Corvette's convertible top folds away completely when not in use and is stored beneath a flush-fitting fiberglass panel behind the driver. Optional hard top cost $231.75 in 1966.

Alloy gearbox and clutch housing

To save weight, the Sting Ray was given an alloy clutch housing and an alloy-cased gearbox. This also improved weight distribution.

Specifications
1966 Chevrolet Corvette Sting Ray

ENGINE

Type: V8, 90°

Construction: Cast-iron block and heads; Single cam, pushrods

Bore and stroke: 4.0 in. x 3.25 in.

Displacement: 327 c.i.

Compression ratio: 11:1

Induction system: Rochester fuel injection or one/two Carter four-barrel carbs

Maximum power: 375 bhp at 6,200 rpm

Maximum torque: 350 lb-ft at 4,000 rpm

Top speed: 135 mph

0-60 mph: 5.6 sec.

TRANSMISSION

Three-speed automatic (optional four-speed manual)

BODY/CHASSIS

Steel ladder frame with two-door convertible or coupe fiberglass body

SPECIAL FEATURES

Innovative retractable headlights.

Soft top folds away neatly into compartment behind seats, with luggage space below.

RUNNING GEAR

Front suspension: Double wishbone, coil springs, anti-roll bar

Rear suspension: Semi-trailing arms, half-shafts and transverse links with transverse leaf spring

Brakes: Vented discs with four-pot calipers (optional cast-iron drums)

Wheels: Five-bolt steel (knock off aluminum optional) 6 in. x 15 in.

Tires: 6.7 in. x 15 in. Firestone Super Sport 170

DIMENSIONS

Length: 175.3 in.   **Width:** 69.6 in.

Height: 49.8 in.   **Wheelbase:** 98 in.

Track: 56.3 in. (front), 57 in. (rear)

Weight: 3,150 lbs.

lip-up headlights

he headlights are otated by two reversible acuum operated otors—a postwar first or an American car.

Triple side vents

Side vent arrangement, like many minor details, changed over the years. The 1965 and '66 models like this one have three vents.

Independent rear suspension

Another Corvette first, the Sting Ray has a crude but effective system with a transverse leaf spring mounted behind the differential.

119

Chevrolet **CORVETTE ZR-1**

With the ZR-1, Chevrolet proved that an exotic mid-mounted engine and $100,000 price tag are not required to offer true supercar performance.

Quad-cam V8
A technological masterpiece, the LT5 was originally intended for boats. Although all-alloy, it weighs more than a cast-iron Chevy small block.

Plastic springs
Like all Corvettes since the launch of the 1963 Coupe, the ZR-1 features transverse leaf springs. These are now made from plastic for reduced weight.

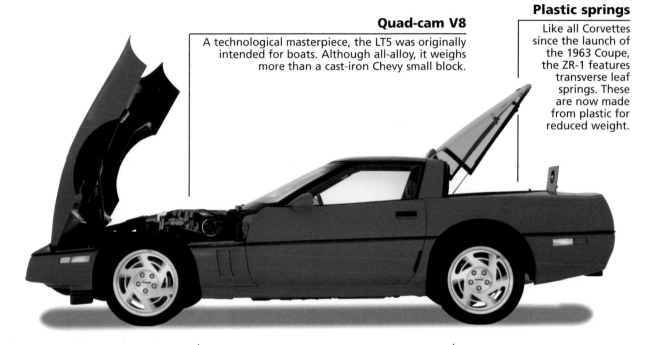

Traction control
Corvettes were often tricky to control on slippery roads. The introduction of ASR (Anti-Slip Regulation) considerably reduced the tendency for the car to slide on wet roads.

Tire-pressure monitor
For 1989 all Corvettes received a tire-pressure monitoring device which warns the driver, by means of a flashing light, if tire pressures are low.

CAGS gear selection
Computer-Aided Gear Selection (CAGS) is a device which skips shifts in low gears at light throttle openings.

Valet key

To prevent certain individuals from experiencing the ZR-1's full performance, a special key can be used to restrict horsepower.

Fiberglass bodywork

The ZR-1, like all Corvettes, retains fiberglass bodywork. The back half of the car had to be widened to fit the ZR-1s large wheels.

Selective ride control

At the touch of a switch the ZR-1 driver can select three different suspension settings: Touring, Sport, or Performance. As speed increases, the shocks are stiffened by a computer that is able to make 10 adjustments per second.

Variable fuel injection

During normal driving, the ZR-1's engine uses only eight primary ports and injectors. With the throttle floored and the engine turning above 3,500 rpm, the eight secondary injectors are brought into action, producing truly awesome performance.

Specifications
1991 Chevrolet Corvette ZR-1

ENGINE

Type: LT5 V8
Construction: Alloy block, heads and cylinder liners
Valve gear: Four valves per cylinder operated by four overhead camshafts
Bore and stroke: 3.90 in. x 3.66 in.
Displacement: 350 c.i.
Compression ratio: 11:1
Induction system: Multi-port fuel injection
Maximum power: 375 bhp at 5,800 rpm
Maximum torque: 371 lb-ft at 4,800 rpm
Top speed: 180 mph
0–60 mph: 5 sec

TRANSMISSION

ZF six-speed manual

BODY/CHASSIS

Separate steel chassis with fiberglass two-door coupe body

SPECIAL FEATURES

A unique feature of the LT5 is the three-stage throttle control.

Prototype ZR-1s retained the original 1984 instrument panel layout.

RUNNING GEAR

Steering: Rack-and-pinion
Front suspension: Double wishbones, transverse plastic leaf springs, and telescopic adjustable shocks
Rear suspension: Upper and lower trailing links, transverse plastic leaf spring, telescopic adjustable shocks, and anti-roll bar
Brakes: Vented discs front and rear, 13 in. dia. (front), 12 in. dia. (rear)
Wheels: Alloy, 17 x 9.5-in. dia. (front), 17 x 11-in. dia. (rear)
Tires: Goodyear Eagle ZR40, 275/40 ZR17 (front), 315/35 ZR17 (rear)

DIMENSIONS

Length: 178.5 in.   **Width:** 73.2 in.
Height: 46.7 in.
Wheelbase: 96.2 in.
Track: 60 in. (front), 62 in. (rear)
Weight: 3,519 lbs.

Chevrolet IMPALA

A striking paint job combined with generous portions of chrome give this 1958 Chevrolet a very nostalgic look. The performance, too, comes from some time-honored, hot-rodding tricks.

Worked V8

With a 400 stroker kit and a .030-inch overbore, this tri-carbed small-block makes almost three time the power output of the straight six it replaces. Its list of modifications reads like that of a race car-spec engine: fully balanced reciprocating assembly, double roller timing chain, fat camshaft, high compression forged pistons, stainless-steel valves and a high-pressure fuel pump. Did we mention it makes more than 400 bhp?

Chromed underpinnings

This car is all about attention to detail. Underneath, nearly everything is chrome plated, including the wishbones, anti-roll bar, motor mounts, springs and rear axle assembly.

Custom exhaust

In order for the engine to fully exploit its power, a low-restriction exhaust system is essential. Custom headers and 2½-inch pipes with Glasspack mufflers not only help increase power but give a low, deep bellow, too.

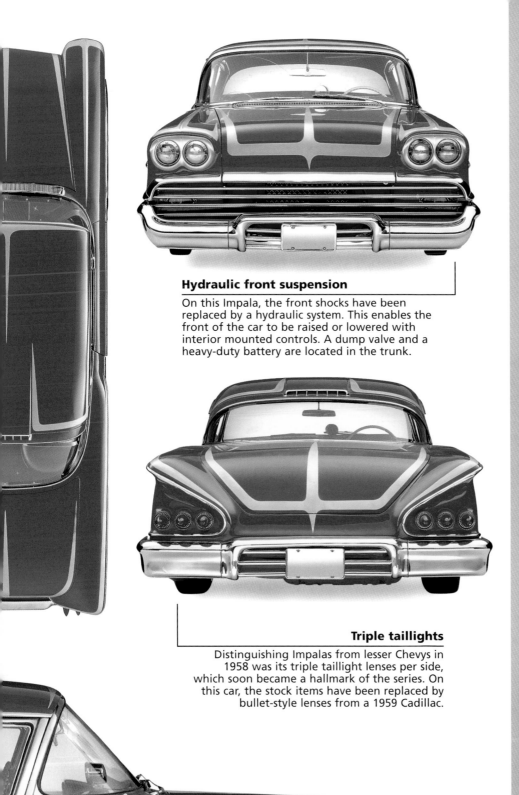

Hydraulic front suspension

On this Impala, the front shocks have been replaced by a hydraulic system. This enables the front of the car to be raised or lowered with interior mounted controls. A dump valve and a heavy-duty battery are located in the trunk.

Triple taillights

Distinguishing Impalas from lesser Chevys in 1958 was its triple taillight lenses per side, which soon became a hallmark of the series. On this car, the stock items have been replaced by bullet-style lenses from a 1959 Cadillac.

Specifications

1958 Chevrolet Impala

ENGINE

Type: V8

Construction: Cast-iron block and heads

Valve gear: Two valves per cylinder operated by a single, centrally-mounted mounted camshaft

Bore and stroke: 4.03 in. x 3.75 in.

Displacement: 383 c.i.

Compression ratio: 10.5:1

Induction system: Three Rochester two-barrel carburetors

Maximum power: 430 bhp at 6,700 rpm

Maximum torque: 420 lb-ft at 3,400 rpm

Top speed: 102 mph

0-60 mph: 6.5 sec.

TRANSMISSION

TH400 three-speed automatic

BODY/CHASSIS

Separate steel chassis with two-door hardtop coupe body

SPECIAL FEATURES

Chrome horizontal bars give the grill a clean appearance.

An aftermarket tach and auxiliary gauges hint at the car's performance.

RUNNING GEAR

Steering: Recirculating ball

Front suspension: Unequal-length wishbones with coil springs, hydraulic rams and anti-roll bar

Rear suspension: Live axle with coil springs and telescopic adjustable shock absorbers

Brakes: Discs (front), drums (rear)

Wheels: Saturn smoothie, 6 x 14 in.

Tires: Coker Classic (front), Commando (rear)

DIMENSIONS

Length: 197.6 in. **Width:** 83.0 in.

Height: 55.0 in. **Wheelbase:** 117.5 in.

Track: 62.5 in. (front), 61.5 in. (rear)

Weight: 3,447 lbs.

Chevrolet MONTE CARLO SS 454

To order an SS 454 you had to check RPO Z20 on the options list. Considering the added performance, this option was a bargain at $420.25. Surprisingly, less than 4,000 buyers chose the option in 1970.

Rally wheels

To go with its high-performance image, all SS 454s had G70-15 wide oval white stripe tires fitted on 7x15-inch Rally wheels.

Big-block muscle

The long 4-inch stroke in Chevrolet's famous cast-iron LS-5 big-block V8 is the reason why this 454-cubic inch Rat motor produces 500 lb-ft. of torque at a very usable 3,200 rpm. Its forged crankshaft is nitride and cross-drilled, making the bottom end virtually bullet proof. Big-valve cast-iron cylinder heads and a Rochester Quadrajet carburetor complete the package.

Front-end style

The bold front end sports a pair of single headlights surrounded by wide chrome bezels. The handsome grill has chrome trim and features a special badge in the center.

Vinyl top

To increase appeal for the luxury car buyer, a special vinyl top was made available as an option. For only $126.40, there was a choice of five distinct colors: black, blue, dark gold, green or white.

Distinctive styling

Built only as a two-door hardtop, the Monte Carlo's exterior styling is very European-looking with its long hood and short deck design. The pronounced fender profile that runs front to back is vaguely reminiscent of the old Jaguar XK models.

ecial suspension

addition to GM's normal practice of
ng unequal length A-arms up front and
olid, live axle at the rear, all SS 454s
ntained a unique Automatic Level
ntrol system with built-in air
npressor.

Optional interior
An optional console could be fitted
between a pair of comfortable bucket
seats upholstered in soft vinyl. Simulated
burred-elm wood inlays were applied
to the instrument panel.

Specifications

1970 Chevrolet Monte Carlo SS 454

ENGINE
Type: V8

Construction: Cast-iron block and heads

Valve gear: Two valves per cylinder operated by a single camshaft, pushrods and rocker arms

Bore and stroke: 4.25 in. x 4.00 in.

Displacement: 454 c.i.

Compression ratio: 10.25:1

Induction system: Rochester Quadrajet four-barrel carburetor

Maximum power: 360 bhp at 4,400 rpm

Maximum torque: 500 lb-ft at 3,200 rpm

TRANSMISSION
GM TurboHydramatic 400 automatic

BODY/CHASSIS
Separate steel body and frame

SPECIAL FEATURES

Discreet badges on the rocker panel
are the only giveaway of the 454.

All production 1970 SS Monte Carlos
were powered by the LS-5 454-cubic
inch V8.

RUNNING GEAR
Steering: Recirculating ball

Front suspension: Unequal length A-arms, telescopic shock absorbers, coil springs and anti-roll bar

Rear suspension: Live solid axle with telescopic shock absorbers and coil springs

Brakes: Discs (front), drums (rear)

Wheels: Rally, 7 x 15 in.

Tires: Goodyear Polyglas, G70-15

DIMENSIONS
Length: 206.0 in   **Width:** 76.0 in.

Height: 52.0 in   **Wheelbase:** 116.0 in

Track: 61.9 in. (front), 61.1 in. (rear)

Weight: 3,860 lbs.

Chevrolet **NOMAD**

This Shoebox-Chevy Nomad combines style with performance. Using a Corvette powerplant and running gear, this 1956 Nomad can surprise many newer performance cars.

Modern paint

The body has been resprayed in two-tone Corvette dark red metallic and tan pearl.

Modified transmission

A 1976 Turbo 400 automatic transmission backs up the sinister LT1 engine. To extract maximum power from the engine, it has a high-stall torque converter.

Custom wheels

No street machine would be complete without aftermarket wheels. This Nomad is fitted with a set of custom chromed 16-inch wheels.

Clean lines

Even in 1956, the Nomad was a fairly clean-looking car. The two-tone paintwork and chrome spears accentuate the classic lines of this Chevrolet.

Corvette front end

The front suspension employs a 1986 Corvette subframe. Not only does it lower the car, giving it a ground-hugging stance, but it greatly improves the car's handling.

Small-block power

For massive performance, this ubiquitous 1970 LT-1 small-block V8 has been bored over .060-inch in and features a forged-steel crank, ported and polished cylinder heads, roller rocker arms plus a B&M supercharger and a Holley carburetor.

Specifications

1956 Chevrolet Nomad

ENGINE

Type: V8

Construction: Cast-iron block and heads

Valve gear: Two valves per cylinder operated by pushrods and rockers

Bore and stroke: 4.06 in. x 3.48 in.

Displacement: 358 c.i.

Compression ratio: 10.5:1

Induction system: B&M supercharger and Holley four-barrel carburetor

Maximum power: 400 bhp at 4,800 rpm

Maximum torque: 320 lb-ft at 3,000 rpm

Top speed: 131 mph

0-60 mph: 5.5 sec.

TRANSMISSION

1976 Turbo HydraMatic 400 with a high-stall torque converter

BODY/CHASSIS

Separate two-door station wagon steel body on X-braced steel frame and Corvette front subframe.

SPECIAL FEATURES

The fuel cap is neatly hidden behind the tail light.

With the rear seat folded down, luggage space is cavernous.

RUNNING GEAR

Steering: Recirculating ball

Front suspension: Double wishbones with plastic transverse leaf spring and shocks

Rear suspension: Trailing arms with plastic transverse leaf spring and shocks

Brakes: Discs (front and rear)

Wheels: Custom Boyds, 15-in. dia.

Tires: Goodyear P22560VR15

DIMENSIONS

Length: 196.7 in. **Width:** 77.2 in.

Height: 53 in.   **Wheelbase:** 115 in.

Track: 59.5 in. (front), 55.8 in. (rear)

Weight: 3,352 lbs.

127

Chrysler **AIRFLOW**

The Airflow was supposed to represent the future, but like so many advanced ideas the public was skeptical of this strange-looking new car, even though it offered new levels of comfort, space and driveability.

Straight-eight power

The straight-eight engine has a healthy power output and masses of torque. In addition, the unit is positioned directly over the front axle, making the hood quite short for a car of this period and allowing more room for passengers.

Aircraft-type construction

The method of construction was inspired by aviation principles. The body is mounted on steel beams and trusses, in a similar way to contemporary aircraft's.

Advanced transmission

The three-speed manual transmission is renowned for its silent operation. It is fitted with helical gears and later examples gained a hypoid rear axle. Above 45 mph, when you lift your foot off the accelerator, overdrive is automatically engaged.

Wind-tunnel-honed body

The Airflow was one of the first cars to be tested in a wind tunnel. The aerodynamic lines helped a 1934 Imperial coupe to complete the flying mile at the Bonneville Salt Flats at 95.6 mph.

Bold nose

The front end of the 1934 model features an amazing 'waterfall' grill, 'shaped by the wind' badging and triple bumper strips. The faired in headlights look curiously like bug eyes, especially on later cars.

A glazing world first

Although most Airflows, like this one, have split windshields, some later-model Imperials boasted a new curved glass design

Puncture-proof tires

By 1936 all Airflows were fitted with new Lifeguard tires with special heavy-duty tubes and a second 'floating' tube inside.

Specifications
1934 Chrysler Airflow Sedan

ENGINE

Type: In-line eight-cylinder
Construction: Cast-iron block and head
Valve gear: Two sidevalves per cylinder
Bore and stroke: 3.25 in. x 4.50 in.
Displacement: 298 c.i.
Compression ratio: Not quoted
Induction system: Two carburetors
Maximum power: 122 bhp at 3,400 rpm
Maximum torque: Not quoted
Top speed: 88 mph
0–60 mph: 19.5 sec.

TRANSMISSION

Three-speed manual

BODY/CHASSIS

Steel girder chassis with four-door steel sedan body

SPECIAL FEATURES

The rear wheel skirts are evocative of the 1930s art deco era.

The rigorously curved surfaces of the Airflow, shaped by Oliver Clark, were unique for 1930s design.

RUNNING GEAR

Steering: worm-and-roller
Front suspension: Beam axle with leaf springs and shock absorbers
Rear suspension: Rigid axle with leaf springs and shock absorbers
Brakes: Drums (front and rear)
Wheels: Steel, 16-in. dia.
Tires: Crossply, 16-in. dia.

DIMENSIONS

Length: 235.0 in.   **Width:** 77.9 in.
Height: 68.9 in.   **Wheelbase:** 146.5 in.
Track: 63.0 in. (front), 61.1 in. (rear)
Weight: 4,166 lbs.

Chrysler **C-300**

America's first mass-produced car to break the 300-bhp ceiling, the C-300 was also incredibly stylish and dominated NASCAR, winning 37 races in the hands of drivers like Buck Baker and Tim Flock.

Stiffened suspension

While the front coil springs of the New Yorker are rated at 480 lbs./in., those on the C-300 are rated at 800 lbs./in. Likewise, the New Yorker's rear leaf springs are rated at 100 lbs./in., whereas the C-300's are 160 lbs./in.

Solid lifters

Chrysler engineers replaced the hydraulic lifters with solid lifters for the 300. Revving up to 5,200 rpm, the heat generated by the engine could 'pump up' hydraulic lifters as they expand and hold the valves open.

Automatics only

All C-300s came with two-speed PowerFlite automatic transmissions. However, experts agree that there was one car (number 1206) that was built with a three-speed manual transmission.

Unique wheels

Chrysler C-300 buyers had a choice of two wheel styles. The standard ones are steel with Imperial wheel covers and unique 300 center caps; or, for an extra $617, buyers could opt for a set of chrome, 48-spoke wheels by Motor Wheel.

Axle ratios

The standard rear axle ratio for the C-300 is a 3.54:1 ring-and-pinion, but steeper cogs were available.

Specifications

1955 Chrysler C-300

ENGINE

Type: V8

Construction: Cast-iron block and heads

Valve gear: Two valves per cylinder operated by a single camshaft with pushrods and rockers

Bore and stroke: 3.81 in. x 3.63 in.

Displacement: 331.1 c.i.

Compression ratio: 8.5:1

Induction system: Two Carter four-barrel carburetors

Maximum power: 300 bhp at 5,200 rpm

Maximum torque: 345 lb-ft at 3,200 rpm

Top speed: 130 mph

0-60 mph: 8.9 sec.

TRANSMISSION

PowerFlite two-speed automatic

BODY/CHASSIS

Separate chassis with steel two-door body

SPECIAL FEATURES

The protruding stalk shifter was only found on 1955 300s.

Fins on the C-300 were little more than extra chrome pieces grafted on.

RUNNING GEAR

Steering: Recirculating-ball

Front suspension: A-arms with coil springs and telescopic shock absorbers

Rear suspension: Live axle with semi-elliptic multileaf springs and telescopic shock absorbers

Brakes: Drums (front and rear)

Wheels: Wire, 15 x 5 in.

Tires: Goodyear Super Cushion Nylon Special tubeless white sidewalls 6-ply, 8.00 x 15

DIMENSIONS

Length: 218.8 in.   **Width:** 79.1 in.

Height: 60.1 in.   **Wheelbase:** 126.0 in.

Track: 60.2 in. (front) 59.6 in. (rear)

Weight: 4,005 lbs.

Chrysler 300 G

Unleashing an overabundance of output from its dual-quad, cross-ram, max-wedge engine, the Chrysler 300 G became a legend on the street. However, its first-class styling and massive size kept its brutality well concealed.

Big-block V8

Created under the guidance of chief engineer Robert M. Rodger, the cross-ram induction system made Chryslers some of the hottest cars in their day. Although a 375-bhp V8 was standard in the 300 G, buyers could step up to an even more potent 400-bhp 413 motor. It had even longer runners on its unusual looking intake manifold.

Larger wheels and tires

For the first time since 1956, the 300 featured 15-inch wheels giving the car a taller stance. They also resulted in improved road holding and ride qualities.

TorqueFlite transmission

Chrysler's proven TorqueFlite automatic transmission is operated by pushbutton controls mounted on the dashboard. A three-speed manual was listed on the options list, but few 300 Gs were ordered with it.

Generous list

As befitting its flagship status, the 300 G came loaded with equipment, including power steering, brakes and windows, a safety cushion dashboard, waterproof ignition, tachometer and front and rear center armrests.

Crisp styling

The 300 G was the last of the 'letter' cars to really bear the hallmarks of what is perhaps Virgil Exner's finest work. Canted fins were dramatic and futuristic but times were changing, and for the 1962 300 H they were discarded completely, marking the end of the tail-fin era.

Stiffer suspension
The 300 G has a stiffer suspension than other Chryslers, making this 4,315-lb. cruiser one of the most nimble big cars of its time.

Popular options
Besides the extensive standard equipment that garnished the 300, popular options included air conditioning, electric mirrors and a Music Master radio.

Specifications
1961 Chrysler 300 G

ENGINE
Type: V8
Construction: Cast-iron block and heads
Valve gear: Two valves per cylinder operated by pushrods and rockers
Bore and stroke: 4.18 in. x 3.75 in.
Displacement: 413 c.i.
Compression ratio: 10.0:1
Induction system: Twin Carter four-barrel carburetors, cross-ram intake manifold
Maximum power: 375 bhp at 5,000 rpm
Maximum torque: 495 lb-ft at 2,800 rpm
Top speed: 130 mph
0-60 mph: 8.4 sec.

TRANSMISSION
TorqueFlite 727 three-speed automatic

BODY/CHASSIS
Steel unitary chassis with two-door convertible body

SPECIAL FEATURES

The 300 G's swivelling seats were a popular feature on lavish Chryslers.

The year 1961 was significant because it was the final appearance of large, pointed fins on 300s.

RUNNING GEAR
Steering: Recirculating ball
Front suspension: Unequal-length A-arms with longitudinal torsion bars and telescopic shock absorbers
Rear suspension: Live axle with semi-elliptic leaf springs and telescopic shock absorbers
Brakes: Drums (front and rear)
Wheels: Steel disc, 15-in. dia.
Tires: Blue Streak, 8.00 x 15

DIMENSIONS
Length: 219.8 in   **Width:** 79.4 in.
Height: 55.6 in.   **Wheelbase:** 126.0 in.
Track: 61.2 in. (front and rear)
Weight: 4,315 lbs.

Chrysler TOWN & COUNTRY

The name Town & Country came from Mr. Boyertown—the man who built the bodies for these special cars. He said the front of the car 'looked town, while the rear looked country,' and the name stuck.

Semi-automatic transmission

Chrysler's fluid-drive transmission was standard on the Town & Country. This semi-automatic unit has two high and two low gears. The fluid drive means acceleration is slightly on the leisurely side.

Exclusively straight eight

Production 1946-1948 Town & Countrys are powered by Chrysler's venerable straight-eight engine sized at 324-cubic inches. With two Ball and Ball carburetors, it produces 135 bhp.

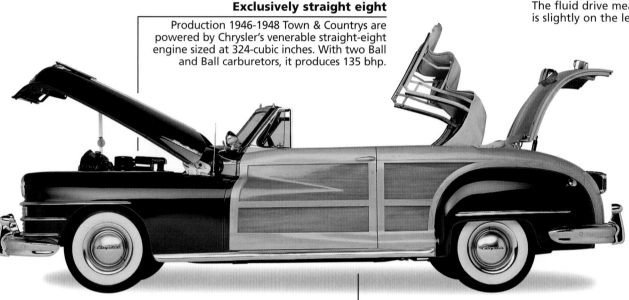

Structural wood

Besides looking great, the wood is structural on the Town & Country. The door, quarter panel and trunk-lid framing are made from white ash, and the inserts are real Honduras mahogany, changed to DI-NOC decals in late 1947.

Fender skirts

Available as a dealer-installed accessory, rear fender wheel well skirts gave the car a more streamlined appearance.

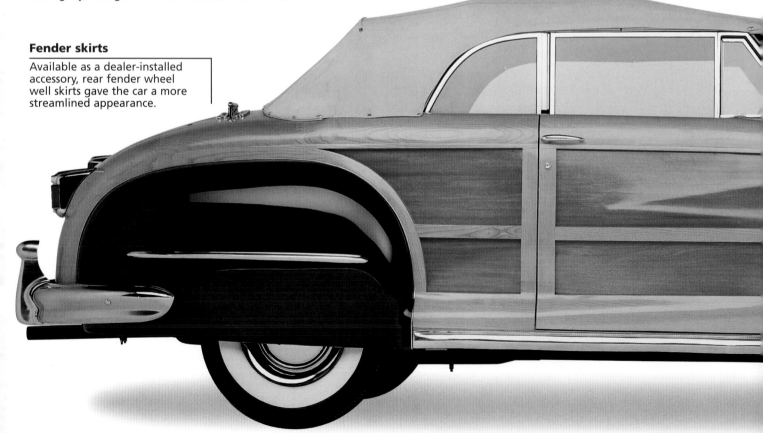

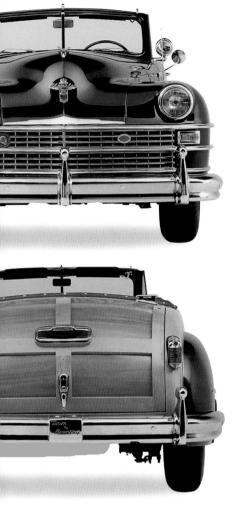

Specifications

1947 Chrysler Town & Country

ENGINE
Type: Inline eight-cylinder

Construction: Cast-iron block and head

Valve gear: Two side valves per cylinder operated by a single block-mounted cam

Bore and stroke: 3.25 in. x 4.88 in.

Displacement: 324 c.i.

Compression ratio: 6.7:1

Induction system: Twin Ball and Ball E7A1 carburetors

Maximum power: 135 bhp at 3,400 rpm

Maximum torque: Not quoted

TRANSMISSION
Fluid-drive four-speed semi-automatic

BODY/CHASSIS
Steel chassis with steel and wood two-door convertible body

SPECIAL FEATURES

Chrysler's fluid-drive semi-automatic transmission is fitted on this car.

Its body and door frames were made from ash with mahogany inserts.

RUNNING GEAR
Steering: Recirculating ball

Front suspension: Unequal-length wishbones with coil springs and telescopic shock absorbers

Rear suspension: Live axle with semi-elliptic leaf springs and telescopic shock absorbers

Brakes: Drums (front and rear)

Wheels: Pressed steel, 15-in. dia.

Tires: 8.20 x 15

DIMENSIONS
Length: 202.9 in. **Width:** 84.2 in.

Height: 66.8 in. **Wheelbase:** 127.5 in.

Track: 64.7 in. (front), 65.7 in. (rear)

Weight: 4,332 lbs.

Long wheelbase

In 1947, the Town & Country was available either as a sedan or convertible. The six-cylinder powered sedans had a 121.5-inch wheelbase, while the eight-cylinder convertibles had 127.5 inches between the wheel centers.

Chrysler TURBINE

The sight and sound of a car powered by a high-revving gas-turbine engine sounded very space-age in 1963. Chrysler's bold experimental Turbine car worked surprisingly well in many areas and looked futuristic to boot.

Turbine engine

Central to the Chrysler is its gas-turbine powerplant, a neat installation under the hood. Able to spin up to 44,600 rpm, its power is available right across the rev band, as is its torque. But it is too thirsty, even though it can run on a wide variety of fuels.

Orange paintwork

All 55 cars were built to basically the same specifications, including orange metallic paint and orange leather upholstery. Most, but not all, also had a black vinyl roof.

Designed by Mr. Thunderbird

The cigar-shaped Turbine body was designed by Elwood Engle, the father of the 1961 Ford Thunderbird. Many similarities exist in the profile of the two designs.

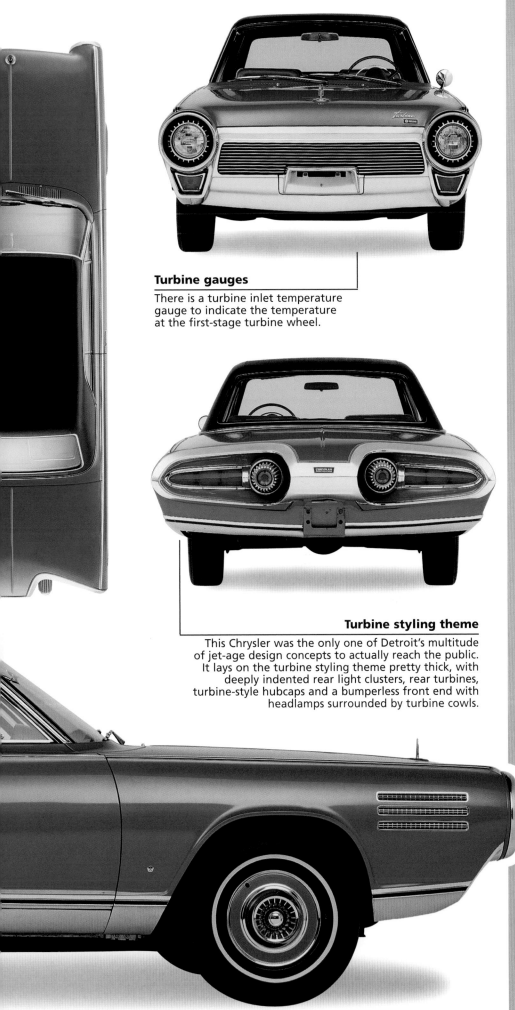

Turbine gauges

There is a turbine inlet temperature gauge to indicate the temperature at the first-stage turbine wheel.

Turbine styling theme

This Chrysler was the only one of Detroit's multitude of jet-age design concepts to actually reach the public. It lays on the turbine styling theme pretty thick, with deeply indented rear light clusters, rear turbines, turbine-style hubcaps and a bumperless front end with headlamps surrounded by turbine cowls.

Specifications

1963 Chrysler Turbine

ENGINE

Type: Gas turbine

Construction: Centrifugal air compressor with vaned power turbine

Valve gear: Compressor turbine operating power turbine

Bore and stroke: N/A

Displacement: N/A

Compression ratio: N/A

Induction system: Pressurized air in flame tube

Maximum power: 130 bhp at 44,600 rpm

Maximum torque: 425 lb-ft at zero rpm output shift speed

TRANSMISSION

Three-speed automatic

BODY/CHASSIS

Separate chassis with steel two-door sedan body

SPECIAL FEATURES

The rear-end styling drew inspiration from Flash Gordon.

Spent gases exit from under the car, as in a conventional engine.

RUNNING GEAR

Steering: Recirculating-ball

Front suspension: Upper and lower wishbones, coil springs and shock absorbers

Rear suspension: Live axle with leaf springs and shock absorbers

Brakes: Drums (front and rear)

Wheels: Steel, 14-in. dia.

Tires: 7.50 x 14

DIMENSIONS

Length: 201.6 in.   **Width:** 72.9 in.

Height: 53.5 in.   **Wheelbase:** 110.0 in.

Track: 59.0 in. (front), 56.7 in. (rear)

Weight: 3,900 lbs.

Citroën DS

When it was introduced in 1955, the revolutionary DS set new standards for family sedans. Though not much to look at, the DS was innovative and very much ahead of its time.

Fiberglass roof
Although the rest of the panels were steel, the bolt-on roof panel was manufactured from fiberglass. Early ID models had unpainted and untrimmed roofs that allowed light to filter into the cabin.

Swivelling headlights
When the headlights were faired in and the system changed to a four-light design, the inner pair turned with the front wheels to illuminate the driver's way through corners.

Pushrod engine
Citroën wanted to have an engine as advanced as the car itself but DS development cost such a fortune it couldn't afford the water- and air-cooled sixes that had been developed for the car. Instead, Citroën installed a modified Light 15 engine.

Hydropneumatic gearchange
The high-pressure hydraulic system was originally intended to power the brakes, the clutch, the steering and even the shifter, but eventually a manual gearshift was used.

Hydropneumatic suspension
The DS's greatest innovation was the hydropneumatic suspension, which relied on a pressurized hydraulic system run by an engine-driven pump. It also operated the power-assisted steering, the brakes and semi-automatic gearshift.

Self jacking
The high-pressure hydraulics gave the DS the ability to rise up on its suspension to allow the driver or mechanic to look underneath. It was also useful for crossing bumpy terrain.

Removable rear panels
The rear fenders of the DS could be detached in a matter of seconds to allow access to the rear wheel or to change a flat tire.

Specifications
1971 Citroën DS21

ENGINE
Type: In-line four cylinder
Construction: Cast-iron block and alloy head
Valve gear: Two valves per cylinder operated by single block-mounted cam, via pushrods and rockers
Bore and stroke: 3.54 in. x 3.36 in.
Displacement: 2,175 cc
Compression ratio: 8.75:1
Induction system: Electronic fuel injection
Maximum power: 108 bhp at 5,500 rpm
Maximum torque: 123 lb-ft at 3,500 rpm
Top speed: 95 mph
0-60 mph: 18.4 sec.

TRANSMISSION
Five-speed manual

BODY/CHASSIS
Steel monocoque with four-door, four-seat sedan body

SPECIAL FEATURES

Roof-guttering leads the eye into an unusually located trumpet-shaped rear indicator.

Rear fenders can be removed by simply unfastening one bolt. The fender must be removed to change the wheel.

RUNNING GEAR
Steering: Rack-and-pinion
Front suspension: Upper and lower control arms, hydropneumatic combined spring/shock units and anti-roll bar
Rear suspension: Trailing arms and combined hydropneumatic spring/shock units
Brakes: Discs front, drums rear
Wheels: Steel disc
Tires: 185-400 Michelin XAS

DIMENSIONS
Length: 189 in. **Width:** 70.5 in.
Wheelbase: 123 in. **Height:** 63 in.
Track: 57 in. (front), 51.3 in. (rear)
Weight: 2,919 lbs.

Inboard front discs
Citroën took advantage of the empty space under the hood next to the transmission by moving the front discs inboard to save on unsprung weight.

Citroën GS BIROTOR

The GS Birotor was not only way ahead of its time, but perhaps too complex to succeed. When the gas crisis struck in 1973, sales of the Birotor fell sharply and Citroën tried to buy many back to avoid the extensive servicing they required.

Rotary engine

A super-smooth water-cooled rotary engine replaced Citroën's air-cooled flat four, the engine found in the conventional GS.

Special color scheme

The brown roof and beige body was a special Birotor color scheme, which was later adopted on the Pallas versions of the GS.

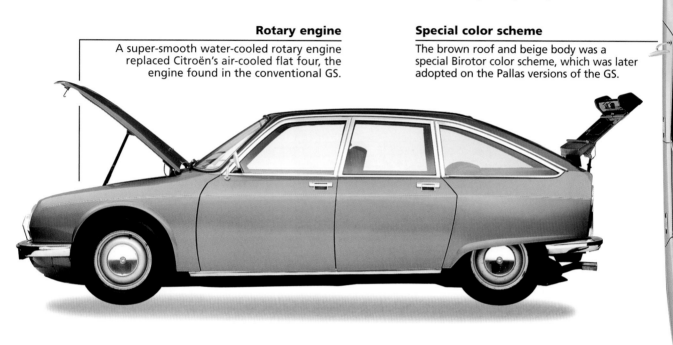

Flared arches

At a glance, the flared arches are the only way you can distinguish a Birotor from a conventional GS. They are needed to accommodate the wider track.

Four-wheel disc brakes

Like the standard GS the Birotor has disc brakes, but the fronts are not in-board; they are mounted in the conventional position and are larger, to make stopping the car much easier.

High-backed seats

Another Birotor feature are the high-backed seats with integral head restraints.

Semi-automatic transmission

The semi-automatic transmission can be operated like a manual, but there is no clutch pedal. A touch-sensitive switch in the gear knob operates the clutch.

Specifications
1975 Citroën GS Birotor

ENGINE
Type: Wankel twin rotary
Construction: Alloy housings; nickel-silicon coated inside
Valve gear: N/A
Bore and stroke: N/A
Displacement: 1,990 cc
Compression ratio: N/A
Induction system: Solex twin-barrel carburetor
Maximum power: 107 bhp at 6,500 rpm
Maximum torque: 101 lb-ft at 3,000 rpm
Top speed: 109 mph
0-60 mph: 10.2 sec.

TRANSMISSION
Three-speed semi-automatic

BODY/CHASSIS
Unitary monocoque construction with steel four-door sedan body

SPECIAL FEATURES

The hydropneumatic suspension can be raised or lowered by a console lever.

To free up much needed luggage space in the trunk, the spare wheel is carried under the hood.

RUNNING GEAR
Steering: Rack-and-pinion
Front suspension: Double wishbones with interconnected hydropneumatic struts and anti-roll bar
Rear suspension: Trailing arms with interconnected hydropneumatic struts
Brakes: Discs, 10.6-in. dia. (front), vented discs, 6.9-in. dia. (rear)
Wheels: Steel, five-bolt fixing, 5.5-in. rim
Tires: Radial, 165 HR14

DIMENSIONS
Length: 150.2 in.   **Width:** 64.6 in.
Height: 53.9 in.   **Wheelbase:** 100.0 in.
Track: 56.3 in. (front), 53.2 in. (rear)
Weight: 2,514 lbs.

Citroën SM

Designed to be a luxury grand tourer for the man who wanted to be different from everyone else, the SM's character was as complex as its unique engineering.

Transmission ahead of engine

To help weight distribution the five-speed transmission is mounted ahead of the engine so all the V6 is behind the front axle line.

Maserati V6 engine

The SM's V6 engine is derived from the Maserati V8 design—it is compact, light, and powerful.

Hatchback design

The fastback styling meant there was no room for a trunk—the SM became one of the world's most expensive hatchbacks.

Trailing arm front suspension

The SM's front suspension has two trailing arms that are sprung and dampened by the usual Citroën hydropneumatic system.

Power brakes

The SM's very high-pressure hydraulic system powers the four disc brakes. The brake feel is closer to a push button than a conventional brake pedal and needs only the slightest touch to produce very effective braking.

Variable ride height

Citroën hydropneumatic suspension can be set to different heights. Here it's at the maximum, which would never have been used on normal roads.

Inboard front discs

To help with unsprung weight, the front disc brakes are mounted inboard next to the transmission.

Power-assisted steering

At low speeds the assistance is great, dropping away as road speed rises. It's very direct with just two turns lock-to-lock and the self-centering action is extremely strong.

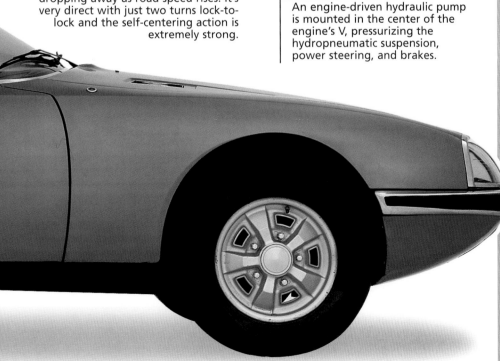

Central hydraulic pump

An engine-driven hydraulic pump is mounted in the center of the engine's V, pressurizing the hydropneumatic suspension, power steering, and brakes.

Specifications
1973 Citroën SM

ENGINE
Type: V6
Construction: Alloy block and cylinder heads; wet liners
Valve gear: Two valves per cylinder operated by four chain-driven overhead camshafts
Bore and stroke: 3.42 in. x 2.95 in.
Displacement: 2,670 cc
Compression ratio: 9.0:1
Induction system: Bosch D-Jetronic fuel injection
Maximum power: 178 bhp at 5,500 rpm
Maximum torque: 171 lb-ft at 4,000 rpm
Top speed: 142 mph
0-60 mph: 8.5 sec

TRANSMISSION
Five-speed manual

BODY/CHASSIS
Unitary construction with two-door, four-seat hatchback body

SPECIAL FEATURES

The SM has a typically quirky Citroën dashboard with oval instruments and trademark single-spoke steering wheel.

As the SM turns through corners one pair of the powerful front lights also turns to illuminate the whole corner. The lights also self-level.

RUNNING GEAR
Steering: Rack-and-pinion
Front suspension: Twin trailing arms with hydropneumatic springs and anti-roll bar
Rear suspension: Trailing arms with hydropneumatic springs. Self levelling front and rear
Brakes: Four-wheel discs
Wheels: Steel, 6 in. x 15 in.
Tires: Michelin XVX 205/70 VR15

DIMENSIONS
Length: 192.8 in.   **Width:** 72.5 in.
Height: 52.1 in.   **Wheelbase:** 116.1 in.
Track: 60.1 in. (front), 52.2 in. (rear)
Weight: 3,197 lbs.

Citroën **TRACTION AVANT**

By forcing his engineers to design and develop the revolutionary front-wheel drive Traction Avant, André Citroën bankrupted the company. However, the result was a car that was way ahead of its time.

Citroën emblem

The double chevron emblem represented meshing gears, an iro considering the weakness of the three-speed transmission.

Wet liner engine

The engine has wet liners—cylinder sleeves inserted into the block and surrounded by the water jacket. These could be replaced where a conventional engine would need to be rebuilt.

Monocoque design

The main structure of the Traction was a steel monocoque. Citroën once demonstrated its great strength by pushing one off a cliff.

Front-wheel dri

It was the first front-wheel drive car to solve the problem of getting universal joints to work reliab on front driveshafts, and the first to go into mass production

Transmission ahead of engine

Since the Traction Avant is a front-wheel drive, the transmission is mounted ahead of the engine. It helped weight distribution, but made for a very long gear linkage which needed precise adjustment to work well.

Michelin radial tires

Michelin took over the company when Citroën went bankrupt— naturally the Traction used Michelin tires. After the war, they were replaced with the new and hard-wearing X radials.

'Floating Power' engine mounts

Citroën wanted the car to be comfortable and refined. Using 'Floating Power' mounts helped to isolate the movement and vibration of the engine and transmission.

Specifications
1952 'Big Fifteen' Citroën 11CV Traction Avant

ENGINE

Type: In-line four cylinder
Construction: Cast-iron block and head with wet liner cylinder sleeves.
Valve gear: Two valves per cylinder operated by single block-mounted camshaft, pushrods and rockers
Bore and stroke: 3.07 in. x 3.93 in.
Displacement: 1,911 cc
Compression ratio: 6.5:1
Induction system: Single Solex 32 PBI downdraft carburetor
Maximum power: 56 bhp at 4,250 rpm
Maximum torque: 90 lb-ft at 2,200 rpm
Top speed: 71 mph
0-50 mph: 16.4 sec.

TRANSMISSION

Three-speed manual

BODY/CHASSIS

Steel monocoque with, at one stage, choice of sedan, coupe or open-roadster body

SPECIAL FEATURES

The wind-shield can be wound open with a handle in the cabin to improve ventilation.

The shifter sprouts from the dashboard in an unconventional fashion for Citroën. It can be difficult to use if it is out of adjustment.

RUNNING GEAR

Steering: Rack-and-pinion
Front suspension: Upper wishbones, lower radius arms, torsion bars and shocks
Rear suspension: Beam axle, trailing arms, radius arms, torsion bars and hydraulic shocks
Brakes: Hydraulically operated drums, 12 in. dia. (front), 9.8 in. dia. (rear)
Wheels: Pressed steel disc
Tires: 6.5 in. x 15 in.

DIMENSIONS

Length: 186.5 in.   **Width:** 70 in.
Height: 61 in.   **Wheelbase:** 21.5 in.
Track: 58.5 in. (front), 57.8 in. (rear)
Weight: 2,349 lbs.

Cord 810/812

The Cord 812 was styled by one of the great car designers, Gordon Buehrig. It was like no other car on the road, thanks to its coffin-like nose, unique radiator grill and pop-up headlights.

V8 engine

Lycoming's V8 is very strong yet relatively light thanks to its alloy cylinder heads. The valve-train is a unique design with upright rockers pivoted below the camshaft actuating the valves mounted in the block and angled at 35 degrees.

Independent front suspension

Helping to give the 812 its superb road holding independent front suspension with trailing arms and a single transverse leaf spring.

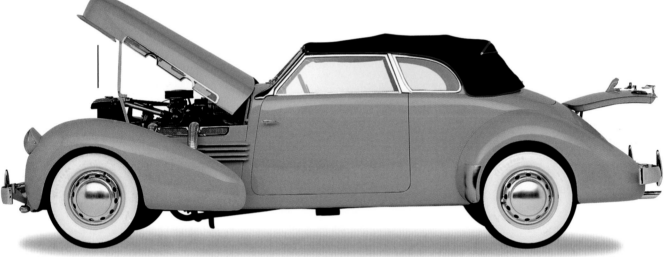

Four-speed transmission

An advanced feature of the 812 is the four-speed manual transmission (unusual for the time). Fourth gear is very tall with over 28 mph per thousand revs, making the Cord ideal for high-speed touring.

Electro-vacuum gear shifter

The Cord uses a Bendix 'Electric Hand' pre-selector gear shifter. This miniature gear linkage relies on the vacuum inside the intake manifold to suck the pistons controlling the movements of the selector rods. It only works with the clutch depressed and the driver's foot off the accelerator.

Drum brakes

Massive 12-inch, hydraulic, centrifuse drums are used on all four wheels.

Pop-up lights

Ordinary round headlights would have spoiled the Cord's bold styling and obstructed airflow, so they were designed to be concealed. In fact, the lights are basically landing light units from Stinson aircraft (also owned by Auburn-Cord-Duesenberg).

Specifications
1937 Cord 812 Supercharged

ENGINE

Type: V8

Construction: Cast-iron block and alloy cylinder heads

Valve gear: Two in-line side valves per cylinder operated by a single block-mounted camshaft with rocker arms and rollers

Bore and stroke: 3.50 in. x 3.75 in.

Displacement: 288.6 c.i.

Compression ratio: 6.3:1

Induction system: Single carburetor with mechanically driven Schwitzer-Cummins supercharger

Maximum power: 190 bhp at 4,200 rpm

Maximum torque: 272 lb-ft at 3,000 rpm

Top speed: 111 mph

0–60 mph: 13.8 sec.

TRANSMISSION

Four-speed manual

BODY/CHASSIS

Welded steel floorpan and side rails with two-door convertible body

SPECIAL FEATURES

Phaetons only differ stylistically from cabriolets by having a rear seat and quarter windows.

A crank mounted on the passenger side of the dash is used to raise and lower the headlights.

RUNNING GEAR

Steering: Gemmer centerpoint

Front suspension: Independent with trailing arms, transverse semi-elliptic leaf spring and friction shock absorbers

Rear suspension: Beam axle with semi-elliptic leaf springs and friction shock absorbers

Brakes: Hydraulically operated drums, 12-in. dia.

Wheels: 16 in. Stamped Steel, 16-in. dia.

Tires: 6.50 x 16

DIMENSIONS AND WEIGHT

Length: 195.5 in.　　**Width:** 71.0 in.

Height: 58.0 in.　　**Wheelbase:** 132.0 in.

Track: 55.9 in. (front), 60.9 in. (rear)

Weight: 4,110 lbs.

Cosworth VEGA

Using electronic fuel injection and four valves per cylinder in a 2-liter engine might have been normal in Europe during the 1970s, but not in the U.S. It's too bad this high-tech hot rod wasn't more successful.

Wide radials

Due to its better performance, the Cosworth deserves bigger tires so it uses with fatter BR70-13 radials as standard equipment.

High-tech horsepower

Small displacement, overhead cams and electronic fuel injection are common on U.S. cars today. But these features made the Cosworth an exotic high-tech hot rod with 110 bhp from its very small 122 cubic inch engine in 1975.

Twin-cam engine

Chevrolet followed the exotic import route and fitted the Vega with a Cosworth-designed twin-cam cylinder head, the first in a U.S. car for many years. When the engine first appeared the power output was an excellent 130 bhp and 115 lb-ft of torque, but in production the figures were much lower.

Four-speed transmission

In attempt to attract buyers of would-be imported small cars, the Cosworth Vega came with a Muncie four-speed transmission.

European styling

Vegas bore styling cues from the larger Camaro®, which was unmistakably European, although this was later marred by big bumpers.

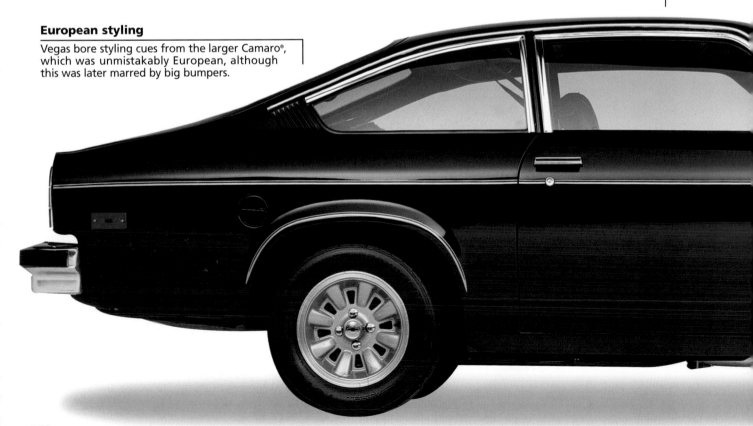

Low rear axle ratio

All 1975 Cosworth Vegas used 3.73:1 rear axle ratios, while in 1976 they used 4.10:1s. The Cosworth's rear suspension is upgraded to handle the engine's power.

Alloy wheels

The standard Vega wheels have been replaced by wider 6-inch alloy wheels.

Specifications

1975 Chevrolet Cosworth Vega

ENGINE
Type: In-line four-cylinder twin-cam
Construction: Light alloy block and head
Valve gear: Four valves per cylinder operated by twin belt-driven overhead camshafts
Bore and stroke: 3.50 in. x 3.14 in.
Displacement: 122 c.i.
Compression ratio: 8.5:1
Induction system: Bendix electronic injection
Maximum power: 110 bhp at 5,600 rpm
Maximum torque: 107 lb-ft at 4,800 rpm
Top speed: 112 mph
0-60 mph: 12.3 sec

TRANSMISSION
Four-speed Muncie

BODY/CHASSIS
Unitary monocoque construction with two-door coupe body

SPECIAL FEATURES

Each Cosworth Vega has a dash-mounted plaque making it exclusive.

The twin-cam alloy engine is highly exotic for a 1970s American compact.

RUNNING GEAR
Steering: Recirculating ball, 16:1 ratio
Front suspension: Double wishbones with coil springs, telescopic shocks and anti-roll bar
Rear suspension: Live axle with upper and lower control arms, coil springs, telescopic shocks and anti-roll bar
Brakes: Discs, 9.9-in. dia. (front), drums, 9-in. dia. (rear)
Wheels: Alloy, 6 in. x 13 in.
Tires: Radial BR70-13 in. x 6 in.

DIMENSIONS
Length: 170.2 in.   **Width:** 65.4 in.
Height: 47.9 in.   **Wheelbase:** 97 in.
Track: 55.2 in. (front), 54.1 in. (rear)
Weight: 2,639 lbs.

Daimler MAJESTIC MAJOR

With its unique blend of dignified lines, relaxed performance and competitive pricing, the Majestic Major was a British favorite for those who liked its adequate power. But this made it a popular and safe driver's car.

Unique V8 power

Though Daimler did produce a popular 2.5-liter V8 for its smaller models, the 4.6-liter V8 engine in the Majestic Major was never fitted to any other model. It has light alloy cylinder heads and hemispherical combustion chambers.

Unique V grills

The bodywork is basically the same as that on the six-cylinder Majestic, itself a development of the 1955 One-O-Four sedan. A major identification mark was the V-grills on either side of the radiator.

Two wheelbase lengths

A 114-inch wheelbase may seem long enough, but the eight-passenger DR450 limousine version is nearly 19 feet long and weighs more than two tons.

Leather interior

The Major has a beautifully crafted interior that resembles a living room rather than an automobile interior. The seats are hand-stitched leather and the dashboard is styled with wood veneer.

Four-wheel disc brakes

Dunlop supplied Daimler with its disc brakes which were fitted to all four wheels. They were just barely adequate to haul down the two tons of metal.

Optional power steering

After early buyers had struggled with the non-assisted steering, power assistance became an option—and a popular one. It was fitted as standard only in 1964.

Leaf-sprung rear axle

The chassis is very conventional. It has coil-sprung front suspension and a live rear axle on semi-elliptic leaf springs.

Specifications

1960 Daimler Major Major

ENGINE

Type: V8

Construction: Cast-iron block and aluminum heads

Valve gear: Two valves per cylinder operated via pushrods and rockers

Bore and stroke: 3.75 in. x 3.15 in.

Displacement: 4,561 cc

Compression ratio: 8.0:1

Induction system: Two SU carburetors

Maximum power: 220 bhp at 5,500 rpm

Maximum torque: 283 lb-ft at 3,200 rpm

Top speed: 120 mph

0–60 mph: 10.3 sec.

TRANSMISSION

Borg-Warner three-speed automatic

BODY/CHASSIS

Separate chassis with steel four-door sedan body

SPECIAL FEATURES

Daimler's distinctive emblem sits atop a fluted grill.

The opulence of the interior includes fold-away wood-veneer tables.

RUNNING GEAR

Steering: Recirculating ball

Front suspension: Semi-trailing arms with lower wishbones, coil springs and telescopic shock absorbers

Rear suspension: Live axle with semi-elliptic springs and telescopic shock absorbers

Brakes: Discs (front and rear)

Wheels: Steel, 16-in. dia.

Tires: 6.70 x 16

DIMENSIONS

Length: 202.0 in. **Width:** 73.25 in.

Height: 62.75 in. **Wheelbase:** 114.0 in.

Track: 57.0 in. (front and rear)

Weight: 4,228 lbs.

Datsun 240Z

Unashamedly created for and targeted at the U.S. market, the 240Z marked the beginning of the modern era of Japanese sports cars. It did almost everything right, and sales went straight through the roof.

High standard of finish

In addition to an attractive price, the Datsun Z's high level of build quality was very impressive. By comparison, European sports cars were not very well put together and could be unreliable in service. The Datsun was a more sensible proposition for everyday use.

Six-cylinder engine

Datsun's punchy in-line six gave impressive performance for a sports car, especially one which sold at such a low price. Unlike some of its rivals, the 240Z's engine was also incredibly strong and reliable.

Hatchback rear

In most sports cars practicality is overlooked, but the 240Z features an opening decklid, complete with spoiler, plus a useful storage area behind the seats. However, space is impeded by the intrusion of the suspension struts and the spare tire.

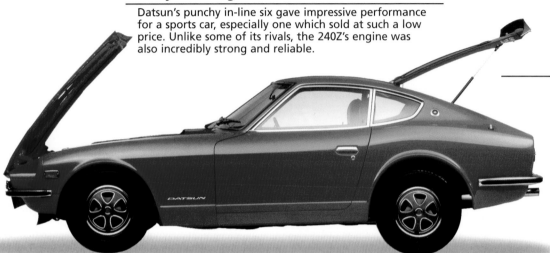

All-independent suspension

While rivals still used live rear axles and leaf springs, the 240Z was updated with an all-independent suspension front and rear giving the Z outstanding cornering ability.

Handsome styling

The smooth styling of the Z was probably its biggest selling point. Count Albrecht Goertz, who conceived the Z, had a solid track record in recognizing what the American public wanted. Goertz's other achievements include the BMW 507 and the Toyota 2000GT.

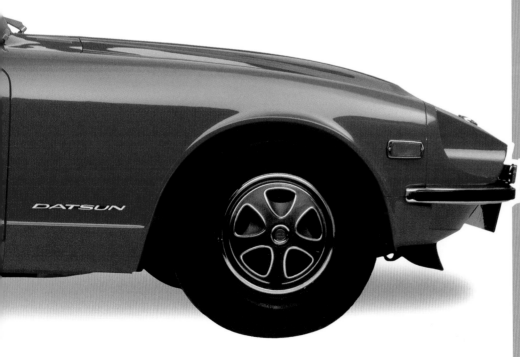

Specifications
1971 Datsun 240Z

ENGINE

Type: In-line six-cylinder

Construction: Cast-iron block and alloy head

Valve gear: Two valves per cylinder operated by a chain-driven single overhead camshaft

Bore and stroke: 3.27 in. x 2.9 in.

Displacement: 2,393 cc

Compression ratio: 9.0:1

Induction system: Two Hitachi HJG 46W carburetors

Maximum power: 150 bhp at 6,000 rpm

Maximum torque: 148 lb-ft at 4,400 rpm

TRANSMISSION

Four- or five-speed manual or three-speed automatic

BODY/CHASSIS

Steel monocoque with two-door coupe body

SPECIAL FEATURES

The straight-six engine is reliable, and easily capable of lasting 150,000 miles.

Very few Datsun Zs retain their original wheels and trims. Most are now fitted with aftermarket alloy wheels.

RUNNING GEAR

Steering: Rack-and-pinion

Front suspension: MacPherson struts with coil springs, telescopic shock absorbers and anti-roll bar

Rear suspension: Chapman struts with coil springs, telescopic shock absorbers and anti-roll bar

Brakes: Discs (front), drums (rear)

Wheels: Steel, 14-in. dia.

Tires: 175 x 14 in.

DIMENSIONS

Length: 162.8 in.   **Width:** 64.1 in.

Height: 50.6 in.   **Wheelbase:** 90.7 in.

Track: 53.3 in. (front), 53.0 in. (rear)

Weight: 2,355 lbs.

De Tomaso MANGUSTA

This is now one of the forgotten supercars, but it would have been a very different story if De Tomaso had given the powerful Mangusta the development its stunning Giugiaro design merited.

Glass engine covers

Giugiaro's solution to engine access was to design two transparent covers which opened up, pivoting from the center. They are an impressive sight when up, but access is awkward nevertheless.

V8 engine

Given De Tomaso's close links with Ford (the later Pantera was a joint Ford/De Tomaso enterprise), it was no surprise that De Tomaso chose to use the 289- and 302-cubic inch Ford V8s. They give plenty of power and are very reliable.

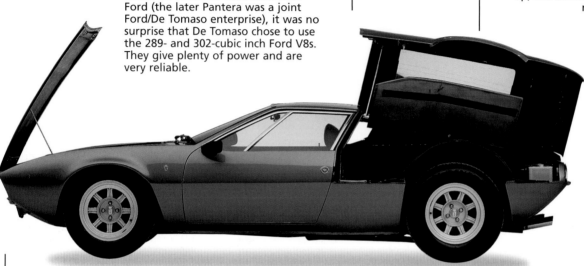

Front radiator

Although De Tomaso mounted the radiator at the front and ran pipes back to the engine to offset the car's weight distribution, the Mangusta was still very rear-heavy.

Rear-biased weight distribution

A combination of the all-iron V8, clutch, final drive and heavy ZF transmission at the back of the car gives the Mangusta a very heavy rear weight bias—as much as 68 percent of the weight at the back.

Giugiaro styling

After he moved on from Bertone, Giorgetto Giugiaro was, for a time, head of styling at Ghia (then owned by De Tomaso). During this time, he designed the body for the Mangusta. It still looks stunning today, more than thirty years after its debut.

Bigger rear tires
With the weight at the back of the car the front and rear tires are different sizes, with 185 HR15s at the front and 225 HR15s at the rear. Time has proven that the car needs even larger, more modern tires for its performance to be safely exploited.

Alloy hood
Strangely, given that the Mangusta's design ensures that it is light at the front, it has an alloy hood which makes the problem worse.

Specifications
1970 De Tomaso Mangusta

ENGINE
Type: V8

Construction: Cast-iron block and heads

Valve gear: Two valves per cylinder operated by single V-mounted camshafts via pushrods and rockers

Bore and stroke: 4.00 in. x 3.00 in.

Displacement: 4,950 cc

Compression ratio: 10.0:1

Induction system: Four-barrel carburetor

Maximum power: 230 bhp at 4,800 rpm

Maximum torque: 310 lb-ft at 2,800 rpm

Top speed: 130 mph

0–60 mph: 6.3 sec

TRANSMISSION
Rear-mounted ZF five-speed manual

BODY/CHASSIS
Sheet steel backbone chassis with engine and transmission as stressed members and alloy and steel two-door coupe body

SPECIAL FEATURES

By way of a nod to Ferrari, the Mangusta has a gated shifter.

The triple line engine vents on the C-pillars are a neat styling touch.

RUNNING GEAR
Steering: Rack-and-pinion

Front suspension: Double wishbones with coil springs, telescopic shock absorbers and anti-roll bar

Rear suspension: Reversed lower wishbone with single transverse link and twin radius arms per side, coil springs, telescopic shock absorbers and anti-roll bar

Brakes: Girling discs, 11.5-in. dia. (front), 11.0-in. dia. (rear)

Wheels: Magnesium alloy, 7 x 15 in. (front), 7.5 x 15 in. (rear)

Tires: 185 HR15 (front), 225 HR15 (rear)

DIMENSIONS
Length: 168.3 in.   **Width:** 72.0 in.

Height: 43.3 in.   **Wheelbase:** 98.4 in.

Track: 54.9 in. (front), 57.1 in. (rear)

Weight: 2,915 lbs.

De Tomaso PANTERA

The Pantera was built tough to survive on the U.S. market, with a simple and strong Ford V8 engine. It proved to be the right approach and the Pantera stayed in production long after it should have become obsolete.

Wishbone suspension

The Pantera featured double-wishbone suspension with telescopic shocks, coil springs and anti-roll bars.

Five-speed transaxle

To better handle the power output of the V8 engine, a strong ZF five-speed transaxle was used, along with a limited slip differential.

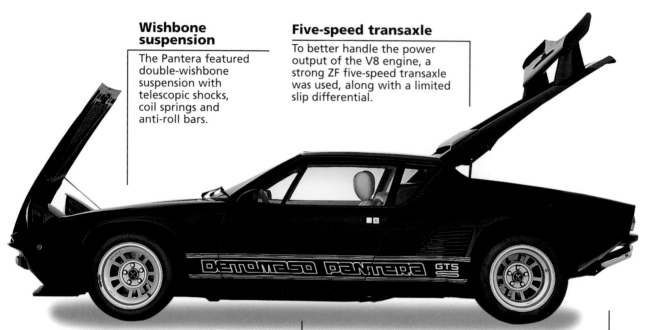

Steel monocoque

As it was intended to be built in large numbers for a supercar (Ford hoped for 5,000 a year), it was designed to be built like a mass-production car, with a unitary steel monocoque.

Ford V8 engine

Because the Pantera was to be sold through Ford in the large U.S. market, it used a Ford Cleveland 5,763 cc V8 overhead valve engine design that was used in many early Mustangs.

Front spoiler

Designed to complement that flamboyant extrovert rear wing, the front spoiler plays its part in cutting down the amount of air that can flow under the car.

Carbon fiber rear spoiler

A rear spoiler was optional on the Pantera to provide extra downforce at very high speeds. By the 1980s that spoiler was made of carbon fiber.

Unequal-size wheels

To carry the large rear tires the rear wheels are 13 inches wide, compared with the slimmer 10-inch wide front wheels.

Extra driving lights

Its headlights were never the Pantera's strong suit and the extra driving lights which could be fitted in front of the air dam were a valuable addition.

Specifications
1986 De Tomaso Pantera GT5S

ENGINE
Type: Ford V8
Construction: Cast-iron block and heads
Valve gear: Two valves per cylinder operated by single block-mounted camshaft via pushrods and rockers
Bore and stroke: 4.01 in. x 3.50 in.
Displacement: 5,763 cc
Compression ratio: 10.5:1
Induction system: Single four-barrel Holley 680 cfm carburetor
Maximum power: 350 bhp at 6,000 rpm
Maximum torque: 451 lb-ft at 3,800 rpm
Top speed: 165 mph
0–60 mph: 5.6 sec

TRANSMISSION
ZF five-speed manual transaxle

BODY/CHASSIS
Steel monocoque two-door, two-seat coupe

SPECIAL FEATURES

Wheel vents in the rear arch extensions redirect cool air to the brakes keeping them from getting too hot and fading at high speeds.

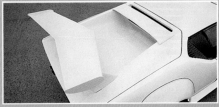

Like the Lamborghini Countach, De Tomaso Panteras came with an optional rear spoiler. It was as much for style as function.

RUNNING GEAR
Steering: Rack-and-pinion
Front suspension: Double wishbones with coil springs, telescopic shocks and anti-roll bar
Rear suspension: Double wishbones, coil springs, telescopic shocks and anti-roll bar
Brakes: 11.7 in. discs (front) vented 11.2 in. discs (rear)
Wheels: Alloy,10 in. x 15 in. (front), 13 in. x 15 in. (rear)
Tires: 285/40 VR15 (front), 345/35 VR15 (rear)

DIMENSIONS
Length: 168.1 in.   **Width:** 77.5 in.
Wheelbase: 99 in.   **Height:** 44.3 in.
Track: 61 in. (front), 62.1 in. (rear)
Weight: 3,202 lbs.

Delahaye 135

Few Delahaye 135s were as outrageous as this example, which has some of the Paris coachbuilders Figoni & Falaschi's most extravagant bodywork in 1930s' style used on the 135's simple chassis.

Narrow track

This 135 looks as though it has a particularly narrow track but that's because the wings stick out so far in order to allow the front wheels to turn.

Six-cylinder engine

The six-cylinder engine used by Delahaye is not nearly as exotic as its bodywork. It is an ordinary in-line cast-iron overhead-valve six, but it is powerful, reliable and easily tuned.

Removable fender skirts

With this type of design the all-enveloping fenders have removable sections to allow the wheels to be changed. Enclosing the wheels theoretically makes the cars more aerodynamic but it was really only a styling feature.

Cotal transmission

The expensive and complicated electrically controlled Cotal epicyclic transmission allows very fast clutchless gear shifts to be made.

Live rear axle

Delahaye kept the rear suspension design simple, with a live axle mounted on top of two semi-elliptic leaf springs along with transversely mounted adjustable shock absorbers.

Design hallmarks

One of Figoni & Falaschi's hallmarks is the way they finished off the point of the rear fenders with a chrome-encased light on each one.

Independent front suspension

Delahaye proved that an excellent design of independent front suspension could be created using a simple transverse leaf spring.

Hinged windshield

It may not look like it, but this windshield can be folded flat if the driver desires.

Specifications
1938 Delahaye 135M

ENGINE

Type: In-line six cylinder
Construction: Cast-iron block and head
Valve gear: Two valves per cylinder operated by single block-mounted camshaft, pushrods and rocker arms
Bore and stroke: 3.31 in. x 2.95 in.
Displacement: 3,557 cc
Induction system: Three Solex Type 40 carburetors
Maximum power: 110 bhp at 3,850 rpm
Maximum torque: 150 lb-ft (approx.)
Top speed: 105 mph
0–60 mph: 14.0 sec.

TRANSMISSION

Electromagnetic Cotal four-speed

BODY/CHASSIS

Steel ladder chassis frame with choice of coachbuilt bodywork

SPECIAL FEATURES

In the Cotal transmission, electro-magnets change the gears according to the position of this miniature shifter. The driver only needs to use the clutch when moving away from a stop.

The Figoni & Falaschi-bodied Delahaye 135 is one of the most elegant and striking cars of the stylish 1930s.

RUNNING GEAR

Steering: Worm-and-nut
Front suspension: Transverse leaf spring with upper transverse and longitudinal links and adjustable friction shocks
Rear suspension: Live axle with semi-elliptic leaf springs and adjustable friction shocks
Brakes: Bendix drums all around
Wheels: Wire spoke 17-in. dia.
Tires: Crossply, 6 x 17 in.

DIMENSIONS

Length: 153.5 in.   **Width:** 60.9 in.
Height: 50 in.   **Wheelbase:** 87.9 in.
Track: 49.29 in. (front), 48.8 in. (rear)
Weight: 2,072 lbs.

DeLorean **DMC**

The official name 'Sports Car' was hardly ever used. It showed a lack of imagination, which the design itself did not. With more development and power it could have been a great success.

V6 engine

DeLorean needed to buy his engines 'off the shelf' and the Renault/Peugeot/Volvo V6 was ideal. It was large, yet light enough so it wouldn't spoil the handling.

'Gullwing' doors

John DeLorean was an admirer of the Mercedes-Benz 300SL, and realized the marketing potential of its 'Gullwing' doors.

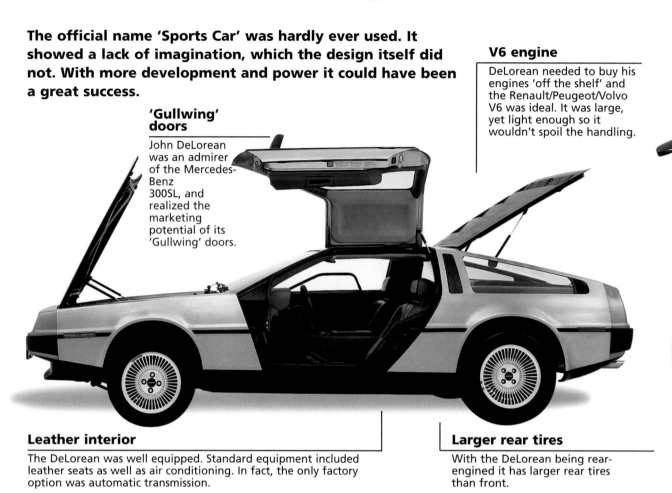

Leather interior

The DeLorean was well equipped. Standard equipment included leather seats as well as air conditioning. In fact, the only factory option was automatic transmission.

Larger rear tires

With the DeLorean being rear-engined it has larger rear tires than front.

Rear weight bias

The rear-mounted engine puts as much as 65 percent of the car's weight over the rear wheels.

Front radiator

With the engine at the back, the logical place for the radiator and the fuel tank is in the front of the car.

Backbone chassis

The backbone chassis is the clearest evidence of Lotus involvement. They had used such a system for years, starting with the original Elan, and its design is very close to the contemporary Esprit's.

Specifications

1981 DeLorean Sports Car

ENGINE

Type: V6

Construction: Alloy block and heads

Valve gear: Two inclined valves per cylinder operated by single chain-driven overhead cam per bank of cylinders

Bore and stroke: 3.58 in. x 2.87 in.

Displacement: 2,849 cc

Compression ratio: 8.8:1

Induction system: Bosch K-Jetronic fuel injection

Maximum power: 145 bhp at 5,500 rpm

Maximum torque: 162 lb-ft at 2,750 rpm

TRANSMISSION

Renault five-speed manual

BODY/CHASSIS

Sheet-steel backbone chassis with fiberglass coupe body covered with stainless steel

SPECIAL FEATURES

To get some fresh air on the road, there are small opening electric windows set in the door.

Relatively low power and low weight means that the rear-mounted engine does not cause poor handling traits.

RUNNING GEAR

Steering: Rack-and-pinion

Front suspension: Double wishbones with coil springs, telescopic shocks, and anti-roll bar

Rear suspension: Semi-trailing arms, coil springs, and telescopic shocks

Brakes: Discs all around, 10.5 in. dia. (front), 10 in. dia. (rear)

Wheels: Alloy 6 in. x 14 in. (front), 8 in. x 15 in. (rear)

Tires: Goodyear NCT 195/60HR14 (front), 235/60HR15 (rear)

DIMENSIONS

Length: 168 in. **Width:** 78.3 in.

Height: 44.9 in. **Wheelbase:** 94.89 in.

Track: 62.6 in. (front), 62.5 in. (rear)

Weight: 2,840 lbs.

DeSoto PACESETTER

DeSotos were always clean, stylish and classic. The Adventurer and Pacesetter, with their 320-bhp Hemi V8s and luxury trim, were flagships, and still look fresh and stylish today.

DeSoto Fireflite Eight

Chrysler's Hemi V8 was an engineering milestone of the 1950s. In the DeSoto Pacesetter it was known as the Fireflite Eight. It had smoother porting and manifold passages and better spark plug and valve location than rival V8s, which helped produce more power.

Coil-sprung suspension

Like rivals of the time, the Pacesetter has independent front suspension with upper and lower wishbones and telescopic shocks. Adventurers and Pacesetters have standard heavy-duty suspension, which slightly improves roadholding.

126-inch wheelbase

The Pacesetter is a full-size car riding a 126-inch wheelbase. In 1957, when Virgil Exner's 'Forward look' cars arrived, the entry-level Firesweep got a shorter 122-inch wheelbase; other DeSotos had a 126-inch wheelbase.

Single color scheme

In its debut year, the Adventurer and the Pacesetter were available only in two-tone white and gold. Special gold badging, interior paneling, grill and wheel covers completed the package. The result was one of the most striking Detroit cars in 1956.

Tailfins

1956 was a pivotal year for Chrysler products, which began sprouting true fins. Those on the Pacesetter were tasteful and mated well with the rest of the body. As the decade wore on, Desotos gained increasingly taller and more outlandish fins.

Convenience options

Pacesetters came with standard power steering, chrome exhaust tips and whitewall tires, which were optional on the Firedome and Fireflite. Air Temp air conditioning, power antenna and Solex safety glass were also available to Pacesetter buyers in 1956.

Specifications

1956 DeSoto Pacesetter

ENGINE

Type: V8

Construction: Cast-iron block and heads

Valve gear: Two valves per cylinder operated by a single camshaft via pushrods and rockers

Bore and stroke: 3.78 in. x 3.80 in.

Displacement: 341 c.i.

Compression ratio: 9.5:1

Induction system: Two Carter four-barrel carburetors

Maximum power: 320 bhp at 5,200 rpm

Maximum torque: 365 lb-ft at 2,800 rpm

Top speed: 115 mph

0–60 mph: 10.2 sec.

TRANSMISSION

PowerFlite two-speed automatic

BODY/CHASSIS

Separate steel chassis with two-door convertible body

SPECIAL FEATURES

Fins were fashionable in 1956 and twin antennas were a popular option.

A dealer installed record player was just one of the DeSoto's unusual options.

RUNNING GEAR

Steering: Recirculating ball

Front suspension: Double wishbones with coil springs and telescopic shock absorbers

Rear suspension: Live axle with semi-elliptic leaf springs and telescopic shock absorbers

Brakes: Drums (front and rear)

Wheels: Pressed steel, 15-in. dia.

Tires: 7.60 x 15

DIMENSIONS

Length: 220.9 in.   **Width:** 76.5 in.

Height: 58.12 in.   **Wheelbase:** 126.0 in.

Track: 60.4 in. (front), 59.6 in. (rear)

Weight: 3,870 lbs.

DeSoto FIREFLITE

Even in their day, these cars were considered flamboyant, to say the least, but this period-modified example takes the idea a step further with its stunning paint finish and classic custom touches.

Custom paint

This Fireflite has been painted using DuPont Sonic Purple as the main color, with the roof and lower rear fenders covered in contrasting Eggshell White. This two-tone combination is well suited to the sweeping lines.

Hemi V8

Although this car originally came with a Hemi V8, the original engine is long gone. In its place is a 1956 330 Hemi. Unlike many other street machines, which have radically modified engines, the owner chose to leave the V8 stock. With 255 bhp, however, performance is still far from sedate.

Swoopy styling

DeSotos were fairly stodgy-looking cars until 1955. Although all Chryslers were restyled that year, the DeSotos benefited most of all. Some even claimed these cars were among the most beautiful automobiles ever to come out of Detroit.

Aftermarket exhaust

In the 1950s and 1960s, it was common for many speed freaks to fit aftermarket exhausts to help the engine produce more power. This DeSoto has a classic stainless-steel system with true dual pipes and glass pack mufflers. This results in an extra 7 bhp and makes for a terrific-sounding engine.

Shaved and smoothed body

A popular modification on many cars of the 1940s and 1950s is to smooth the body, accentuating the sheet metal contours. On this Fireflite, the body has been nosed and decked, and all emblems and the door handles have been removed.

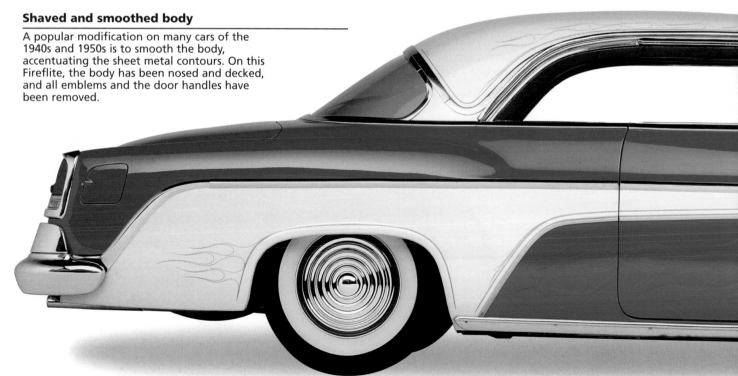

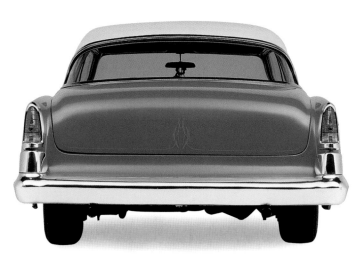

Toothy grill

The distinctive grill treatment is a trademark of DeSotos from 1953 to 1955. This car's owner has retained it but has modified the front bumper.

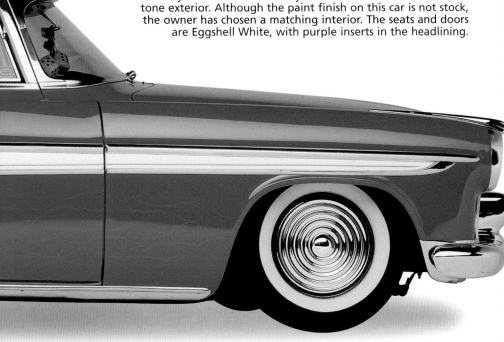

Two-tone interior

Many 1950s cars had factory interiors that matched the two-tone exterior. Although the paint finish on this car is not stock, the owner has chosen a matching interior. The seats and doors are Eggshell White, with purple inserts in the headlining.

Specifications

1955 DeSoto Fireflite Sportsman

ENGINE

Type: V8

Construction: Cast-iron block and heads

Valve gear: Two valves per cylinder operated by a singe camshaft via pushrods and rockers

Bore and stroke: 3.72 in. x 3.80 in.

Displacement: 330.4 c.i.

Compression ratio: 10.0:1

Induction system: Dual four-barrel carburetors

Maximum power: 255 bhp at 5,200 rpm

Maximum torque: 340 lb-ft at 2,800 rpm

Top speed: 118 mph

0–60 mph: 8.2 sec.

TRANSMISSION

TorqueFlite three-speed automatic

BODY/CHASSIS

Separate steel chassis with two-door hardtop body

SPECIAL FEATURES

Half-moon headlight covers are a typical custom feature for this kind of car.

In DeSotos, the Hemi V8 was known as the Firedome Eight.

RUNNING GEAR

Steering: Recirculating ball

Front suspension: Unequal-length wishbones with coil springs and telescopic shock absorbers

Rear suspension: Live axle with semi-elliptic multi-leaf springs and telescopic shock absorbers

Brakes: Drums (front and rear)

Wheels: Steel discs, 5 x 14 in.

Tires: F70-14

DIMENSIONS

Length: 204.0 in.   **Width:** 85.4 in.

Height: 58.9 in.   **Wheelbase:** 126.0 in

Track: 65.7 in. (front), 63.2 in. (rear)

Weight: 3,930 lbs.

Dodge CHALLENGER R/T SE

Smoothly styled and an able performer in R/T guise, the Challenger was well received when new, and remains today as one of the most sought-after early muscle cars.

Mopar Power

Although the 383 was standard fare, the big 440 Magnum was an ideal choice for those into serious racing. Adding the Six-Pack option with three two-barrel carburetors resulted in 390 bhp and 490 lb-ft of torque. A good running Six Pack was a threat to just about anything with wheels.

Special Edition

An SE, or Special Edition, package was basically a luxury trim package on the Challenger. It added a vinyl roof with a smaller rear window, upgraded interior appointments and exterior trim. It could be ordered on both base and R/T models.

Manual transmission

Although the standard Challenger transmission was a three-speed manual, R/Ts ordered with the 440 or Hemi got the robust TorqueFlite automatic transmission. A handful were, however, fitted with four-speed manuals, complete with Hurst shifters with a wood-grain Pistol-Grip shift handle.

Standard R/T hood

Most Challenger R/Ts left the factory with a performance hood, which included dual scoops and a raised center section. For $97.30, however, buyers could order a Shaker hood scoop that attached directly to the air cleaner.

Dana Sure-Grip differential

A good way to reduce quarter-mile ETs was to order the Per-formance Axle Package with a 3.55:1 ring and pinion with a Sure-Grip limited-slip differential. Steeper 4.10:1 cogs could be specified as part of the Super Track Pak.

Heavy-duty suspension

he R/T was the standard performance model, it has a heavy-duty suspension with thicker front torsion bars and stiffer rear leaf springs, plus a beefy front anti-roll bar.

Wide wheels

For the early 1970s, 6-inch-wide wheels were considered large. The Rallye rims fitted to the R/T are only 14 inches in diameter, shod in F-70 14 Goodyear Polyglas tires. Bigger G-60 15 tires and 15-inch Rallyes could be ordered resulting in slightly improved grip.

Specifications

1970 Dodge Challenger R/T-SE 440

ENGINE

Type: V8

Valve gear: Two valves per cylinder operated by a single V-mounted camshaft via pushrods, rockers and hydraulic lifters

Bore and stroke: 4.32 in. x 3.75 in.

Displacement: 440 c.i.

Compression ratio: 10.1:1

Induction system: Three Holley two-barrel carburetors

Maximum power: 390 bhp at 4,700 rpm

Maximum torque: 490 lb-ft at 3,200 rpm

TRANSMISSION

Four-speed manual

BODY/CHASSIS

Unitary steel chassis with steel body panels

SPECIAL FEATURES

All Challengers came with a racing-style fuel filler cap, which is also found on the bigger intermediate Charger.

As it was the performance model, the R/T got a full set of gauges.

RUNNING GEAR

Steering: Recirculating ball

Front suspension: A arms with longitudinal torsion bars, telescopic shock absorbers and anti-roll bar

Rear suspension: Live axle with semi-elliptic leaf springs, telescopic shock absorbers and anti-roll bar

Brakes: Drums, 11.0-in. dia. (front and rear)

Wheels: Stamped steel, 14x6 in.

Tires: Fiberglass belted, F-70 14

DIMENSIONS

Length: 192 in.   **Width:** 76.1 in.

Height: 50.9 in.   **Wheelbase:** 110.0 in.

Track: 59.7 in. (front), 60.7 in. (rear)

Weight: 3,437 lbs.

Dodge CHARGER

Although previous Dodge muscle machines were outstanding performers, they lacked a racy image. The slick Charger changed all that and thrust hot Mopars into the spotlight during the mid-1960s.

Drum brakes

Like most muscle cars of the time, the Charger came from the factory with four-wheel drum brakes. All Hemi-equipped cars came with front discs as standard.

The hemispherical edge

Launched in 1964 and offered in street trim from 1966, the Hemi was the engine to beat. With solid valve lifters, dual quad carburetion and massive hemispherical combustion chambers, it was more powerful and efficient than rival big-blocks.

Heavy-duty suspension

The Hemi required a heavy-duty suspension. The front torsion bars were increased to 0.92 in. in diameter and a front anti-roll bar was fitted to reduce body roll. Even so, the nose-heavy car can become a handful around corners with an inexperienced driver at the wheel.

Slippery styling

Although its shape is visually appealing, the Charger's slippery lines were important for high speed aerodynamics in NASCAR races. It proved to be so successful this year that David Pearson took the NASCAR championship in 1966 driving a Hemi Charger.

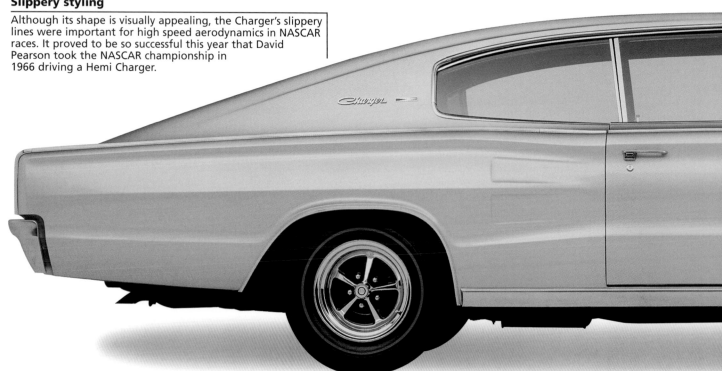

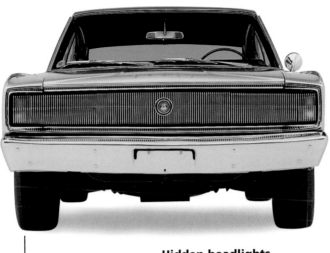

Hidden headlights

A standard feature of early Chargers are the hidden headlights. The doors concealing them are activated by vacuum canisters.

Futuristic cabin

One of the Charger's main selling points was the interior. Strictly a four-seater, due to the long centre console, the cabin also features deeply set gauges with brushed metal housings. The rear seats can be folded flat to free up rear luggage space.

Specifications

1966 Dodge Charger

ENGINE

Type: V8

Construction: Cast-iron block and heads

Valve gear: Two valves per cylinder operated by a single camshaft with pushrods and rockers

Bore and stroke: 4.25 in. x 3.75 in.

Displacement: 426 c.i.

Compression ratio: 10.25:1

Induction system: Twin Carter AFB four-barrel carburettors

Maximum power: 425 bhp at 5000 rpm

Maximum torque: 490 lb-ft at 4000 rpm

Top speed: 134 mph

0–60mph: 5.3 sec

TRANSMISSION

Four-speed manual

BODY/CHASSIS

Steel unitary chassis with two-door fastback body

SPECIAL FEATURES

Magnum steel wheels were a popular option among Charger buyers.

RUNNING GEAR

Steering: Recirculating ball

Front suspension: Unequal-length wishbones with longitudinal torsion bars, telescopic shock absorbers

Rear suspension: Live axle with semi-elliptic leaf springs and telescopic shock absorbers

Brakes: Discs (front), Drums (rear)

Wheels: Magnum 500 steel, 14 in. dia.

Tyres: Blue Streak, 8.25 in. x 14 in.

DIMENSIONS

Length: 203.6 in.

Width: 75.2 in.

Height: 53.8 in.

Wheelbase: 117.0 in.

Track: 59.3in. (front), 58.5 in. (rear)

Weight: 3990 lbs.

Dodge CHARGER DAYTONA

The Charger Daytona's outrageous look was no styling gimmick; the sharp extended nose and huge rear wing really did make the car far more aerodynamic and quicker around the track.

426-c.i. Hemi

The street version of the Hemi gave less power than the higher tuned race engines, with their outputs between 575 and 700 bhp. Also, they ran with iron heads, lower compression ratios, and later hydraulic rather than solid tappets which kept the potential engine speeds lower.

Four-speed transmission

Street versions of the Charger Daytona came with a standard three-speed manual, but the racers were equipped with a close-ratio, four-speed with a Hurst shifter. Customers could specify a four-speed as a no-cost option or opt for the TorqueFlite three-speed auto.

Two four-barrel carburetors

For the street Hemi engine there were two Carter four-barrel carburetors, arranged to open progressively. Just two barrels of the rear carb open at low throttle.

Extended nose

The new nose was made of Fiberglass and was some 17 inches long. It made the car more aerodynamically efficient. The poor fit, that is a feature of all Charger Daytonas and Plymouth Superbirds, clearly had no effect on the aerodynamics of this 200-mph car.

Unitary construction

Although it looks like a classic example of a traditional body-on-frame piece of American design, the Charger Daytona is a unitary vehicle, with the bodywork acting as the chassis.

Pop-up lights

With the addition of the sharp extended nose, the standard headlights were covered and had to be replaced by a new arrangement of pop-up light pods, with each having two headlights.

Rear wing

That distinctive rear wing is mounted more than two feet above the trunk lid, so there is room for the trunk to open. But its real benefit is to allow it to operate in clean air.

Specifications

1969 Dodge Charger Daytona

ENGINE

Type: V8

Construction: Cast-iron block and heads

Valve gear: Two valves per cylinder operating in hemispherical combustion chambers opened by a single V-mounted camshaft with pushrods, rockers and solid lifters

Bore and stroke: 4.25 in. x 3.75 in.

Displacement: 426 c.i.

Compression ratio: 10.25:1

Induction system: Two Carter AFB 3084S carburetors

Maximum power: 425 bhp at 5,600 rpm

Maximum torque: 490 lb-ft at 4,000 rpm

TRANSMISSION

Four-speed manual

BODY/CHASSIS

Unitary monocoque construction with steel body panels and fiberglass nose section

SPECIAL FEATURES

The aerodynamic fiberglass nose houses the unique pop-up headlights.

The black rear wing distinguishes the Charger from the Plymouth Superbird.

RUNNING GEAR

Steering: Recirculating-ball

Front suspension: A-arms with longitudinal torsion bars, telescopic shock absorbers and anti-roll bar

Rear suspension: Live axle with asymmetrical leaf springs and telescopic shock absorbers

Brakes: Drums, 11.0-in. dia. (front), 11.0-in. dia. (rear)

Wheels: Stamped steel, 14 in. x 6 in.

Tires: F70 x 14

DIMENSIONS

Length: 208.5 in.   **Width:** 76.6 in.

Height: 53.0 in.   **Wheelbase:** 117.0 in.

Track: 59.7 in. (front), 59.2 in. (rear)

Weight: 3,671 lbs.

Dodge SUPER BEE

With its enormous cop-baiting hood and loud paint, the Super Bee Six Pack is certainly no street sleeper. It is, however, a true high performance machine, able to take on any challenger on the street or at the strip.

Fibreglass bonnet

The feature that probably brings more attention than any other element of the car is the hood. It is a one-piece fiberglass affair with a massive functional scoop.

Six Pack 440 engine

In normal driving, the engine requires only the fuel from the center carburetor. However, when the accelerator pedal meets the floorboard, the front and rear carburetors feed the engine more fuel. With this engine, the Super Bee can run the ¼-mile in a shade under 14 seconds.

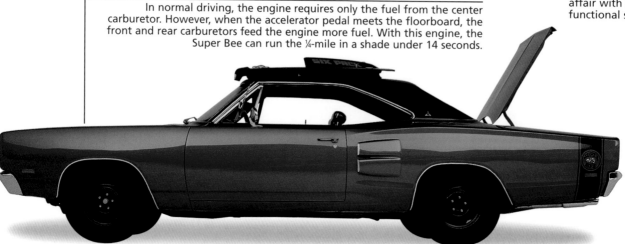

Heavy-duty suspension

Super Bee Six Packs are fitted with the same heavy-duty torsion bar suspension used on Hemi-powered Chryslers. This gives them surprisingly good roadholding for what is, after all, primarily a straight line rocket.

Hardtop styling

Introduced in 1968, the second-generation Coronet is one of the best-looking intermediates of the period. When launched early in 1968, the Super Bee was available only as a pillared coupe, though a hardtop version arrived later in the year.

Rugged rear end

Back in the 1960s, ultra-low rear axle ratios were available from the factory on many muscle cars. In 1969, Super Bee Six Packs came with 4.10:1 gearing in an almost bulletproof Dana rear end – this enables the driver to really exploit the power and torque of the six-barrel engine.

Dual exhaust

One of the signature factory performance enhancers in the 1960s was dual exhaust. It released the engine's back pressure, enabling the engine to make more power.

Specifications

1969 Dodge Super Bee 440

ENGINE

Type: V8

Construction: Cast-iron block and heads

Valve gear: Two valves per cylinder operated by a single camshaft via pushrods and rockers

Bore and stroke: 4.32 in. x 3.75 in.

Displacement: 440 c.i.

Compression ratio: 10.5:1

Induction system: Three Holley two-barrel carburetors (Six Pack)

Maximum power: 390 bhp at 4700 rpm

Maximum torque: 490 lb-ft at 3200 rpm

Top speed: 130mph

0–60mph: 6.0 sec

TRANSMISSION

Four-speed manual

BODY/CHASSIS

Steel unitary chassis with two-door hardtop coupe body

SPECIAL FEATURES

Because of its bare-bone image, the only wheels that the Super Bees came with were these low-budget black steel wheels with chrome lug nuts.

The one-piece, lift-off fiberglass bonnet is held in place by four tie-down pins and made routine oil checks a two-person job.

RUNNING GEAR

Steering: Recirculating ball

Front suspension: Unequal length wishbones with longitudinally mounted torsion bars, telescopic shock absorbers and anti-roll bar

Rear suspension: Dana 60 rear axle with semi-elliptic leaf springs and telescopic shock absorbers

Brakes: Drums (front and rear)

Wheels: Steel discs, 7 in. x 14 in.

Tyres: F70-14

DIMENSIONS

Length: 206.6 in.

Width: 76.7 in.

Height: 54.8 in.

Wheelbase: 117.0 in.

Track: 59.5 in. (front), 58.5 in. (rear)

Weight: 4100 lbs.

Dodge VIPER GTS

In a world where the premiere performance cars are thought to come from Maranello, Italy and Stuttgart, Germany, its great to know that, with the Viper GTS, the U.S. has a supercar that can crush both Ferrari and Porsche.

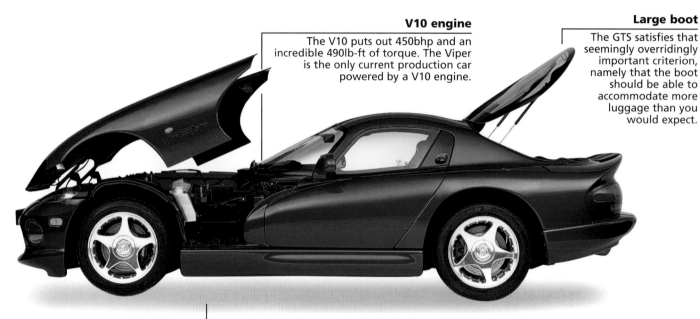

V10 engine

The V10 puts out 450bhp and an incredible 490lb-ft of torque. The Viper is the only current production car powered by a V10 engine.

Large boot

The GTS satisfies that seemingly overridingly important criterion, namely that the boot should be able to accommodate more luggage than you would expect.

Six-speed transmission

The Viper was one of the first road cars to use a six-speed transmission. However, in reality, the six-speed unit was specified to obtain an improved fuel economy rating to satisfy tough fuel consumption standards. Both fifth and sixth are overdrive gears.

Huge brakes

Vented disc brakes at all four corners are among the largest used on any production car. They measure 13 in. across and can stop the GTS from very high speeds.

Sleeker shape

Compared to the RT/10 roadster, the GTS has smoother, more aerodynamic lines and a drag figure of 0.39. Body panels are not interchangeable with the roadster.

Polished alloy wheels
The alloy wheels have a beautifully polished finish and are huge – 17 in. diameter and 10 in. wide at the front and 13 in. at the rear.

Plastic bodywork
The body of the GTS is made almost entirely of composite materials, with some steel strengthening in the doors. This suits the low-volume production of the Viper. The GTS weighs 42.2 lbs. less than the RT/10 roadster.

Specifications
1998 Dodge Viper GTS

ENGINE
Type: V10

Construction: Aluminium cylinder block and heads

Valve gear: Two valves per cylinder operated by a single chain-driven camshaft

Bore and stroke: 4 in. x 3.88 in.

Displacement: 488 c.i.

Compression ratio: 9.6:1

Induction system: Sequential fuel injection

Maximum power: 450 bhp at 5200 rpm

Maximum torque: 490 lb-ft at 3700 rpm

Top speed: 288 km/h (179 mph)

0–60mph: 4.7 sec

TRANSMISSION
Six-speed manual

BODY/CHASSIS
Monocoque tubular backbone chassis with composite two-door coupe body

SPECIAL FEATURES

Huge 17 in. five-spoke wheels were fitted on Viper roadsters in 1995.

RUNNING GEAR
Steering: Rack-and-pinion

Front suspension: Unequal length wishbones with coil springs, shocks and anti-roll bar

Rear suspension: Unequal length wishbones with coil springs, shocks and anti-roll bar

Brakes: Vented discs, 13 in. dia. (front and rear)

Wheels: Alloy, 17 in. dia.

Tyres: 275/40 ZR17 (front), 335/35 ZR17 (rear)

DIMENSIONS
Length: 175.1 in.

Width: 75.7 in.

Height: 44 in.

Wheelbase: 96.2 in.

Track: 59.6 in. (front), 60.6 in. (rear)

Weight: 3384 lbs.

Duesenberg MODEL J

Duesenberg was the only American automaker to win a Grand Prix and put that experience to good use in building racing-inspired engines to power cars like the Model J.

Solid front axle

Though the Duesenberg brothers were fantastic engineers, they still had no problems about using a solid front axle.

Swivelling spotlights

An intriguing feature on the Model J are the spotlights that turn along with the steering wheel so the lights follow the direction of the car.

Bodies made to order

Customers could choose to have any body they liked fitted to the Model J. Coachbuilders like Le Baron, Rollston, and Weymann built bodies to complement Duesenberg's own offerings. This model is a LeGrande convertible.

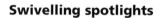

Straight-eight engine

It's an impressive technical feat to make a twin-cam straight-eight. The camshafts and crankshaft are very long and need to be well supported.

Hydraulic brakes

Duesenberg pioneered hydraulic brakes in motor racing, so it's no surprise that the Model J has huge 15-inch hydraulic drum brakes.

Luggage trunk

The rear luggage compartment was nothing more than a trunk strapped to the rear of the car.

Single stop light

In the late-1920s, it was not compulsory to have two brake lights, but this Duesenberg's single huge white stop light is still very unusual.

Specifications
1929 Duesenberg Model J

ENGINE

Type: Straight-eight twin cam
Construction: Cast-iron block and head
Valve gear: Four valves per cylinder operated by two chain-driven overhead camshafts
Bore and stroke: 3.74 in. x 4.76 in.
Displacement: 420 c.i.
Compression ratio: 5.2:1
Induction system: Single updraft Schebler carburetor
Maximum power: 265 bhp at 4,250 rpm
Top speed: 116 mph
0–60 mph: 11.0 sec. approx.

TRANSMISSION

Three-speed manual

BODY/CHASSIS

Wide choice of coachbuilt bodies on steel ladder chassis.

SPECIAL FEATURES

The Model J has a clockwork mechanism that controls the automatic chassis lubrication and the warning lights which tell the driver to change the oil.

The flamboyant chrome flexible exhaust pipes are actually decorative covers over conventional pipes.

RUNNING GEAR

Steering: Cam-and-lever
Front suspension: Solid axle with semi-elliptic leaf springs and friction shocks
Rear suspension: Live axle with semi-elliptic leaf springs and friction shocks
Brakes: Hydraulically operated drums all round, 15 in. dia.
Wheels: Wire spoked, 9 in. x 16 in.
Tires: 9 in. x 16 in. dia. crossply

DIMENSIONS

Length: 188 in.   **Width:** 67.9 in.
Height: 61 in.   **Wheelbase:** 142.5 in.
Track: 56 in. (front and rear)
Weight: 4,895 lbs.

Duesenberg SJ

With a stiffened-up engine and a blower fitted, Duesenberg's supremely accomplished Model J was transformed into the exclusive and powerful SJ. Only the extraordinarily wealthy could afford one.

Aircraft-quality engine

The undoubted centerpiece of any Duesenberg is its engine. The fabulous straight eight was extremely advanced, boasting twin overhead camshafts and four valves per cylinder. The basic engine was built by Lycoming to Fred Duesenberg's specifications.

Power brakes

The brakes were as advanced as the rest of the car's specification. With oversized shoes, braking power was impressive and was made easier by standard vacuum assistance.

Custom bodywork

In the best coachbuilt traditions, Duesenberg supplied only the chassis. Customers were expected to patronize independent coachbuilders to create whatever body-work struck their fancy. With its sporty bias, the SJ's performance suited a roadster or convertible body.

h use of aluminum

s many production SJs measured more than 0 feet long, there was aturally some concern to keep weight down. Therefore, many parts were made from aluminum, including some of the engine, dash, crankcase, water ump, intake manifold, brake shoes and gas tank.

Snaking pipes

One of the hallmarks of the SJ is its dramatic and beautifully plated exhaust headers emerging from the side of the engine. However, elaborate pipework like this does not necessarily mean the car is an SJ—the ordinary Model J was often fitted with such plumbing, even if there wasn't a supercharger.

Supercharger

A centrifugal blower was added to the traight eight to deliver crushing performance on a mildly higher compression ratio. Power shot up to 320 ohp, making it easily the most powerful auto production engine in the world.

Specifications
Duesenberg SJ

ENGINE

Type: Inline eight

Construction: Cast-iron cylinder block and head

Valve gear: Four valves per cylinder operated by double chain-driven camshafts

Bore and stroke: 3.70 in. x 4.50 in.

Displacement: 420 c.i.

Compression ratio: 5.7:1

Induction system: Single Schebler carburetor plus supercharger

Maximum power: 320 bhp at 4,200 rpm

Maximum torque: 425 lb-ft at 2,400 rpm

Top speed: 130 mph

0–60 mph: 8.5 sec.

TRANSMISSION

Three-speed manual

BODY/CHASSIS

Separate chassis with convertible bodywork

SPECIAL FEATURES

A fold out rumble is available to fit two additional passengers.

As part of the effort to reduce weight, even the dashboard is aluminum.

RUNNING GEAR

Steering: Cam-and-lever

Front suspension: Beam axle with leaf springs and shock absorbers

Rear suspension: Live axle with leaf springs and shock absorbers

Brakes: Drums (front and rear)

Wheels: Wire, 19-in. dia.

Tires: Crossply, 9 in. x 16 in.

DIMENSIONS

Length: 222.5 in.

Width: 72.0 in.

Height: 70.0 in.

Wheelbase: 142.5 in.

Track: 37.5 in. (front), 58.0 (rear)

Weight: 5,000 lbs.

Edsel CITATION

There are many reasons the Edsel failed in the marketplace, but perhaps the greatest was poor quality control. This factor alone sent buyers scurrying almost immediately to other makes.

V8 engine

The Citation V8 was tuned for torque, as the output of 475 lb-ft at only 2,900 rpm indicates. Even the smaller 361 engine used in the Ranger and Pacer put out an impressive 303 bhp and 400 lb-ft of torque. That engine had its combustion chambers in the head, unlike the bigger 401 unit.

Convertible top

There was a choice of four colors available for the vinyl-covered convertible top on the Citation: black (seen here), white, turquoise and copper. The top folded down flush with the rear deck and was power-operated like most convertibles of the era. It had a flexible plastic rear window.

Mercury chassis

There were three different wheelbase lengths for 1958 Edsels: 116 inches for wagons; 118 inches for Pacer and Ranger coupes, sedans and convertibles; and 124 inches for Corsairs and Citations. The latter two actually rode on a Mercury chassis and were built on the same assembly line as the slightly plusher Mercurys.

Recirculating-ball steering

The recirculating-ball steering could be ordered with or without power assistance (an $85 option). If you went without, the steering ratio was altered accordingly to make the wheel easier to turn. There were 5.25 turns lock to lock, compared with 4.25 when power was added.

ower seats

n Edsel Citation convertible was a luxury
ehicle and there was the $76 option of four-
ay power adjustable front seats which were
ormed by a 30/70 divided front bench seat.

Specifications

1958 Edsel Citation

ENGINE

Type: V8

Construction: Cast-iron block and heads

Valve gear: Two valves per cylinder operated by single V-mounted camshaft

Bore and stroke: 4.20 in. x 3.70 in.

Displacement: 410 c.i.

Compression ratio: 10.5:1

Induction system: Single four-barrel carburetor

Maximum power: 345 bhp at 4,600 rpm

Maximum torque: 475 lb-ft at 2,900 rpm

Top speed: 105 mph

0–60 mph: 9.7 sec

TRANSMISSION

Three-speed automatic

BODY/CHASSIS

Separate curbed-perimeter chassis frame with center X-brace and convertible body

SPECIAL FEATURES

A station seeking radio with an electric antenna was an expensive ($143.90) option.

One interesting gimmick on 1958 Edsels was the Cyclops Eye rotating-drum speedometer.

RUNNING GEAR

Steering: Recirculating-ball

Front suspension: Double wishbones with coil springs, telescopic dampers and anti-roll bar

Rear suspension: Live axle with semi-elliptic leaf springs and telescopic shock absorbers

Brakes: Drums, 11.0-in. dia. front, 11.0-in. dia. rear

Wheels: Pressed steel disc, 14 in. dia.

Tires: 8.50 -14

DIMENSIONS

Length: 218.8 in.   **Width:** 79.8 in.

Height: 57.0 in.   **Wheelbase:** 124.0 in.

Track: 59.4 in front, 59.0 in rear

Weight: 4,311 lbs.

Ferrari 250GT CALIFORNIA

When the first California Spyder appeared in 1957, it looked a little out of proportion, but the short-wheelbase model, which appeared in 1960, was much more attractive. Its Pininfarina lines were perfect, with the top up or down.

V12 engine

For the later short-wheelbase versions of the California, Ferrari installed an improved version of the 3.0-liter, V12 engine—the 168F, with 280 bhp. Changes included moving the spark plugs to the outside of the V, better-shaped combustion chambers and conventional coil valve springs instead of the hairpin type.

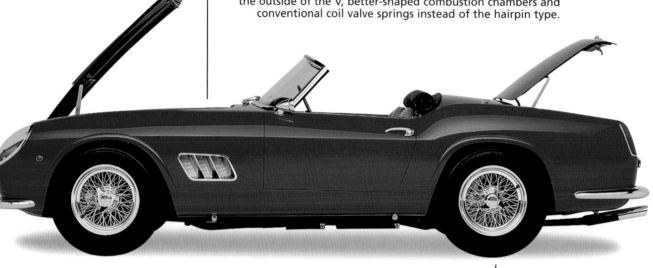

Wire wheels

Disc-type wheels were never used on Ferraris of this era—the California is fitted with very expensive Borrani wire-spoke wheels. These are strong and light, as well as extremely elegant.

Steel body

Although some of the early California long-wheelbase models were sold with an alloy hood and trunk, the later production run of short-wheelbase cars were almost all fitted with all-steel bodywork.

Hood scoop

Both the long-wheelbase and short-wheelbase versions have distinctive hood scoops, but on the shorter cars, they are recessed farther into the hood, which is one way of telling the two versions apart. This model is a short wheelbase variant.

Standard spotlights

The two small Marchal spotlights that were mounted above the bumper in the grill were standard. The headlight design varies; the majority have curved Plexiglas covers over the round head-lights, but approximately 25 cars were built without the covers.

Disc brakes

Huge, alloy-finned drums were used on the long-wheelbase models, but despite their size these are not very effective. It was only a matter of time before Ferrari switched to disc brakes.

Specifications

1960 Ferrari 250 GT California

ENGINE

Type: V12

Construction: Alloy block and heads

Valve gear: Two valves per cylinder operated by a single, chain-driven overhead camshaft and rockers

Bore and stroke: 2.87 in. x 2.31 in.

Displacement: 2,953 cc

Compression ratio: 9.2:1

Induction system: Three Weber 42 DCL twin-choke downdraft carburetors

Maximum power: 280 bhp at 7,000 rpm

Maximum torque: 203 lb-ft at 5,500 rpm

Top speed: 150 mph

0–60 mph: 7.0 sec.

TRANSMISSION

Four-speed manual

BODY/CHASSIS

Separate tubular-steel chassis with steel two-seat, two-door convertible body

SPECIAL FEATURES

Wide Borrani wire wheels with knockoff spinners are seen on the majority of Ferrari 250s. Fender vents are functional.

Unlike most supercars, the California Spyder has ample trunk space.

RUNNING GEAR

Steering: Worm-and-sector

Front suspension: Double wishbones with coil springs, telescopic shock absorbers and anti-roll bar

Rear suspension: Live axle with semi-elliptic leaf springs, radius arms and telescopic shock absorbers

Brakes: Dunlop discs (front and rear)

Wheels: Borrani knockoff wire, 6 x 15 in.

Tires: 185 x 15

DIMENSIONS

Length: 165.4 in.   **Width:** 67.7 in.

Height: 53.9 in.   **Wheelbase:** 94.5 in.

Track: 54.0 in. (front), 54.1 in. (rear)

Weight: 2,315 lbs.

Ferrari 330 GT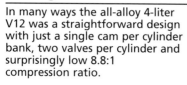

With real 150-mph performance, room for four passengers and one of the sweetest engines on the market, the Ferrari 330 GT was the epitome of luxurious freeway mile-eaters.

V12 engine

In many ways the all-alloy 4-liter V12 was a straightforward design with just a single cam per cylinder bank, two valves per cylinder and surprisingly low 8.8:1 compression ratio.

Four-seat interior

One of the major attractions of the 330 GT was its ability to seat four adults in comfort, making it ideal for long-distance touring. In Ferrari circles, this makes it less desirable.

Worm-and-roller steering

When the 330 GT was made Ferrari had yet to concede that rack-and-pinion steering was the best system for a high-performance car and kept the existing worm-and-roller arrangement, with 3.5 turns lock to lock.

Overdrive transmission

The first batch of Ferrari 330 GT Americas came with a manual four-speed transmission with overdrive on top gear only. This long final gearing was ideally suited to the V12's characteristics, helping it along to 150 mph plus. From 1965 onward a new five-speed transmission was fitted.

Disc brakes

Like Jaguar, Ferrari eventually conceded that disc brakes were really the only way to stop high-performance cars effectively, so large discs were fitted on the 330 GT.

Leaf-sprung rear suspension

When the 330 GTC two-seat version was introduced, it featured double wishbone rear suspension, complete with coil springs. However, the GT relied on conventional semi-elliptic leaf springs.

Specifications

1967 Ferrari 330 GT

ENGINE
Type: V12

Construction: Alloy block and heads with cast-iron dry liners

Valve gear: Two valves per cylinder operated by single overhead cam per bank of cylinders with rockers

Bore and stroke: 3.03 in. x 2.80 in.

Displacement: 3,967 cc

Compression ratio: 8.8:1

Induction system: Three Weber 40 DFI twin-choke carburetors

Maximum power: 300 bhp at 6,600 rpm

Maximum torque: 415 lb-ft at 5,000 rpm

Top speed: 152 mph

0–60 mph: 6.3 sec

TRANSMISSION
Four-speed manual with overdrive

BODY/CHASSIS
Separate tubular-steel chassis with steel two-door coupe body

SPECIAL FEATURES

Side vents on the front fenders exhaust hot air from the crowded engine bay.

Early 330 GT Americas have the elegant twin-headlamps design.

RUNNING GEAR
Steering: Worm-and-roller

Front suspension: Double wishbones with coil springs, telescopic shock absorbers and anti-roll bar

Rear suspension: Live axle with semi-elliptic leaf springs, torque arms and shock absorbers

Brakes: Discs all around, 12.4-in. dia. front, 11.74-in. dia. rear

Wheels: Wire center lock, 7 in. x 14 in.

Tires: 205 HR14

DIMENSIONS
Length: 189.0 in. **Width:** 69.0 in.
Height: 52.0 in. **Wheelbase:** 104.2 in.
Track: 55.0 in. front, 54.7 in. rear
Weight: 3,180 lbs.

185

Ferrari **360 MODENA**

With the arrival of the latest Porsche 911, Ferrari was forced to raise its game. With the stunning new 360 Modena, the company has done just that. Fantastic looks and technology to match put it at the top of the supercar league.

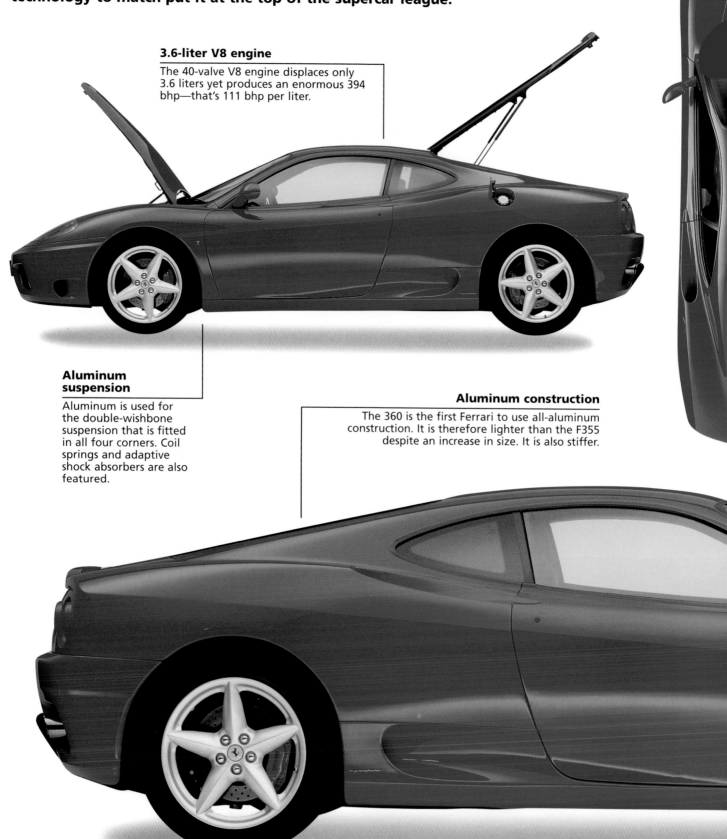

3.6-liter V8 engine
The 40-valve V8 engine displaces only 3.6 liters yet produces an enormous 394 bhp—that's 111 bhp per liter.

Aluminum suspension
Aluminum is used for the double-wishbone suspension that is fitted in all four corners. Coil springs and adaptive shock absorbers are also featured.

Aluminum construction
The 360 is the first Ferrari to use all-aluminum construction. It is therefore lighter than the F355 despite an increase in size. It is also stiffer.

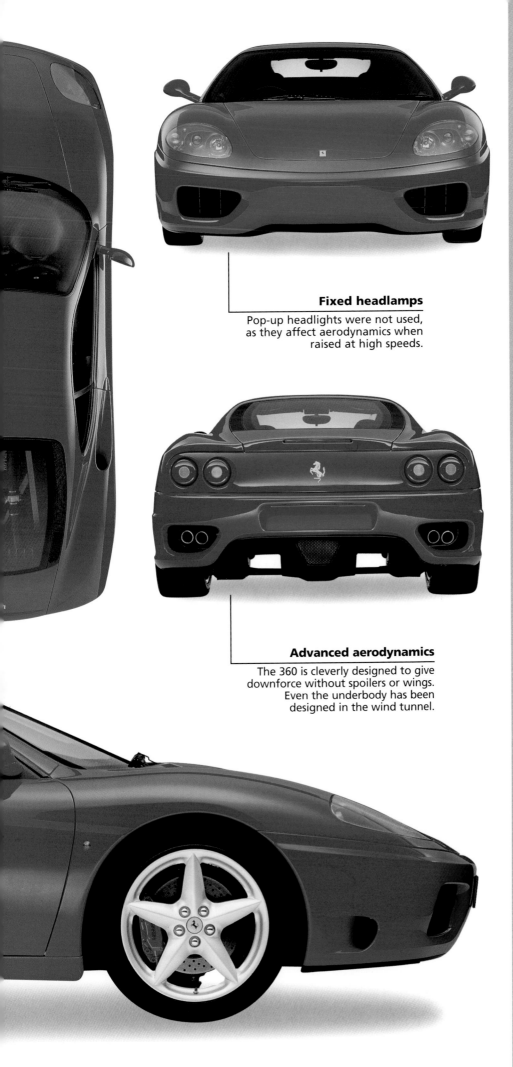

Fixed headlamps

Pop-up headlights were not used, as they affect aerodynamics when raised at high speeds.

Advanced aerodynamics

The 360 is cleverly designed to give downforce without spoilers or wings. Even the underbody has been designed in the wind tunnel.

Specifications

1999 Ferrari 360 Modena

ENGINE

Type: V8

Construction: Alloy block and heads

Valve gear: Five valves per cylinder operated by two overhead camshafts per cylinder bank

Bore and stroke: 3.40 in. x 3.16 in.

Displacement: 3,586 cc

Compression ratio: 11.0:1

Induction system: Bosch multipoint fuel injection

Maximum power: 394 bhp at 8,500 rpm

Maximum torque: 275 lb-ft at 4,750 rpm

Top speed: 185 mph

0–60 mph: 4.5 sec

TRANSMISSION

Six-speed semi-automatic

BODY/CHASSIS

Aluminum spaceframe/monocoque

SPECIAL FEATURES

Despite all-new styling, the traditional round rear lights are retained.

Once again, Pininfarina has penned stunning lines for a Ferrari.

RUNNING GEAR

Steering: Rack-and-pinion

Front suspension: Double wishbones with coil springs, adaptive shock absorbers and anti-roll bar

Rear suspension: Double wishbones with coil springs, adaptive shock absorbers and anti-roll bar

Brakes: Vented discs (front and rear)

Wheels: Alloy, 18-in. dia.

Tires: 215/45 ZR18 (front), 275/40 ZR18 (rear)

DIMENSIONS

Length: 176.3 in.   **Width:** 75.7 in.

Height: 47.8 in.   **Wheelbase:** 102.4 in.

Track: 65.7 in. (front), 63.7 in. (rear)

Weight: 3,065 lbs.

Ferrari 500 SUPERFAST

Pininfarina's design for the Superfast is nothing short of a masterpiece with its perfectly proportioned flowing lines and long graceful tail. Yet at the same time it is muscular enough to radiate sheer power.

Overdrive

The first 25 Superfasts used a four-speed manual transmission with overdrive to make even 150 mph seem relaxed. The overdrive operates on top gear and gives over 25 mph per 1,000 rpm.

V12 engine

Although a single camshaft gives an ideal combustion-chamber shape, it does not allow for a centrally mounted spark plug, so the plugs are side-mounted.

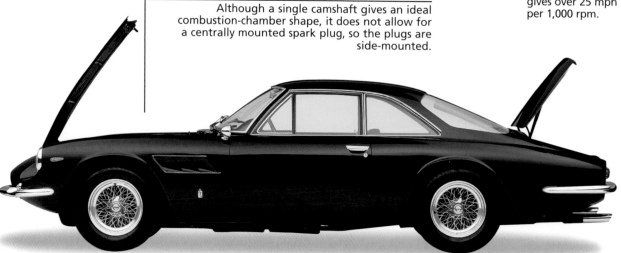

Wishbone front suspension

A double-wishbone front suspension was standard Ferrari equipment by this time. Transverse leaf springs were abandoned in 1956. The 410 Superamerica was the first Ferrari to use conventional coil springs, telescopic shocks and an anti-roll bar.

Four-wheel discs

The 170-mph Superfast requires large brakes. Therefore it is fitted with 12.4-inch diameter discs at the front and 11.7-inch discs at the rear. Twin-vacuum servo assistance insures that enough pressure can be applied.

Separate chassis

Ferrari used a separate chassis frame on all its cars, but for short production run models like the Superfast, it would certainly have made no sense to tool up to make either a stamped floorpan or monocoque body/chassis.

Side vents

The huge V12 engine needs good ventilation to keep under-hood temperatures down. Consequently, the Superfast has a large radiator grill and two large side vents to expel hot air.

Specifications
1965 Ferrari 500 Superfast

ENGINE
Type: V12

Construction: Alloy block with pressed-in cast-iron wet liners and alloy heads

Valve gear: Two valves per cylinder operated by a single overhead camshaft per bank of cylinders

Bore and stroke: 3.46 in. x 2.68 in.

Displacement: 4,962 cc

Compression ratio: 8.8:1

Induction system: Six Weber 40 DC2/6 carburetors

Maximum power: 400 bhp at 6,500 rpm

Maximum torque: 351 lb-ft at 4,750 rpm

Top speed: 174 mph

0–60 mph: 7.6 sec.

TRANSMISSION
Four-speed manual with overdrive

BODY/CHASSIS
Separate tubular-steel body with steel two-door coupe body

SPECIAL FEATURES

Aside from the 365 California, the 500 Super-fast was the last Ferrari to have wire wheels.

The tail of the 500 is understated but perfectly proportioned.

RUNNING GEAR
Steering: Worm-and-roller

Front suspension: Double wishbones with coil springs, telescopic shock absorbers and anti-roll bar

Rear suspension: Live rear axle with semi-elliptic leaf springs, radius arms and telescopic shock absorbers

Brakes: Dunlop discs, 12.4-in. dia. (front), 11.7-in. dia. (rear)

Wheels: Borrani wire spoke, 15-in. dia.

Tires: 205-15

DIMENSIONS
Length: 189.8 in.	**Width:** 70.1 in.
Height: 50.4 in.	**Wheelbase:** 104.3 in.

Track: 55.0 in. (front), 54.7 in. (rear)

Weight: 3,087 lbs.

Ferrari **DAYTONA**

The end of an era...but what a way to go! The combination of Pininfarina's perfectly proportioned body and a 4.4 liter Ferrari V12 makes it an instant classic, not to mention one of the world's fastest cars.

Quad-cam V12

The 365 GTB/4 model name helps explain the engine. The 365 stands for the size of each cylinder (which multiplied by the number of cylinders gives its 4.4 liter displacement).The 4 stands for the number of camshafts.

Rear-mounted transmission

The five-speed transmission shares the same alloy housing as the final drive. Because this is a two-seater with a short cabin, the length of gear linkage from the driver to the transmission is not excessive.

Engine air vents

After cool air has passed through the tiny front opening and through the V12's big radiator, it leaves the car via the two unobtrusive sunken vents in the hood.

Square-tube chassis

In the late-1960s, Ferrari was a very traditional manufacturer, so the Daytona's chassis is made up of many small-diameter square section tubes welded together. It is strong but heavy.

Front-to-rear torque tube

The engine and rear-mounted transmission are rigidly connected by a torque tube that houses the driveshaft.

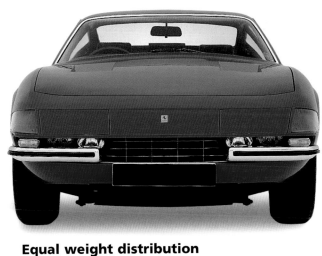

Equal weight distribution

By setting the V12 back in the chassis and moving the transmission to the rear, Ferrari achieved a near-perfect 52/48 weight distribution without the complexity of a mid-engined car.

Wishbone suspension

Double wishbone suspension is fitted all around. To help the packaging, the rear spring/shock units are mounted above the top wishbone.

Alloy and steel body

The doors, hood and trunk lid are made of weight-saving alloy. The rest of the bodywork is steel.

Specifications
1970 Ferrari 365 GTB/4 Daytona

ENGINE
Type: V12
Construction: Alloy block and heads with wet liners
Valve gear: Two valves per cylinder operated by four gear-driven overhead camshafts
Bore and stroke: 3.19 in. x 2.8 in.
Displacement: 4,390 cc
Compression ratio: 9.3:1
Induction system: Six Weber 40DCN 20 downdraft carburetors
Maximum power: 352 bhp at 7,500 rpm
Maximum torque: 330 lb-ft at 5,500 rpm
Top speed: 174 mph
0–60 mph: 5.6 sec

TRANSMISSION
Rear-mounted, five-speed manual

BODY/CHASSIS
Steel square tube separate chassis with alloy and steel two-door coupe or convertible body

SPECIAL FEATURES

Wrap-around front direction indicators were often mimicked after the Daytona's launch.

Four round tail lights and four exhausts tell you you've just been overtaken by a Daytona.

RUNNING GEAR
Steering: Recirculating ball
Front suspension: Double wishbones with coil springs, telescopic shocks and anti-roll bar
Rear suspension: Double wishbones with coil springs, telescopic shocks and anti-roll bar
Brakes: Vented discs, 11.3 in. dia. (front), 11.6 in. dia. (rear)
Wheels: Alloy, 7.5 in. x 15 in.
Tires: 215/7015

DIMENSIONS
Length: 174.2 in.   **Width:** 69.3 in.
Wheelbase: 94.5 in.   **Height:** 49 in.
Track: 56.7 in. (front), 56.1 in. (rear)
Weight: 3,530 lbs.

Ferrari **F40**

The F40 was designed to be the fastest car that could be driven on European roads. It was the most exciting street-legal Ferrari in 20 years—so exciting that none could be brought to the U.S. for use on the road.

Ground effect

The F40 has a flat bottom, carefully shaped nose and strategically placed air intakes that lead to zero lift in front and downforce at the rear.

Modular wheels

Modular wheels are all light alloy, bolted together with nuts on the inside. Pirelli P-Zero ZR-rated tires were designed for the F40.

Adjustable suspension

Rear suspension has easily adjustable camber (tilting the top of the wheel inward or outward) to tailor handling to suit the driving conditions.

Dual turbos

Dual turbos use exhaust gas to drive them. The compressed air feeds through an intercooler before it enters the engine—the denser the air, the higher the power.

Rear wing

Rear downforce is created by the inverted aerofoil section rear wing.

Three-liter twin-turbo V8

Double overhead cams for each bank of cylinders are driven by a toothed belt. The cylinder heads have two intake and two exhaust valves per cylinder.

Shock absorbers

Front and rear shock absorbers lower height at about 50 mph, improving aerodynamics and handling.

Triple exhaust pipes

Three exhaust pipes exit in the center: one for each bank of cylinders, one for the turbo wastegates.

Cockpit

Brakes and steering have no power boost so that the driver can feel the controls better. There is a choice of three seat sizes.

Dual fuel tanks

Dual fuel tanks have quick-fill caps, 30-gallon capacity. Fuel is fed into the engine by Marelli-Weber fuel injection.

Specifications

1992 Ferrari F40

ENGINE

Type: V8, 90°

Construction: Light alloy, heads, block, Nikasil cylinder liners

Bore and stroke: 3.32 in. x 2.74 in.

Displacement: 2,936 cc

Compression ratio: 7.8:1

Induction system: Two IHI turbos, intercoolers, Marelli-Weber fuel injection, two injectors per cylinder

Ignition: distributorless Marelli-Weber

Maximum power: 478 bhp at 7,000 rpm

Maximum torque: 423 lb-ft at 4,000 rpm

Top speed: 201 mph

0–60 mph: 4.2 sec

TRANSMISSION

Transaxle: Five speeds forward + reverse (non-synchro optional); pump lubricated; limited slip differential

BODY/CHASSIS

Carbon fiber and Kevlar body panels with welded steel tube cage and suspension mounts

SPECIAL FEATURES

The engine cover is louvered to allow the heat generated by the big V8 and twin turbochargers to be dispersed.

If 478 bhp wasn't enough, a factory kit could add an additional 200 bhp.

RUNNING GEAR

Front suspension: Unequal length wishbones with coil-over shock absorbers, anti-roll bar

Rear suspension: Unequal length wishbones, coil-over shock absorbers, anti-roll bar

Brakes: Vented discs, multi-piston calipers front and rear, separate handbrake caliper

Wheels: Modular light alloy 17 in.

DIMENSIONS

Length: 171.5 in.

Width: 77.5 in.

Height: 44.5 in.

Wheelbase: 96.5 in.

Track: 62.7 in. (front), 63.2 in. (rear)

Weight: 2,425 lbs.

Ferrari DINO

The Dino did more than just combine a small race-bred quad-cam V6 in a beautiful lightweight alloy body—it was mid-engined and set new standards of handling for street-legal Ferrari sports cars.

V6 quad-cam engine

By the time this 246 GT was produced, the engine block was made of iron. Ferrari shared the V6 engine with Fiat who used it in its own front-engined Dino.

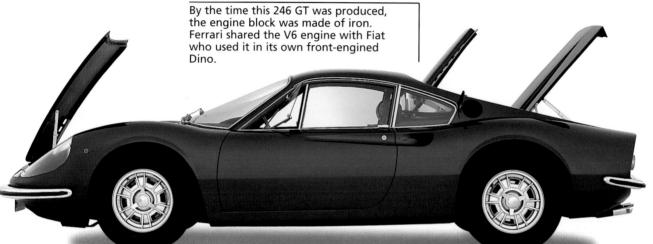

Front-mounted radiator

Although there appears to be no room for it, the Dino's radiator is mounted in the nose, where it had to be angled to fit under the shallow nose.

Side air vents

Although the radiator is in the front, side air vents are still needed to feed air to the engine and oil cooler.

Alloy wheels

Ferrari used wire wheels from 1947 right up until the 1960s when alloys became standard.

Flying buttress design

Styling the back of a mid-engine car is difficult because it is necessary to leave access space. One solution is to have 'flying buttresses' where the line of the cabin is continued towards the rear of the car, but there's space between the two sides.

Vented disc brakes

Dinos have very effective vented disc brakes and they are the same size on all four wheels because the Dino's weight distribution is almost perfect.

Wishbone suspension

Like most high-performance cars, the Dino uses double wishbones with an anti-roll bar in the front and rear.

Steel bodywork

In 1969, Ferrari switched from alloy bodies to steel. That made the cars noticeably heavier than the original 206 GT but engine size and power were increased to compensate.

Specifications
1971 Ferrari Dino 246 GT

ENGINE

Type: V6

Construction: Cast-iron block and alloy cylinder heads

Valve gear: Two valves per cylinder operated by twin chain-driven overhead cams per bank of cylinders

Bore and stroke: 3.67 in. x 2.36 in.

Displacement: 2,418 cc

Compression ratio: 9.0:1

Induction system: Three Weber 40DCN carburetors

Maximum power: 195 bhp at 5,000 rpm

Maximum torque: 166 lb-ft at 5,500 rpm

Top speed: 148 mph

0–60 mph: 7.3 sec.

TRANSMISSION

Five-speed manual

BODY/CHASSIS

Tubular steel chassis with steel two-door coupe body

SPECIAL FEATURES

Dino's simple door handles help leave the car's beautiful lines uncluttered.

Plastic headlight covers were popular with European manufacturers but became illegal in the U.S. and fell out of fashion.

RUNNING GEAR

Steering: Rack-and-pinion

Front suspension: Double wishbones, coil springs, telescopic shocks and anti-roll bar

Rear suspension: Double wishbones, coil springs, telescopic shocks and anti-roll bar

Brakes: Four-wheel vented discs, 10.6 in. dia.

Wheels: Cast alloy 6.5 in. x 14 in.

Tires: 205/70 VR14

DIMENSIONS

Length: 166.5 in. **Width:** 67 in.

Height: 45 in. **Wheelbase:** 92 in.

Track: 55.5 in. (front), 56 in. (rear)

Weight: 2,611 lbs.

Fiat **124 SPIDER**

Built for 19 years, mainly for the U.S. market, the 124 Spider brought new levels of sophistication to the affordable sports car class and became an instant classic upon its demise in 1985.

Five-speed transmission

Five-speed transmissions were normally found only in highly exotic cars from the likes of Maserati and Ferrari, but Fiat brought the delights of slick, five-speed driving to a new generation of sports car drivers.

Twin-cam engine

Designed by Aurelio Lampredi, the 124's classic twin-cam engine is smooth and spirited and became the mainstay of Fiat's and Lancia's mid-range sedans in the 1970s and 1980s, growing from 1.4 to 2.0 liters.

Disc brakes

Like the humble 124 sedan—but unlike many other sports cars—the 124 has four-wheel disc brakes with a servo-assisted booster.

Versatile top

When many other sports car drivers were struggling with build-it-yourself tops that resembled tents, the Fiat's could be raised with one hand from the driver's seat.

Pininfarina bodywork

Fiat commissioned Pininfarina to style and build the Spider's steel body. The cars were built on a very large scale at Pininfarina's Turin factory and were later marketed by Pininfarina, too.

Well-located live rear axle

With its lightweight casing, Panhard rod and coil springing, the live axle is able to handle mid-corner bumps extremely well.

Specifications
1974 Fiat 124 Spider

ENGINE
Type: In-line four-cylinder

Construction: Cast-iron block and alloy cylinder head

Valve gear: Two valves per cylinder operated by twin belt-driven overhead camshafts

Bore and stroke: 3.31 in. x 3.12 in.

Displacement: 1,756 cc

Compression ratio: 8.0:1

Induction system: Single Weber twin-choke carburetor

Maximum power: 93 bhp at 6,200 rpm

Maximum torque: 92 lb-ft at 3,000 rpm

Top speed: 112 mph

0–60 mph: 12.2 sec.

TRANSMISSION
Five-speed manual or three-speed automatic

BODY/CHASSIS
Unitary monocoque construction with steel roadster body

SPECIAL FEATURES

Throughout its production run the Spider retained opening vent windows.

Fiat's lusty twin-cam four provides the power behind the 124 Spider.

RUNNING GEAR
Steering: Worm-and-roller

Front suspension: Double wishbones with coil springs, shocks and anti-roll bar

Rear suspension: Live axle with parallel trailing arms, Panhard rod, coil springs, shocks and anti-roll bar

Brakes: Fiat-Bendix discs, 9.0-in.

Wheels: Alloy, 5 x 13 in.

Tires: 165/70 SR13

DIMENSIONS
Length: 156.3 in.   **Width:** 63.5 in.

Height: 49.3 in.   **Wheelbase:** 89.8 in.

Track: 53.0 in. (front), 52.0 in. (rear)

Weight: 2,540 lbs.

Fiat 130 COUPE

Although the Fiat 130 Coupe was futuristic-looking for 1971, its styling pre-empted the angular body shapes associated with 1970s cars. It was also evident that Fiat could actually build high-quality, large cars.

V6 Engine
The 130's strong, free-revving V6 has good torque but that doesn't make the car wildly quick—0–60 mph takes around 11 seconds and it has a top speed of 120 mph.

Automatic transmission
The majority of 130 Coupes have Borg-Warner's Model 12 automatic transmission that tends to make the car a little under-geared and suffer from poor gas mileage, but which suits its smooth personality. A few models use the slick ZF five-speed manual transmission.

Pininfarina badges
The Pininfarina badge means the famous design house didn't just style the body but built it, too. It then sent the completed bodywork to the Rivalta Fiat factory.

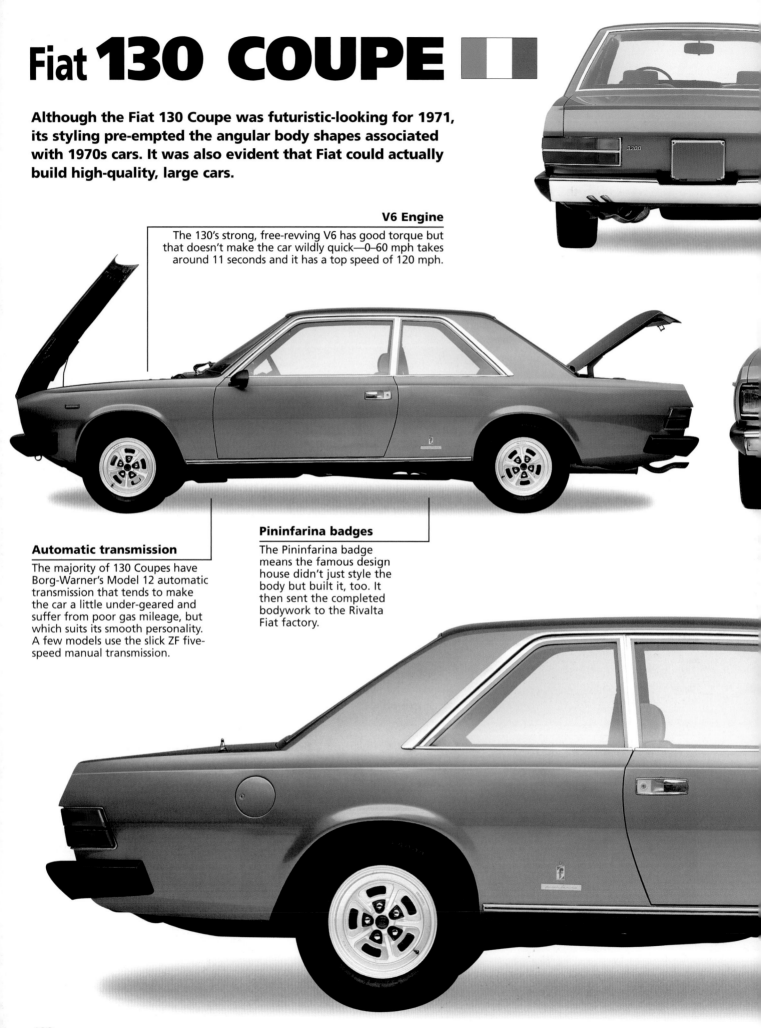

Luxurious interior

When it was introduced the 130 Coupe was considered to have one of the most luxurious interiors of any car in the world. It featured thick velour upholstery and real wood trim. Apart from the steering wheel, the dashboard is the same as the one found in the sedan. Because the Coupe is based on the same wheelbase as the sedan, there is plenty of room in the back.

Unique headlights

The 130 Coupe's infamously oblong headlights were never fitted to any other production car.

Specifications

1973 Fiat 130 Coupe

ENGINE
Type: V6

Construction: Iron block, alloy heads

Valve gear: Single overhead camshaft

Bore and stroke: 4.02 in. x 2.60 in.

Displacement: 3,325cc

Compression ratio: 9.0:1

Induction system: Weber Carburetor

Maximum power: 165 bhp at 5,500 rpm

Maximum torque: 184 lb-ft at 3,400 rpm

Top speed: 120 mph

0–60 mph: 11.4 sec.

TRANSMISSION
Three-speed automatic

BODY/CHASSIS
Unitary monocoque construction with steel, two-door coupe body

SPECIAL FEATURES

The 130 features normal horns for town use and strident air horns for fast, open-road driving.

Shades were fitted in the rear and are mounted on the speaker shelf.

RUNNING GEAR
Steering: Worm-and-roller

Front suspension: Double wishbones with torsion bars, telescopic shock absorbers and anti-roll bar.

Rear suspension: Wishbones and lateral and trailing links with coil springs, telescopic shock absorbers and anti-roll bar.

Brakes: Vented discs, 10.8 in. (front), 10.3 in. (rear)

Wheels: Cromadora cast alloy, 5-stud fixing, 6.5-in. rim

Tires: 205/70 VR14

DIMENSIONS
Length: 190.6 in.　　**Width:** 69.3 in.

Height: 54.3 in.　　**Wheelbase:** 107.1 in.

Track: 57.8 in. (front and rear)

Weight: 3,528 lbs.

Fiat 1500

Fiat turned to Pininfarina for the styling of its Spider. The result was a very clean, timeless and balanced design that still looked fresh many years after it was introduced.

Four-cylinder engine

Because the valve gear was arranged to give a crossflow head with intake on one side and exhaust on the other, Fiat's simpler pushrod design could rival the efficiency of a twin-cam head despite theoretical disadvantages, such as the weight of the valve gear.

Radial tires

Although the Pirelli Cinturato 145-14 tires seem very small by today's standards, they suited the character of the car and were a compromise between handling and roadholding.

Convertible top

Having decided to make a serious attempt at selling its cars in the U.S. market, Fiat knew it would have to come up with a good convertible-top design as a selling point. The designers made sure it was easy to raise and lower, requiring just one arm while sitting in the driver's seat.

Wishbone front suspension

Upper and lower wishbones were used at the front. The coil spring/shock unit was mounted above the top wishbones, a more space-efficient arrangement that also helped to improve the handling.

Single carburetor

The four-cylinder engine is fed through a single twin-barrel Weber 28/36 DCD carburetor. It works well to give economical running at low rpms, with enough power for high-speed motoring.

Live rear axle

Rear-suspension design follows the live-rear axle layout of the 1500 sedan. However, instead of having four 1.97-inch wide leaves in the rear semi-elliptic springs, the Spider has six.

Specifications

Fiat 1500 Spider

ENGINE

Type: Inline four cylinder

Construction: Cast-iron block and alloy head

Valve gear: Two angled valves per cylinder operated by a single block-mounted cam with pushrods and rockers

Bore and stroke: 3.07 in. x 3.18 in.

Displacement: 1,481 cc

Compression ratio: 8.8:1

Induction system: Single Weber 28/36 DCD carburetor

Maximum power: 72 bhp at 5,200 rpm

Maximum torque: 87 lb-ft at 3,200 rpm

Top speed: 91 mph

0–60 mph: 14.7 sec.

TRANSMISSION

Four-speed manual

BODY/CHASSIS

Unitary monocoque construction with steel two-door convertible body

SPECIAL FEATURES

Like many sports cars of the early 1960s, the 1500 has a dash-mounted rear-view mirror.

1500 engines used alloy heads and a pushrod valvetrain.

RUNNING GEAR

Steering: Worm-and-roller

Front suspension: Double wishbones with coil springs, telescopic shock absorbers and anti-roll bar

Rear suspension: Live axle with semi-elliptic leaf springs and telescopic shock absorbers

Brakes: Discs, 9.38-in. dia. (front), alloy-cased drums, 10.6-in. dia. (rear)

Wheels: Pressed steel discs, 14-in. dia.

Tires: 145-14

DIMENSIONS

Length: 160.8 in.   **Width:** 59.8 in.

Height: 51.0 in.   **Wheelbase:** 92.1 in.

Track: 48.1 in. (front), 48.4 in. (rear)

Weight: 2,115 lbs.

Fiat 600 MULTIPLA

In Italy, the Multipla became an icon, a jack-of-all-trades that could act as a people carrier, small truck, taxi, camper or regular sedan. Its styling and layout may look odd but it worked well—and at a bargain price.

Rear-mounted engine

The small four-cylinder powerplant sits at the rear of the car and is easily accessible for servicing. It is unusual in that it incorporates the transmission within it as a single unit, saving weight and complexity.

'Suicide' front doors

Like many European small car designs of this era, the front doors hinge at the rear to provide better access for the driver and front passenger. The obvious safety implications of this setup led to the nickname 'suicide' doors.

600-based styling

The Multipla's family lineage is obvious because the lower half of the rear body is identical to the Fiat 600 sedan. The rear engine lid is also the same. However, the body is some 8 inches taller overall and 2 inches wider.

Forward control

To maximize interior space, the driver is seated at the very front of the car. This posed problems for the steering, which had to have a right-angle joint between the driver's legs.

600 chassis

It may look like a mini truck but the Multipla is based on the platform of a Fiat 600 sedan. The wheelbase and rear engine/suspension are identical, although the steering, track and front suspension are altered.

Fiat 1100 front suspension

To cope with the extra weight over the front axle, the transverse leaf spring suspension of the 600 was substituted by the coil springs and anti-roll bar from the larger 1100 sedan.

Specifications
1957 Fiat 600 Multipla

ENGINE

Type: In-line four-cylinder

Construction: Cast-iron block and aluminum cylinder head

Valve gear: Two valves per cylinder operated by a single camshaft

Bore and stroke: 2.36 in. x 2.20 in.

Displacement: 633 cc

Compression ratio: 7.0:1

Induction system: Single Weber carburetor

Maximum power: 22 bhp at 4,600 rpm

Maximum torque: 29 lb-ft at 2,800 rpm

Top speed: 62 mph

0–60 mph: 54.0 sec.

TRANSMISSION

Four-speed manual

BODY/CHASSIS

Unitary monocoque construction with steel four-door minivan body

SPECIAL FEATURES

The compact four-cylinder engine is mounted at the rear.

This diminutive Multi-Purpose Vehicle (MPV) has three rows of seats.

RUNNING GEAR

Steering: Worm-and-roller

Front suspension: Wishbones with coil springs, telescopic shocks and anti-roll bar

Rear suspension: Semi-trailing arms with coil springs and telescopic shocks

Brakes: Drums (front and rear)

Wheels: Steel, 12-in. dia.

Tires: 5.20 x 12 in.

DIMENSIONS

Length: 140.8 in. **Width:** 57.0 in.

Height: 62.3 in. **Wheelbase:** 78.75 in

Track: 48.3 in. (front), 45.5 in. (rear)

Weight: 1,624 lbs.

Fiat DINO

Powered by a Ferrari engine, the Fiat Dino resulted from the requirement to build 500 road cars in order to race in Formula 2. It is one of Fiat's most desirable cars.

Basic cabin

Despite the Spider's up-market pretensions, the interior of the car is surprisingly stark and not unlike that of the much cheaper 124 Spider—another Pininfarina design.

Five-speed transmission

The original transmission in the 2.0-liter models was too fragile for the bigger 2.4-liter engine, and so the later cars use a ZF transmission with closer ratios.

Sophisticated rear suspension

Although the 2.0-liter had a live rear axle, Fiat adopted an independent semi-trailing arm and strut system for the 2.4-liter version, which is also used by the big Fiat 130 sedan. This results in much improved ride and handling.

Pininfarina bodywork

The shapely body of the two-seat Spider was styled and built by Pininfarina of Turin. Fiat supplied the unitary floorpan, which is based on a shortened version of the 2300S Coupe chassis.

Alloy wheels

The Dino's Cromadora alloy wheels are of the knock-off type on the 2.0-liter version, but are conventionally bolted on the later 2.4. The Ferrari Dino 246 GT uses the same design.

Parts bin details

The attractive rear circular lights of the Dino Spider are the same as those fitted to the humble Fiat 850 Coupe.

Specifications

1970 Fiat Dino 2400

ENGINE

Type: V6

Construction: Cast-iron block and alloy heads

Valve gear: Two valves per cylinder operated by two overhead camshafts per cylinder bank

Bore and stroke: 3.64 in. x 2.36 in.

Displacement: 2,418 cc

Compression ratio: 9.0:1

Induction system: Three Weber carburetors

Maximum power: 180 bhp at 6,600 rpm

Maximum torque: 159 lb-ft at 4,600 rpm

Top speed: 130 mph

0–60 mph: 7.7 sec.

TRANSMISSION

ZF five-speed manual

BODY/CHASSIS

Unitary steel chassis with Pininfarina bodywork

SPECIAL FEATURES

Later cars have a five-speed ZF transmission.

Dinos feature cowled headlights with large wraparound turn signal lamps.

RUNNING GEAR

Steering: ZF worm and roller

Front suspension: Wishbones with coil springs and anti-roll bar

Rear suspension: Coil springs with struts, semi-trailing arms and anti-roll bar

Brakes: Girling discs (front and rear)

Wheels: Cromadora alloys, 14-in. dia

Tires: 205/70 14

DIMENSIONS

Length: 161.8 in. **Width:** 67.6 in.

Height: 50.0 in. **Wheelbase:** 89.8 in.

Track: 53.9 in. (front), 53.6 in. (rear)

Weight: 2,579 lbs.

Ford MODEL 81A

Hot-rodding is a labor of love. The time and effort required to turn a humble 1938 Ford into a refined highway cruiser is beyond the reach of most people. However, the outcome—a truly unique car—is worth it.

Chevrolet small-block V8

The 350-cubic inch Chevrolet engine has been modified for optimum street performance. The addition of an Edelbrock four-barrel carburetor and performance engine tuning has increased the power output to 345 bhp.

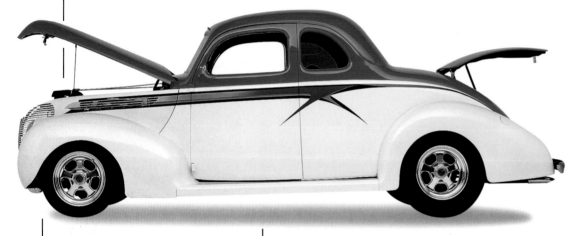

DeLuxe grill

The simplest way of distinguishing the 1938 DeLuxe and Standard models is the front grill. On DeLuxe versions, the top is sculpted into two pronounced arcs, whereas the grill on the Standard car has a horizontal top.

Mustang front suspension

The lowered front suspension is taken from the Ford Mustang II. The independent arrangement with coil springs and telescopic shocks offers more stability and greater comfort than the stock solid axle.

Outlandish color scheme

To augment the car's styling, this rod is painted pink over white with customized graphics consisting of a pearl-foil blue stripe with candy silver, purple, gray, burgundy and gold.

Luxurious interior

One of the great things about building your own car is being able to add the fittings that you want. This car has a natural-wood dash with Ford SVO gauges, burgundy and mauve pleated door and seat panels, air conditioning and a CD player.

Modern disc brakes

Braking is one area where big advances in technology have been made since the 1930s. Brakes from that era often lack bite and feel. To cope with the extra performance, this car has been fitted with front disc brakes.

Specifications

1938 Ford Model 81A DeLuxe Coupe

ENGINE

Type: V8

Construction: Cast-iron block and heads

Valve gear: Two valves per cylinder operated by a single camshaft with pushrods and rockers

Bore and stroke: 4.00 in. x 3.48 in.

Displacement: 350 c.i.

Compression ratio: 9.5:1

Induction system: Single four-barrel carburetor

Maximum power: 345 bhp at 5,600 rpm

Maximum torque: 360 lb-ft at 4,000 rpm

Top speed: 122 mph

0–60 mph: 6.1 sec.

TRANSMISSION

Four-speed automatic

BODY/CHASSIS

Separate steel chassis with two-door coupe body

SPECIAL FEATURES

To complete the slick customized look, 15-inch alloy wheels have been fitted.

The billet side mirrors follow the "streamlined appearance" theme.

RUNNING GEAR

Steering: Recirculating-ball

Front suspension: Independent with coil springs and telescopic shock absorbers

Rear suspension: Parallel leaf springs, live axle with telescopic shock absorbers

Brakes: Discs (front), drums (rear)

Wheels: Aluminum, 15 x 6 in. (front), 15 x 8 in. (rear)

Tires: 165/40-15 (front), 205/60-15 (rear)

DIMENSIONS

Length: 155.3 in.   **Width:** 71.3 in.

Height: 62.4 in.   **Wheelbase:** 112.0 in.

Track: 56.9 in. (front), 59.0 in. (rear)

Weight: 2,350 lbs.

Dramatic-looking in its day, the Crown Victoria was not a great commercial success, and this, coupled with the new maximum-volume policy instigated by Ford, sounded the death knell for the bubbletop.

Lifeguard luxuries

Ford began touting safety in the mid-1950s, and the Crown Victoria boasted such features as a padded dashboard and sun visors, a deep-dish steering wheel, a breakaway rearview mirror and factory-installed seatbelts. All these items were grouped under the Lifeguard package.

Y-block power

Three versions, displacing 272, 292 and 312 cubic inches, of the new-for-1952 Y-block were available in the Crown Victoria. The top 312 unit, shared with the Thunderbird, put out 225 bhp with a four-barrel carburetor if teamed with the Ford-O-Matic automatic transmission.

Automatic transmission

The three-speed, Ford-O-Matic unit was a popular option and was smoother and more refined than arch rival Chevrolet's two-speed Powerglide.

Roof band

The Crown Victoria has a wraparound chromed roof band, which gives a tiara effect. The band adds no structural strength to the body, but gives the car a very 1950s, luxurious look.

Bubbletop roof

Costing an extra $70, the optional glass roof panel was heavily tinted, but on hot days it acted like a greenhouse, making the inside of the cabin unbearably hot. A zip-out headliner helped to reduce the problem.

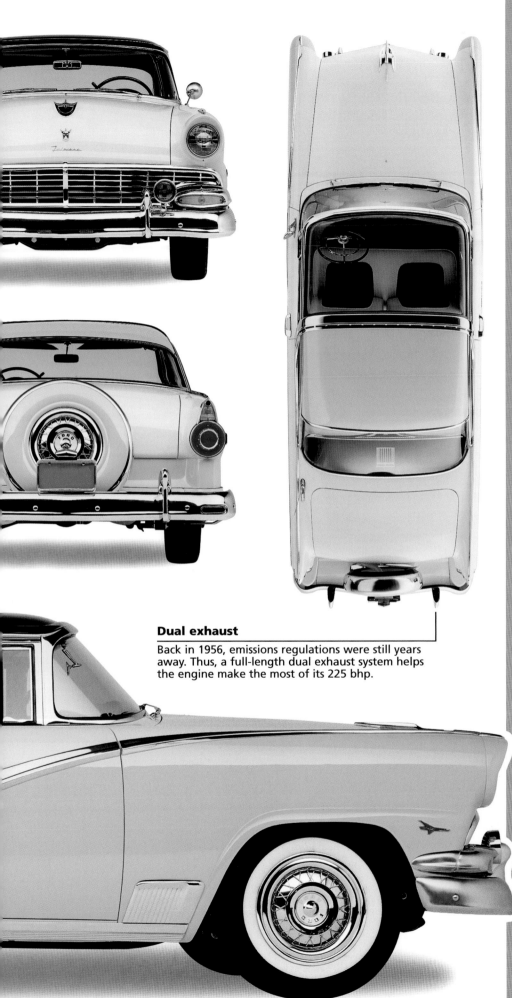

Dual exhaust

Back in 1956, emissions regulations were still years away. Thus, a full-length dual exhaust system helps the engine make the most of its 225 bhp.

Specifications

1956 Ford Crown Victoria

ENGINE

Type: V8

Construction: Cast-iron block and heads

Valve gear: Two valves per cylinder operated by a single camshaft with pushrods and rockers

Bore and stroke: 3.8 in. x 3.44 in.

Displacement: 312 c.i.

Compression ratio: 8.4:1

Induction system: Holley four-barrel carburetor

Maximum power: 225 bhp at 4,600 rpm

Maximum torque: 317 lb-ft at 2,600 rpm

TRANSMISSION

Ford-O-Matic three-speed automatic

BODY/CHASSIS

Separate steel chassis with two-door hardtop body

SPECIAL FEATURES

The Continental kit hinges to the left to gain access to the trunk.

 A rear-mounted antenna was a dealer-installed option.

RUNNING GEAR

Steering: Recirculating ball

Front suspension: Double wishbones with coil springs and telescopic shock absorbers

Rear suspension: Live axle with semi-elliptic leaf springs and telescopic shock absorbers

Brakes: Drums (front and rear)

Wheels: Pressed steel, 15-in. dia.

Tires: 7.10 x 15

DIMENSIONS

Length: 198.5 in. **Width:** 75.9 in.

Height: 52.5 in. **Wheelbase:** 155.0 in.

Track: 58.0 in. (front), 56.0 in. (rear)

Weight: 3,299 lbs.

Ford **DELUXE V8**

Durability and affordability were the hallmarks that established Ford, and though the V-8 boasted both of those qualities, its performance was the most impressive feature.

V8 engine

Crucial to Ford's success in the 1930s was its V8 powerplant. When other car makers had only fours and sixes, Ford could justly claim superiority with not one but two different V8 engines.

V-grill

The distinctive V-shaped grill arrived in 1935 and developed into the streamlined profile see on this 1939 Deluxe four-door sedan. The 1939 has vertical gri bars in place of the horizontal bars of the 1940 Deluxe.

Steel roo

Early V8 models had a fabric roof inser but in 1937 Ford began using a fu steel roof pane

Deluxe interiors

All Deluxe models came with a woodgrain dashboard and a centrally mounted clock.

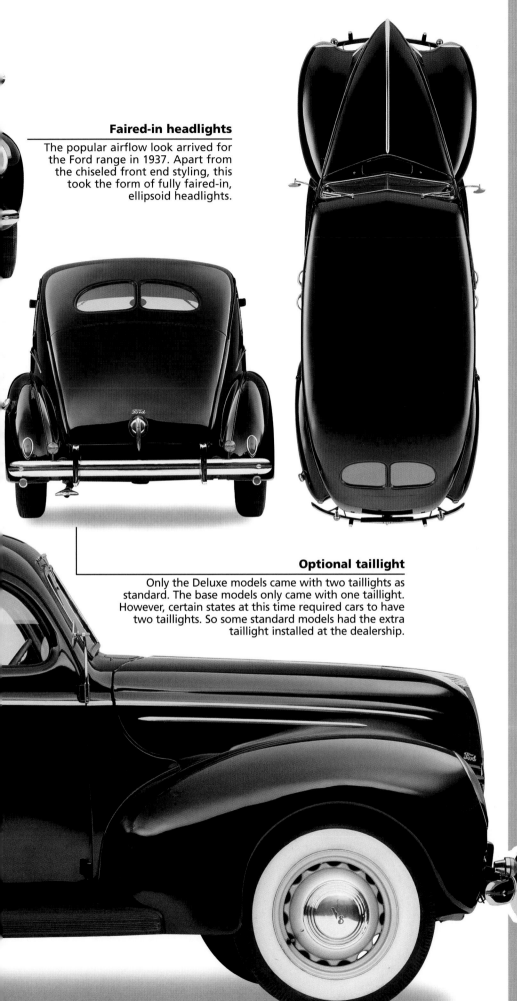

Faired-in headlights

The popular airflow look arrived for the Ford range in 1937. Apart from the chiseled front end styling, this took the form of fully faired-in, ellipsoid headlights.

Optional taillight

Only the Deluxe models came with two taillights as standard. The base models only came with one taillight. However, certain states at this time required cars to have two taillights. So some standard models had the extra taillight installed at the dealership.

Specifications
1939 Ford Deluxe V8

ENGINE

Type: V8

Construction: Cast-iron cylinder block and heads

Valve gear: Two side-mounted valves per cylinder operated by a single camshaft

Bore and stroke: 3.06 in. x 3.75 in.

Displacement: 221 c.i.

Compression ratio: 6.2:1

Induction system: Single carburetor

Maximum power: 85 bhp at 3,800 rpm

Maximum torque: 155 lb-ft at 2,200 rpm

Top speed: 87 mph

0–60 mph: 17.4 sec.

TRANSMISSION

Three-speed manual

BODY/CHASSIS

Separate chassis with steel two-door or four-door sedan, coupe or convertible body

SPECIAL FEATURES

Suicide-type rear doors were offered on four-door sedans in 1939.

Ellipsoid headlights were faired into the front fenders.

RUNNING GEAR

Steering: Worm-and-roller

Front suspension: Beam axle with transverse leaf spring and shocks

Rear suspension: Live axle with transverse leaf spring and shocks

Brakes: Drums (front and rear)

Wheels: Steel, 17-in dia.

Tires: 6 x 16 in.

DIMENSIONS

Length: 179.5 in.   **Width:** 67.0 in.

Height: 68.6 in.   **Wheelbase:** 112.0 in.

Track: 55.5 in. (front), 58.3 in. (rear)

Weight: 2,898 lbs.

Ford **ESCORT RS1600**

Remarkably, Ford did not make the dramatically faster and better RS1600 look any different than a standard car. Only keen observers would spot the lower ride height, cambered front wheels and tiny RS badges.

Front discs

The RS1600 uses the same braking system as the Escort Twin Cam, which means it has fairly large 9.6-inch diameter front discs. The rear brakes are nine-inch diameter drums, which were considered good enough.

Twin-cam engine

Just as the Lotus twin-cam engine was a development of an existing Ford block, the more powerful BDA engine was a similar approach by Cosworth. The 1.6-liter BDA could easily be bored out to give up to 1.8 liters, or even as much as 2.0 liters.

Rear battery

Shoe-horning a twin-cam engine into the Escort's engine bay meant there was no room for the battery, so it migrated to the rear of the car where it was mounted in the trunk. This had the welcome incidental effect of improving the weight distribution, although the RS1600 still felt too light in the rear.

Flared wheel arches

At first glance it is not obvious, but Ford had to make the wheel arches slightly flared to clear the 165-13 tires. The change can be best seen from the front three-quarter angle.

Strut front suspension

The existing MacPherson-strut front suspension was modified with lower and stiffer springs and struts. In addition, the front wheels were given 1.5 degrees of negative camber to greatly improve front-end grip during hard cornering.

Specifications

1971 Ford Escort RS1600

ENGINE

Type: In-line four-cylinder

Construction: Cast-iron block and alloy cylinder head

Valve gear: Four valves per cylinder operated by twin belt-driven overhead camshafts

Bore and stroke: 3.20 in. x 3.05 in.

Displacement: 1,601 cc

Compression ratio: 10.0:1

Induction system: Two Weber 40 DCOE carburetors

Maximum power: 120 bhp at 6,500 rpm

Maximum torque: 112 lb-ft at 4,000 rpm

Top speed: 114 mph

0–60 mph: 8.3 sec.

TRANSMISSION

Four-speed manual

BODY/CHASSIS

Unitary monocoque construction with steel two-door sedan body

SPECIAL FEATURES

Sporty Escorts can be identified by their two-piece front fenders.

Oil coolers were standard on race-prepped Escort RS1600s.

RUNNING GEAR

Steering: Rack-and-pinion

Front suspension: MacPherson struts with lower control arms and anti-roll bar

Rear suspension: Live axle with semi-elliptic leaf springs, trailing arms and telescopic shock absorbers

Brakes: Discs, 9.6-in. dia. (front), drums 9.0-in. dia. (rear)

Wheels: Pressed-steel disc, 5.5 x 13 in.

Tires: Radial, 165-13

DIMENSIONS

Length: 160.0 in.   **Width:** 61.8 in.

Height: 53.0 in.   **Wheelbase:** 94.5 in.

Track: 50.8 in. (front), 52.0 in. (rear)

Weight: 1,965 lbs.

Ford FAIRLANE

The 1957 Fairlane boasts tasteful styling for the period—a factor in its favor nowadays. Fords from this era are rarer than their popularity at the time might suggest.

Modern paint

The body of this restored and customized car has been resprayed in yellow and white acrylic paint.

Thunderbird engine

The base engine for the 1957 Fairlane was a modest six-cylinder. This car has received a useful increase in power by fitting a 255-bhp Thunderbird V8.

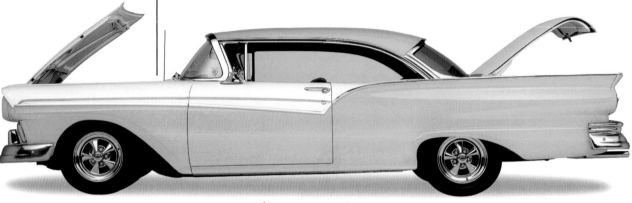

Automatic transmission

The Ford-O-Matic three-speed automatic transmission was optional on 1957 models and provides easy gear shifts.

Custom trim

The upholstery is black and charcoal velour, with yellow piping on the seats and rear package tray. Other additions include Auto Meter gauges, air-conditioning, and a powerful stereo.

Safety interior

Ford began its safety drive in 1956. This car is fitted with a dished steering wheel, padded dash, break-away rear-view mirror, and crash-proof door locks.

Specifications

1957 Ford Fairlane 500

ENGINE

Type: V8

Construction: Cast-iron cylinder block and cylinder heads

Valve gear: Two valves per cylinder operated by a single camshaft

Bore and stroke: 3.90 in. x 3.44 in.

Displacement: 312 c.i.

Compression ratio: 9.7:1

Induction system: Single Holley carburetor

Maximum power: 255 bhp at 4,600 rpm

Maximum torque: 354 lb-ft at 2,800 rpm

Top speed: 120 mph

0–60 mph: 10.2 sec.

TRANSMISSION

Ford-O-Matic three-speed automatic

BODY/CHASSIS

Separate chassis with steel two-door coupe bodywork

SPECIAL FEATURES

In 1957, the Fairlane had single rear lights; twin lights were fitted in 1958.

Chrome valve covers and air cleaner, and headers liven up the T-bird V8.

RUNNING GEAR

Steering: Recirculating ball

Front suspension: Independent with coil springs and telescopic shocks

Rear suspension: Rigid axle with leaf springs and telescopic shocks

Brakes: Four-wheel drums

Wheels: Cragar, 15-in. dia.

Tires: 235/60 x 15 in.

DIMENSIONS

Length: 207.5 in.   **Width:** 77 in.

Height: 56.5 in.   **Wheelbase:** 118 in.

Track: 59 in. (front), 56.4 in. (rear)

Weight: 3,400 lbs.

Partial dechroming

In order to give this car clean and uncluttered lines, much of the chrome trim has been removed.

Classic styling

Unlike the gaudy and contrived excesses of some late-1950s cars, the Fairlane was quite simple and understated.

Ford FALCON

It may resemble a 1963 Falcon, but this car is almost totally custom fabricated. Perhaps the most interesting thing about it is that the shell is actually from a convertible, with a hardtop from another Falcon grafted on.

Lightweight bumpers

Shaving as many pounds as possible was of primary concern when building this car. That approach extends to the bumpers, which are fiberglass items and have been sectioned to make them fit as close to the body as possible.

Killer V8

With a genuine 500 cubic inches and a huge 1050-cfm carburetor, this engine makes a tremendous amount of horsepower, more than 700, in fact. This enables the bantam weight Falcon to scream down the quarter-mile in just 9.2 seconds.

Strut front suspension

Stock Falcons came with a short-long-arm front suspension and coil-over shocks, but both the stock chassis and IFS have been replaced by a pair of Morrison struts. In the interest of weight transfer, the anti-roll bar has been omitted and lightweight wheels, with skinnies, have been fitted.

Custom interior

A whole new interior has been fabricated from aluminum sheeting, including the dash and the transmission tunnel (on which sits a B&M shifter for the Powerglide transmission). Safety is courtesy of a roll cage and Simpson twin harnesses.

Free-flowing exhaust

To expel the spent gases as quickly as possible, the big motor has a pair of Hooker 2½-inch diameter headers bolted to it. Besides getting rid of the spent gases, they help the engine make a truly thunderous trip down the strip.

Specifications
1963 Ford Falcon Sprint

ENGINE
Type: V8

Construction: Cast-iron block with alloy heads

Valve gear: Two valves per cylinder operated by a single V-mounted camshaft with pushrods and rockers

Bore and stroke: 4.39 in. x 4.125 in.

Displacement: 500 c.i.

Compression ratio: 13.5:1

Induction system: Holley Dominator 1050-cfm four-barrel carburetor

Maximum power: 710 bhp at 7,000 rpm

Maximum torque: 685 lb-ft at 5,200 rpm

Top speed: 230 mph

0–60 mph: 2.8 sec

TRANSMISSION
Powerglide two-speed automatic

BODY/CHASSIS
Tubular-steel chassis with two-door hardtop body

SPECIAL FEATURES

Lexan glass is used for all windows to save as much weight as possible.

Wheelie bars help keep the car straight off the tree.

RUNNING GEAR
Steering: Rack-and-pinion

Front suspension: Morrison struts, lower control arms and telescopic shock absorbers

Rear suspension: Live axle, four-bar links, coil springs, telescopic shock absorbers and Panhard rod

Brakes: Discs (front and rear)

Wheels: Centerline lightweight

Tires: BFGoodrich radial T/A (front), Goodyear Drag Slicks (rear)

DIMENSIONS
Length: 183.7 in. **Width:** 70.8 in.

Height: 51.5 in. **Wheelbase:** 109.5 in.

Track: 56.9 in. (front), 48.5 in. (rear)

Weight: 2,015 lbs.

Ford GALAXIE 500XL

When it came to racing, Ford always rolled up its sleeves and attacked the competition at full throttle. This 1963 lightweight Galaxie was one of 50 cars that clearly illustrated how seriously Ford took winning drag races.

Stripped out interior

All of the unnecessary items in the interior such as the radio, heater, all sound deadeners, carpeting and clock were removed. In addition, Econoline van seats replace the plush cushions.

427 V8 engine

Introduced halfway through 1963, the 427 ultimately emerged as Ford's most legendary and fearsome powerplant of the 1960s.

Fastback styling

The big Galaxies were also used for stock car racing. The fastback roof, in addition to looking stylish, helped to reduce aerodynamic drag on stock car oval tracks and increased the maximum speed by more than 10 mph.

Manual transmission

All lightweight Galaxies were only available with a 4-speed transmission. Since saving weight was a primary concern, the transmission casings and bell-housings were made of aluminum instead of steel.

Six-cylinder suspension

This car uses the lighter chassis found under the 300 Series Galaxies that used six cylinder motors. It is made of lighter gauge steel and weighs considerably less than the standard 500XL chassis.

The lightweight package

All lightweight Galaxies were designed for one purpose—drag racing. These cars are so radical that they weren't the least bit street-able. The drag cars came with a high 12.2:1 compression ratio, different 2nd and 3rd gears in the transmission and a 4.56:1 rear axle ratio. This car was not for the faint hearted.

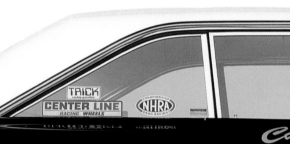

The 700-lb. diet

All lightweight Galaxies used fiberglass fenders, doors, trunk lids and hoods, while the steel bumpers were replaced with aluminum parts.

Specifications

1963 Ford Galaxie 500XL

ENGINE

Type: V8

Construction: Cast-iron block and heads

Valve gear: Two valves per cylinder operated by pushrods and rockers

Bore and stroke: 4.23 in x 3.78 in

Displacement: 427 c.i.

Compression ratio: 12.2:1

Induction system: Twin reverse-mounted Holley 600 cfm four-barrel carburetors

Maximum power: 425 bhp at 6,000 rpm

Maximum torque: 480 lb-ft at 3,700 rpm

TRANSMISSION

Borg-Warner T-10 four-speed

BODY/CHASSIS

Lightweight perimeter steel chassis with two-door steel and fiberglass hardtop body

SPECIAL FEATURES

In true 1960s style, this Galaxie 500XL features a Borg-Warner T-10 four-speed transmission.

The gas cap is hidden by a flip-up lid in the taillight panel.

RUNNING GEAR

Steering: Recirculating ball

Front suspension: Unequal length wishbones with coil springs and telescopic shock absorbers

Rear suspension: Live rear axle fitted with 4.56:1 gears with semi-elliptical leaf springs and telescopic shock absorbers

Brakes: Drums (front and rear)

Wheels: Centerlines, 15-in. dia.

Tires: BFG radials (front), Mickey Thompson slicks (rear)

DIMENSIONS

Length: 199.3 in. **Width:** 82.4 in.

Height: 54.3 in. **Wheelbase:** 119.0 in.

Track: 63.6 in. (front), 62.7 in. (rear)

Weight: 3,772 lbs.

Ford **GT40**

Fast and immensely strong, the GT40 showed what a production car company could do when it wanted to go racing, particularly with Carroll Shelby, father of the AC Cobra, running the racing program.

Final specification

Although this car first raced in 1965, it was later brought up to the final racing specs, those of the Le Mans-winning cars of 1968 and '69.

Mid-engined design

By the 1960s, it was obvious that a successful racing car had to be mid-engined and Ford followed suit. The engine is behind the driver, mounted lengthwise, and by 1968, the displacement of the small-block engine had risen to 302 cubic inches. With Gurney-Weslake-developed cylinder heads, as on this car, power output was up to 435 bhp.

Front-mounted radiator

Ford decided to keep the radiator in its conventional position rather than mounting it alongside or behind the engine as on some modern mid-engined designs.

Four-speed transmission

The first racers are equipped with a four-speed Colotti transmission with right-hand change. Road cars have a ZF five-speed box with conventional central shifter.

Opening side windows

GT40s get incredibly hot inside and although the main side windows do not open, there are small hinged windows to allow air to pass through the cockpit.

Fiberglass body

The GT40's body played no structural role, so it was made from fiberglass and consisted basically of two large hinged sections, which gave the best access during pit stops.

Radiator outlet

By 1968, the air passing through the radiator was exhausted through this one large vent. It has a small upturned lip on the leading edge to accelerate air flow through the radiator.

Competition record

This car was one of the first driven at Le Mans, in 1965 by Bob Bondurant, but it failed to finish after cylinder head gasket failure. Three years later, it came fourth in the 1000 km at Spa Francorchamps.

Magnesium suspension components

The GT40 is a heavyweight racing car, but some effort was still made to save weight—the magnesium suspension uprights, for example.

Halibrand wheels

The wide Halibrand wheels are made from magnesium, so they are very light. The design also provides good cooling for the disc brakes. They are a knock-off design for quick changes at pit stops.

Specifications
1967 Ford GT40 MkIII (road spec)

ENGINE

Type: V8
Construction: Cast-iron block and heads
Valve gear: Two valves per cylinder operated by single camshaft via pushrods and rockers
Bore and stroke: 4 in. x 2.87 in.
Displacement: 289 c.i.
Compression ratio: 10.5:1
Induction system: Single four-barrel Holley carburetor
Maximum power: 306 bhp at 6,000 rpm
Maximum torque: 328 lb-ft at 4,200 rpm
Top speed: 165 mph
0–60 mph: 5.5 sec

TRANSMISSION

Five-speed ZF manual transaxle

BODY/CHASSIS

Sheet steel central semi-monocoque with front and rear subframes and fiberglass two-door, two-seat GT body

SPECIAL FEATURES

The GT40 was made as low as possible to help its aerodynamics. On this car, to help fit a driver with helmet into the cockpit, this bump was added onto the roof.

To help achieve a low overall height, the exhaust pipes run over the top of the transmission.

RUNNING GEAR

Steering: Rack-and-pinion
Front suspension: Double wishbones with coil springs, telescopic shocks and anti-roll bar
Rear suspension: Trailing arms and wishbones with coil springs, telescopic shocks and anti-roll bar
Brakes: Discs, 11.5 in. dia. (front), 11.2 in. dia. (rear)
Wheels: Halibrand magnesium 6.5 in. x 15 in. (front), 8.5 in. x 15 in. (rear)
Tires: 5.5 in. x 15 in. (front), 7 in. x 15 in. (rear)

DIMENSIONS

Length: 169 in. **Width:** 70 in.
Height: 40 in. **Wheelbase:** 95.3 in.
Track: 55 in. (front), 53.5 in. (rear)
Weight: 2,200 lbs.

Ford **LOTUS CORTINA**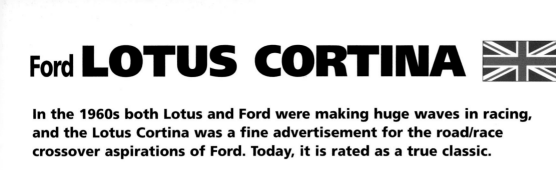

In the 1960s both Lotus and Ford were making huge waves in racing, and the Lotus Cortina was a fine advertisement for the road/race crossover aspirations of Ford. Today, it is rated as a true classic.

Lotus engine
The heart of the Lotus Cortina is its engine. With a healthy power output of 105 bhp, it transforms the Cortina into a real performance machine.

Modified suspension
While the MacPherson strut front end is almost standard (only with stiffer springs and shocks), the leaf-sprung rear end is completely changed. It consists of an A-frame attached to the differential with trailing arms pivoting from the old leaf-spring mountings. As a result, the ride height is much lower than normal.

Lightweight drivetrain
Colin Chapman was called in to re-engineer the transmission to match the new engine. The close-ratio four-speed manual unit from the Elan is used, but the clutch housing, differential casing and remote gearshift extension are made from light alloy.

Sensible styling
Ford of England often played it safe regarding styling. The Cortina may not be much to look at, but this was exactly what the public wanted.

Aluminum body parts

When launched, the Lotus Cortina boasted lightweight aluminum panels. These included the skins on the doors, hood and trunk lid. However, in July 1964 these reverted to ordinary steel, and you had to pay extra if you wanted light alloy panels.

Unique paint scheme

The distinctive paintwork of the Lotus Cortina became its trademark. Virtually all cars were delivered from Lotus' Cheshunt factory in England painted in Ermine White with a Sherwood Green flash applied by Lotus.

Specifications
1964 Ford Lotus Cortina

ENGINE
Type: In-line four-cylinder

Construction: Cast-iron block and aluminum head

Valve gear: Two valves per cylinder operated by dual overhead camshafts

Bore and stroke: 3.25 in. x 2.87 in.

Displacement: 1,558 cc

Compression ratio: 9.5:1

Induction system: Twin Weber downdraft carburetors

Maximum power: 105 bhp at 5,500 rpm

Maximum torque: 108 lb-ft at 4,000 rpm

Top speed: 106 mph

0–60 mph: 9.9 sec

TRANSMISSION
Four-speed manual

BODY/CHASSIS
Integral chassis with two-door steel sedan body

SPECIAL FEATURES

Auxiliary driving lights are fitted to many Lotus Cortinas and together with the stripes add a dash of sportiness.

Minilite wheels were a popular aftermarket addition to British sports cars in the 1960s, and the Lotus Cortina was no exception.

RUNNING GEAR
Steering: Recirculating ball

Front suspension: MacPherson struts with coil springs, shock absorbers, track control arms and anti-roll bar

Rear suspension: Live axle with A-frame, coil springs, trailing arms and shock absorbers

Brakes: Discs (front), drums (rear)

Wheels: Steel, 13-in. dia.

Tires: 6.00 x 13

DIMENSIONS
Length: 168.3 in.   **Width:** 62.5 in.

Height: 53.7 in.   **Wheelbase:** 98.4 in.

Track: 51.5 in. (front), 50.5 in. (rear)

Weight: 2,038 lbs.

Ford MODEL T

Probably the single most important technical advance in motoring history, the Model T brought car ownership to the masses. Henry Ford's vision of an integrated production line is still used in automobile factories today.

Gearbox

The Model T was nothing like a modern car. You had two forward gears, which you selected by pulling an outside lever and then pressing a foot pedal, where the clutch is on a modern car, in order to change gear. Reverse gear was selected using the middle pedal.

Windscreen wipers

Model T drivers had to use a very rudimentary way of keeping their screens clear. Wipers didn't exist, but part of the screen could be lifted up so the driver could reach out and clean it with his hand.

Starting handle

Until an electric starter was introduced in 1919, Model T owners had to turn the engine by hand in order to get it to fire. The handle slotted in beneath the radiator grille and you had to turn on a tap to get fuel to the engine first.

Mudguards

This model features streamlined rear mudguards as it's a two-seater coupe. Saloon models had the guards integrated into the rear body, while van bodies sat over the axle to create a wheelarch. Basic and racing models had exposed wheels, but these were vulnerable to damage from road debris.

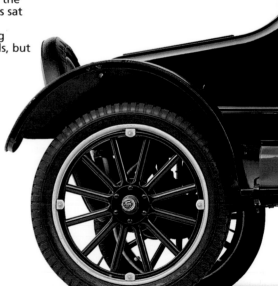

Hand throttle

The three foot pedals were for changing gear, engaging reverse and braking, with the brake where the gas pedal can be found on a modern car. To accelerate, drivers had to use a lever on the steering wheel to increase the amount of fuel entering the engine.

Quarter-elliptical leaf springs

Most contemporary cars came with semi-elliptic leaf springs as standard, but the Model T had smaller quarter-elliptic ones instead. This kept production costs to a minimum, but the trade-off was a harsh and bumpy ride quality.

Rear brakes

The right-hand foot pedal operated the cable brake, which applied itself to the front wheels only. It slowed the car down, but emergency stops were out of the question as it would heat up and fail completely. The rear brakes were more efficient and were operated with a hand lever.

Under the hood

The Model T engine was typical of its time. The 2.9-litre four-cylinder unit ran at low compression and had a realtively small output of just 20bhp, but it had enormous reserves of torque and could pull from very low speeds.

Central fuel

The fuel tank of a Model T is a simple round barrel. It was mounted under the driving seat as it was most protected from damage here, which explains the car's rather high driving position. Most owners carried a spare can of motor spirit on the running board.

Specifications
1908 Ford Model T

ENGINE
Engine: Four cylinder in-line
Construction: Cast iron block and cylinder head
Valve gear: Two valves per cylinder, mounted in block
Bore and stroke: 3.74 in. x 3.97 in.
Capacity: 2,895cc
Compression ratio: 4.5:1
Carburettor: One Holley direct unit
Power: 20bhp @ 1,800rpm
Top speed: 42mph
0–60mph: Not applicable

TRANSMISSION
Two-speed manual

BODY/CHASSIS
Chassis available in two lengths, wide range of bodies on offer.

SPECIAL FEATURES

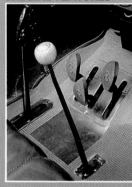

Totally confusing: The left-hand pedal operates the forward gearbox, the middle pedal is used to select reverse and the right-hand pedal applies the brakes.

Front and rear, the Model T was equipped with quarter-elliptic leaf springs in order to cut production costs.

RUNNING GEAR
Steering: Direct linkage
Front suspension: Subframe, diagonal crosstubes, quarter-elliptic leaf springs
Rear suspension: Subframe, diagonal crosstubes, quarter-elliptic leaf springs
Brakes: Foot pedal operating cable to front, hand-operated cable linkage to rear
Wheels: Wooden, 30-spoke
Tires: 3.5 x 30 solid tyres

DIMENSIONS
Length: 140.0 in. Width: 66.0 in.
Height: Dependent on selected bodywork
Wheelbase: 100.5 in.
Track: 57.0 in. (front), 57.5 in. (rear)
Weight: 1475 lb. (applies to chassis and front bodywork only)

Ford MUSTANG 1966

If you like the looks but not the performance, what can you do?
Build your ideal car, of course. With nearly 400 bhp and a chassis
that can handle the power, this Mustang would be your dream car.

Supercharged engine

To get phenomenal performance from the
Mustang, a 32-valve, all-alloy 4.6 liter "modular"
Ford V8 engine, from a late-model Mustang
Cobra, has been fitted. The power has been
upped to 392 bhp by the addition of a Kenne
Bell supercharger running at 6 pounds of boost.

Tangerine dream

Completing the modified look is the
tangerine pearl custom paint scheme.
The side scallops are finished in a blend
of gold pearl and candy root beer.

Billet grill

A lot of attention
has been paid to
the look of this car.
This is illustrated by
the six-bar chrome
front grill and the
five-bar rear fascia,
which incorporates
900 LEDs.

Four-wheel disc brakes

To balance the enhanced
performance, disc brakes have
been installed. At the front these
are 11 inches in diameter with
9-inch ones at the rear.

Custom interior

As much work has gone into customizing the interior as modifying the mechanicals of this car. There are two shades of leather upholstery, cream and biscuit. There is also a wool carpet from a Mercedes, as well as modified 1965 T-Bird front seats.

Upgraded suspension

As with many modified first-generation Mustangs, this car uses the coil-sprung front suspension from the Mustang II. A chrome 9-inch rear axle combines with a Global West stage III suspension system out back.

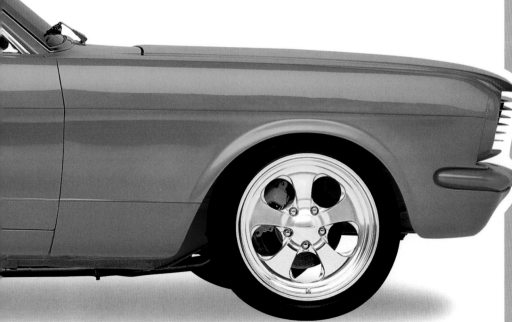

Specifications
1966 Ford Mustang

ENGINE
Type: V8

Construction: Alloy block and heads

Valve gear: Four valves per cylinder operated by four chain-driven overhead cams.

Bore and stroke: 3.61 in. x 3.60 in.

Displacement: 281 c.i.

Compression ratio: 9.8:1

Induction system: Multipoint fuel injection with Kenne Bell twin-screw whipple supercharger

Maximum power: 392 bhp at 5,800 rpm

Maximum torque: 405 lb-ft at 4,500 rpm

Top speed: 141 mph

0–60 mph: 4.3 sec.

TRANSMISSION
Three-speed automatic

BODY/CHASSIS
Steel chassis with steel body

SPECIAL FEATURES

Even the trunk has been upholstered in matching fabrics.

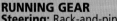

Budnick alloy wheels are a fine addition to the car.

RUNNING GEAR
Steering: Rack-and-pinion

Front suspension: A-arms with coil springs and telescopic shock absorbers

Rear suspension: Live rear axle with leaf springs and telescopic shock absorbers

Brakes: Discs, 11-in. dia. (front), 9-in. dia. (rear)

Wheels: Alloy, 17 x 7 in. (front); 17 x 8 in. (rear)

Tires: Toyo 215/45ZR17 (front), 245/45ZR17 (rear)

DIMENSIONS
Length: 176.0 in.   **Width:** 71.0 in.

Height: 50.3 in.   **Wheelbase:** 108.0 in.

Track: 58.6 in. (front and rear)

Weight: 2,358 lbs.

Ford **MUSTANG BOSS 302**

This one-of-a-kind, pristine Boss 302 road racer combines a high-tech chassis and suspension with some very exotic and rare engine and drivetrain components.

Reworked engine

Standard Boss 302s are rated at 290 bhp, but this one, with its multiple-carburetor free-flowing cylinder heads and exhaust manifolds, is rated at an impressive 400 bhp.

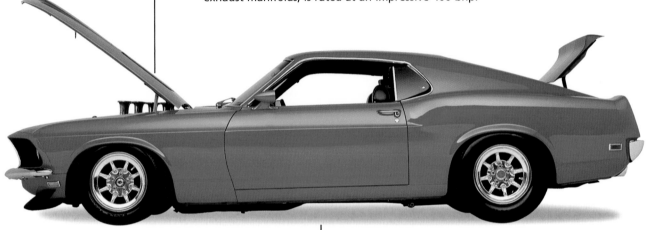

Interior alterations

Although this Boss retains the original high-back bucket seats, four-point harnesses, a Mallory tachometer and Grant steering wheel have been added.

Big wheels and tires

During the 1969 season the factory Boss 302s ran with Minilite wheels. A set of these classic wheels, which have been chromed and shod with modern Goodyear tires, are fitted to this racer.

Stock body

Despite the radical internal modifications the body remains fairly stock, with no spoilers or unnecessary additions.

Lowered suspension

For better handling and stability, this Boss has been lowered with relocated control arms and reversed-rolled rear leaf springs.

Original paint

The policy of keeping the exterior appearance of this 302 as original as possible even extends to the paintwork. It is painted in Calypso Coral, a factory available color on Boss 302s in 1969. The black stripes however, have been added by the owner.

Uprated transmission

A Ford 9-inch rear end with a 4.11:1 set of gears sends the power to the rear wheels. A 5.43:1 Detroit Locker rear end can be installed if required.

Specifications
1969 Ford Mustang Boss 302

ENGINE
Type: V8

Construction: Cast-iron block and heads

Valve gear: Two valves per cylinder operated by a single camshaft via pushrods and rockers

Bore and stroke: 4 in. x 3 in.

Displacement: 302 c.i.

Compression ratio: 10.5:1

Induction system: Eight Autolite carburetors giving 2,850 cfm

Maximum power: 400 bhp at 6,500 rpm

Maximum torque: 343 lb-ft at 4,300 rpm

TRANSMISSION
Borg-Warner T-10 four-speed manual

BODY/CHASSIS
Steel monocoque with two-door body

SPECIAL FEATURES

Eight carburetor stacks poke through the hood.

Chromed Minilite spoked wheels add a period look to this custom racer.

RUNNING GEAR
Steering: Recirculating ball

Front suspension: Unequal length wishbones with coil springs, telescopic shocks and anti-roll bar

Rear suspension: Live axle with multi-leaf springs, telescopic shocks and anti-roll bar

Brakes: Power discs (front and rear)

Wheels: Minilite spoked magnesium, 8 x 15 in.

Tires: Goodyear Gatorback P225/50 ZR15

DIMENSIONS
Length: 187 in. **Width:** 72 in.

Height: 47 in.   **Wheelbase:** 108 in.

Track: 66 in. (front), 61.8 in. (rear)

Weight: 3,209 lbs.

Ford **MUSTANG GT/CS**

CS stands for California Special, and as its name suggests, this limited-edition Mustang was a regional promotional model. It featured all the GT performance and handling features, plus a few of its own.

Big 390 V8

In many ways, the 390 was the ideal engine for the Mustang in 1968. It's smooth, tractable and packs a substantial wallop, thanks to its incredible 403lb-ft of torque.

Hardtop styling

To order the GT/CS, you had to start with the base hardtop coupe and then add the GT package and California Special trim option. The latter included special side scoops, Shelby-style taillights, a plain grill and special emblems.

Floating front calipers

A notable improvement of the 1968 Mustangs were floating calipers on the optional front disc brakes. These provide more balanced power compared to fixed calipers.

Safety features

The 1968 Mustang has an energy-absorbing dash and steering column, dual circuit brakes and a double-laminated windshield.

Heavy-duty suspension

The GT equipment includes uprated suspension, which in 1960s Detroit consisted of stiffened springs and shocks, plus a beefier front anti-roll bar.

Dual exhaust

1968 GTs also got a standard dual exhaust system, with (for just this year) quad tips protruding through the rear valance.

Specifications

1968 Ford Mustang GT/CS

ENGINE

Type: V8

Construction: Cast-iron block and heads

Valve gear: Two valves per cylinder operated by a single V-mounted camshaft with pushrods and rockers

Bore and stroke: 4.05 in. x 3.78 in.

Displacement: 390 c.i.

Compression ratio: 10.5:1

Induction system: Single Holley four-barrel downdraft carburetor

Maximum power: 280 bhp at 4400 rpm

Maximum torque: 403 lb-ft at 2600 rpm

Top speed: 120mph

0–60mph: 7.5 sec

TRANSMISSION

C6 Cruise-O-Matic three-speed automatic

BODY/CHASSIS

Steel unitary chassis with steel body panels

SPECIAL FEATURES

These side scoops are found only on 1968 CS, HCS and Shelby Mustangs.

A neat option were the turn signal repeaters in the bonnet scoops.

RUNNING GEAR

Steering: Recirculating-ball

Front suspension: Unequal-length A-arms, coil springs, telescopic shock absorbers and anti-roll bar

Rear suspension: Live axle, semi-elliptic leaf springs and telescopic shock absorbers

Brakes: Discs (front), drums (rear)

Wheels: 14 in. x 7 in. stamped steel

Tires: Goodyear Polyglas E70-14

DIMENSIONS

Length: 183.6 in.

Width: 68.9 in.

Height: 51.2 in.

Wheelbase: 108.0 in.

Track: 58.5 in. (front and rear)

Weight: 2635 lbs.

Ford **MUSTANG MACH 1**

The Mach 1 line, which began in 1969, enhanced the sporty qualities of the Mustang, picking up on some of the themes of Carroll Shelby's modifications. The 1973 Mach 1 boasted a variety of enhancements.

Standard V8 power

All Mustangs for 1973 came with a six-cylinder engine as standard except the Mach 1, with its 302 c.i. V8. Because it had an emissions-restricted output of 136bhp, ordering one of the optional V8 engines was an attractive choice.

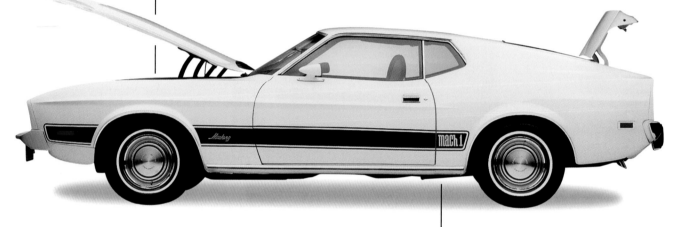

Competition suspension

Justifying its reputation as the sporty member of the Mustang group, the Mach 1 received a standard competition suspension, with heavy-duty front and rear springs and revalved shock absorbers.

SportsRoof style

The Mach 1 was offered in one body style only, a fastback coupe known as the SportsRoof. This is characterized by a near-horizontal rear roof line, in contrast to the cut-away style of the Mustang hardtop coupe. The rear window is tinted on the Mach 1 and a rear spoiler was optional.

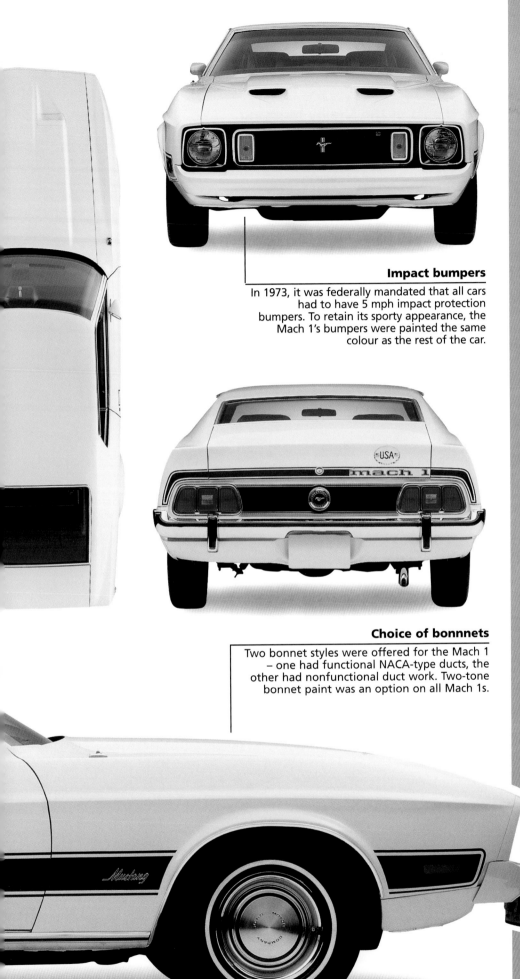

Specifications

1973 Ford Mustang Mach 1

ENGINE

Type: V8

Construction: Cast-iron block and heads

Valve gear: Two valves per cylinder operated by a single camshaft with pushrods and rocker arms

Bore and stroke: 4.00 in. x 3.00 in.

Displacement: 302 c.i.

Compression ratio: 8.5:1

Induction system: Single Motorcraft two-barrel carburettor

Maximum power: 136 bhp at 4200 rpm

Maximum torque: 232 lb-ft at 2200 rpm

Top speed: 110 mph

0–60mph: 10 sec

TRANSMISSION

Three-speed automatic

BODY/CHASSIS

Unitary monocoque construction with steel two-door coupe body

SPECIAL FEATURES

Fold-down rear seats allow access to the boot from inside. It also permits more room to carry unusually long items.

RUNNING GEAR

Steering: Recirculating ball

Front suspension: Wishbones with lower trailing links, coil springs, shock absorbers and anti-roll bar

Rear suspension: Live axle with semi-elliptic leaf springs, shock absorbers and anti-roll bar

Brakes: Discs (front), drums (rear)

Wheels: Steel, 14 in. dia.

Tires: E70 x 14 in.

DIMENSIONS

Length: 189.0 in.

Width: 74.1 in.

Height: 50.7 in.

Wheelbase: 109.0 in.

Track: 61.5 in. (front), 59.5 in. (rear)

Weight: 3090 lbs.

Impact bumpers

In 1973, it was federally mandated that all cars had to have 5 mph impact protection bumpers. To retain its sporty appearance, the Mach 1's bumpers were painted the same colour as the rest of the car.

Choice of bonnnets

Two bonnet styles were offered for the Mach 1 – one had functional NACA-type ducts, the other had nonfunctional duct work. Two-tone bonnet paint was an option on all Mach 1s.

Ford SHELBY MUSTANG GT500

If bigger was better, the GT500 was the best of the Shelby Mustang line. There was no way you could have added a bigger engine to the car, and that made sure it was the most powerful of all.

Fibreglass bonnet
A new fiberglass bonnet with functional air scoops helps to accommodate the big engine and also reduces the car's weight.

Power steering
With so much weight over the nose and with wide tyres, power steering was a very good idea. In fact you had no choice – it was a standard feature, as were the power brakes and shoulder harnesses.

Front heavy
That huge cast-iron V8 naturally made the GT500 front heavy, with a weight distribution of 58 per cent front and 42 per cent rear. It was just as well that the hood was fiberglass.

V8 engine
With the GT500, Shelby went for the biggest engine he could fit in the bay, the Police Interceptor type 428 c.i. V8. It filled the engine compartment so fully you couldn't even see the spark plugs.

Wide tyres
The GT500 needed to put as much rubber on the road as possible to cope with its power. Shelby opted for Goodyear Speedway E70-15s, a popular choice for muscle cars of the era that were rated at 140 mph.

Alloy wheels
Steel wheels were a standard feature, but these Shelby alloys were available as an option. They are very desirable today.

Adjustable shocks
The standard shocks were thrown out and replaced by Gabriel adjustables. However, the car left the Shelby works with what was considered the optimum settings.

Unique tail lights

The back of the car was distinguished from the standard Mustang fastback by different tail lights, two very wide ones replacing the two sets of triple lights. Above the lights, the trunk lid was another Shelby fiberglass part.

Specifications
1967 Ford Shelby Mustang GT500

ENGINE
Type: V8
Construction: Cast-iron block and heads
Valve gear: Two valves per cylinder operated by single block-mounted camshaft via pushrods, rockers and hydraulic lifters
Bore and stroke: 4.13 in. x 3.98 in.
Displacement: 428 c.i.
Compression ratio: 10.5:1
Induction system: Two Holley four-barrel carburettors
Maximum power: 355 bhp at 5400 rpm
Maximum torque: 420 lb-ft at 3200 rpm
Top speed: 132 mph
0–60mph: 7.0 sec

TRANSMISSION
Ford Cruise-O-Matic three-speed automatic or four-speed manual

BODY/FRAME
Unitary steel with two-door coupe body

SPECIAL FEATURES

The bonnet scoops added by Shelby were changed with each model year. They became more prominent after these rather subtle scoops on this 1967 car.

RUNNING GEAR
Steering: Recirculating ball
Front suspension: Double wishbones with adjustable Gabriel shock absorbers and 1-in. dia. anti-roll bar
Rear suspension: Live axle with semi-elliptic leaf springs
Brakes: Discs, 11.3 in. dia. (front), drums, 10 in. dia. (rear)
Wheels: Shelby alloy, 7 in. x 15 in.
Tyres: E70-15 (front and rear)

DIMENSIONS
Length: 86.6 in.
Width: 70.9 in.
Height: 49 in.
Wheelbase: 108 in.
Track: 58 in. (front and rear)
Weight: 3520 lbs.

Ford **FAIRLANE SKYLINER**

For three years Ford was the only car company brave enough to make a true mass-production car with a foldaway steel roof. It cost millions to develop, and is a real treat to see today.

Powerful V8

In 1959 the Skyliner came with a standard 292-cubic inch Mercury V8. With gas selling for around 20 cents a gallon at the time, big-blocks were popular. This car is fitted with a 352-cubic inch unit producing 300 bhp.

Folding rear deck

When the roof is folded away in the trunk, the deck is fully extended. When the roof is up, however, the end of the deck lid folds away. The end section of the deck is moved by an electric motor.

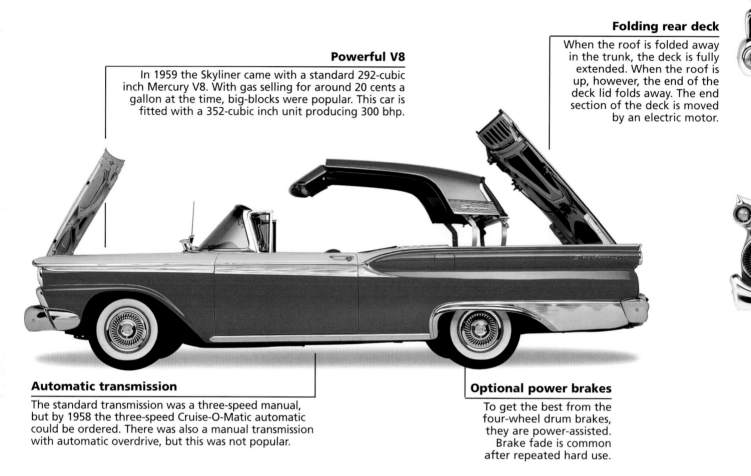

Automatic transmission

The standard transmission was a three-speed manual, but by 1958 the three-speed Cruise-O-Matic automatic could be ordered. There was also a manual transmission with automatic overdrive, but this was not popular.

Optional power brakes

To get the best from the four-wheel drum brakes, they are power-assisted. Brake fade is common after repeated hard use.

Seven electric motors

To operate the roof, seven electric motors are required. The biggest is in the trunk and operates the two very long screw jacks that raise and lower the roof. Thirteen switches, 10 solenoids, eight circuit breakers and over 600 feet of wiring serve the electric motors.

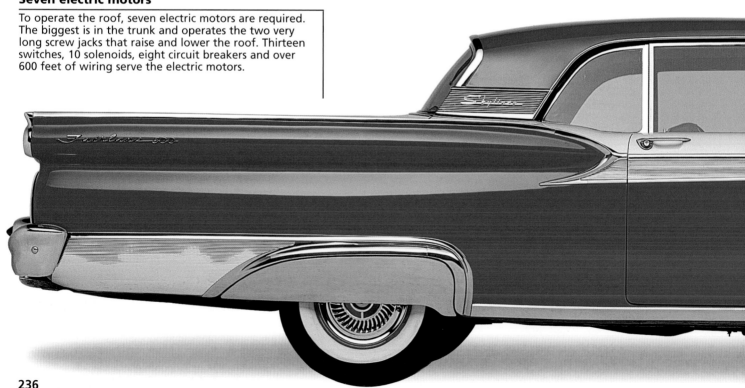

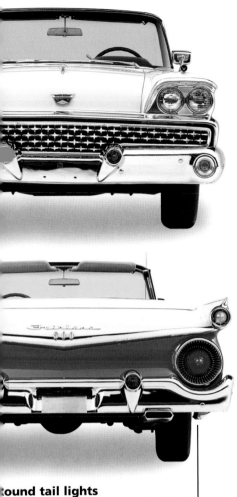

Round tail lights
One of the best styling changes made to 1959 Fords was to replace the four protruding taillights in the rectangular housings by single, large round lights. These became a trademark on early-1960s Fords.

Two-tone paintwork
The side trim of the 1957 model lent itself to a two-tone finish, and the 1958 model, with a long chrome-edged side panel, was ideal for a three-tone treatment. This panel became almost a stripe on the 1959 model.

Specifications
1959 Ford Skyliner

ENGINE
Type: V8

Construction: Cast-iron block and heads

Valve gear: Two valves per cylinder operated by a single V-mounted camshaft via pushrods and rockers

Bore and stroke: 4.00 in. x 3.50 in.

Displacement: 352 c.i.

Compression ratio: 9.6:1

Induction system: Four-barrel Holley carburetor

Maximum power: 300 bhp at 4,600 rpm

Maximum torque: 381 lb-ft at 2,800 rpm

TRANSMISSION
Three-speed Cruise-O-Matic automatic

BODY/CHASSIS
Steel X-frame chassis with steel two-door convertible body

SPECIAL FEATURES

When the roof is up, the trunk is quite spacious.

With the top up the Skyliner looks like a normal hardtop car.

RUNNING GEAR
Steering: Recirculating ball

Front suspension: Double wishbones with coil springs and telescopic shock absorbers

Rear suspension: Live axle with semi-elliptic leaf springs and telescopic shock absorbers

Brakes: Drums (front and rear)

Wheels: Steel discs, 14-in. dia

Tires: 6.00 x 14

DIMENSIONS
Length: 208.1 in. **Width:** 76.6 in.

Height: 56.5 in. **Wheelbase:** 118.0 in.

Track: 59.0 in. (front), 56.5 in. (rear)

Weight: 4,064 lbs.

Ford THUNDERBIRD

The T-Bird was one of the smallest and most striking cars Ford built in the U.S. in many years. Ford called it a 'personal luxury' car rather than a sports car. It was never intended to be a serious rival to Jaguars or Ferraris.

Choice of transmissions

There was a choice of three different transmissions: a three-speed Fordomatic automatic or the three-speed manual; and perhaps the best option—a manual transmission with high overdrive ratios.

Cooling flaps

The 1955 models had poor ventilation, so Ford added a flap in the front fenders which could be opened to let cold air into the footwells.

Wrap-around windshield

Like the Chevy Corvette, which came out two years before it, the T-Bird has a wrap-around-type front windshield, a design which avoided the blind spot caused by conventional front windshield pillars.

V8 engine

From the beginning, the Thunderbird had a V8 engine. The prototype had only a 256-cubic inch engine with 160 bhp, but that was enlarged for production and became steadily more powerful year by year. By 1957, the most powerful engine—apart from the rare supercharged V8—was the 285-bhp, 312-cubic inch V8.

14/15-inch wheels

For its first two years, the Thunderbird ran on tall, 15-inch wheels. For the 1957 model year, they changed to 14-inch wheels which made the cars look sleeker.

Stretched rear

The original 1955 Thunderbird is very short, so the spare wheel had to be carried above the bumper. For 1957, Ford redesigned the back of the car to make the trunk longer so the spare wheel could be carried inside.

Open hardtop or convertible

As standard, the Thunderbird came with a bolt-on fiberglass hardtop. The car could also be ordered with a folding rayon convertible top instead of the hardtop, or in addition to it, for an extra $290.

Specifications
1957 Ford Thunderbird

ENGINE

Type: V8

Construction: Cast-iron block and heads

Valve gear: Two valves per cylinder operated via pushrods and rockers from a single block-mounted camshaft

Bore and stroke: 3.74 in. x 3.31 in.

Displacement: 292 c.i.

Compression ratio: 8.1:1

Induction system: two- or four-barrel carburetor

Maximum power: 212 bhp at 4,400 rpm

Maximum torque: 297 lb-ft at 2,700 rpm

TRANSMISSION

Three-speed manual with optional overdrive or three-speed Fordomatic automatic

BODY/CHASSIS

Separate cruciform steel chassis with steel two-door body: choice of removable hardtop or convertible roof

SPECIAL FEATURES

Exhausts exiting through holes in the bumper are a typical 1950s American styling feature.

From 1956, the hardtop was available with 'porthole' windows to improve rear three-quarter vision.

RUNNING GEAR

Steering: Power-assisted recirculating ball

Front suspension: Double wishbones, coil springs and telescopic shocks

Rear suspension: Live axle with semi-elliptic leaf springs and telescopic shocks

Brakes: Drums front and rear with optional power assistance

Wheels: Steel 14 in. dia.

Tires: Crossply, 7.5 in. x 14 in.

DIMENSIONS

Length: 181.4 in.   **Width:** 70.3 in.

Height: 51.6 in.   **Wheelbase:** 102 in.

Track: 56 in. (front and rear)

Weight: 3,050 lbs.

Rear fenders

Setting the 1957 T-Bird apart from the 1955 and 1956 cars was the introduction of tail fins. This was the start of the fin era in the U.S., but those on the Thunderbirds are a little more restrained than those on some other models of the period.

Ford TORINO COBRA

From any angle, the Torino Cobra has presence. It also has unrivaled handling, comfort and 0–60 mph acceleration. Other muscle cars may be quicker, but few offered so much in a single, tailor-made package.

Wicked 429

In standard form the 429 engine is rated at 360 bhp, although the Cobra Jet version produces 370 bhp thanks to a hotter camshaft, free-flowing cylinder heads and a high-riser intake manifold. The baddest engine option was the 375 bhp version with four-bolt mains, forged pistons, solid cam and larger carburetor. This model happens to be the intermediate model with 370 bhp.

Four-speed transmission

Backing the 429 engine is a standard four-speed transmission, including a Hurst T-shaped shifter. This combination made the Cobra a threat to any car on the street, even with the most average driver behind the wheel.

Beefed-up suspension

Like most muscle machines of its period, the Cobra has standard suspension which has been uprated with a thicker front anti-roll bar and stiffer springs and shocks. The 2-inch wider track results in one of the best-handling muscle cars.

Swoopy styling

The 1970-1971 Torinos are arguably the best-looking, with their fluid styling and fastback roof. Although they look aerodynamic, tests in stock car racing proved that the older 1969 styling was more efficient and therefore Ford continued using 1969 Talladegas on the big NASCAR ovals.

Low rear axle gearing

If equipped with the Drag Pack, Torino Cobras came with either Traction-Lok 3.91:1 rear axle ratio or with the deadly Detroit locker 4.30:1 gears.

Ram Air induction

With the addition of the shaker scoop, the engine became known as the 429 Cobra Jet Ram Air. The scoop attaches directly to the engine's air cleaner.

Specifications

1970 Ford Torino Cobra

ENGINE

Type: V8

Construction: Cast-iron block and heads

Valve gear: Two valves per cylinder operated by pushrods and rockers

Bore and stroke: 4.36 in. x 3.59 in.

Displacement: 429 c.i.

Compression ratio: 11.3:1

Induction system: Single Holley four-barrel carburetor

Maximum power: 370 bhp at 5,400 rpm

Maximum torque: 450 lb-ft at 3,400 rpm

Top speed: 118 mph

0–60 mph: 5.9 sec.

TRANSMISSION

Borg-Warner T10 four-speed with Hurst shifter

BODY/CHASSIS

Unitary steel monocoque with two-door fastback body

SPECIAL FEATURES

The Ram Air induction quickly forced cool air into the carburetor.

A four-speed manual is standard, as is this Hurst T-handle shifter.

RUNNING GEAR

Steering: Recirculating ball

Front suspension: Unequal length wishbones with coil springs, telescopic shock absorbers and anti-roll bar

Rear suspension: Live 9-in. axle with multi-leaf springs and staggered telescopic shock absorbers

Brakes: Discs, 10-in. dia. (front), finned drums, 9-in. dia. (rear)

Wheels: Steel, 15-in. dia.

Tires: ZBF Goodrich Radial T/A, F60-15

DIMENSIONS

Length: 203.6 in.   **Width:** 80.0 in.

Height: 49.3 in.   **Wheelbase:** 117.0 in.

Track: 60.3 in. (front), 58.4 in. (rear)

Weight: 4,000 lbs.

Graham **HOLLYWOOD** 🇺🇸

Graham-Paige chose the four-door Beverly Sedan shape rather than the two-door convertible from the various Cord bodystyles because it was intended to make the car a popular, mass-market contender.

Side-valve engine

The Graham-Paige company had used six-cylinder, side-valve engines supplied by Continental since the late 1920s when the three Graham brothers took over Paige-Detroit to form Graham-Paige. The 218-cubic inch six used for the Graham Hollywood was by no means the largest. Previous models featured a 287-cubic inch six.

Pod headlights

The idea behind the Graham Hollywood was to produce a simpler, and less expensive car than the Cord. One of the complicated items to be dispensed with was the pop-up headlights. The lights were replaced by free-standing units mounted in pods on top of the fenders.

Three-speed transmission

While the Cord has a complicated remote electromagnetic-vacuum gear shifter with its own miniature gate (a system that could also be used as a pre-selector transmission), the Graham Hollywood uses a much simpler conventional manual unit. Like many Detroit cars of the time, the transmission has a column shift.

Split windshield

Technology to produce compound curved glass had not been perfected in 1940. Even Cadillacs had split windshields, and the Cord and Graham Hollywood followed suit. The design is mirrored in the back window, which is also a two-piece split unit.

Live rear axle

With a switch from front to rear drive, the Cord beam rear axle was replaced by a live unit and differential, located and sprung on semi-elliptic leaf springs like most contemporary automobiles.

Specifications
1941 Graham Hollywood

ENGINE

Type: Inline six-cylinder

Construction: Cast-iron block and alloy head

Valve gear: Two inline sidevalves per cylinder operated by a single block-mounted camshaft and solid valve lifters

Bore and stroke: 3.25 in. x 4.38 in.

Displacement: 218 c.i.

Compression ratio: 7.1:1

Induction system: Single Carter carburetor with Graham supercharger

Maximum power: 124 bhp at 4,000 rpm

Maximum torque: 182 lb-ft at 2,400 rpm

Top speed: 89 mph

0–60 mph: 14.6 sec.

TRANSMISSION

Three-speed manual

BODY/CHASSIS

Separate box-section steel frame with four-door sedan body

SPECIAL FEATURES

A split rear window is standard on all Graham Hollywoods.

In addition to fixed headlights, the Graham also has a different grill.

RUNNING GEAR

Steering: Worm-and-roller

Front suspension: Beam axle with semi-elliptic leaf springs and telescopic shock absorbers

Rear suspension: Live axle with semi-elliptic leaf springs and telescopic shock absorbers

Brakes: Drums (front and rear)

Wheels: Pressed steel discs, 5 x 16 in. dia.

Tires: Bias-ply, 6.00 x 16

DIMENSIONS

Length: 190.5 in.   **Width:** 71.0 in.

Height: 60.5 in.   **Wheelbase:** 115.0 in.

Track: 57.5 in. (front), 61.0 in. (rear)

Weight: 3,240 lbs.

Hispano-Suiza H6B

The style and appearance of the Hispano-Suiza H6B depended entirely on what sort of bodywork the customer wanted. That could range from elegant open tourers to formal closed sedans.

Updraft carburetor

For such a superbly designed engine, the breathing is still restricted. Fuel is fed through a double Solex updraft carburetor with a long pipe to one end of the intake manifold, making fuel delivery uneven to all of the cylinders. The exhaust manifold on the other side of the head is also poorly shaped.

Six-cylinder engine

Hispano-Suiza's great model H airplane engine powered the fast SPAD fighters of World War I. Most of the quality was found in its 6.6-liter six-cylinder, alloy-cased, wet-liner car engine. The valve adjustment is very clever and also follows airplane engine design.

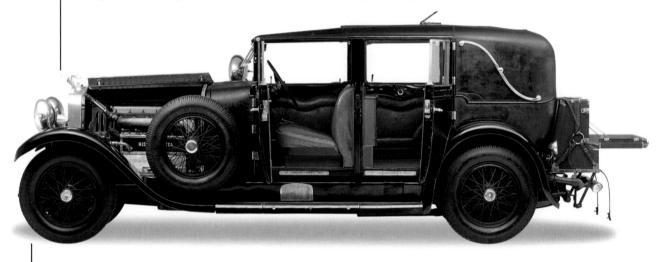

Solid front axle

The H6B has a solid-beam axle under the chassis rails. It is both suspended and located by semi-elliptic leaf springs. There is a shorter section of spring ahead of the axle to give better location.

Servo brakes

A small drum is driven off the transmission with its brake shoe attached to the brake pedal. The lining is also attached by a rod to the other brakes and as the brake is applied, the rotating drum grabs and moves the lever to the other brakes.

Wire wheels

There was no doubt that the H6B would have anything other than center-lock wire spoke wheels. They had to be large to allow room for the enormous brake drums and to give the ground clearance required in the days when roads were very poor.

Specifications
1920 Hispano-Suiza H6B

ENGINE

Type: In-line six-cylinder

Construction: Alloy crankcase with forged-steel liners and alloy head

Valve gear: Two valves per cylinder operated by a single overhead camshaft

Bore and stroke: 3.94 in. x 5.51 in.

Displacement: 6,597 cc

Compression ratio: 4.5:1

Induction system: Twin Solex carburetors

Maximum power: 135 bhp at 3,000 rpm

Maximum torque: Not quoted

Top speed: 85 mph

0–60 mph: 18.9 sec.

TRANSMISSION

Three-speed

BODY/CHASSIS

Separate channel-section steel perimeter chassis with four-door sedan body

SPECIAL FEATURES

Despite their size, the headlights are only moderately effective.

Trunk had a literal meaning back in the early 20th century.

RUNNING GEAR

Steering: Screw-and-nut

Front suspension: Beam axle with semi-elliptic leaf springs and friction shock absorbers

Rear suspension: Live axle with semi-elliptic leaf springs and torque tube; later with friction shock absorbers

Brakes: Alloy-cased drums, 15.75-in. dia. (front and rear)

Wheels: Wire spoke, 26-in. dia.

Tires: 35 x 5 in.

DIMENSIONS

Length: 192.0 in   **Width:** 73.2 in.

Height: 73.3 in.   **Wheelbase:** 146.0 in

Track: 57.0 in. (front), 57.0 in. (rear)

Weight: 4,250 lbs.

Honda **NSX-R**

Don't be fooled by its looks. The NSX-R retains the beautiful Ferrari-inspired lines of the standard NSX road car, but underneath there is a blueprinted engine and suspension almost as stiff as a racing car's.

V6 engine

For the Type-R, the 3.0-liter DOHC V6 was fully balanced and blueprinted to withstand competition use. Advertised power and torque remained virtually unchanged at 280 bhp and 209 lb-ft.

Alloy wheels

Not only are the NSX's wheels made from alloy, but they are forged rather than cast to give extra strength. They are also lighter than typical cast-aluminum wheels. The spare tire was deleted to save weight.

VTEC-variable valve timing and lift

By 5,800 rpm, the intake and exhaust valves open farther and longer, thus increasing the engine's power. A hydraulically actuated mechanism locks the cam followers to follow the high lift cam profile.

Weight-saving program

To save 268 lbs., Honda took drastic measures. It scrapped the air conditioning, underseal, stereo, the standard seats and other pieces of electrical equipment.

Wishbone rear suspension

Very wide-based wishbones are used at the rear, and what looks like a steering track rod on each side is in fact an adjustable arm to change the toe angle of the wheels. This gives a measure of passive rear-wheel steer, toeing-in under cornering load.

Alloy body

There was little scope to lighten the body, except for the plastic-covered steel bumpers. For the best compromise between strength and weight, they were changed to alloy.

Specifications

1993 Honda NSX Type-R

ENGINE

Type: V6

Construction: Alloy block and heads

Valve gear: Four valves per cylinder operated by two belt-driven overhead camshafts per bank of cylinders with VTEC-variable valve lift

Bore and stroke: 3.54 in. x 3.07 in.

Displacement: 2,997 cc

Compression ratio: 10.2:1

Induction system: Electronic fuel injection

Maximum power: 280 bhp at 7,300 rpm

Maximum torque: 209 lb-ft at 5,400 rpm

Top speed: 169 mph

0–60 mph: 5.1 sec

TRANSMISSION

Five-speed manual

BODY/CHASSIS

Aluminum-alloy monocoque with alloy two-door coupe body

SPECIAL FEATURES

The rear window lifts up to give better access to the NSX's midmounted engine.

The alloy wheels are unique to the NSX Type-R and are ultra-lightweight.

RUNNING GEAR

Steering: Rack-and-pinion

Front suspension: Double wishbones with coil springs, telescopic shock absorbers and anti-roll bar

Rear suspension: Double wishbones with coil springs, telescopic shock absorbers and anti-roll bar

Brakes: Vented discs, 11.1-in. dia.

Wheels: Alloy 6.5 x 15 in. (front), 8.0 x 16 in. (rear)

Tires: 205/50 ZR15 (front), 225/50 ZR16 (rear)

DIMENSIONS

Length: 173.4 in. **Width:** 71.3 in.

Height: 46.1 in. **Wheelbase:** 99.6 in.

Track: 59.4 in. (front), 60.2 in. (rear)

Weight: 2,712 lbs.

HRG **1100/1500**

The HRG was also a formidable performer in off-road motoring events such as trials. Along with the pre-war Frazer Nash, it is the quintessential, no-nonsense, British sports car.

Singer-derived engine

The basic engine block almost invariably came from Singer, a good choice at the time since the engines are well-suited to the sporty role. HRG performed its own head work and fitted a new crankshaft that reduced the stroke so capacity fell below the 1.5-liter limit in motorsports.

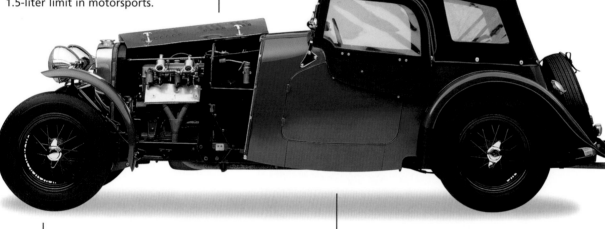

Good ground clearance

Trialing enthusiasts were grateful for the generous ground clearance offered by the HRG chassis. At six inches, this was enough to ford the sort of mud tracks found in trial events and enough to dodge protruding rocks.

Wire wheels

The HRG has classic wire wheels. Initially, these came in vintage-style measurements: 17 inches in diameter and shod with very narrow 4.75-inch tires. However, later cars have 16-inch wheels and 5.50-inch tires.

Two wheelbase lengths

Depending on engine size, the HRG chassis came in two lengths. The 1100 model uses a 99.5-inch wheelbase; the larger 1500 model measures in at 103 inches and is correspondingly longer overall.

Vintage bodystyle

In style, the bodywork is a throwback to the early 1930s. Each HRG was built by hand, using aluminum formed into various styles around the same theme. There are cutaway doors and a squared-off tail. There is even a surprising amount of luggage room behind the two bucket-type seats.

Specifications
1939 HRG 1500

ENGINE
Type: Inline four-cylinder

Construction: Cast-iron block and head

Valve gear: Two valves per cylinder operated by a single overhead camshaft

Bore and stroke: 2.68 in. x 4.06 in.

Displacement: 1,496 cc

Compression ratio: 7.0:1

Induction system: Two SU carburetors

Maximum power: 61 bhp at 4,800 rpm

Maximum torque: 77 lb-ft at 2,800 rpm

Top speed: 84 mph

0–60 mph: 18.1 sec.

TRANSMISSION
Four-speed manual

BODY/CHASSIS
Separate chassis with aluminum two-door sports body

SPECIAL FEATURES

An old-fashioned grease gun is included in the engine bay.

The HRG uses the common twin SU carburetor setup.

RUNNING GEAR
Steering: Worm-and-roller

Front suspension: Beam axle with quarter-elliptic leaf springs and shock absorbers

Rear suspension: Live axle with semi-elliptic leaf springs and shock absorbers

Brakes: Drums (front and rear)

Wheels: Wires, 17-in. dia.

Tires: 4.75 x 17

DIMENSIONS
Length: 144.0 in. **Width:** 55.0 in.

Height: 52.0 in. **Wheelbase:** 103.0 in.

Track: 48.0 in. (front), 45.0 in. (rear)

Weight: 1,620 lbs.

Hudson HORNET

The 'Step-Down' Hudson range was a real revolution. The Hornet's innovative body/chassis construction offered fine handling while its huge engine was highly tunable. It was America's finest from the early 1950s.

Choice of body styles

The Hornet was sold in three basic body styles: a four-door sedan – easily the most popular – a two-door coupe and a two-door Convertible Brougham. The convertible is the rarest, selling only 550 examples in its most popular year (1951).

Straight-six engine

While the 'Big Three' Detroit automakers were discovering the V8 engine, Hudson stuck to its straight-six. It expanded its Super Six engine to 308 cubic inches and provided enough torque and power to challenge and beat the V8 powerplants in NASCAR racing.

'Step-Down' construction

The floorpan of the body sits below the chassis in a semi-unitary construction called Monobilt. Passengers have to step over the chassis rails to get in, leading to the nickname 'Step-Down'. There is still over 8 inches of ground clearance.

Enclosed rear wheels

Because the construction used dual rear chassis outriggers, one either side of each of the rear wheels, it was natural to adopt fully-enclosed rear wheels. Changing wheels is a challenge, though, as they had to drop right down.

Low roofline

The most dramatic part of the Hornet's overall shape is its ultra-low roofline. The windows resemble tapering slits and the sloping line is echoed by a similarly-profiled body side moulding. The low roofline was made possible by keeping the 'Step-Down' floor low.

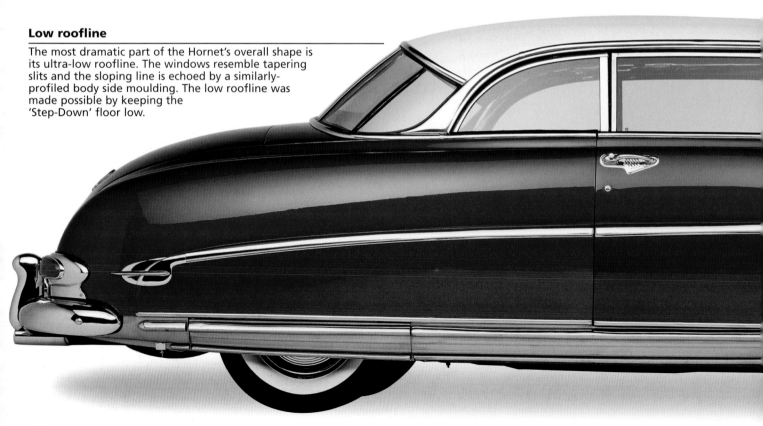

Specifications

1952 Hudson Hornet

ENGINE

Type: In-line six-cylinder

Construction: Cast-iron block and aluminum cylinder head

Valve gear: Two valves per cylinder operated by a single camshaft

Bore and stroke: 3.81 in. x 4.50 in.

Displacement: 308 c.i.

Compression ratio: 7.2:1

Induction system: Single carburetor

Maximum power: 145 bhp at 3,800 rpm

Maximum torque: 257 lb-ft at 1,800 rpm

TRANSMISSION

Four-speed manual or three-speed automatic

BODY/CHASSIS

Steel unitary construction with steel coupe, convertible or four-door sedan body

SPECIAL FEATURES

Twin carburetors gave the powerful 1952 Twin H Hornets their name.

The sun visor was a popular dealer-installed item in the early 1950s.

RUNNING GEAR

Steering: Recirculating ball

Front suspension: Wishbones with coil springs and telescopic shock absorbers

Rear suspension: Live axle with semi-elliptic leaf springs and telescopic shock absorbers

Brakes: Drums (front and rear)

Wheels: Steel, 15-in. dia.

Tires: 5 x 15 in.

DIMENSIONS

Length: 201.5 in.   **Width:** 77.1 in.

Height: 60.4 in.   **Wheelbase:** 123.9 in.

Track: 58.5 in. (front), 55.5 in. (rear)

Weight: 3,600 lbs.

Streamlined shape

Chief designer Art Kibiger knew that the Monobilt body could not easily be updated, so he designed a car that would stay current as long as possible. It was much lower and wider than other Detroit offerings and received a rapturous reception.

Hudson SUPER SIX

No expense was spared during the creation of this one-of-a-kind Hudson Super Six. The list of modifications is almost endless, and the result is a striking and unique car.

Custom hinges
Even the trunk-lid hinges have been altered, with the deck lid hinging to the right on opening.

Sun visor
Despite the radical contemporary modifications, this Hudson is fitted with a period 1940s sun visor. On this car it is perfectly blended into the roof line.

Special wheels
Full dish aluminum wheels, like those used on Bonneville flats racers, are fitted and stand out against the dark paintwork.

Shaved doors
The doors have been 'shaved' of their handles and locks. Thanks to modern electronics, this lead sled uses a device that electronically activcates latches hidden inside the doors to allow easy entry.

Fastback shape
Fastbacks were in vogue in the late 1940s. At the time of its introduction the 'step-down' Hudson had one of the sleekest shapes around. A low center of gravity ensures good handling.

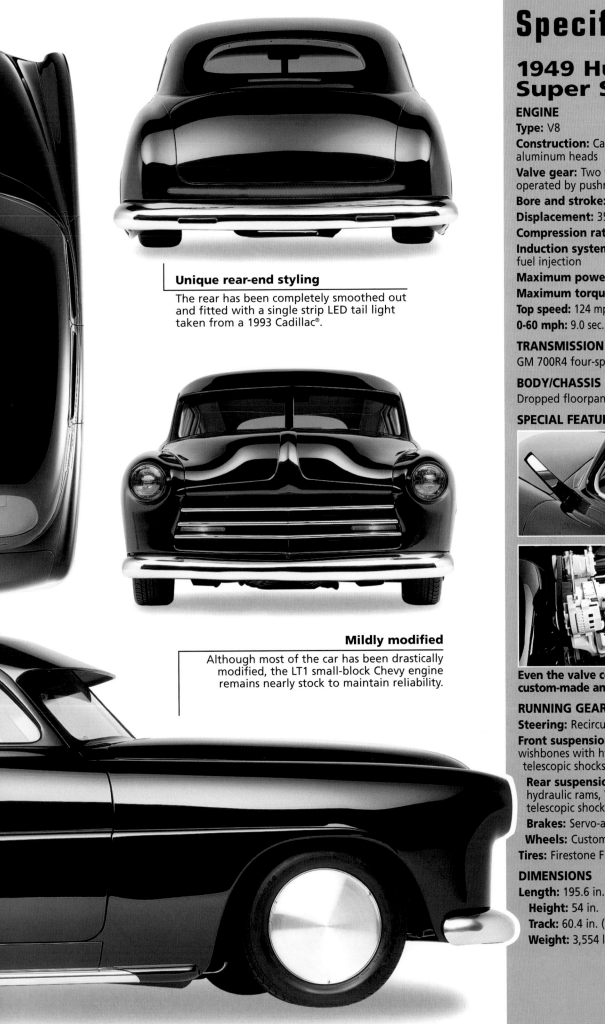

Unique rear-end styling

The rear has been completely smoothed out and fitted with a single strip LED tail light taken from a 1993 Cadillac®.

Mildly modified

Although most of the car has been drastically modified, the LT1 small-block Chevy engine remains nearly stock to maintain reliability.

Specifications

1949 Hudson Super Six

ENGINE
Type: V8

Construction: Cast-iron block with aluminum heads

Valve gear: Two valves per cylinder operated by pushrods and rockers

Bore and stroke: 4 in. x 3.48 in.

Displacement: 350 c.i.

Compression ratio: 10.5:1

Induction system: Multiport electronic fuel injection

Maximum power: 310 bhp at 5,000 rpm

Maximum torque: 340 lb-ft at 2,400 rpm

Top speed: 124 mph

0-60 mph: 9.0 sec.

TRANSMISSION
GM 700R4 four-speed automatic

BODY/CHASSIS
Dropped floorpan monocoque

SPECIAL FEATURES

Flip-out door mirrors are a unique feature on this customized lead sled.

Even the valve covers have been custom-made and include Hudson script.

RUNNING GEAR
Steering: Recirculating ball

Front suspension: Unequal length wishbones with hydraulic rams and telescopic shocks

Rear suspension: Live axle with hydraulic rams, Watt linkage, and telescopic shocks

Brakes: Servo-assisted drums

Wheels: Custom alloy, 15-in. dia.

Tires: Firestone Firehawk F670-15.

DIMENSIONS
Length: 195.6 in. **Width:** 73.4 in.

Height: 54 in. **Wheelbase:** 124 in.

Track: 60.4 in. (front), 57.6 in. (rear)

Weight: 3,554 lbs.

Hudson **TERRAPLANE**

Even though Terraplanes were not intended to be the most flamboyant and stylish cars on the road, features like the attractive grill helped make these cars stand out in a crowd.

Side-valve engine

In an L-head sidevalve engine like the 3.5-liter Hudson six, both the intake and exhaust valves are on one side of the engine. Effectively, they work upsidedown, compared with an overhead-valve engine, with the combustion chambers in the head but to one side of the engine over the valves.

Low-pressure tires

To make its cars as comfortable as possible, Hudson had a tendency to fit larger, wider tires than its rival companies. These also ran at a relatively low pressure to improve the ride.

Welded-on body

Although the Terraplane had an unusual and immensely strong steel chassis for its time, Hudson made the whole car stiffer by welding on the all-steel bodywork at more than 30 points rather than simply bolting it in place like other manufacturers were doing.

Solid front axle

Hudson's normal front-suspension system was more complicated than most. It fitted a radius arm on each side that was bolted to a solid axle. These ran back from the axle to pivots on the frame and provided better location than the semi-elliptic leaf springs could manage by themselves. They also provide a measure of antidive under severe braking.

Reserve brake system

In case the hydraulic system failed (and these were the days before dual circuits), Hudson developed Duo-Automatic as a safety feature. Should the pedal get near the floor, it operates a cable to activate the rear brakes.

Specifications
1936 Hudson Terraplane

ENGINE
Type: Inline six cylinder

Construction: Cast-iron block and head

Valve gear: Two valves operated by single camshaft mounted on side of block

Bore and stroke: 3.0 in. x 5.0 in.

Displacement: 212 c.i.

Compression ratio: 6.0:1

Induction system: Single downdraft Carter carburetor

Maximum power: 88 bhp at 3,800 rpm

Maximum torque: Not quoted

Top speed: 80 mph

0–60 mph: 23.2 sec.

TRANSMISSION
Three-speed manual

BODY/CHASSIS
Separate channel-section frame with X-brace and welded-on steel body

SPECIAL FEATURES

The Hudson Terraplane was known for its ornate details such as this interesting grill ornament.

A fold-out rear rumble seat can easily accommodate two people in total comfort.

RUNNING GEAR
Steering: Worm-and-sector

Front suspension: Solid axle with radius rods, semi-elliptic leaf springs and telescopic shock absorbers

Rear suspension: Live axle with semi-elliptic leaf springs and telescopic shock absorbers

Brakes: Drums (front and rear)

Wheels: Pressed steel, 16-in. dia.

Tires: 6.00 x 16

DIMENSIONS
Length: 195.0 in.   **Width:** 70.0 in.

Height: 70.8 in.   **Wheelbase:** 115.0 in.

Track: 56.0 in. (front), 57.5 in. (rear)

Weight: 2,740 lbs.

Invicta S-TYPE

Invicta showed what could be done with outsourced components. Separate manufacturers supplied the mechanics and the bodywork but everything came together to make a 1930s supercar with lots of character.

Coachbuilt bodies

Different bodies could be specified for the 4½ Litre's chassis, but the S-type typically had long, low bodywork built either by Vanden Plas or Carbodies Coachbuilders.

Six-cylinder engine

The Meadows company supplied engines to a number of car makers. Tuning was easy because of its advanced, crossflow design with exhaust and intake manifolds on different sides of the engine.

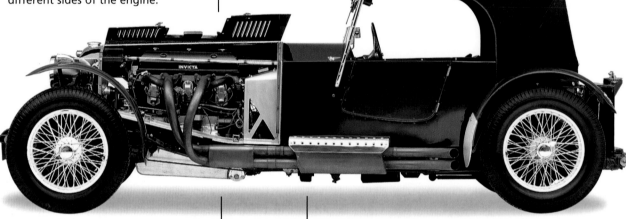

Four-speed transmission

With so much torque the engine can use top gear at virtually any speed. But to get the best from the transmission, double clutching is necessary.

Flexible exhaust pipes

The flexible exhaust pipes are very stylish. They are connected to the exhaust manifold and project out of one side of the long hood. The hood is hinged in the center and can be opened from either side.

Underslung chassis

The standard Invicta 4½ is a tall, upright model, but the S-type is much more low slung and streamlined. This is achieved by designing the chassis rails to curve under the rear axle. This arrangement requires very stiff springs and limited wheel travel to stop the axle from hitting the chassis.

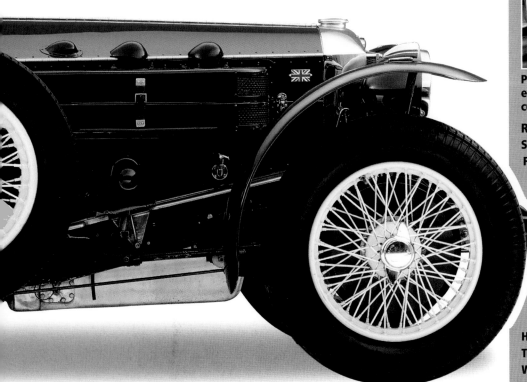

Specifications
1930 Invicta S-Type

ENGINE

Type: Meadows in-line six cylinder

Construction: Alloy block and head

Valve gear: Two valves per cylinder operated by a single block-mounted camshaft via pushrods and rockers

Bore and stroke: 3.48 in. x 4.75 in.

Displacement: 4,467 cc

Compression ratio: 8:1

Induction system: Twin SU carburetors

Maximum power: 115 bhp at 3,200 rpm

Maximum torque: Not quoted

Top speed: 100 mph

0–60 mph: 14.4 sec.

TRANSMISSION

Meadows four-speed manual

BODY/CHASSIS

Steel ladder-frame chassis with separate open coachbuilt body

SPECIAL FEATURES

The side mounted handbrake is easily accessible. It is located outside the car, right next to the spare tire.

Protective covers over the side-mounted exhaust pipes prevent burns on over-curious passengers.

RUNNING GEAR

Steering: Marles worm-and-roller

Front suspension: Beam axle with semi-elliptic leaf springs and adjustable shocks

Rear suspension: Live axle with semi-elliptic leaf springs and adjustable friction shock absorbers

Brakes: Mechanically operated finned drums (front and rear)

Wheels: Wire spoke

Tires: Dunlop 19.0 x 6.00 in.

DIMENSIONS

Length: 156.0 in.   **Width:** 60.0 in.

Height: 52.0 in.   **Wheelbase:** 118.0 in.

Track: 52.0 in. (front and rear)

Weight: 3,248 lbs.

Iso **GRIFO**

Iso may not have the heritage of some of its rivals, but for a brief moment in the 1960s, the Italian company produced one of the fastest production supercars in the world.

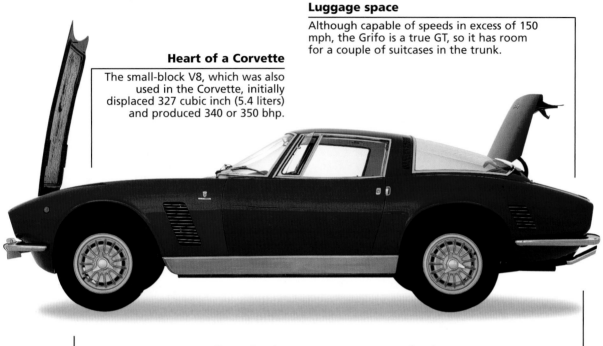

Heart of a Corvette

The small-block V8, which was also used in the Corvette, initially displaced 327 cubic inch (5.4 liters) and produced 340 or 350 bhp.

Luggage space

Although capable of speeds in excess of 150 mph, the Grifo is a true GT, so it has room for a couple of suitcases in the trunk.

Alloy wheels

Most Grifos are fitted with these handsome cast-alloy wheels, complete with knock-off spinners.

Dual exhaust

To exploit the V8s power, dual exhaust is mandatory and gives a fantastic exhaust note.

Excellent visibility

A large rear window offers great visibility and came with a standard built-in defroster.

Wishbone suspension

The Grifo followed 1960s supercar practice by using unequal length wishbones and coil springs.

Elegant shape

The Grifo was designed by a young Giorgetto Giugiaro, who has been responsible for many of the world's most elegant cars.

Specifications

1967 Iso Grifo

ENGINE

Type: V8

Construction: Cast-iron block and heads

Valve gear: Two valves per cylinder operated by pushrods and rocker arms

Bore and stroke: 4.0 in. x 3.25 in.

Displacement: 5,359 cc

Compression ratio: 10.5:1

Induction system: Single four-barrel Holley carburetor

Maximum power: 350 bhp at 5,800 rpm

Maximum torque: 360 lb-ft at 3,600 rpm

Top speed: 163 mph

0–60 mph: 6.4 sec.

TRANSMISSION

ZF five-speed manual

BODY/CHASSIS

Monocoque two-door coupe

SPECIAL FEATURES

Side scoops on the front fenders are functional and vent hot air from the engine bay.

Bertone was responsible for building the beautiful coupe body.

RUNNING GEAR

Steering: Burman recirculating ball

Front suspension: Upper and lower wishbones with coil springs and telescopic shocks

Rear suspension: De Dion axle with coil springs, telescopic shocks, anti-roll bar, Watt linkage, and radius arms

Brakes: Servo-assisted disc brakes all around

Wheels: Cast-alloy knock-off

Tires: Pirelli Cinturato 205HS/15

DIMENSIONS

Length: 174.7 in.   **Width:** 69.5 in.

Height: 47 in.   **Wheelbase:** 106.3 in.

Track: 55.5 in. (front and rear)

Weight: 3,036 lbs.

Jaguar **D-TYPE**

Jaguar's D-type broke new ground with its semi-monocoque construction and aerodynamic design. It was perfectly at home on the fast circuit of Le Mans, where it won for three consecutive years (1955–1957).

Dry-sump lubrication

Although the D-type's XK engine is essentially identical to that used in Jaguar's roadgoing sports cars, it has a dry sump rather than a conventional wet one. The oil is kept in a separate tank and circulated by a pump, which prevents oil surge during high-speed cornering.

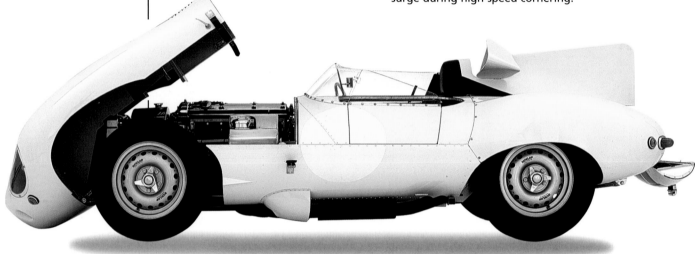

Disc brakes front and rear

Jaguar pioneered the use of disc brakes in motor racing with the C-type. The Dunlop system was also used in the D-type, being employed both front and rear.

Two-seater bodywork

Racing regulations decreed that the D-type had to be a two-seater. In reality, it raced with just a driver; a fixed cover was put over the second seat to aid aerodynamics.

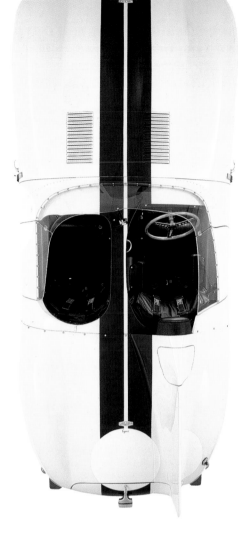

Rear stabilizing fin

Part of the aerodynamic package designed by ex-Bristol Aircraft aerodynamicist Malcolm Sayer is the fin that runs back from behind the driver's headrest. This provides important directional stability when racing on very fast circuits like Le Mans.

Monocoque center section

To give it the very stiff but light structure needed for a racing car, the D-type pioneered the use of an alloy monocoque to replace the spaceframe chassis used on the C-type. It is not a full monocoque, however, as the engine and front suspension are held in a separate subframe.

Specifications

1957 Jaguar D-type*

ENGINE

Type: In-line six

Construction: Cast-iron block and alloy head

Valve gear: Two valves per cylinder operated by two overhead camshafts

Bore and stroke: 3.27 in. x 4.17 in.

Displacement: 3,442 cc

Compression ratio: 9.0:1

Induction system: Three Weber sidedraft carburetors

Maximum power: 250 bhp at 6,000 rpm

Maximum torque: 242 lb-ft at 4,000 rpm

Top speed: 162 mph

0–60 mph: 5.4 sec.

TRANSMISSION

Four-speed manual

BODY/CHASSIS

Center monocoque with separate front subframe

SPECIAL FEATURES

The spare wheel is stored in a small trunk which hinges down for access.

A leather strap on each side keeps the clamshell hood secured.

RUNNING GEAR

Steering: Rack-and-pinion

Front suspension: Double wishbones with longitudinal torsion bars and telescopic shock absorbers

Rear suspension: Live axle with single transverse torsion bar, trailing links, single A-bracket and telescopic shock absorbers

Brakes: Dunlop discs (front and rear)

Wheels: Dunlop light alloy Center-lock, 5.5 x 16 in.

Tires: Dunlop racing, 6.50 x 16 in.

DIMENSIONS

Length: 154.0 in. **Width:** 65.4 in.

Height: 44.0 in. **Wheelbase:** 90.0 in.

Track: 50.0 in. (front), 48.0 in. (rear)

Weight: 2,460 lbs.

* Model illustrated is a Lynx replica

Jaguar **E-TYPE LIGHTWEIGHT**

Following the racing success of the great Jaguar C-Type and D-Type was never going to be easy, and the E-Type had to be radically transformed by lightening it significantly to be competitive.

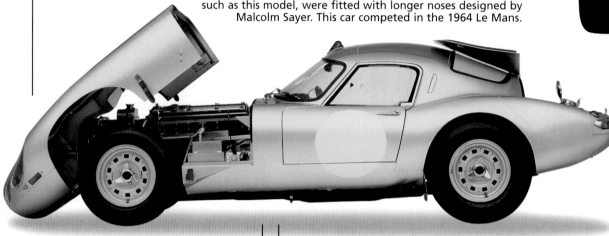

Alternative nose treatments

Most Lightweights had a hood like that of the roadgoing E-Type, except that it was made of aluminum. Several race cars, such as this model, were fitted with longer noses designed by Malcolm Sayer. This car competed in the 1964 Le Mans.

Bigger brakes

Even the standard roadgoing E-Type had all-around disc brakes, so all the Lightweight needed were slightly larger brake discs and uprated calipers.

Choice of rear axle formats

Some Lightweights used the conventional Power-Lok differential, but others used ZF or Thornton units. There was a choice of rear axle ratios depending on how you planned to use the E-Type.

Fixed hardtop

The Lightweights were all based on the lighter open-topped body but to add extra rigidity they were all fitted with an aluminum non-removable hardtop. Usually the shape echoed that of the road car's hardtop, but an alternative 'low-drag' fastback was also designed by aerodynamicist Malcolm Sayer for fast events such as Le Mans. The shape of the roof on this Lindner Nocker Lightweight was unique.

All-aluminum body

While the roadgoing E-Type had a steel monocoque and body panels, the Lightweight used aluminum exclusively throughout. This reduced the car's overall weight by nearly 500 lbs.

No bumpers

In an effort to save weight, no bumpers were fitted front or rear. Other weight-saving omissions included badges, brightwork, sliding windows and a stripped-out interior.

Uprated suspension

Much of the suspension was shared with the highly effective roadgoing E-Type. However, certain components were uprated. Up front, stiffer torsion bars and anti-roll bar, uprated shock absorbers and special upper and lower fulcrum housings were used. At the rear there was a stiffer cage bottom plate, lightened hub carriers, modified wishbones, shock absorbers with integral bump-stops and stiffer mountings.

Specifications

1963 Jaguar E-Type Lightweight

ENGINE

Type: In-line 6-cylinder

Construction: Aluminum cylinder block and head

Valve gear: Two valves per cylinder operated by twin chain-driven overhead camshafts

Bore and stroke: 3.43 in. x 4.17 in.

Displacement: 3,781 cc

Compression ratio: 9.5:1

Induction system: Lucas mechanical fuel injection

Maximum power: 344 bhp at 6,500 rpm

Maximum torque: 314 lb ft at 4,750 rpm

Top speed: 157 mph

0–60 mph: 5.0 sec.

TRANSMISSION

Four or five-speed manual

BODY/CHASSIS

Unitary monocoque construction with aluminum fixed hardtop coupe body

SPECIAL FEATURES

A racing-type fuel filler allows quick mid-race fuel stops.

The blue light over the windshield is for signaling to the pits.

RUNNING GEAR

Steering: Rack-and-pinion

Front suspension: Wishbones with torsion bars, anti-roll bar and telescopic shock absorbers

Rear suspension: Lower wishbone, upper driveshaft link, radius arms, coil springs, anti-roll bar and telescopic shock absorbers

Brakes: Discs (front and rear)

Wheels: Alloy 15-in dia.

Tires: 5.50 x 15 (front), 6.00 x 15 (rear)

DIMENSIONS

Length: 175.3 in.   **Width:** 65.2 in.

Height: 48.0 in.   **Wheelbase:** 96.0 in.

Track: 50.0 in. (front), 50.0 in. (rear)

Weight: 2,220 lbs.

Jaguar MK 2

There is something about the shape of a Mk 2 that excites Jaguar enthusiasts. In addition, it is rewarding to drive and comfortable to be in, and has charm and grace aplenty.

XK power
Jaguar's acclaimed straight-six XK engine powers the Mk 2. Available in 2.4-, 3.4- and 3.8-liter sizes, the biggest one made the Mk 2 the quickest Bitish four-door sedan on the market in its day.

Stylish wheel
Although the Mk was available wit steel wheels with traditional Jagua hub caps and a body colored finish, th more stylish optio was a set of chrome wires. These suit th Mk 2's sport temperament

Choice of transmission
A four-speed manual transmission with overdrive is standard for the Mk 2, although many customers chose a three-speed automatic. Unlike the smaller-engined versions, the 3.8-liter Mk 2 has a standard limited-slip differential.

Luxury interior

Inside, the Mk 2 reached new levels of luxury. The upholstery is almost entirely leather and the floors have rich pile carpeting. Standard equipment includes a sports car-like instrument display, center console and foldaway tables for rear passengers.

Classic styling

Many people regard the Mk 2 as Jaguar's most elegant sedan. It has slimmer pillars, a much larger glass area, separate chromed window frames and more chrome than the earlier Mk 1.

Unibody construction

Unlike separate-chassis Jaguars of the 1950s, the Mk 2 uses monocoque construction. It is extremely rigid with two long box-sections welded to a ribbed steel floorpan, linked by transverse crossmembers and bulkheads.

Specifications

1960 Jaguar Mk 2 3.8

ENGINE

Type: In-line six-cylinder

Construction: Cast-iron cylinder block and alloy head

Valve gear: Two valves per cylinder operated by two overhead camshafts

Bore and stroke: 3.42 in. x 4.17 in.

Displacement: 3,781 cc

Compression ratio: 8.0:1

Induction system: Two SU sidedraft carburetors

Maximum power: 220 bhp at 5,500 rpm

Maximum torque: 240 lb-ft at 3,000 rpm

Top speed: 125 mph

0-60 mph: 9.2 sec.

TRANSMISSION

Four-speed manual with overdrive or three-speed automatic

BODY/CHASSIS

Unitized chassis with steel four-door sedan body

SPECIAL FEATURES

Wide wire wheels were a popular option on the Mk 2.

A classic Jaguar grill features vertical chrome bars. On early Mk 2s it is flanked by twin driving lights.

RUNNING GEAR

Steering: Recirculating ball

Front suspension: Wishbones with coil springs, shock absorbers and anti-roll bar

Rear suspension: Live axle with radius arms, leaf springs, Panhard rod and shock absorbers

Brakes: Discs (front and rear)

Wheels: Steel or wires, 15-in. dia.

Tires: 6.40 x 15 in.

DIMENSIONS

Length: 180.8 in.   **Width:** 66.75 in.

Height: 57.5 in.   **Wheelbase:** 107.4 in.

Track: 55.0 in. (front), 53.4 in. (rear)

Weight: 3,400 lbs.

265

Jaguar **XJ13**

Even as Jaguar drew the curtains on its racing program in the 1950s, insiders were planning a spectacular comeback. The XJ13 was the result, but politics and changing regulations caused its demise.

Stressed engine

Following the lead of the Lotus 25 Formula 1 car, the XJ13's engine is a stressed part of the monocoque structure.

Unique V12 engine

The XJ13 engine is a complex, double overhead camshaft racing unit, while the eventual roadgoing V12 used in the E-Type S3 is a much more practical single overhead camshaft design and is far more reliable.

Ultra wide tires

For maximum grip, the XJ13 was fitted with 10-inch front tires and 13.6 rear tires. It was very unusual for a car of the 1960s to have tires this wide.

Six ZF transmissions

Jaguar had six ZF 5DS25/2 transaxles made for the XJ13 because it was easier to change the transmission than just the differential. Each of the six units had a different final drive ratio.

Alloy wheels

The magnesium alloy wheels were cast especially for the XJ13, and featured knock-on spinners. When the car was restored in the mid-1970s, an entirely new set of wheels were fitted as the existing ones were showing signs of fatigue.

Timeless elegance

The XJ13's graceful lines were styled by Malcolm Sayer, the very gifted designer of the great C-Type and D-Type racers of the 1950s. He also penned the immortal E-Type. The overall shape is very aerodynamically efficient, with a low body and minimal frontal area. It is claimed that its drag coefficient is superior to that of the Ford GT40.

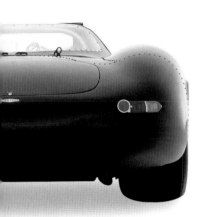

Aluminum monocoque

The key to the XJ13's light weight is its superb monocoque made entirely of aluminum. It is fully stressed and clothed in light alloy bodywork by Abbey Panels of Coventry, England. The engine is mounted directly to the monocoque, and doesn't use rubber bushings.

Specifications
1966 Jaguar XJ13

ENGINE

Type: V12

Construction: Aluminum cylinder block and heads

Valve gear: Two valves per cylinder operated by two chain-driven overhead camshafts per bank

Bore and stroke: 3.42 in. x 2.75 in.

Displacement: 4,991 cc

Compression ratio: 10.4:1

Induction system: Lucas fuel injection

Maximum power: 502 bhp at 7,600 rpm

Maximum torque: 365 lb-ft at 5,500 rpm

Top speed: 161 mph

0–60 mph: 4 sec.

TRANSMISSION

Five-speed manual

BODY/CHASSIS

Aluminum monocoque with two-door open-roof coupe body

SPECIAL FEATURES

The intake tubes dominate the view of the engine from the rear.

For maximum grip the one-off Jag uses 15-inch alloys with 10-inch wide tires in the front and 13.6-inch tires on the rear.

RUNNING GEAR

Steering: Rack-and-pinion

Front suspension: Double wishbones with coil springs, shocks and anti-roll bar

Rear suspension: Trailing links with fixed length driveshafts, bottom A-frame with coil springs, shocks and anti-roll bar

Brakes: Vented discs (front and rear)

Wheels: Magnesium alloy, 15-in. dia.

Tires: Dunlop Racing, 4.75/10.00 x 15 (front), 5.30/13.60 x 15 (rear)

DIMENSIONS

Length: 176.4 in.   **Width:** 73 in.

Height: 37.9 in.   **Wheelbase:** 95.9 in.

Track: 55.9 in. (front), 55.9 in. (rear)

Weight: 2,477 lbs.

Jaguar **XJ220**

Elegant and smooth, the XJ220 took its styling cues from the XJ13, a still-born Jaguar racer of the 1960s. But under the skin it's right up to date, with state-of-the-art racing technology.

Baggage space

This is a car for traveling light. The rear end is full of engine, and the front is full of radiators to cool it. The trunk is just big enough for a briefcase or two.

Transparent engine cover

The hood on the XJ220 is a lift-up glass panel that puts the powerful turbo motor permanently on show.

Aluminum-honeycomb chassis

Designed to be simple and easy to produce (because the first XJ220 was built in Jaguar engineers' spare time), the chassis is bonded together with adhesive, not welded.

Luxury interior

Leather seats, lush carpets and a top-level sound system ensure that XJ220 owners know they're in a Jaguar.

Aluminum body

Lightweight aluminum is used for the body. Each car was hand-assembled before being painted one of five standard colors—all metallics. Cars were available in silver, grey, blue, green and maroon.

V6 turbo engine

Light and compact, the engine was designed for Jaguar's IMSA race cars in the late-1980s. Adapted for road use, it produces 542 bhp, more than the big V12 originally planned for the car.

King-size wheels and tires

Specially-designed tires and wheels are so big there's no room for a spare. If a tire goes flat, it's filled with a special aerosol mixture and can be driven up to 60 miles at 30 mph.

Aerodynamic styling

Designed to look as elegant as a Jaguar should, the XJ220 is also aerodynamically efficient. At high speeds, the car develops over nearly 600 lbs. of downforce to hold it on the road.

Street legal

The XJ220 is legal for road use in most parts of the world, but not in the U.S. Jaguar never exported any cars to the States, although 10 were sent there for a TV race series in 1993.

Specifications
1993 Jaguar XJ220

ENGINE
Type: V6 turbocharged, 60°
Construction: Aluminum alloy block and heads
Bore and stroke: 3.7 in. x 3.3 in.
Displacement: 3,494 cc
Compression ratio: 8.3:1
Induction system: Electronic injection with twin Garrett turbochargers with air-to-air intercoolers and wastegate control
Maximum power: 542 bhp at 7,200 rpm
Maximum torque: 475 lb-ft at 4,500 rpm
Top speed: 208 mph
0–60 mph: 3.8 sec.

TRANSMISSION
Transaxle: FF Developments all-synchromesh, five-speed manual transaxle with triple-cone synchronizer on first and second gears; Viscous control limited-slip differential

BODY/CHASSIS
Aluminum alloy honeycomb monocoque with alloy two-door, two-seat body

SPECIAL FEATURES

Stylish air outlets for radiator compartment at front.

Vents behind doors feed air to engine's twin intercoolers.

RUNNING GEAR
Front suspension: Independent, double unequal-length wishbones, push-rod and rocker-operated spring/shock units, anti-roll bar
Rear suspension: Independent, unequal-length double wishbones, rocker-operated twin spring/shock units, anti-roll bar
Brakes: Vented 13 in. (front), 11.8 in. (rear), four-piston calipers
Wheels: Die-cast aluminum alloy. 9 in. x 17 in. (front), 10 in. x 18 in. (rear)
Tires: 255/45 ZR17 (front), 345/35 ZR18 (rear)

DIMENSIONS
Length: 194 in.   **Width:** 87.4 in.
Height: 45.3 in.
Wheelbase: 103.9 in.
Track: 67.3 in. (front), 62.5 in. (rear)
Weight: 3,241 lbs.

Jaguar XJ6

There was nothing that could come remotely close to the XJ6 for the price. This car was so significant that current Jaguar sedans still bear similar styling cues.

Rack-and-pinion steering

Jaguar had been quick to adopt rack-and-pinion steering on its sports and racing cars but the revious large sedan, the huge Mk X, had recirculating ball steering. This was replaced on the XJ6 by sharper and more responsive rack-and-pinion steering.

Twin-cam engine

One of the world's greatest engines powers this milestone sedan. For the XJ6 Series I it was built in 2.8-liter and 4.2-liter forms.

Bolt-on fenders

Although the XJ6 has a modern unitary-construction monocoque, the front fenders can be unbolted for ease of repair. The monocoque is heavily reinforced with box-section cross members while more box-section chassis rails carry the rear subframe.

Inboard rear discs

The rear disc brakes are mounted inboard next to the differential for reduced unsprung weight.

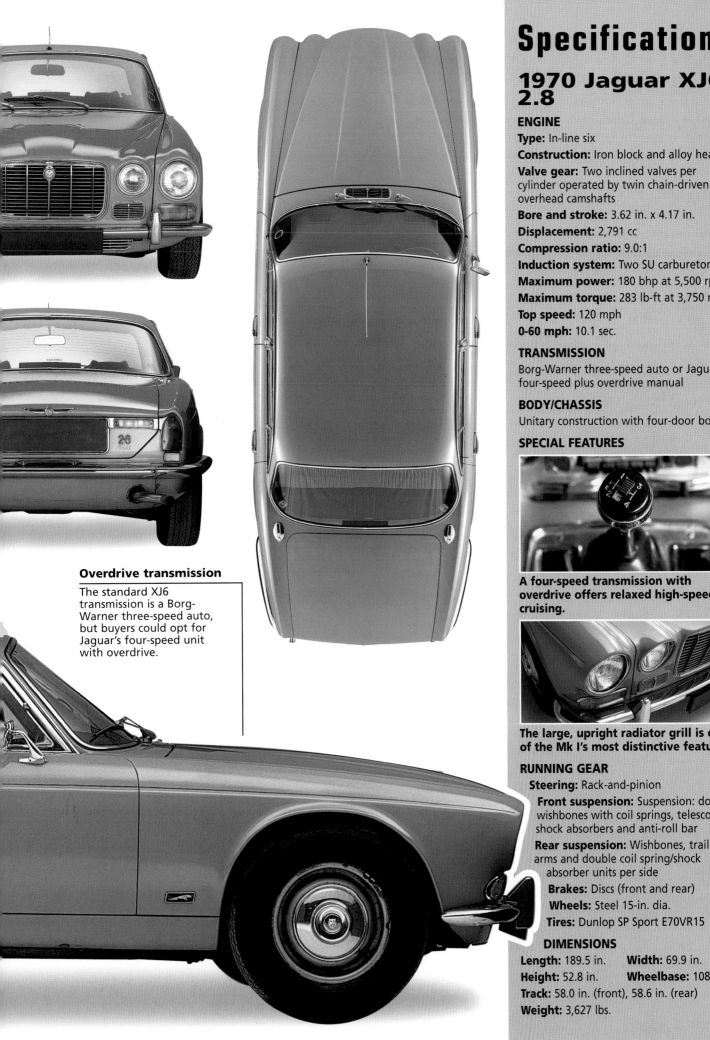

Specifications

1970 Jaguar XJ6 2.8

ENGINE

Type: In-line six

Construction: Iron block and alloy head

Valve gear: Two inclined valves per cylinder operated by twin chain-driven overhead camshafts

Bore and stroke: 3.62 in. x 4.17 in.

Displacement: 2,791 cc

Compression ratio: 9.0:1

Induction system: Two SU carburetors

Maximum power: 180 bhp at 5,500 rpm

Maximum torque: 283 lb-ft at 3,750 rpm

Top speed: 120 mph

0-60 mph: 10.1 sec.

TRANSMISSION

Borg-Warner three-speed auto or Jaguar four-speed plus overdrive manual

BODY/CHASSIS

Unitary construction with four-door body

SPECIAL FEATURES

A four-speed transmission with overdrive offers relaxed high-speed cruising.

The large, upright radiator grill is one of the Mk I's most distinctive features.

RUNNING GEAR

Steering: Rack-and-pinion

Front suspension: Suspension: double wishbones with coil springs, telescopic shock absorbers and anti-roll bar

Rear suspension: Wishbones, trailing arms and double coil spring/shock absorber units per side

Brakes: Discs (front and rear)

Wheels: Steel 15-in. dia.

Tires: Dunlop SP Sport E70VR15

DIMENSIONS

Length: 189.5 in.   **Width:** 69.9 in.

Height: 52.8 in.   **Wheelbase:** 108.8 in.

Track: 58.0 in. (front), 58.6 in. (rear)

Weight: 3,627 lbs.

Overdrive transmission

The standard XJ6 transmission is a Borg-Warner three-speed auto, but buyers could opt for Jaguar's four-speed unit with overdrive.

Jaguar XJC 🇬🇧

Jaguar's speciality is sporty sedans and luxurious sports cars. The XJC was a unique attempt to marry the two in one enticing package. It was elegant, refined, exclusive and—with its V12 engine—a superb cruiser.

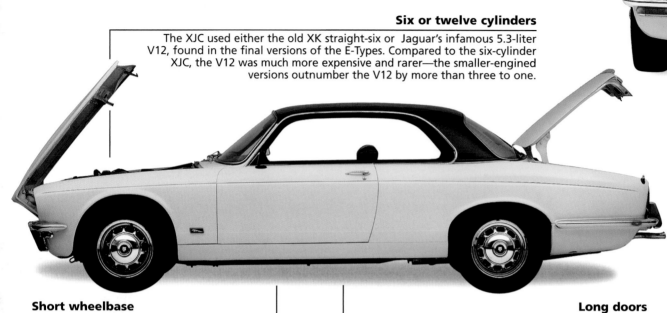

Six or twelve cylinders

The XJC used either the old XK straight-six or Jaguar's infamous 5.3-liter V12, found in the final versions of the E-Types. Compared to the six-cylinder XJC, the V12 was much more expensive and rarer—the smaller-engined versions outnumber the V12 by more than three to one.

Short wheelbase

Based on the short wheelbase XJ6 sedan, the coupe was also unique in that it was the only XJ to marry the V12 engine with the 108.8-inch wheelbase chassis.

Long doors

Compared to the XJ sedan, the coupe's doors were four inches longer and substantially heavier. An absence of vent windows also gave it a neater side profile.

Unique roofline

Having a unique roofline gave rise to some problems, particularly wind noise and water leaks. Neither problem was ever properly addressed by Jaguar.

Black vinyl roof

All XJ coupes had a black vinyl roof. This was less to do with aesthetics and more to do with craftiness. Chopping the front and rear roof sections of a sedan to make the coupe roofline left an unsightly seam that had to be covered up—and a vinyl roof was the cost-efficient solution.

Pillarless glass

The opportunity was taken to rid the XJ coupe of a central pillar and so do away with a glass pillar divider. Both front and rear windows could wind away out of sight to allow completely open sides.

Smaller cabin

Although the wheelbase remained the same as the sedan, rear seat room was tighter. Still, compared to most coupe competitors the XJC was very spacious.

Specifications

1976 Jaguar XJ 4.2 C

ENGINE

Type: In-line six-cylinder

Construction: Cast-iron block and head

Valve gear: Two valves per cylinder operated by twin chain-driven overhead camshafts

Bore and stroke: 3.65 in. x 4.17 in.

Displacement: 4,235 cc

Compression ratio: 7.8:1

Induction system: Two SU carburetors

Maximum power: 176 bhp at 4,750 rpm

Maximum torque: 219 lb-ft at 2,500 rpm

Top speed: 139 mph

0-60 mph: 8.8 sec.

TRANSMISSION

Borg Warner three-speed automatic

BODY/CHASSIS

Unitary monocoque construction chassis with two-door steel coupe body

SPECIAL FEATURES

Series III XJs are distinguished by higher mounted bumpers.

All XJC coupes had vinyl roof coverings to hide metal seams.

RUNNING GEAR

Steering: Rack-and-pinion

Front suspension: Double wishbones with coil springs, telescopic shock absorbers and anti-roll bar

Rear suspension: Lower wishbones and radius arms with twin coil springs and telescopic shock absorbers

Brakes: Vented discs (front and rear)

Wheels: Steel or alloy 15-in. dia.

Tires: 205/70 VR15

DIMENSIONS

Length: 189.5 in.   **Width:** 69.3 in.

Height: 54.1 in.   **Wheelbase:** 108.8 in.

Track: 58.0 in. (front), 58.5 in. (rear)

Weight: 3,696 lbs.

Jaguar **XK120**

Where the pre-war Jaguar SS100 had been the absolutely typical 1930s sports car, the XK120 looked to the future. It was in a class of its own because none of its rivals could come close in looks or performance.

Wishbone front suspension

Engine apart, the XK120's most advanced feature is its double-wishbone front suspension with torsion bars and telescopic shock absorbers instead of lever arm devices.

Twin-cam engine

The XK twin-cam six, which started life in the XK120, went on to power the C- and D-type racers, the XK140 and XK150, and the Jaguar sedans up to and beyond the XJ6.

Fitted rear luggage

To make the best possible use of the Jaguar's trunk space, fitted luggage was an option.

Alloy bodywork

Very early XK120s have all aluminum-alloy bodywork, joined to the chassis in 12 places. The alloy panels were soon replaced by steel.

Connolly leather seats

On the cars fitted with leather trim, high-quality Connolly leather is used for the seats and the trim around the doors.

Live rear axle

The XK120 uses a traditional live axle located and sprung on semi-elliptic leaf springs with lever arm shocks.

Rear wheel skirts

The removable wheel skirts are for style and aerodynamic efficiency, but they can only be fitted with steel disc wheels because the spinners on the wire wheels project too far.

No rear bumper

To begin with, only these small rear over-riders were fitted, but later XK models grew larger and larger bumpers.

Removable windshield

On the roadster, the windshield can be completely removed if you really want wind-in-the-hair motoring. The windshield pillars unbolt from the bodywork. On the coupe and convertible model, the windshield pillars are part of the bodywork.

Specifications
1951 Jaguar XK120 M

ENGINE

Type: In-line six
Construction: Cast-iron block, aluminum alloy cylinder head
Valve gear: Two valves per cylinder operated by twin overhead camshafts
Bore and stroke: 3.26 in. x 4.17 in.
Displacement: 3,442 cc
Compression ratio: 8.0:1
Induction system: Two SU H6 carburetors
Maximum power: 180 bhp at 5,300 rpm
Maximum torque: 203 lb-ft at 4,000 rpm
Top speed: 121 mph
0-60 mph: 11.3 sec.

TRANSMISSION

Four-speed manual

BODY/CHASSIS

Separate box section chassis with steel open-roadster body

SPECIAL FEATURES

XK120's curvaceous and wind-cheating lines were a revelation in 1948.

The rear wheels are covered by skirts which improve the aerodynamics.

RUNNING GEAR

Steering: Recirculating ball
Front suspension: Double wishbones with longitudinal torsion bars and telescopic shocks
Rear suspension: Live axle with semi-elliptic leaf springs and lever arm shocks
Brakes: Drums (front and rear)
Wheels: Steel disc or wire spoke, 16-in. dia.
Tires: Crossply 6 in. x 16 in.

DIMENSIONS

Length: 174 in. **Width:** 62 in.
Height: 53 in. **Wheelbase:** 102 in.
Track: 51 in. (front), 50 in. (rear)
Weight: 3,039 lbs.

Jaguar **XJR-S**

Needing to capitalize on its Le Mans success of 1988, Jaguar wanted a sportier high-performance car than was already in the line-up. To keep costs low, Jaguar transformed the XJS into the XJR-S instead of building a whole new model.

Three-speed auto
Only a three-speed automatic transmission was used in the XJR-S. Unfortunately, a sporty manual transmission was not available in this model.

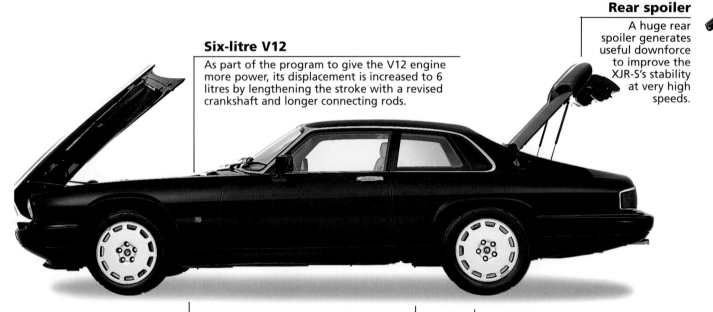

Six-litre V12
As part of the program to give the V12 engine more power, its displacement is increased to 6 litres by lengthening the stroke with a revised crankshaft and longer connecting rods.

Rear spoiler
A huge rear spoiler generates useful downforce to improve the XJR-S's stability at very high speeds.

Uprated suspension
The suspension is uprated with shorter, stiffer, coil springs and Bilstein shocks complementing the bigger wheels and lower-profile tires.

Revised styling
In 1991 Jaguar restyled the XJS and the XJR-S followed suit, with softer lines to the rear windows.

Larger rear tyres
Where the XJS uses the same size tires all around, the XJR-S has larger, 245/55 tires on 16 in. rather than 15 in. wheels. The front tires are smaller 225/50s.

Forged alloy wheels
One major difference between the XJS and XJR-S is the larger, 8 in. x 16 in. forged-alloy wheels fitted to the XJR-S. They are designed to provide some air flow to the brakes.

Integrated bumper and spoiler

To improve aerodynamic efficiency and stability, the XJR-S has a chin spoiler integrated into the body-colored front fender.

Restyled taillights

Another feature of the 1991 restyle was the move from separate tail lights that joined the top of the rear wing to these wide rectangular lights.

Recalibrated power steering

Traditionally Jaguars have always had strong power assistance, which made the steering extremely light. The XJR-S was recalibrated for a more direct, heavier feel.

Specifications
1992 Jaguar XJR-S

ENGINE
Type: V12
Construction: Alloy block and heads, wet cylinder liners
Valve gear: Two valves per cylinder operated by single chain-driven camshaft per bank of cylinders
Bore and stroke: 3.54 in. x 3.07 in.
Displacement: 366 c.i.
Compression ratio: 11.0:1
Induction system: Zytek sequential electronic fuel injection
Maximum power: 333 bhp at 5250 rpm
Maximum torque: 365 lb-ft at 3650 rpm
Top Speed: 155 mph
0–60mph: 4.8 seconds

TRANSMISSION
Three-speed automatic

BODY/CHASSIS
Steel monocoque with two-door coupé body

SPECIAL FEATURES

Rear seats are luxurious but leg room is a little limited.

RUNNING GEAR
Steering: Rack-and-pinion
Front suspension: Double wishbones with coil springs, Bilstein telescopic shocks and anti-roll bar
Rear suspension: Lower wishbone with upper link and radius arms, coil springs and Bilstein telescopic shocks
Brakes: Vented discs, 11.2 in. dia. (front), 10.3 in. dia. (rear)
Wheels: Forged alloy, 8 in. x 16 in.
Tyres: Dunlop D40 M2, 225/50 ZR16 (front), 245/55 ZR16 (rear)

DIMENSIONS
Length: 189.8 in.
Width: 70.6 in.
Height: 49.2 in.
Wheelbase: 102 in.
Track: 58.6 in. (front), 59.2 in. (rear)
Weight: 4023 lbs.

Jaguar **XKR**

Like the E-Type, the XKR convertible has perfect looks to go with the performance. It lacks the immediate visual impact of the 1960s icon, but is still one of the most dramatic-looking cars around.

Huge brakes

This amount of power and weight takes some controlling, and Jaguar's solution is huge, 12-inch-diameter vented discs front and rear. The XKR has uprated higher-friction pads to cope with the higher temperatures.

Quad-cam V8

The four-cam 32-valve engine is a lightweight all-alloy unit with the pistons running on Nikasil-coated bores. This dispenses with the need for liners and enables it to take increased power with few modifications. Each cylinder has its own individual coil.

Traction control

Despite the huge tires, traction control is standard on the XKR. When one rear wheel begins to spin, braking is applied.

Power top

It takes just the press of a button and the Jaguar's lined insulated top folds away in 20 seconds. It also features a zip-out heated glass rear window.

Leather interior

Standard interior equipment for the XKR includes leather-faced, multi-adjustable, power front seats; maple trim; climate control; a six-CD changer and cruise control. A memory function for the driver's seat is optional.

Larger rear wheels
Partly to accommodate the huge brakes and partly for style, the XKR has very tall, 18-inch wheels.

Hood vents
For supercharged engines that run at higher temperatures, extra engine-bay cooling really helps. For this reason, the XKR has twin hood vents.

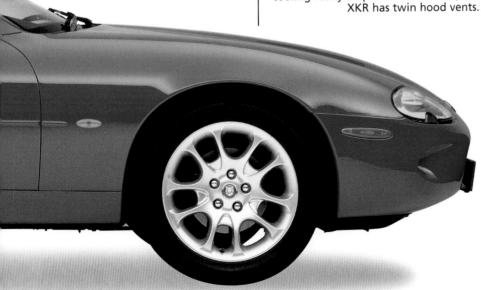

Specifications
1999 Jaguar XKR

ENGINE
Type: V8

Construction: Alloy block and heads

Valve gear: Four valves per cylinder operated by twin chain-driven overhead camshafts per bank of cylinders

Bore and stroke: 3.38 in. x 3.38 in.

Displacement: 3,996 cc

Compression ratio: 9.0:1

Induction system: Electronic fuel injection with Eaton mechanically driven supercharger

Maximum power: 370 bhp at 6,150 rpm

Maximum torque: 387 lb-ft at 3,600 rpm

Top speed: 155 mph

0–60 mph: 5.1 sec.

TRANSMISSION
Five-speed automatic

BODY/CHASSIS
Unitary monocoque construction with steel coupe or convertible body

SPECIAL FEATURES

Jaguar's customary J-gate is retained, but Mercedes-Benz supplies the transmission.

The chrome mesh grill distinguishes the XKR from the basic XK8.

RUNNING GEAR
Steering: Rack-and-pinion

Front suspension: Double wishbones with coil springs, Bilstein shock absorbers and anti-roll bar

Rear suspension: Double wishbones with coil springs, Bilstein shock absorbers and anti-roll bar

Brakes: Vented discs (front and rear)

Wheels: Alloy, 8 x 18 in. (front), 9 x 18 in. (rear)

Tires: Pirelli P Zero, 245/45 ZR18 (front), 255/45 ZR18 (rear)

DIMENSIONS
Length: 187.4 in.   **Width:** 79.3 in.

Height: 51.4 in.   **Wheelbase:** 101.9 in.

Track: 59.2 in. (front), 58.9 in. (rear)

Weight: 3,850 lbs.

Jensen INTERCEPTOR

The Jensen Interceptor, launched in 1966 at the London Motor Show, is by far the company's best-remembered product and its biggest seller. The car was so good that it was reborn in the early 1980s.

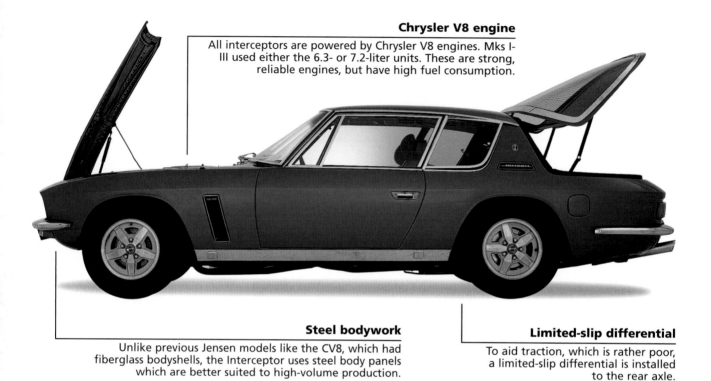

Chrysler V8 engine
All interceptors are powered by Chrysler V8 engines. Mks I–III used either the 6.3- or 7.2-liter units. These are strong, reliable engines, but have high fuel consumption.

Steel bodywork
Unlike previous Jensen models like the CV8, which had fiberglass bodyshells, the Interceptor uses steel body panels which are better suited to high-volume production.

Limited-slip differential
To aid traction, which is rather poor, a limited-slip differential is installed to the rear axle.

Glass hatchback
The bulbous back window is not only attractive, but also functional. The whole unit lifts up to provide space for luggage.

Adjustable shocks
Despite its archaic rear leaf springs, the Interceptor has adjustable telescopic shocks to help smooth out the ride.

Italian styling
The shape was originally penned by Touring of Milan and adapted by Vignale to produce the Interceptor.

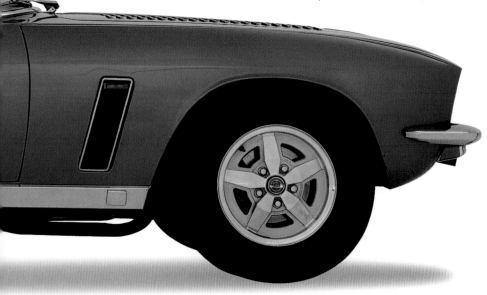

Specifications
1968 Jensen Interceptor

ENGINE
Type: V8

Construction: Cast-iron block and heads

Valve gear: Two valves per cylinder operated by hydraulic tappets, pushrods and rockers

Bore and stroke: 4.25 in. x 3.38 in.

Displacement: 6,276 cc

Compression ratio: 10.0:1

Induction system: Single Carter AFB four-barrel carburetor

Maximum power: 330 bhp at 4,600 rpm

Maximum torque: 450 lb-ft at 2,800 rpm

Top speed: 137 mph

0–60 mph: 6.4 sec.

TRANSMISSION
Chrysler TorqueFlite 727 automatic

BODY/CHASSIS
Tubular and welded sheet steel monocoque with two-door body

SPECIAL FEATURES

The Mk II Interceptor has a different front bumper with the parking lights positioned beneath it.

Fender extractor vents aid engine cooling and help to distinguish the Interceptor from the four-wheel drive FF, which has two vents per side.

RUNNING GEAR
Steering: Recirculating ball

Front suspension: Independent wishbones with coil springs and telescopic shocks

Rear suspension: Live rear axle with semi-elliptical leaf springs, telescopic shocks and a Panhard rod

Brakes: Girling discs, 11.4-in. dia. (front), 10.7-in. dia. (rear)

Wheels: Rostyle pressed steel, 15-in. dia.

Tires: Dunlop 185 x 15

DIMENSIONS
Length: 188 in.   **Width:** 70 in.

Height: 53 in.   **Wheelbase:** 105 in.

Track: 56 in. (front and rear)

Weight: 3,696 lbs.

Jowett JAVELIN

To a post-war nation being fed warmed-over remnants of dull 1930s automobiles, the sleek, advanced Javelin was a breath of fresh air. It might have been expensive, but it was probably the most desirable British sedan of its day.

Six-seat interior

For a car that measured only 14 feet long, the Javelin is extremely roomy inside—front and rear bench seats comfortably fit six adults. Legroom is particularly generous because the axles are positioned to the extreme ends of the car, and access is excellent with four perpendicular doors.

Generous equipment

The Javelin was well equipped for 1947. A built-in jacking system, ashtrays and interior mirror were standard. Deluxe models included leather trim, a spotlight, picnic trays and a walnut-faced radio.

Aerodynamic shape

Engineers discovered aerodynamics in the 1930s and Jowett was one of the first companies to embrace the new science in a popular car.

Large trunk
Under the sloping rear styling is a deceptively large trunk. The lid hinges upward for access to an extremely generous load bay. A built-in toolbox is also supplied.

Independent front suspension
Wishbones and torsion bars made up the independent front suspension, which was very effective by the standards of the day.

Flat-four engine
In the immediate post-war period, Jowett's choice of a horizontally-opposed four-cylinder engine was brave and innovative. It was torquey, but early models were unreliable.

Specifications
1950 Jowett Javelin

ENGINE
Type: Horizontally-opposed four-cylinder

Construction: Aluminum cylinder block and cast-iron heads

Valve gear: Two valves per cylinder operated by a single camshaft

Bore and stroke: 2.85 in. x 3.54 in.

Displacement: 1,486 cc

Compression ratio: 7.25:1

Induction system: Two Zenith carburetors

Maximum power: 50 bhp at 4,100 rpm

Maximum torque: 76 lb-ft at 2,600 rpm

Top speed: 80 mph

0-60 mph: 25.4 sec.

TRANSMISSION
Four-speed manual

BODY/CHASSIS
Integral chassis with four-door steel sedan body

SPECIAL FEATURES

The deluxe model boasted a number of options such as picnic trays.

Flush-fitting, easy-release door handles were a major style innovation.

RUNNING GEAR
Steering: Rack-and-pinion

Front suspension: Live axle, transverse wishbones with torsion bars and shock absorbers

Rear suspension: Transverse torsion bars with shock absorbers

Brakes: Drums (front and rear)

Wheels: Steel, 16-in. dia.

Tires: 5.25 x 16

DIMENSIONS
Length: 168.0 in. **Width:** 61.0 in.

Height: 60.5 in.

Wheelbase: 102.0 in.

Track: 51.0 in. (front), 49.0 in. (rear)

Weight: 2,254 lbs.

Kaiser DARRIN

Howard Dutch Darrin conceived this unusual sports car and sold the idea to Henry Kaiser, who was facing big losses with his automobile empire. However, it lasted only one season and sold a mere 435 examples.

Willys engine

Kaiser used the six-cylinder, 161-cubic inch, Willys F-head engine, tuned to develop 90 bhp. At the time, this was enough for reasonable performance because the car's weight was so low.

Sliding doors

A patent was taken out on the novel-opening doors. Once the door handle is turned, the narrow doors move inward and slide into the front fenders. No other car ever used this system.

Overdrive transmission

Those sliding doors may have been unique, but the Darrin stood out from most cars of the time in another way. It relied on a floorshifted manual transmission with three forward speeds plus an overdrive.

Henry J chassis

To get a 100-inch wheelbase suitable for a sports car, Kaiser turned to its Henry J model. This had a conventional specification with coil springs in the front and left springs at the rear. Four-wheel drums safely bring the car to a stop.

Fiberglass bodywork

Howard Darrin was a fiberglass pioneer. He was well ahead of Chevrolet when he produced the prototype for the Kaiser Darrin in 1952. By then, however, companies such as Glasspar had plastic shells in production.

Stylized grill

The distinctive concave grill retains typical Kaiser styling. The very small 'mouth' has vertical chrome teeth, a V at its lower edge and a rounded top that follows the shape of the hood.

Specifications
1954 Kaiser Darrin

ENGINE
Type: In-line six-cylinder
Construction: Cast-iron block and head
Valve gear: Two valves per cylinder operated by a single camshaft
Bore and stroke: 3.12 in. x 3.50 in.
Displacement: 161 c.i.
Compression ratio: 7.6:1
Induction system: Single Carter carburetor
Maximum power: 90 bhp at 4,200 rpm
Maximum torque: 135 lb-ft at 1,600 rpm

TRANSMISSION
Three-speed manual with overdrive

BODY/CHASSIS
Separate chassis with fiberglass two-door convertible body

SPECIAL FEATURES

The sleek rear end incorporates the unusually shaped trunklid.

The front doors completely slide into the front fender. This patented design is the most novel feature of the Kaiser Darrin.

RUNNING GEAR
Steering: Worm-and-roller
Front suspension: A-arms with coil springs and shock absorbers
Rear suspension: Live axle with leaf springs and shock absorbers
Brakes: Drums (front and rear)
Wheels: Steel, 15-in. dia.
Tires: 5.90 x 15

DIMENSIONS
Length: 184.0 in.　**Width:** 67.5 in.
Height: 52.7 in.　**Wheelbase:** 100.0 in.
Track: 54.0 in. (front and rear)
Weight: 2,250 lbs.

Kaiser **MANHATTAN**

With a fortified Chevy V8, radical chassis modifications and elegant styling, customs don't come any more exclusive than this Kaiser. Best of all, it can cover 0-60 mph in just over 3 seconds.

Worked mouse

The most popular engine among hot rodders is the small-block Chevy. Nestling between the framerails of this Kaiser is a 400 motor, destroked to 377 cubic inches. With custom-machined heads, aluminum pistons, a high-lift camshaft, twin Holley carburetors and a supercharger, this Kaiser can achieve 9.8-second ¼-mile times.

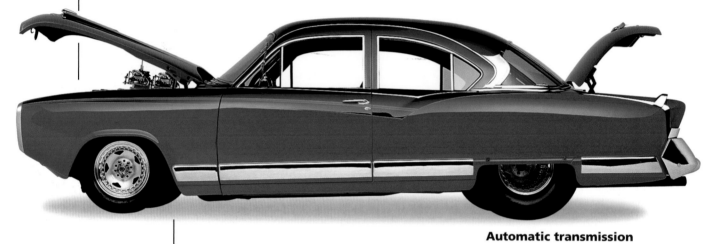

Automatic transmission

In the past, most drivers who ran their cars at the strip preferred manual transmissions, but, today, automatic units can provide more precise shifting, shaving a few tenths of a second off the ET (elapsed time). This one has a rugged GM TurboHydramatic 350 three-speed with a Hurst quarter shifter.

Radical rear end

On pro street cars, builders fill the rear fenderwells with as much rubber as possible. In order to achieve this, the rear subframe has been narrowed, Alston full wheel tubs has been welded on and a narrowed rear axle on upper and lower parallel links fitted. The 9-inch Ford differential has a Detroit Locker limited-slip differential with low 4.86:1 gears.

Low beltline

When the facelifted Kaiser was revealed in 1951, it boasted a lower beltline than contemporary Detroit sedans and more glass for greater visibility. Changes for 1954 included a concave grill, inspired by Harley Earl's Buick XP 300, and larger taillights. Two-door Manhattans, like this one, represent just five percent of 1954 production.

Custom-fabricated chassis

This Kaiser Manhattan came from the factory with a steel box-section chassis. This has been replaced with a tubular racing-style frame with a steel integral roll cage.

Sumptuous interior

Besides the customary full set of Auto Meter gauges, this Manhattan has a Budnik steering wheel, pink and purple tweed upholstery, custom front sport bucket seats and an Alpine stereo with compact disc player and amplifier.

Specifications

1954 Kaiser Manhattan

ENGINE

Type: V8

Construction: Cast-iron block and aluminum cylinder heads

Valve gear: Two valves per cylinder operated by a single camshaft with pushrods and rockers

Bore and stroke: 4.13 in. x 3.48 in.

Displacement: 377 c.i.

Compression ratio: 7.6:1

Induction system: Two Holley four-barrel carburetors and roots style supercharger

Maximum power: 630 bhp at 6,400 rpm

Maximum torque: 335 lb-ft at 4,200 rpm

Top speed: 167 mph

0-60 mph: 3.2 sec.

TRANSMISSION

GM TurboHydramatic three-speed automatic

BODY/CHASSIS

Steel tubular chassis with steel two-door sedan body

SPECIAL FEATURES

Kaiser was the first manufacturer to adopt dual-purpose taillights.

A 671 supercharger and twin 660-cfm carburetors sit atop the Chevy V8.

RUNNING GEAR

Steering: Recirculating ball

Front suspension: Unequal length A-arms with coil springs and telescopic shock absorbers

Rear suspension: Narrowed live axle mounted on upper and lower parallel links with coil springs and telescopic shock absorbers

Brakes: Drums (front and rear)

Wheels: Centerline Convo Pro, 4 x 15 in. (front), 15 x 15 in. (rear)

Tires: Mickey Thompson, 7.50 x 15 in. (front), 5 x 15 in. (rear)

DIMENSIONS

Length: 201.8 in.   **Width:** 73.2 in.

Height: 55.7 in.   **Wheelbase:** 118.5 in.

Track: 55.0 in. (front), 48.1 in. (rear)

Weight: 3,330 lbs.

Lagonda RAPIDE

The Rapide name recalled the glorious LG45 and V12 Lagondas of the 1930s, though in most respects the new Lagonda was a modern, cutting-edge car. Its construction followed Touring's 'superleggera' principles.

Italian styling

The Milanese styling house Touring had done an excellent job of designing the Aston Martin DB4 and so it was called in to design the Rapide. Its efforts here were more controversial, especially at the front end.

Traditional grill

The outline of the main air intake grill reflects the traditional Lagonda design. However, its overall effect is rather convoluted, thanks to an odd center bar in the main grill and ungainly side grills.

'Superleggera' construction

Touring of Milan pioneered the 'superleggera' method of construction, which was used for the Rapide. Basically, the aluminum body panels are unstressed and mounted on a solid frame constructed with channels and round tubes welded to the main chassis frame. This increases stiffness and keeps the car's overall weight down.

Auto or manual transmission

As standard, the Rapide came with a Borg-Warner torque converter and three-speed automatic transmission. To satisfy more sporty drivers, an all-synchromesh, four-speed, manual transmission was optional.

de Dion rear axle

To save space, the well located live rear axle of the DB4 was abandoned in favor of a de Dion layout. For the same reason, transverse torsion bars were used in place of coil springs. A Watt linkage provides lateral location and trailing arms locate the de Dion longitudinally.

Luxury interior

All five passengers enjoy true luxury travel. The seats are deeply upholstered in leather, and the front pair is fully adjustable. There is thick floor carpeting, twin heaters for front and rear and power windows all around.

Quad headlights

One of the controversial aspects of the styling was the headlight treatment. Lucas 'mixed' lights were fitted in oval shrouds, the outer pair measuring seven inches across, the inner pair five inches. The effect is dramatic but rather fussy for some enthusiast's tastes.

Specifications

1962 Lagonda Rapide

ENGINE

Type: In-line six-cylinder

Construction: Aluminum block and cylinder head

Valve gear: Two valves per cylinder operated by double overhead camshafts

Bore and stroke: 3.78 in. x 3.62 in.

Displacement: 3,995 cc

Compression ratio: 8.25:1

Induction system: Two Solex carburetors

Maximum power: 236 bhp at 5,000 rpm

Maximum torque: 265 lb-ft at 4,000 rpm

Top speed: 130 mph

0-60 mph: 8.9 sec.

TRANSMISSION

Four-speed manual or three-speed automatic

BODY/CHASSIS

Platform steel chassis with aluminum four-door sedan body

SPECIAL FEATURES

What was considered odd styling in 1961 now has idiosyncratic appeal.

Aston Martin's hallmark fender vents appear on a Lagonda for the first time.

RUNNING GEAR

Steering: Rack-and-pinion

Front suspension: Upper and lower wishbones with coil springs, telescopic shock absorbers and anti-roll bar

Rear suspension: De Dion axle with Watt linkage, trailing arms, torsion bars and telescopic shock absorbers

Brakes: Discs (front and rear)

Wheels: Steel, 15-in. dia.

Tires: 7.10 x 15

DIMENSIONS

Length: 195.5 in. **Width:** 69.5 in.

Height: 56.0 in. **Wheelbase:** 114.0 in.

Track: 54.0 in. (front), 55.5 in. (rear)

Weight: 3,780 lbs.

Lamborghini COUNTACH

Design a car as dramatic as the Countach and you just have to make it perform the way it looks. It looked like the fastest car in the world and Lamborghini made sure it was.

Radiator ducts

Air flows into the huge ducts and electric fans blow the cool air across the side-mounted radiators.

Mid-mounted V12

The long V12 engine is mounted lengthwise with the transmission ahead of the engine. It was a change from Lamborghini's previous supercar, the Miura, which has its V12 engine mounted transversely.

Upright opening doors

Lamborghini could have made the Countach's doors open in the normal way, but that would have had nothing like the dramatic impact of doors that opened straight up, each supported on a single gas strut.

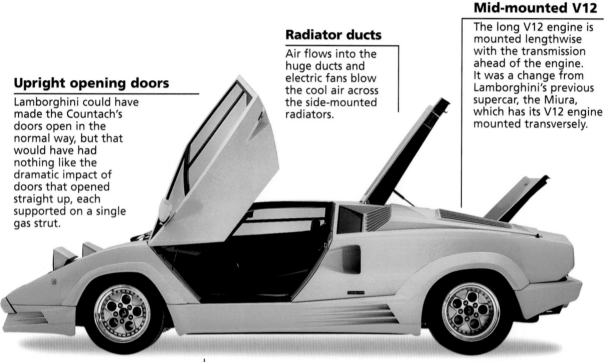

Split-rim alloy wheels

The circle of tiny bolts around each wheel shows that the Countach runs on split-rim alloys. The difference in size between front and rear wheels is enormous: the rears are 12-inches wide and the fronts 8.5 inches.

Flared wheel arches

The original Countach had no wheel-arch flares. They had to be added in 1978 when larger wheels and wider tires were fitted.

Optional rear wing

This car does without the optional rear wing which is as much for style as aerodynamic effect.

Alloy and fiberglass body

The Countach's exotic body is alloy with the exception of the fiberglass floor. None of the bodywork is structural.

Pirelli P Zero tires

The first Countachs ran on Michelin XWX tires, but in 1978 Lamborghini re-engineered the car to run on Pirelli P7s. The Anniversary model uses the latest advanced Pirelli P Zero tires.

Front spoiler

A deeper front spoiler was added in 1978 to improve high-speed stability. The front suspension geometry was altered at the same time. The two openings in the spoiler are there to keep the brakes cool.

Specifications

1990 Lamborghini Countach QV Anniversary

ENGINE

Type: V12
Construction: Alloy block and heads
Valve gear: Four valves per cylinder operated by four chain-driven overhead cams
Bore and stroke: 3.38 in. x 2.95 in.
Displacement: 5,167 cc
Compression ratio: 9.5:1
Induction system: Six Weber 44 DCNF downdraft carburetors
Maximum power: 455 bhp at 7,000 rpm
Maximum torque: 369 lb-ft at 5,200 rpm
Top speed: 178 mph
0–60 mph: 5.2 sec.

TRANSMISSION

Five-speed manual

BODY/CHASSIS

Tubular steel spaceframe chassis with alloy and fiberglass two-door, two-seat body

SPECIAL FEATURES

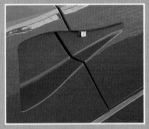

NACA-style ducts were first used in aircraft and were very efficient at channeling air in at high speed.

You could drive the Countach flat out without the optional rear wing, usually chosen only for dramatic effect.

RUNNING GEAR

Steering: Rack-and-pinion
Front suspension: Double wishbones, coil springs, telescopic shocks and anti-roll bar
Rear suspension: Wishbones, trailing arms, double coil springs/shocks per side, and anti-roll bar
Brakes: Vented discs 11.8 in. dia. (front), 11 in. dia. (rear)
Wheels: Split-rim alloys, 8.5 in. x 15 in. (front), 12 in. x 15 in. (rear)
Tires: Pirelli P Zero, 225/50 VR15 (front), 345/35 VR15 (rear)

DIMENSIONS

Length: 162.9 in.   **Width:** 78.7 in.
Height: 42.1 in.   **Wheelbase:** 96.5 in.
Track: 58.7 in. (front), 63.2 in. (rear)
Weight: 3,188 lbs.

Lamborghini DIABLO

Twelve years since the Diablo was introduced, it's still a rare and thrilling sight. One look at Marcello Gandini's masterpiece tells you it really will go way beyond 190 mph.

No spare wheel

There's no room for even a space saver spare tire. Lamborghini's explanation? "Diablo drivers do not change wheels by the side of the road."

Twin rear radiators

Two radiators are needed to cool the big V12. Mounted at the rear of the engine bay, each is assisted by a large electric fan.

Forward-hinged doors

Like the Countach before it, the Diablo has long doors with single hinges that lift up and forward, each supported on a single gas strut.

Side-mounted oil coolers

The vents on the lower side panels feed air to the two oil coolers which are mounted directly ahead of the rear wheels.

Larger rear wheels

The Diablo needs massive tires to feed its power to the road and the 1991 model was equipped with large very low-profile Pirelli P Zero 335/35 ZR17s on 13 inch x 17 inch split rim alloy wheels.

Poor rear vision

Like most mid-engined supercars, the Diablo has extremely limited rear vision through the small rear window.

Alloy, composite and steel body

The Diablo's bodyshell is made from a mixture of materials. The roof is steel for strength, but the fenders and doors are alloy and a new composite material was used for the nose, engine cover, rockers and bumpers.

World's widest supercar

At 80.3 inches, the Diablo is wider than even Ferrari's bulky Testarossa, making it the widest supercar in the world.

Engine cooling vents

Once air has passed through the engine's twin radiators it exits through these large vents at the rear of the car.

Ventilation scoops

Cabin ventilation is provided via two small scoops in front of the windshield but, unlike the Countach, the Diablo is air conditioned.

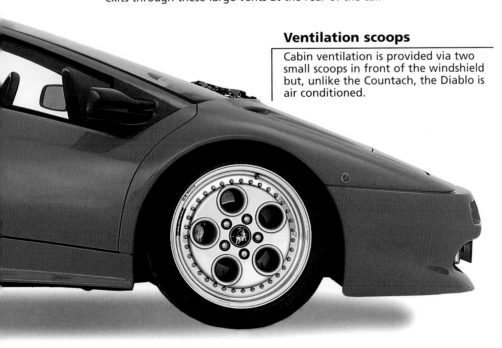

Specifications
1991 Lamborghini Diablo

ENGINE

Type: Sixty-degree V12
Construction: Light alloy block and heads
Valve gear: Four valves per cylinder operated by four chain-driven overhead camshafts
Bore and stroke: 3.43 in. x 3.15 in.
Displacement: 5,729 cc
Compression ratio: 10.0:1
Maximum power: 492 bhp at 7,000 rpm
Maximum torque: 428 lb-ft at 5,200 rpm
Top speed: 205 mph
0–60 mph: 4.3 sec.

TRANSMISSION

Five-speed manual

BODY/CHASSIS

Steel square-tube spaceframe chassis with two-door, two-seat coupe body in alloy, steel and carbon fiber

SPECIAL FEATURES

The vertically opening doors are a clever way of creating as much impact as gullwing doors, but without the same extremely difficult sealing problems.

RUNNING GEAR

Steering: Rack-and-pinion
Front suspension: Double wishbones with coil springs, telescopic shocks and anti-roll bar
Rear suspension: Double wishbones with twin coaxial spring shock units per side, and anti-roll bar
Brakes: Vented discs, 13 in. dia. (front), 11.2 in. dia. (rear)
Wheels: Multi-piece alloy, 8.5 in. x 17 in. (front), 13 in. x 17 in. (rear)
Tires: Pirelli P Zero 245/40 ZR17 (front), 335/35 ZR17 (rear)

DIMENSIONS

Length: 175.6 in.   **Width:** 80.3 in.
Height: 43.5 in.   **Wheelbase:** 104.3 in.
Track: 60.6 in. (front), 64.6 in. (rear)
Weight: 3,475 lbs.

Lamborghini MIURA

Only three years after Lamborghini started making cars, the company produced the most exotic supercar the world had ever seen. It was as advanced as it was stunning, with its 4-liter V12 engine mounted behind the driver.

Transverse V12

To make the Miura as compact as possible the engine is mounted transversely, making it the first transverse V12 supercar.

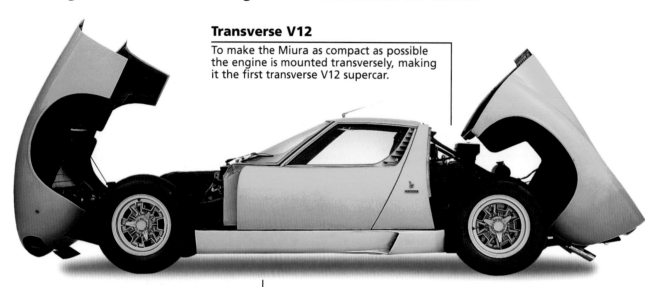

Transmission behind engine

With a transverse engine, there is no space for the transmission to be mounted in the usual place. The Miura's transmission is behind the engine, with the transmission and engine sharing the same oil.

Slatted engine cover

The great heat generated by a large V12 running fast in a small engine bay was vented through the open slatted engine cover, which did little to improve the view through the rear-view mirror.

Alloy and steel bodywork

The main body section of the Miura is fabricated from steel for strength. Some panels, such as the engine cover and front section of the bodywork, are alloy to save weight.

Door frame air vents

One of the main styling features is the air vents—for the engine compartment—which are actually built into the door frame.

Tip forward lights

When not in use, the headlights fold back to follow the line of the bodywork, a styling feature used years later by Porsche on the 928.

Top-mounted anti-roll bar

The Miura follows racing car practice in many ways. For example, its rear anti-roll bar runs from the bottom wishbones up over the chassis.

Front-mounted radiator

Although the engine is mid-mounted, the radiator stays in the conventional place at the front where it is easier to cool with the help of two electric fans. It is angled to fit under the Miura's low sloping nose.

Specifications
1970 Lamborghini P400S

ENGINE

Type: V12
Construction: Light alloy block and heads
Valve gear: Two valves per cylinder operated by four chain-driven overhead camshafts
Bore and stroke: 3.23 in. x 2.44 in.
Displacement: 3,929 cc
Compression ratio: 10.7:1
Induction system: Four Weber downdraft carburetors
Maximum power: 370 bhp at 7,700 rpm
Maximum torque: 286 lb-ft at 5,500 rpm
Top speed: 172 mph
0–60 mph: 6.9 sec.

TRANSMISSION

Five-speed manual

BODY/CHASSIS

Steel monocoque platform with steel and alloy two-door, two-seat coupe body

SPECIAL FEATURES

Stylized vents behind the doors provide air to the mid-mounted engine. The door handle is cleverly shaped to blend in with the styling.

The sloping headlights have distinctive 'eyebrows'; purely a styling feature.

RUNNING GEAR

Steering: Rack-and-pinion
Front suspension: Double wishbones with coil springs, telescopic shocks and anti-roll bar
Rear suspension: Double wishbones, with coil springs, telescopic shocks and anti-roll bar
Brakes: Solid discs, 11.8 in. dia. (front),12.1 in. dia. (rear)
Wheels: Magnesium 7 in. x 15 in.
Tires: Pirelli Cinturato GT70 VR15

DIMENSIONS

Length: 171.6 in.   **Width:** 71 in.
Height: 42 in.   **Wheelbase:** 98.4 in.
Track: 55.6 in. (front and rear)
Weight: 2,850 lbs.

Lancia THEMA 8.32

Before Lancia fitted the Ferrari V8, the fastest car in the Thema range was the fierce four-cylinder Turbo. By normal standards this car was quick; compared to the 8.32 it looked like it was traveling in reverse.

MacPherson strut suspension

Along with coil springs and electronically-controlled damping, the Thema uses MacPherson strut suspension at all four corners. Anti-roll bars are used front and rear.

Ferrari V8

Lancia took the quad-cam V8 from the Ferrari 308 and mounted it transversely in the front of the Thema. It produced 215 bhp—a little down on the Ferrari's 240-bhp output.

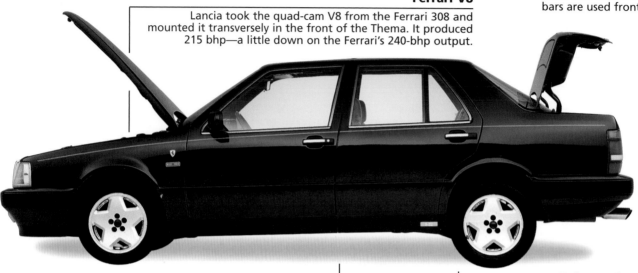

Shared platform

The Thema is built on the Type 4 platform, shared with the Alfa Romeo 164, Fiat Croma and Saab 9000.

Unique wheels

Five-spoke alloy wheels are unique to the 8.32 and help set it apart from lesser Themas.

Luxury interior

With leather and wood trim on a long list of standard equipment, the Thema 8.23's interior has more of a luxury than a sporty bias. Despite its sporty pretensions it can seat five in total comfort.

Powerful brakes

The 8.32 uses vented front and solid rear disc brakes. It also uses a three-channel anti-lock braking system.

Big trunk

The trunk has a volume of 19.3 cubic feet, but a relatively small opening restricts the size of loads that can be carried.

Specifications

1990 Lancia Thema 8.32

ENGINE

Type: V8

Construction: Alloy block and heads

Valve gear: Four valves per cylinder operated by four overhead camshafts

Bore and stroke: 3.27 in. x 2.80 in.

Displacement: 2,927 cc

Compression ratio: 10.5:1

Induction system: Bosch KE3 Jetronic fuel injection

Maximum power: 215 bhp at 6,750 rpm

Maximum torque: 210 lb-ft at 4,500 rpm

TRANSMISSION

Five-speed manual

BODY/CHASSIS

Unitary monocoque construction four-door steel sedan body

SPECIAL FEATURES

The neat trunk lid spoiler is unique to the Thema 8.32.

The Ferrari-designed V8 was built by motorcycle manufacturer Ducati.

RUNNING GEAR

Steering: Rack-and-pinion

Front suspension: MacPherson struts with coil springs, telescopic shock absorbers and anti-roll bar

Rear suspension: MacPherson struts with coil springs, telescopic shock absorbers and anti-roll bar

Brakes: Vented discs (front), solid discs (rear)

Wheels: Alloy, 6 x 15 in.

Tires: 205/55 VR15

DIMENSIONS

Length: 180.7 in.   **Width:** 69.3 in.

Height: 55.9 in.   **Wheelbase:** 104.7 in.

Track: 58.7 in. (front), 58.3 in. (rear)

Weight: 3,087 lbs.

Lancia DELTA INTEGRALE

Rally stars lined up to drive the Integrale. This car dominated world rallying for six years, and it comes as no surprise to discover that it is still one of the most coveted road cars of recent times.

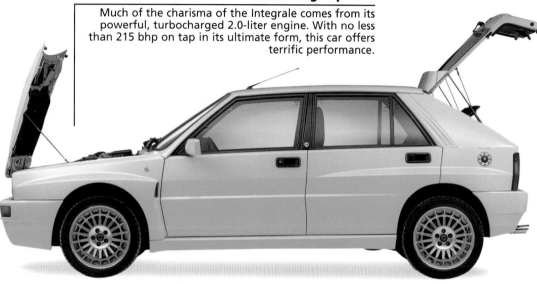

Turbocharged power

Much of the charisma of the Integrale comes from its powerful, turbocharged 2.0-liter engine. With no less than 215 bhp on tap in its ultimate form, this car offers terrific performance.

Torque-split four-wheel drive

The secret of the Integrale's pace and safety is its four-wheel drive system. This uses a torque split system with a planetary center differential incorporating a viscous coupling and a rear Torsen unit. The torque is permanently fed to all four wheels in a 47:53 percent front/rear split.

Pumped-up muscles

One of the most distinctive features of the Integrale is its very wide wheel arches. These are needed to clear the 7-inch cast-alloy wheels and wide tires. Other identifying features of the bodywork include a vented hood, small side skirts and an adjustable spoiler at the top of the tailgate.

Sporty cabin

Lancia's tradition for excellent interiors has been continued in the Integrale. The Recaro seats, Momo leather steering wheel and unique instrumentation are just right, however. Standard equipment includes power windows, mirrors and door locks, not to mention a sunroof.

Generous disc brakes

To ensure the Integrale stops as well as it accelerates, Lancia specified 11-inch vented discs up front and 10-inch solid discs at the rear.

Delta bodyshell

Because Group A rally regulations required that competition cars should be based on production car bodyshells, the Integrale uses the shell of the Delta—a rather ordinary hatchback launched in 1979. It is amazing how such an ordinary base model could be transformed into one of the best cars in the world.

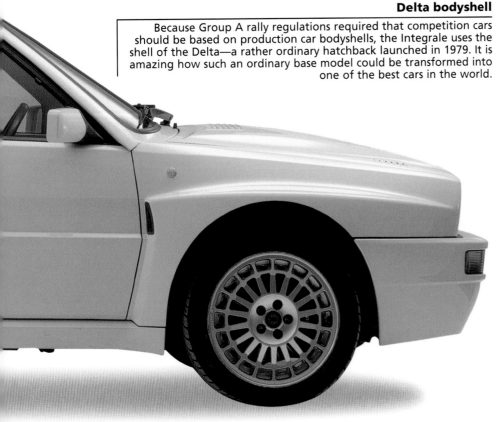

Specifications
1993 Lancia Delta Integrale Evoluzione 2

ENGINE

Type: In-line four-cylinder

Construction: Cast-iron block and aluminum head

Valve gear: Four valves per cylinder operated by belt-driven double overhead camshafts

Bore and stroke: 3.3 in. x 3.54 in.

Displacement: 1,995 cc

Compression ratio: 8.0:1

Induction system: Fuel injection

Maximum power: 210 bhp at 5,750 rpm

Maximum torque: 227 lb ft at 2,500 rpm

Top speed: 137 mph

0–60 mph: 5.7 sec.

TRANSMISSION

Five-speed manual

BODY/CHASSIS

Steel monocoque five-door hatchback

SPECIAL FEATURES

Distinctive blister wheel arches cover wide wheels and tires.

The angle of the small spoiler at the top of the tailgate is adjustable.

RUNNING GEAR

Steering: Rack-and-pinion

Front suspension: MacPherson struts with lower wishbones, coil springs, shock absorbers and anti-roll bar

Rear suspension: MacPherson struts with transverse links, coil springs, shock absorbers and anti-roll bar

Brakes: Vented discs, 11-in. dia (front), solid discs, 10-in. dia. (rear)

Wheels: Alloy, 16-in. dia.

Tires: 205/45 ZR16

DIMENSIONS

Length: 153.5 in.   **Width:** 69.7 in.

Height: 53.7 in.   **Wheelbase:** 97.6 in.

Track: 59.0 in. (front and rear)

Weight: 2,954 lbs.

Lancia FULVIA COUPE

The top of the Fulvia range is the Coupe 1.6 HF. Its larger, tuned engine can produce up to 132 bhp, and it was campaigned successfully in rallying, taking the 1972 world title.

Wider wheels
Six-inch wide alloy wheels are fitted to the 1.6 HF necessitating distinctive plastic fender flares to cover them.

V4 engine
Lancia fitted its last V4 engine to the Fulvia. It started out with 1,091 cc and 58 bhp but eventually grew to 1,584 cc and 132 bhp.

Beam axle
The rear beam axle is suspended on semi-elliptic leaf springs and has extra location provided by a Panhard rod.

Five-speed transmission
Launched in 1968, the 1.6-liter HF was always fitted with a five-speed transmission as standard. The rest of the Fulvia range made do with a four-speeder until the Series 2 was launched in 1969.

Steel and alloy panels
The HF is lighter than the other production Fulvia Coupes, thanks to the use of alloy body panels and Plexiglas windows.

Quad headlights

The Fulvia Coupe was always fitted with quad headlights. The larger, inner pair on this car indicate that it is a Fulvia Rallye 1.6 HF. On later Series 2 cars, the outer pair is raised to comply with light height regulations.

Specifications
1970 Lancia Fulvia 1.6 HF

ENGINE
Type: V4

Construction: Alloy block and head

Valve gear: Two valves per cylinder operated by two overhead camshafts

Bore and stroke: 3.23 in. x 2.95 in.

Displacement: 1,584 cc

Compression ratio: 10.5:1

Induction system: Two Solex carburetors

Maximum power: 115 bhp at 6,000 rpm

Maximum torque: 113 lb-ft at 4,500 rpm

Top speed: 112 mph

0–60 mph: 9.0 sec.

TRANSMISSION
Five-speed manual

BODY/CHASSIS
Unitary monocoque construction with steel two-door coupe body

SPECIAL FEATURES

A distinctive feature of the Fulvia is the center-mounted hood vent.

The Fulvia's V4 engine is slightly inclined toward the left.

RUNNING GEAR
Steering: Worm-and-sector

Front suspension: Unequal length wishbones with a transverse leaf spring, telescopic shock absorbers and anti-roll bar

Rear suspension: Beam axle with semi-elliptic leaf springs, Panhard rod, telescopic shock absorbers and anti-roll bar

Brakes: Discs (front and rear)

Wheels: Alloy, 5 x 14 in.

Tires: 165 SR-14

DIMENSIONS
Length: 156.5 in. **Width:** 61.2 in.

Height: 51.2 in. **Wheelbase:** 91.7 in.

Track: 54.7 in. (front), 52.6 in. (rear)

Weight: 1,874 lbs.

Lancia **RALLY 037**

The Lancia Rally 037 is one of those special breed of cars designed to compete in the exciting Group B rally championship. It is hugely effective and terrifyingly fast.

Huge rear spoiler

The huge rear spoiler had to be homologated, but it was really only necessary on the more powerful competition cars which needed to maximize their traction.

Twin-cam engine

The 037's engine is a development of the long-stroke 2-liter twin-cam which powered the successful Fiat Abarth 131 rally cars, but the iron block has a new alloy cylinder head with four valves per cylinder.

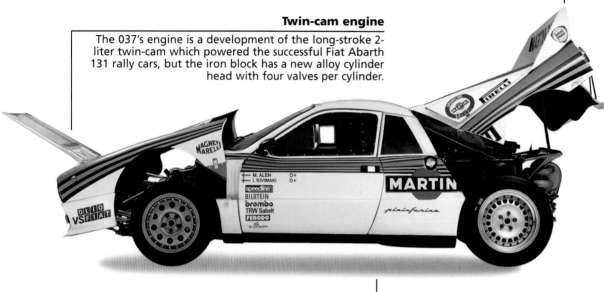

Montecarlo center section

For the sake of convenience, the center section of the Lancia Beta Montecarlo is used for the 037. Competition models required the front and rear track to be wider than that on the Montecarlo. Naturally, wider bodywork had to be grafted on.

ZF transmission

Lancia's existing transmissions were not strong enough for the supercharged engine in competition spec. The more robust German ZF five-speed was used instead.

Supercharger

Lancia chose supercharging to eliminate turbo lag and get instant throttle response. Supercharging requires similar changes to turbocharging, including reducing the compression ratio.

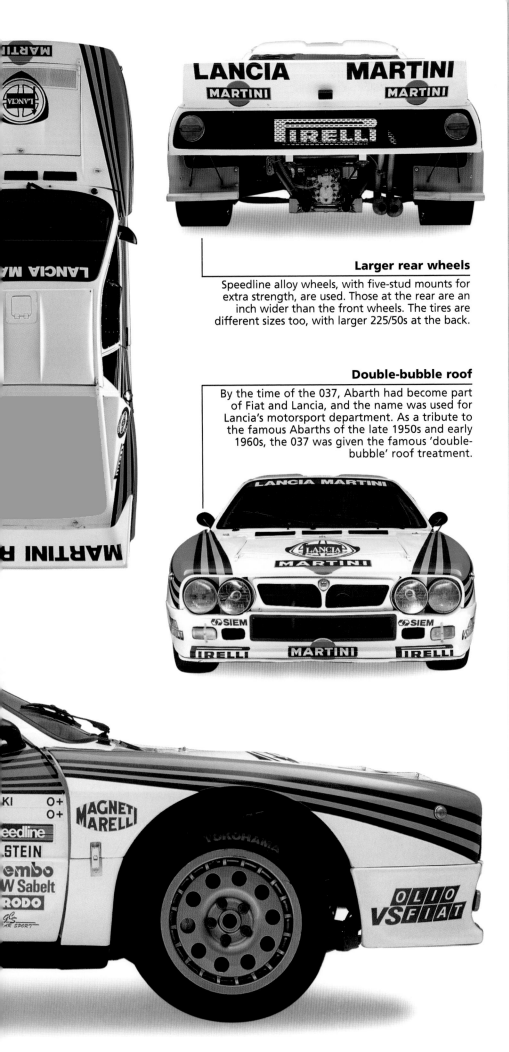

Larger rear wheels

Speedline alloy wheels, with five-stud mounts for extra strength, are used. Those at the rear are an inch wider than the front wheels. The tires are different sizes too, with larger 225/50s at the back.

Double-bubble roof

By the time of the 037, Abarth had become part of Fiat and Lancia, and the name was used for Lancia's motorsport department. As a tribute to the famous Abarths of the late 1950s and early 1960s, the 037 was given the famous 'double-bubble' roof treatment.

Specifications

1985 Lancia Rally 037 Evo 2

ENGINE

Type: In-line four

Construction: Cast-iron block and alloy cylinder head

Valve gear: Four valves per cylinder operated by twin overhead camshafts

Bore and stroke: 3.35 in. x 3.66 in.

Displacement: 2,111 cc

Compression ratio: 7.5:1

Induction system: Fuel injection with Abarth Volumex supercharger

Maximum power: 325 bhp at 8,000 rpm

Maximum torque: Not quoted

Top speed: 140 mph

0–60 mph: 6 sec.

TRANSMISSION

ZF five-speed manual

BODY/CHASSIS

Steel center section with tubular-steel subframes and steel/Kevlar body

SPECIAL FEATURES

In ultimate Evo 2 form the Fiat/Lancia twin-cam engine produces 325 bhp.

Large scoops behind the side windows provide cooling air for the engine.

RUNNING GEAR

Steering: Rack-and-pinion

Front suspension: Double wishbones with coil springs, telescopic shock absorbers and anti-roll bar

Rear suspension: Double wishbones with coil springs and dual shock absorbers

Brakes: Vented discs, 11.8-in. dia. (front and rear)

Wheels: Speedline alloy, 8 x 16 in. (front), 9 x 16 in. (rear)

Tires: Pirelli P7, 205/55 VR16 (front), 225/50 VR16 (rear)

DIMENSIONS

Length: 154.1 in.   **Width:** 72.8 in.

Height: 49.0 in.   **Wheelbase:** 96.1 in.

Track: 59.4 in. (front), 58.7 in. (rear)

Weight: 2,117 lbs.

Lancia STRATOS

The Stratos looks almost as strange as the show car that gave it its name, yet it is extremely versatile. Not only was it a World Championship Rally-winning car, but also a successful road racer and a desirable roadgoing sports car.

Fiberglass body

None of the Stratos' body panels are load bearing, so they are made of fiberglass, keeping its weight to a minimum.

Ferrari Dino engine

By the time the Stratos was developed, Lancia had access to Ferrari engines and used its V6 'Dino' quad-cam V6 engine.

Removable bodywork

Quick and easy mechanical access is vital in a rally car, so the front and rear sections of the Stratos lifts clear for maintenance. Both panels can also be completely removed quickly.

Short wheelbase

Mid-engined cars like the Stratos are normally very nimble and maneuverable, but the Stratos is more agile than most due to its short wheelbase.

Central spoiler

The tiny central spoiler is enough to provide extra downforce, supplementing the rear wing which helps keep the back of the car firmly on the road.

Wishbone front suspension

Classic twin-wishbone suspension is used in the front. The front wheel arches are bulged at the top to allow long wheel travel required in rallying.

Vented disc brakes

Very effective brakes were required, so the Stratos has vented four-wheel discs, for improved stops.

Front-mounted radiator

The rear-mounted engine is cooled by a radiator in the front, with two electric fans, accounting for its louvered hood.

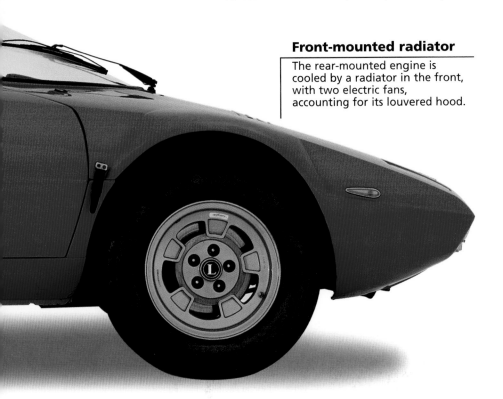

Specifications
1974 Lancia Stratos

ENGINE

Type: V6, quad cam

Construction: Cast-iron block and alloy cylinder heads

Valve gear: Two valves per cylinder operated by four chain-driven overhead camshafts

Bore and stroke: 3.64 in. x 2.36 in.

Displacement: 2,418 cc

Compression ratio: 9.0:1

Induction system: Triple Weber carburetors

Maximum power: 190 bhp at 7,000 rpm

Maximum torque: 166 lb-ft at 5,500 rpm

Top speed: 140 mph

0–60 mph: 7 sec

TRANSMISSION

Five-speed manual

BODY/CHASSIS

Fiberglass two-door, two-seat coupe body with folded sheet-steel frame

SPECIAL FEATURES

The wraparound roof spoiler provides additional downforce and also helps guide air into the engine bay.

Rear bodywork lifts up as one panel.

RUNNING GEAR

Steering: Rack-and-pinion

Front suspension: Twin wishbones with coil springs, telescopic shocks and anti-roll bar

Rear suspension: MacPherson struts and anti-roll bar

Brakes: Vented discs, 9.9 in. dia. (front and rear)

Wheels: Alloy, 14-in. dia.

Tires: 205/70 VR14

DIMENSIONS

Length: 146 in. **Width:** 68.9 in.

Height: 68.9 in. **Wheelbase:** 85.5 in.

Track: 56.3 in. (front), 57.5 in. (rear)

Weight: 2,161 lbs.

Land Rover SERIES 1 🇬🇧

The Series I may have been basic, but it was supposed to be. The Land Rover had to be reliable, easy to service, and able to maintain its go-anywhere reputation. A worldwide legend was very quickly born.

Basic specification

Inexpensive, rugged and basic were Land Rover's basic principles and the specification was deliberately trimmed down. However, Rover shelved a plan to leave items like doors, roof, spare tire, and passenger seat as options.

Green paint

Series 1 Land Rovers only came painted in Sage Green. A darker green arrived in 1949. The list of paint choices was further increased in 1954 with the addition of blue and gray.

Two wheelbase choices

It was obvious that the Land Rover was capable of carrying more than the short bodywork permitted on the initial 80-inch wheelbase, so a longer chassis was developed and made available in 1953. It was 21 inches longer than the SWB chassis (which by then had grown to 86 inches). Three years later, they were both stretched another two inches.

Aluminum bodywork

Shortages of steel in the post-war period forced Rover to adopt aluminum for its bodywork. Although it was more expensive, it was the ideal material—lightweight and easily formed by hand.

Jeep-inspired chassis

The tough, steel, ladder-frame chassis complete with leaf-sprung rigid axles was clearly developed from the Willys Jeep.

Choice of body styles

Most early Land Rovers were custom made, but there were two basic body styles. The first—and by far the more popular—was an extremely simple pickup with half-doors. The station wagon body with curvaceous paneling was more utilitarian, but not as popular as the pickup.

Specifications

1955 Land Rover Series 1

ENGINE

Type: In-line four-cylinder

Construction: Cast-iron block and head

Valve gear: Two valves per cylinder with intake valve mounted over exhaust valve

Bore and stroke: 3.06 in. x 4.13 in.

Displacement: 1,997 cc

Compression ratio: 6.7:1

Induction system: Single Solex carburetor

Maximum power: 52 bhp at 4,000 rpm

Maximum torque: 101 lb-ft at 1,500 rpm

Top speed: 60 mph

0–60 mph: Not quoted

TRANSMISSION

Four-speed manual with two-speed transfer box

BODY/CHASSIS

Separate chassis with aluminum two-door open body

SPECIAL FEATURES

If the Series 1 can't drive out of a compromising situation, this winch will allow it to pull itself out.

This truck is equipped with these unusual windshield-mounted pop-up turn signals.

RUNNING GEAR

Steering: Recirculating ball

Front suspension: Live axle with semi-elliptic leaf springs and telescopic shock absorbers

Rear suspension: Live axle with semi-elliptic leaf springs and telescopic shock absorbers

Brakes: Drums (front and rear)

Wheels: Steel, 16-in. dia.

Tires: 6.00 x 16

DIMENSIONS

Length: 140.8 in.   **Width:** 62.5 in.

Height: 76.0 in.   **Wheelbase:** 86.0 in.

Track: 50.0 in. (front and rear)

Weight: 2,968 lbs.

Lincoln CONTINENTAL

At 227 inches long and weighing 5,192 lbs., the Continental Mk IV was no lightweight. In fact, it was so big that owners in certain parts of the country were required to place clearance lights on their cars for use on the road.

Power top

The Lincoln's power-operated soft top retracts behind the rear seats and is hidden under a metal tonneau cover, giving it a neat top-down appearence. An unusual option was available in 1958. If the car was parked outside with its top down and it started to rain, the top would automatically raise. Ford had many problems with this option which resulted in its ultimate demise in 1959.

Monster big-block V8

Weighing more than 5,000 lbs., the Mk IV needed a massive engine to move it around. Nestling between the fenders is a monster 430-cubic inch V8, producing 350 bhp and an earth-moving 490 lb-ft of torque.

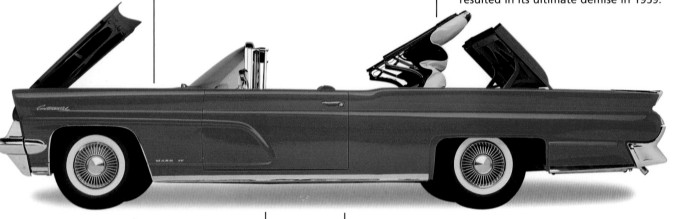

Automatic transmission

By 1959, most buyers expected automatic transmissions. Thus, the Mk IV came with a Ford Turbo-drive three-speed automatic operated with the column-shifter.

Unitary construction

A surprising feature for 1958-1960 Continentals and Lincolns was the adoption of unitary construction, making them stiffer and stronger than rival luxury cars.

Breezway rear window

With the top up, the 'Breezway' rear window gives a distinctive inverted profile. This style feature allows a smaller window, plus it reduces glare from sunlight and helps to keep the interior cool.

Independent front suspension

The Mk IV uses typical 1950s Detroit suspension at the front, with unequal length wishbones, coil springs and telescopic shocks. Air suspension was offered for 1958, but few buyers chose it.

Panoramic windshield

First seen on the 1953 Cadillac Eldorado, the panoramic windshield was a feature of most U.S.-built cars by 1959. These provide excellent forward vision due to moving the A-pillars further back.

Specifications

1959 Lincoln Continental Mk IV

ENGINE

Type: V8

Construction: Cast-iron block and heads

Valve gear: Two valves per cylinder operated by a single camshaft with pushrods and rockers

Bore and stroke: 4.30 in. x 3.70 in.

Displacement: 430 c.i.

Compression ratio: 10.0:1

Induction system: Holley 4150 four-barrel carburetor

Maximum power: 350 bhp at 4,400 rpm

Maximum torque: 490 lb-ft at 2,800 rpm

Top speed: 118 mph

0–60 mph: 10.4 sec.

TRANSMISSION

Turbo-drive three-speed automatic

BODY/CHASSIS

Unitary monocoque construction steel coupe body

SPECIAL FEATURES

A 'Breezway' power window allowed open air driving for the rear passengers.

Compared to rival 1959 luxury cars, the fins on the Mk IV are quite modest.

RUNNING GEAR

Steering: Recirculating ball

Front suspension: Unequal length wishbones with coil springs and telescopic shock absorbers

Rear suspension: Live axle with semi-elliptic leaf springs and telescopic shock absorbers

Brakes: Drums (front and rear)

Wheels: Steel disc, 14-in. dia.

Tires: 9.50 x 15 in.

DIMENSIONS

Length: 227.1 in.   **Width:** 80.1 in.

Height: 56.7 in.   **Wheelbase:** 131.0 in

Track: 61.0 in. (front and rear)

Weight: 5,192 lbs.

Lincoln ZEPHYR

The Zephyr was a curious mixture of new technology—with unitary construction and smooth styling—combined with the old, including mechanical drum brakes and beam axle suspension front and rear.

V12 engine

The Zephyr V12 is a compromise as it is based on the flathead V8. Quiet and refined, it is tuned for torque, not horsepower. The biggest problem is reliability and, consequently, many owners chose to replace the V12 with later Mercury flathead V8s.

Beam axles

Due to the stubbornness of Henry Ford, the Zephyr retained beam-axle suspensio with transverse leaf springs. To improve the handling, adjustable hydraulic shocks were offered.

Three-speed transmission

Geared more for torque than power, the V12 is perfectly mated to the three-speed manual transmission. Synchromesh is fitted to second and top gear to make shifting easier.

Unitary construction

Adopting aircraft techniques, the Zephyr has a light, steel-covered girder-like framework onto which the body is welded. This results in a lighter structure than most rival luxury cars of the time.

Vacuum wipers

There is no electric motor for the windshield wipers, so they are powered by the inlet manifold vacuum. The speed of the wipers varies with engine load, resulting in a slower wiper speed up hills.

Steel disc wheels

By 1936, most American automobile manufacturers had abandoned wire wheels in favor of discs, and the Zephyr was no exception.

Two-speed axle

From 1936 to 1940 a two-speed Columbia rear axle was offered. This effectively doubles the number of gears, giving six forward speeds.

Specifications
1939 Lincoln Zephyr

ENGINE

Type: V12

Construction: Cast-iron block and alloy heads

Valve gear: Two sidevalves per cylinder operated by a side-mounted camshaft

Bore and stroke: 2.75 in. x 3.75 in.

Displacement: 267 c.i.

Compression ratio: 7.2:1

Induction system: Single two-barrel downdraft carburetor

Maximum power: 110 bhp at 3,900 rpm

Maximum torque: 180 lb-ft at 3,500 rpm

Top speed: 87 mph

0–60 mph: 16.0 sec.

TRANSMISSION

Three-speed manual

BODY/CHASSIS

Unitary steel construction with four-door convertible sedan body.

SPECIAL FEATURES

A special V12 engine was commissioned for the Zephyr.

The spare tire mount can be hinged outward for easier luggage access.

RUNNING GEAR

Steering: Worm-and-roller

Front suspension: Beam axle with transverse semi-elliptic leaf spring and hydraulic shock absorbers

Rear suspension: Live axle with transverse semi-elliptic leaf spring and hydraulic shock absorbers

Brakes: Drums (front and rear)

Wheels: Steel discs, 16-in. dia.

Tires: 7.00 x 16 in.

DIMENSIONS

Length: 210.0 in.   **Width:** 73.0 in.

Height: 67.0 in.   **Wheelbase:** 122.0 in.

Track: 55.5 in. (front), 58.25 in. (rear)

Weight: 3,790 lbs.

Lotus ELAN

The Lotus Elan Sprint was one of the fastest sports cars built. Its speed, agility and compact dimensions mean it is now one of the most sought after of all classic Lotus models.

Twin-cam engine
Based on the Ford Cortina, the Elan's engine was originally supposed to have a smaller 1,340-cc capacity. It was designed by Harry Mundy, the technical editor of *Autocar* magazine.

Four- and five-speed transmissions
Most Elans came with the Ford four-speed, but in search of better high-speed cruising, a few later Sprints used the Lotus five-speed transmission (commonly found in the +2S 130), which used Austin internals.

Backbone chassis
Chapman's original intention was to make the Elan a fiberglass monocoque like the Elite. In fact, Elan prototypes used a separate chassis so that they could be built quickly for testing. They worked so well, however, that the production cars were built with separate chassis.

Fiberglass body

Lotus was a pioneer of fiberglass bodyshells. Fiberglass is ideal for low-volume production and has the advantages of strength, light weight and rust resistance.

Pop-up headlights

The Elan's pop-up headlights were a first on a production car and were a device intended to meet California headlight height regulations. They are vacuum-operated.

Advanced suspension

Chapman mixed and matched many parts to produce probably the best-handling and best-riding sports car of its generation. The front suspension parts are shared with the Triumph Herald, with coil springs and patented 'Chapman struts' at the rear.

Specifications

Lotus Elan Sprint

ENGINE

Type: In-line four

Construction: Cast-iron block and alloy cylinder head

Valve gear: Two valves per cylinder operated by twin overhead camshafts

Bore and stroke: 3.25 in. x 2.86 in.

Displacement: 1,558 cc

Compression ratio: 10.3:1

Induction system: Two Weber carburetors

Maximum power: 126 bhp at 6,500 rpm

Maximum torque: 113 lb-ft at 5,500 rpm

Top speed: 118 mph

0–60 mph: 7.0 sec.

TRANSMISSION

Four-speed manual

BODY/CHASSIS

Fiberglass body with steel backbone chassis

SPECIAL FEATURES

The hood bulge was incorporated to accommodate larger carburetors.

Pop-up headlights were a rarely seen feature in the 1960s.

RUNNING GEAR

Steering: Rack-and-pinion

Front suspension: Double wishbones with coil springs, telescopic shock absorbers and anti-roll bar

Rear suspension: Independent by Chapman struts, lower wishbones, coil springs and telescopic shock absorbers

Brakes: Discs (front and rear)

Wheels: Steel, 4.5 x 13.0 in.

Tires: Radials, 165 x 13

DIMENSIONS

Length: 145.0 in. **Width:** 56.0 in.

Height: 45.2 in. **Wheelbase:** 84.0 in.

Track: 45.0 in. (front), 48.4 in. (rear)

Weight: 1,515 lbs.

Lotus ESPRIT V8

You have to look closely to tell the difference between the Esprit S4 and the V8 because Lotus spent all the money it could afford on doubling the car's number of cylinders and turbochargers.

Twin intercoolers

To lower the temperature of the intake air (making it denser and helping combustion and power) each turbocharger has an intercooler.

Split-rim wheels

The V8 Esprit comes equipped with OZ Racing split-rim alloys which are different sizes front and rear, the fronts being 'only' 8.5-inches wide.

New V8 engine

This is the first production Lotus V8, a 349-bhp all-alloy quad-cam design. A more powerful version powers Lotus's new racing Elise at events like the 24 Hours of Le Mans.

Upgraded ABS

One significant change between four-cylinder and V8 Esprits is the switch to Kelsey-Hayes four-channel ABS, which gives some of the most impressive braking in the world.

Kevlar reinforcement

Kevlar is used to reinforce the roof pillars to improve roll-over protection and increase their strength without making them thicker. Kevlar is also used in the sills to help make the whole structure stiffer.

Renault transmission

Lotus first used Renault parts in the Europa in the 1960s and turned to Renault once again in the Esprit. The V8 uses a transmission derived from that used in the fast GTA and A610 Renault Alpine sports cars.

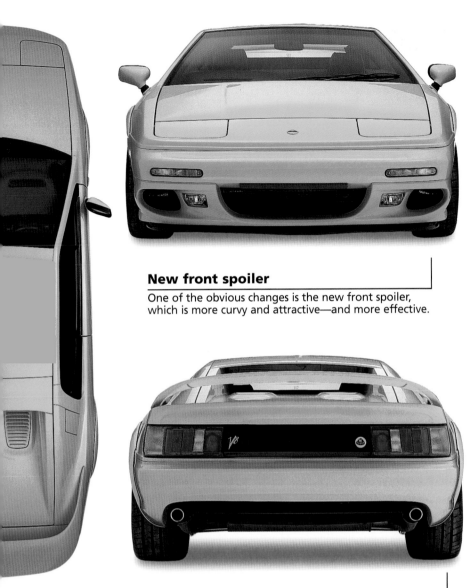

New front spoiler

One of the obvious changes is the new front spoiler, which is more curvy and attractive—and more effective.

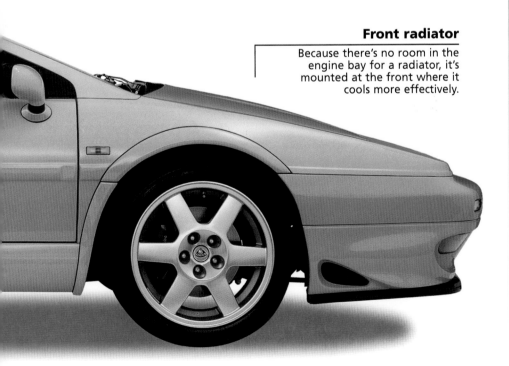

Huge tires

The V8's tires are much larger than those used on the first Esprit over 20 years ago, particularly at the back of the car where they are 285/35 ZR18s running on wheel rims 10 inches wide.

Front radiator

Because there's no room in the engine bay for a radiator, it's mounted at the front where it cools more effectively.

Specifications

1997 Lotus Esprit V8

ENGINE

Type: V8
Construction: Alloy block and heads
Valve gear: Four valves per cylinder operated by four overhead camshafts and hydraulic lifters
Bore and stroke: 3.19 in. x 3.27 in.
Displacement: 3,506 cc
Compression ratio: 8.0:1
Induction system: Electronic fuel injection with twin Garrett T25 turbochargers
Maximum power: 349 bhp at 6,500 rpm
Maximum torque: 295 lb-ft at 4,250 rpm
Top speed: 172 mph
0–60 mph: 4.2 sec

TRANSMISSION

Five-speed manual

BODY/CHASSIS

Sheet steel fabricated backbone chassis with fiberglass two-door coupe body

SPECIAL FEATURES

V8 uses two turbochargers, one for each bank of cylinders, to give the engine better throttle response than if it used a larger single turbo.

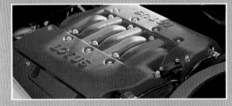
One of the easiest ways to tell the V8 apart is by its new front spoiler with its larger air intakes.

RUNNING GEAR

Steering: Rack-and-pinion
Front suspension: Double wishbones with coil springs, telescopic shocks and anti-roll bars
Rear suspension: Upper and lower links, coil springs, telescopic shocks and anti-roll bar
Brakes: Vented discs, 11.7 in. dia. (front), 11.8 in. dia. (rear); ABS
Wheels: OZ Racing split-rim alloys, 8.5 in. x 17 in. (front), 10 in. x 18 in. (rear)
Tires: 235/40 ZR17 (front), 285/35 ZR18 (rear)

DIMENSIONS

Length: 173.9 in.   **Width:** 78 in.
Height: 45.3 in.   **Wheelbase:** 95.3 in.
Track: 59.8 in. (front and rear)
Weight: 2,968 lbs.

Maserati **BIRDCAGE**

The Birdcage was the ultimate front-engined spaceframe racing car. Despite its clever design, progress left the car behind and the opportunities it had for winning races—before it became obsolete—were almost all wasted.

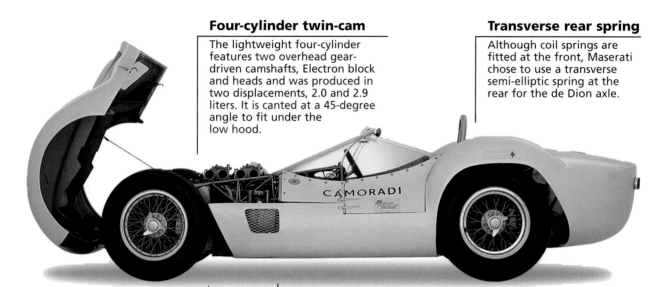

Four-cylinder twin-cam

The lightweight four-cylinder features two overhead gear-driven camshafts, Electron block and heads and was produced in two displacements, 2.0 and 2.9 liters. It is canted at a 45-degree angle to fit under the low hood.

Transverse rear spring

Although coil springs are fitted at the front, Maserati chose to use a transverse semi-elliptic spring at the rear for the de Dion axle.

Disc brakes

The Birdcage was the first Maserati racer to use disc brakes. By the time the Tipo 60 and 61 were built, every top-ranked European racing car was using disc rather than drum brakes.

Alloy bodywork

Maserati had great experience in producing alloy bodywork over a separate chassis and there was never any question of the Birdcage having anything but an alloy body.

Spaceframe chassis

Maserati used a complicated network of small tubes welded together and triangulated wherever possible to produce a light but very strong structure.

Rear transaxle

To help make the weight distribution as equal as possible the five-speed transmission is mounted at the back, along with the differential in an alloy-cased transaxle.

Wishbone front suspension

The classic system of double wishbones, coil springs, telescopic shocks and anti-roll bar was the standard form of front suspension for racing cars in the late 1950s and 1960s.

Cockpit cooling scoop

This particular Birdcage has a scoop added to channel cooling air to the cockpit, even though it's an open car.

De Dion rear axle

The de Dion axle—where the axle tube connects both wheels but curves around the transaxle which is fixed to the chassis—reduces unsprung weight compared to an old-fashioned live axle.

Specifications
1960 Maserati Birdcage Tipo 61

ENGINE
Type: In-line four cylinder
Construction: Electron alloy block and head with cast-iron wet liners
Valve gear: Two inclined valves per cylinder operated by twin gear-driven overhead camshafts
Bore and stroke: 3.94 in. x 3.62 in.
Displacement: 2,890 cc
Compression ratio: 9.0:1
Induction system: Two Weber 52 DCOE sidedraft carburetors
Maximum power: 250 bhp at 7,000 rpm
Maximum torque: Not quoted
Top speed: 165 mph
0–60 mph: Not quoted

TRANSMISSION
Five-speed rear-mounted transaxle

BODY/CHASSIS
Tubular steel spaceframe chassis with open alloy sports racing bodywork

SPECIAL FEATURES

Metal gear shifter gate has a lock to prevent the inadvertent selection of reverse.

The four-into-one exhaust header design is ideal for maximum power.

RUNNING GEAR
Steering: Rack-and-pinion
Front suspension: Double wishbones, coil springs, telescopic shocks and anti-roll bar
Rear suspension: De Dion axle, twin parallel trailing arms per side, transverse leaf spring and telescopic shocks
Brakes: Four-wheel discs
Wheels: Borrani wire spoke 16-in. dia.
Tires: Crossply, 4.5 in. x 16 in. (front), 6.5 in. x 16 in. (rear)

DIMENSIONS
Length: 149.6 in.   **Width:** 59.1 in.
Height: 39.4 in.   **Wheelbase:** 86.6 in.
Track: 49.2 in. (front), 47.2 in. (rear)
Weight: 1,649 lbs.

Maserati BORA

The Bora, which is the Italian name for a strong wind, has a slippery shape and slices through the air at speeds of up to 160 mph thanks to its 310 bhp quad-cam V8 engine.

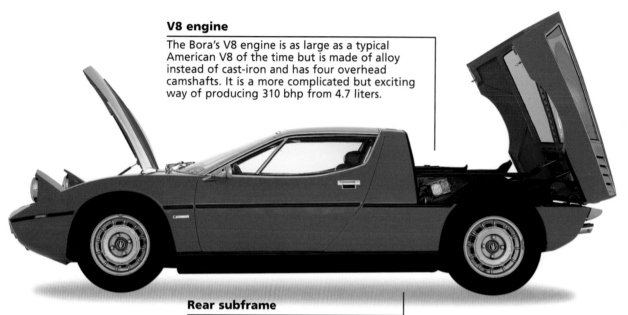

V8 engine

The Bora's V8 engine is as large as a typical American V8 of the time but is made of alloy instead of cast-iron and has four overhead camshafts. It is a more complicated but exciting way of producing 310 bhp from 4.7 liters.

Rear subframe

At the rear, a welded-up square tube structure is used to support the engine, transmission and rear suspension.

Early alloy bodies

The very first Boras were produced with hand-crafted alloy bodies, a skill Maserati was well versed in. Standard production Boras, however, have steel bodies.

Transmission behind engine

German manufacturers ZF supplied the transmission, which is mounted behind the engine toward the tail of the car. This requires a longer and more complicated gear linkage.

Vented discs

Both front and rear brakes are discs, as is common on Italian supercars of the 1970s. They are also vented to improve cooling and to prevent fade.

Aerodynamic shape

Even though the Bora never went anywhere near a wind tunnel, designer Giorgetto Giugiaro achieved a drag coefficient of just 0.30.

Front-mounted radiator

Unlike later mid-engined cars, the Bora has a front-mounted radiator with electric fans.

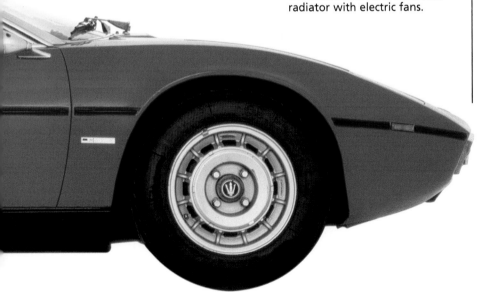

Specifications
1973 Maserati Bora

ENGINE

Type: V8

Construction: Light alloy block and heads

Valve gear: Two inclined valves per cylinder operated by four chain-driven overhead camshafts via bucket tappets

Bore and stroke: 3.69 in. x 3.35 in.

Displacement: 4,719 cc

Compression ratio: 8.5:1

Induction system: Four Weber DCNF/14 downdraft carburetors

Maximum power: 310 bhp at 6,000 rpm

Maximum torque: 325 lb-ft at 4,200 rpm

Top speed: 160 mph

0–60 mph: 6.5 sec

TRANSMISSION

Five-speed ZF manual

BODY/CHASSIS

Steel unitary construction front sections with square-tube rear frame; steel two-door coupe body

SPECIAL FEATURES

The flat rear end or 'Kamm tail' was a popular feature on 1970s supercars.

The Bora was an early Giorgetto Giugiaro design.

RUNNING GEAR

Steering: Rack-and-pinion

Front suspension: Double wishbones with coil springs, telescopic shocks and anti-roll bar

Rear suspension: Double wishbones with coil springs, telescopic shocks and anti-roll bar

Brakes: Vented discs (front and rear), with Citroën high-pressure hydraulics

Wheels: Alloy, 7.5 in. x 15 in.

Tires: Michelin 215/70 VR15

DIMENSIONS

Length: 170.4 in.   **Width:** 68.1 in.

Height: 44.6 in.   **Wheelbase:** 102 in.

Track: 58 in. (front), 57 in. (rear)

Weight: 3,570 lbs.

Maserati GHIBLI

Maserati claimed the Ghibli could reach 174 mph, the same as the more famous Ferrari Daytona, but no one ever quite reached that speed in magazine road testing.

Dry sump lubrication

The V8 engine does not have a conventional oil pan under the engine. The oil is held in a separate tank and pumped around the engine. This had two advantages; the engine could be lower and there was no oil surge under hard cornering.

Quad-cam V8

The most advanced feature of the Ghibli is the quad-cam engine. It is all alloy with four chain-driven overhead camshafts and four Weber carburetors.

Pop-up headlights

These are common today but few cars had pop-up lights in the 1960s. They helped to lower the car's noseline.

Twin-caliper disc brakes

The Ghibli has effective brakes because the front discs are vented and have two calipers which give a larger pad area than single calipers would.

Reinforced tubular-steel chassis

Like all Italian supercars of the era, the Ghibli has a tubular-steel chassis reinforced with welded-on sheet steel to make some sections even stronger.

Steel body

Maserati was not really interested in saving weight with the Ghibli because it had plenty of power, so the body is steel instead of alloy.

Wishbone front suspension

Maserati had made great racing cars so it's no surprise that racing-type twin-wishbone front suspension with an anti-roll bar is used on the Ghibli.

Live rear axle

Despite its exotic looks and performance, Maserati persisted with an old-fashioned live rear axle supported on simple leaf springs for the Ghibli.

Ghia styling

Ghia is now a part of Ford, but was an independent coachbuilder in the 1960s. Giugiaro was chief designer before he moved on to greater fame with Ital Design.

Specifications
1968 Maserati Ghibli

ENGINE
Type: V8, quad cam
Construction: Alloy block with wet liners and alloy cylinder heads
Valve gear: Two valves per cylinder operated by four chain-driven overhead cams
Bore and stroke: 369 in. x 3.35 in.
Displacement: 4,719 cc
Compression ratio: 8.5:1
Induction system: Four Weber 42 DCNF carburetors
Maximum power: 370 bhp at 5,500 rpm
Maximum torque: 326 lb-ft at 4,000 rpm
Top speed: 154 mph
0–60 mph: 6.8 sec.

TRANSMISSION
Five-speed manual

BODY/CHASSIS
Steel two-door 2+2 coupe with tubular-steel chassis

SPECIAL FEATURES

The side vents cool the engine and keep the Ghibli from looking too slab sided.

Lockable fuel filler flaps were built into the Ghibli's rear quarters on both sides to fill the car's twin tanks.

RUNNING GEAR
Steering: Recirculating ball
Front suspension: Twin wishbones with coil springs, shocks and anti-roll bar
Rear suspension: Live axle with semi-elliptic leaf springs, radius arms, Panhard rod and telescopic shocks
Brakes: Vented discs (front), solid discs (rear)
Wheels: Alloy 7.5 in. x 15 in.
Tires: Crossply 205 x 15 in.

DIMENSIONS
Length: 180.7 in. **Width:** 70.9 in.
Wheelbase: 100.4 in. **Height:** 46.6 in.
Track: 56.7 in. (front), 55.4 in. (rear)
Weight: 3,745 lbs.

Maserati MISTRAL

The Mistral marked the end of an era for Maserati—it was the company's last straight-six sports car. Despite having only six cylinders, the Mistral had excellent performance, particularly in its final 4.0-liter form.

Tubular-steel chassis

At the time the Mistral was introduced, all Maseratis were built with a separate tubular-steel chassis. In the Mistral's case this features an array of relatively small-diameter tubes in place of fewer, but larger, main chassis members.

Wishbone front suspension

The front suspension is compact with concentric coil spring/shock absorber units mounted between the unequal-length wishbones.

Frua styling

Pietro Frua styled the Mistral and it proved to be the best of all his designs. He virtually recreated it for a different manufacturer in the form of the AC 428.

Aluminum-alloy bodywork

Contrary to some accounts which describe the Mistral as having mainly steel bodywork with alloy doors, hood and trunk lid, all the body panels are made of aluminum.

Disc brakes

By the mid-1960s virtually all European high-performance cars used disc brakes. The Mistral is no exception, with Girling discs front and rear.

Live rear axle

The most traditional part of the specification is the rear suspension, which employs a live axle located by semi-elliptic leaf springs and assisted by a single torque reaction arm.

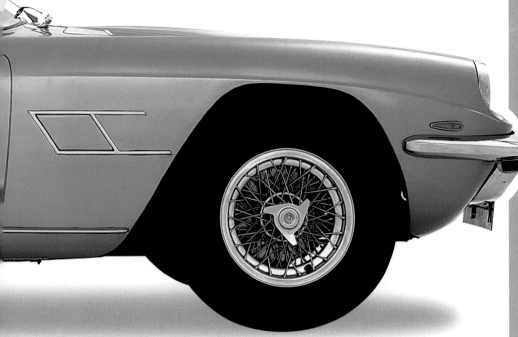

Specifications

1967 Maserati Mistral

ENGINE

Type: In-line six

Construction: Aluminum-alloy block and head

Valve gear: Two valves per cylinder operated by two chain-driven overhead camshafts via bucket tappets and shims

Bore and stroke: 3.46 in. x 4.33 in.

Displacement: 4,014 cc

Compression ratio: 8.8:1

Induction system: Lucas mechanical fuel injection

Maximum power: 255 bhp at 5,200 rpm

Maximum torque: 267 lb-ft at 3,500 rpm

Top speed: 147 mph

0–60 mph: 6.5 sec.

TRANSMISSION

ZF five-speed manual

BODY/CHASSIS

Tubular-steel chassis with coupe or convertible aluminum-alloy body

SPECIAL FEATURES

Tear-drop marker lights supplement the main units under the bumper.

The scoop in the fender is mechanically-operated, allowing cool air into the car.

RUNNING GEAR

Steering: Recirculating ball

Front suspension: Double wishbones with coil springs, telescopic shock absorbers and anti-roll bar

Rear suspension: Live axle with semi-elliptic leaf springs, telescopic shock absorbers, single torque reaction arm and anti-roll bar

Brakes: Discs, 12.05-in. dia. (front), 11.5-in. dia (rear)

Wheels: Borrani wire, 7 x 15 in.

Tires: 225/70 VR15

DIMENSIONS

Length: 177.2 in.   **Width:** 64.9 in.

Height: 49.2 in.   **Wheelbase:** 94.5 in.

Track: 54.7 in. (front), 53.3 in. (rear)

Weight: 2,866 lbs.

Mazda **MIATA**

Recognized around the world as the car that brought back sports car fun, the Miata is brilliant in its simplicity. It is the all-purpose, popular sports car champion.

Classic body styling

Many people compare the Miata with the late, great Lotus Elan. Its shape and proportions are very similar and the general feel is also remarkably consistent with the sports car classics of the 1960s.

Simple top

Anyone used to fiddling with old convertibles will find the new Mazda's top quite simple. You don't even have to unbuckle your seat belt—just press two buttons, fold back the two levers and push the top back.

Twin-cam engine

With an aluminum twin-cam cylinder head and cast-iron block, the four-cylinder engine was state of the art rather than cutting edge. A three-way catalytic converter keeps emissions to a minimum.

Double wishbone suspension

Few cars that are not used on the race track or come from a Ferrari showroom have independent suspension all around with unequal-length double wishbones. This helps to give the Miata extremely capable handling.

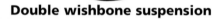

Rack-and-pinion steering

The high-geared, power-assisted rack-and-pinion steering is incredibly fast-reacting. It means you can almost 'feel' your way around bends by simply flexing your wrists.

Powerplant sub-frame

Mazda put the engine, transmission and final drive in a separate subframe. This increases rigidity and isolates the major moving parts to make driving more refined.

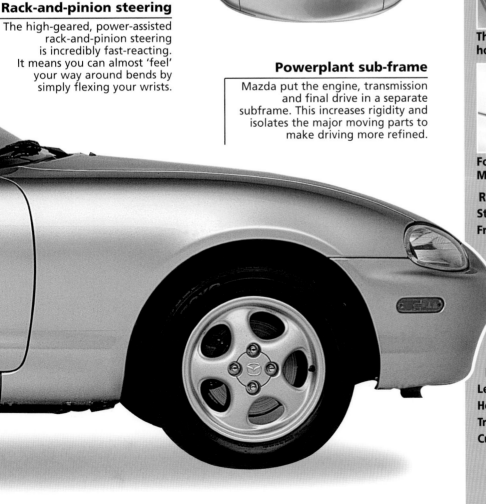

Specifications

1998 Mazda Miata 1.8

ENGINE
Type: In-line four

Construction: Cast-iron block and aluminum alloy head

Valve gear: Four valves per cylinder operated by twin overhead camshafts

Bore and stroke: 3.26 in. x 3.34 in.

Displacement: 1,839 cc

Compression ratio: 9.0:1

Induction system: Multi-point electronic fuel injection

Maximum power: 140 bhp at 6,500 rpm

Maximum torque: 119 lb-ft at 5,500 rpm

TRANSMISSION
Five-speed manual or four-speed automatic

BODY/CHASSIS
Steel monocoque with separate engine/transmission subframe and two-door roadster body with some aluminum and plastic panels

SPECIAL FEATURES

The new 1.8-liter engine has more horsepower than the previous unit.

For a more modern look, the new Miata no longer has pop-up lights.

RUNNING GEAR
Steering: Power-assisted rack-and-pinion

Front suspension: Unequal length double wishbones with coil springs, shocks and anti-roll bar

Rear suspension: Unequal length double wishbones with shocks and anti-roll bar

Brakes: Vented discs front, discs rear

Wheels: Cast-alloy, 14-in. dia.

Tires: 185/60 HR14

DIMENSIONS
Length: 155.3 in. **Width:** 66 in.

Height: 47.3 in. **Wheelbase:** 89.2 in.

Track: 55.9 in. (front), 57 in. (rear)

Curb weight: 2,108 lbs.

McLaren F1

McLaren managed to build the world's best supercar in its very first attempt with the Gordon Murray-designed F1. Unlike most other street-legal supercars, it was good enough to win Le Mans.

Plasma-coated glass

Plasma sprayed onto the inside of the outer glass laminate provides a tint and a heating element to defrost or defog the windshield extremely fast.

Luggage storage

Because space in the front luggage compartment is limited, there are other clever compartments, such as those ahead of the rear wheels, to increase total luggage space.

BMW V12 engine

McLaren commissioned the quad-cam V12 engine from BMW. Light, compact and powerful, its output rose from 550 bhp in 1994 to 668 bhp, all without turbochargers.

'Brake and balance' spoiler

Under heavy braking the spoiler rises at an angle of 30 degrees, generating rear downforce and overcoming the usual pitching.

Formula 1 brakes

The F1's huge vented brakes made by Brembo are as effective as Formula 1 brakes before they were made of carbon fiber.

Six-speed transmission

Six speeds allow the McLaren to have the first five ratios close together and a high 'overdrive' sixth for relaxed high-speed travel.

Survival cell

If the F1 crashes at very high speeds, the occupants are protected by a survival cell; an extremely strong cockpit made of carbon fiber.

Ground effects

Air passing through the venturi tunnels under the F1 drops in pressure, generating 'ground effect' and sucking the car firmly down on the road at high speeds.

Central driver's seat

The driver sits in the center to get the best view and control and also the best weight distribution. Passengers sit on either side, and slightly behind him.

Impact absorbing muffler

The muffler is huge, with a capacity of 65 liters and it has a dual purpose, also acting as a crumple zone in the case of a rear impact.

Specifications
1995 McLaren F1

ENGINE

Type: V12 quad cam by BMW
Construction: Alloy block and heads
Valve gear: Four valves per cylinder operated by four chain-driven overhead cams with variable intake timing
Bore and stroke: 3.39 in. x 3.43 in.
Displacement: 6,064 cc
Compression ratio: 10.5:1
Maximum power: 627 bhp at 7,300 rpm
Maximum torque: 479 lb-ft at 4,000 rpm
Top speed: 231 mph
0–60 mph: 3.2 sec.

TRANSMISSION

Six-speed manual

BODY/CHASSIS

Carbon fiber two-door, three-seat coupe with carbon fiber and Nomex/alloy honeycomb monocoque chassis

SPECIAL FEATURES

The rear spoiler rises under heavy braking, increasing rear downforce and stopping the nose diving.

The driver sits in the center of the car, with a full racing harness rather than a normal seat belt.

RUNNING GEAR

Steering: Rack-and-pinion
Front suspension: Twin wishbones, coil springs, shocks and anti-roll bar
Rear suspension: Twin wishbones with coil springs and shocks
Brakes: Brembo discs, 13.1 in. dia. (front), 12 in. (rear)
Wheels: Magnesium 9 in. x 17 in. (front), 11.5 in. x 17 in. (rear)
Tires: 235/45 ZR17 (front) and 315/40 ZR17 (rear)

DIMENSIONS

Length: 169 in. **Width:** 72 in.
Height: 45 in. **Wheelbase:** 107 in.
Track: 62 in. (front), 58 in. (rear)
Weight: 2,245 lbs.

Mercedes 300SL

The dramatic looks of the world's first postwar supercar were dictated by the racing car chassis under the body which made the Gullwing doors essential.

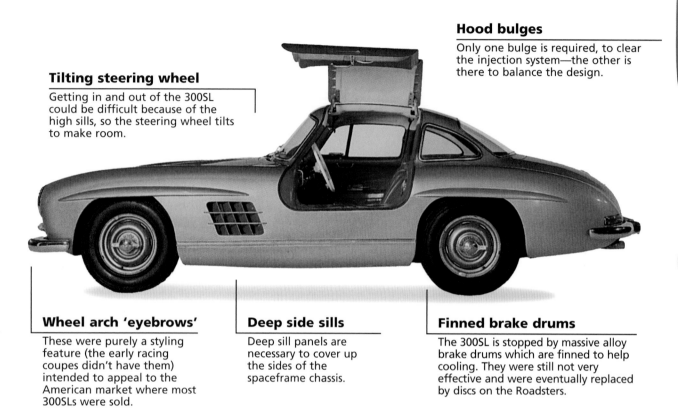

Hood bulges
Only one bulge is required, to clear the injection system—the other is there to balance the design.

Tilting steering wheel
Getting in and out of the 300SL could be difficult because of the high sills, so the steering wheel tilts to make room.

Wheel arch 'eyebrows'
These were purely a styling feature (the early racing coupes didn't have them) intended to appeal to the American market where most 300SLs were sold.

Deep side sills
Deep sill panels are necessary to cover up the sides of the spaceframe chassis.

Finned brake drums
The 300SL is stopped by massive alloy brake drums which are finned to help cooling. They were still not very effective and were eventually replaced by discs on the Roadsters.

Air extractors
To get a good flow of air through the cabin, twin extractors are incorporated into the rear of the roof.

Alloy doors

To ease the strain on the roof-mounted hinges, the doors are made from alloy rather than steel. It also helps save weight overall, as do the alloy hood and trunk lid.

Flush fitting door handles

The door handles are almost too small to notice. The end is pushed in to reveal the whole handle. Handles like these inspired the designers of the Fiat Barchetta in the 1990s.

Sedan engine

Apart from its pioneering use of fuel injection, the specification of the 300SL's engine was quite ordinary due to its sedan origins.

Specifications
1955 Mercedes 300SL

ENGINE
Type: Straight-six
Construction: Cast-iron block and head
Valve gear: Two valves per cylinder operated by single overhead camshaft
Bore and stroke: 3.35 in. x 3.46 in.
Displacement: 2,996 cc
Compression ratio: 8.5:1
Induction system: Bosch mechanical fuel injection
Maximum power: 240 bhp at 6,100 rpm
Maximum torque: 216 lb-ft at 4,800 rpm
Top speed: 165 mph
0–60 mph: 9 sec.

TRANSMISSION
Four-speed manual

BODY/CHASSIS
Steel and alloy two-door coupe with steel spaceframe chassis

SPECIAL FEATURES

Engines in early cars tended to overheat so these large vents were added to allow hot engine-bay air to escape.

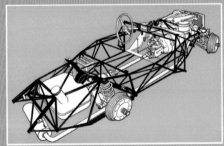

Spaceframe chassis was made light and strong, and was based on that of SL racers.

RUNNING GEAR
Steering: Recirculating ball
Front suspension: Twin wishbones with coil springs and telescopic shocks
Rear suspension: Swinging half axles with coil springs and telescopic shocks
Brakes: Drums all around
Wheels: Steel discs 5 in. x 15 in.
Tires: Crossply 6.7 in. x 15 in.

DIMENSIONS
Length: 178 in.   **Width:** 70 in.
Height: 49.7 in.   **Wheelbase:** 94 in.
Track: 54.5 in. (front), 56.5 in. (rear)
Weight: 2,850 lbs.

Mercedes 540K

The 500 and 540K Mercedes were built in a large range of styles with the beautiful Special Roadsters some of the rarest. More conservative designs like this 1943 500K Cabrio were more common.

Straight-eight engine

The Mercedes in-line, eight-cylinder engine was a very simple design: cast-iron with two valves per cylinder where rivals such as Bentley had four-valve-per-cylinder designs.

Independent front suspension

The Mercedes looked old-fashioned enough to have a solid front axle but in fact it features a new and effective double wishbone and coil spring independent front suspension.

Clutchless gearshifter

If the driver did not wish to use the clutch he could shift from third to fourth by moving the shifter to the right and then up, parallel to third and releasing the throttle pedal.

Separate chassis

The Mercedes chassis looks as though it belongs to a truck. It is massive, with deep box section side members. The advantage of a separate chassis is that it allowed a huge range of coachbuilt bodies to be built on it.

Servo-assisted brakes

One feature where the big Mercedes is advanced is in having servo assistance for its hydraulically-operated drum brakes.

Sprung steel bumpers

Strong sprung steel bumpers were designed to absorb an impact and then spring back into shape.

Electric windshield wipers

The motors are installed on to the windshield instead of being mounted under the hood.

Dual exhaust

To further exploit power, dual exhaust pipes are used, each carrying the exhaust gases from four of the eight cylinders.

Specifications
1938 Mercedes-Benz 540K

ENGINE
Type: In-line eight cylinder
Construction: Monobloc with cast-iron head and block in unit
Valve gear: Two parallel valves per cylinder operated by single block-mounted camshaft, pushrods and rockers
Bore and stroke: 3.46 in. x 4.37 in.
Displacement: 5,401 cc
Compression ratio: 6.13:1
Induction system: Single Mercedes updraft carburetor with Roots-type supercharger
Maximum power: 115 bhp normally aspirated, 180 bhp at 3,500 rpm with supercharger engaged
Maximum torque: Not quoted
Top speed: 105 mph
0–60 mph: 17.0 sec.

TRANSMISSION
Four-speed manual with semi-automatic change on top two gears

BODY/CHASSIS
Separate ladder frame chassis with variety of bodies

SPECIAL FEATURES

Mounted on the side of the windshield is an adjustable light for reading road signs.

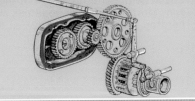

The crankshaft-driven supercharger is activated by a clutch.

RUNNING GEAR
Steering: Worm-and-nut
Front suspension: Double wishbones with coil springs and hydraulic shocks
Rear suspension: Swing axles with trailing arms, hydraulic shocks and twin coil springs per side
Brakes: Lockheed hydraulic drums all round
Wheels: Wire spoke, 17-in. dia.
Tires: Dunlop crossply, 7 x 17 in.

DIMENSIONS
Length: 207 in.   **Width:** 75 in.
Height: 62.5 in.   **Wheelbase:** 129.5 in.
Track: 59.5 in. (front), 58.8 in. (rear)
Weight: 5,516 lbs.

Mercedes-Benz 190SL

Great looks and amazing build quality make the Mercedes-Benz 190SL a superb classic car buy, even if it is more of a boulevard cruiser than an all-out, high-performance sports car.

Supercar styling
The 190SL was sold on its looks. The strong resemblance to the exotic 300SL supercar helped sales tremendously. It outsold the more expensive car by nearly ten to one.

Four-cylinder engine
Despite its sporty looks, the 190SL uses only a 1.9-liter four-cylinder engine to move its 2,550 lbs. It gives 120 bhp. An aftermarket company, Judson, offered an aftermarket supercharger to boost power further.

Wishbone front suspension
Like most post-war sports cars, the 190SL uses double-wishbone front suspension with coil springs and telescopic shock absorbers.

Swing axle rear suspension
The rear end comprises a swing axle with a low center pivot. This ensures a lower roll center and reduces the likelihood of the outside wheel 'jacking up.' It is an effective system, giving good handling.

Hard or soft top
The 190SL was sold as a Roadster (with soft-top only) or a Coupe (with hard-top only), but they are rarely described that way. Most were sold as Roadsters and sold with the optional hardtop. The differences between the two cars are minimal.

Specifications

1956 Mercedes-Benz 190SL

ENGINE

Type: In-line four-cylinder

Construction: Cast-iron block and head

Valve gear: Two valves per cylinder operated by a single overhead camshaft

Bore and stroke: 3.35 in. x 3.29 in.

Displacement: 1,897 cc

Compression ratio: 8.5:1

Induction system: Two Solex twin-choke carburetors

Maximum power: 120 bhp at 5,700 rpm

Maximum torque: 105 lb-ft at 3,200 rpm

Top speed: 106 mph

0–60 mph: 11.2 sec.

TRANSMISSION

Four-speed manual

BODY/CHASSIS

Unitary monocoque construction with steel roadster body

SPECIAL FEATURES

These distinctive wheelwell blisters are also a feature on the 300SL.

The 190SL is a simple two-seater. The space behind the seats is best used for extra luggage.

Unitary build

The 190SL uses a steel monocoque but with a few aluminum parts to reduce weight.

RUNNING GEAR

Steering: Recirculating ball

Front suspension: Double wishbones with coil springs and telescopic shock absorbers

Rear suspension: Low-pivot swing axle with coil springs and telescopic shock absorbers

Brakes: Alfin drums (front and rear)

Wheels: Pressed steel, 5 x 13 in.

Tires: 6.40 x 13 in.

DIMENSIONS

Length: 166.1 in.   **Width:** 68.5 in.

Height: 52.0 in.   **Wheelbase:** 94.5 in.

Track: 56.2 in. (front), 58.1 in. (rear)

Weight: 2,550 lbs.

Mercedes-Benz 600

With the 600, Mercedes aimed to beat Rolls-Royce at its own game with a car that set new standards in luxury travel for those who could afford it. At the time, the 600 was one of the most complex and expensive cars in the world.

V8 engine

This iron-block, overhead-camshaft engine was designed specifically to be used in the 600. It was intended to provide smooth, effortless operation combined with more performance than almost any other sedan in the world.

Four-speed automatic transmission

This is a strengthened version of the familiar four-speed Mercedes automatic transmission that was already becoming the favored option on most of the company's passenger cars.

Four-wheel disc brakes

Given its 130-mph capability, the heavy 600 sedan needed the best brakes money could buy. Mercedes realized this and fitted four-wheel discs that have separate hydraulic circuits front and rear. Each front disc has twin calipers.

Rear passenger luxury

As 600s were conceived for the most prestigious of customers, the rear section of the cabin is fitted with a host of convenience features. Radio controls are duplicated for rear-seat passengers, there are separate heating and ventilation systems, and there is an intercom for communication with the driver.

Air suspension

Rolling bag-type air suspension is a key feature of the 600. Pressurized at 260 psi, it is self-leveling by means of two sensing valves, front and rear. There are soft and hard settings, worked from a steering-column control. In addition, the suspension can be raised up to 2 inches for extra ground clearance.

Long and 'normal' wheelbase

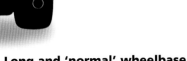

The sedan version of the 600 has a 126-inch wheelbase and the limousine a 153.5-inch wheelbase. There are four- and six-door versions of the limo and a handful were built with State Landaulet bodywork.

Modern, brutal styling

The square, uncompromising styling of the 600 isn't liked by everybody, but its very simplicity means it has never really gone out of fashion; it looked as modern in 1981 as it did in 1963.

Specifications

1963 Mercedes-Benz 600

ENGINE
Type: V8
Construction: Cast-iron block and alloy heads
Valve gear: Two valves per cylinder operated by single overhead camshafts
Bore and stroke: 4.06 in. x 3.74 in.
Displacement: 6,332 cc
Compression ratio: 9.0:1
Induction system: Bosch electronic fuel injection
Maximum power: 300 bhp at 4,100 rpm
Maximum torque: 434 lb-ft at 3,000 rpm
Top speed: 130 mph
0–60 mph: 9.4 sec.

TRANSMISSION
Four-speed automatic

BODY/CHASSIS
Unitary monocoque construction with steel four-door sedan

SPECIAL FEATURES

This pressed-steel hubcap design is featured on most Mercedes-Benz models made in the 1960s.

Mercedes-Benz's prominent, upright headlight arrangement emphasizes the car's square-cut styling.

RUNNING GEAR
Steering: Recirculating ball
Front suspension: Double wishbones with air springs and anti-roll bar
Rear suspension: Low-pivot swing axle with trailing arms each side and air springs
Brakes: Dunlop/ATE discs,11.3-in. dia. (front), 11.6-in. dia.(rear)
Wheels: Steel, 15-in. dia.
Tires: Fulda super sport, 9.00 x 15 in.

DIMENSIONS
Length: 218.0 in. **Width:** 76.8 in.
Height: 59.5 in. **Wheelbase:** 126.0 in.
Track: 62.5 in. (front), 62.0 in. (rear)
Weight: 5,380 lbs

Mercedes **450 SEL 6.9**

Many automobile road testers believed that the 450 SEL 6.9 was the best car in the world when it was new. Its huge V8 endowed it with sports car-humbling performance and its elegantly engineering made it a real driver's car.

6.9-liter engine

At 6,834 cc, the V8 motor was easily the largest produced by Mercedes-Benz since 1945. In Europe the output was 286 bhp, though in the U.S., emissions restrictions knocked 36 bhp off that figure.

Vacuum central locking

The main advantage of Mercedes-Benz's vacuum-operated central locking system over conventional power setups is that it was extremely quiet. It was also more reliable in service.

Four-wheel disc brakes

The 450 SEC 6.9 takes full advantage of four-wheel disc brakes. There are 10.9-inch vented discs up front and 11.0-inch solid discs at the rear while a vacuum servo provides power assistance. Along with other S-Class models, the 450 SEC 6.9 became one of the first cars to be offered with ABS. It was introduced as an option in 1979.

Split air-conditioning

The driver and front passenger have separate temperature controls so that a different ambience can be created on each side of the cabin.

Self-leveling suspension

The 6.9 has standard self-leveling suspension, using a system of hydropneumatics. Remote gas-filled reservoirs are connected to the struts, so whatever the load, the ride height is always maintained. A switch on the fascia can also alter the ride height smoothing out even the roughest terrain.

Specifications
1977 Mercedes-Benz 450 SEL 6.9

ENGINE
Type: V8

Construction: Cast-iron block and aluminum cylinder heads

Valve gear: Two valves per cylinder operated by a single overhead camshaft per bank

Bore and stroke: 4.21 in. x 3.74 in.

Displacement: 6,834 cc

Compression ratio: 8.0:1

Induction system: Bosch mechanical fuel injection

Maximum power: 250 bhp at 4,000 rpm

Maximum torque: 360 lb-ft at 2,500 rpm

Top speed: 140 mph

0–60 mph: 7.1 sec.

TRANSMISSION
Three-speed automatic

BODY/CHASSIS
Unitary monocoque construction with steel four-door sedan body

SPECIAL FEATURES

Like other 1970s Mercedes, the 450 SEL has the trademark ribbed taillights.

The V8 engine has a very large bore and is capable of revving quite high.

RUNNING GEAR
Steering: Recirculating ball

Front suspension: Double wishbones with hydropneumatic struts and anti-roll bar

Rear suspension: Semi-trailing arms with hydropneumatic struts and anti-roll bar

Brakes: Discs (front and rear)

Wheels: Alloy, 14-in. dia.

Tires: 215/70 VR14

DIMENSIONS
Length: 210.0 in.   **Width:** 73.6 in.

Height: 55.5 in.   **Wheelbase:** 116.5 in.

Track: 59.9 in. (front), 59.3 in. (rear)

Weight: 4,390 lbs.

Mercury COUGAR ELIMINATOR

This is Mercury's version of the high-performance Mustang. More refined than its baby brother, it still keeps the Ford heritage with bright paint, side stripes, spoilers, a hood scoop, and big block power.

'High Impact' paintwork

'High Impact' exterior colors was the order of the day in 1970. The Cougar was available in bright blue, yellow and Competition Orange as seen here.

Staggered shocks

Axle tramp can be a serious problem with smaller-sized performance Fords from this era, especially those with big engines. The Cougar Eliminator has staggered rear shock absorbers to help overcome this problem.

Cobra Jet engine

The Eliminator is available with either the 290-bhp Boss 302 or the more stout 428 Cobra Jet with a conservatively rated 335 bhp. This example is powered by the larger 428, often thought of as one of the finest muscle car engines ever produced.

Interior trim

Although more luxurious than the Mustang, the Eliminator is a base model Cougar and has vinyl upholstery. Full instrumentation is standard and includes a tachometer.

Drag Pak

This Eliminator is garnished with the legendary 'Drag Pak' option, which includes the 428 Super Cobra Jet engine, an oil cooler, and ultra-low rear-end gearing (3.91:1 or 4.30:1). This makes the Cougar one of the fastest accelerating muscle cars.

Restyled front

For 1970 the Cougar received a revised front grill with vertical bars and a more pronounced nose. The tail panel was also slightly altered.

Sequential turn indicators

The rear indicators, which are also combined with the brake lights, flash in sequence when the driver flicks the lever. These are also found on contemporary Shelby Mustangs.

Specifications
1970 Mercury Cougar Eliminator

ENGINE

Type: V8

Construction: Cast-iron block and heads

Valve gear: Two valves per cylinder operated by pushrods and rockers

Bore and stroke: 4.0 in. x 3.5 in.

Displacement: 428 c.i.

Compression ratio: 10.6:1

Induction system: Four-barrel carburetor

Maximum power: 335 bhp at 5,200 rpm

Maximum torque: 440 lb-ft at 3,400 rpm

Top speed: 106 mph

0–60 mph: 5.6 sec.

TRANSMISSION

C-6 Cruise-O-Matic

BODY/CHASSIS

Steel monocoque two-door coupe body

SPECIAL FEATURES

The headlights are concealed behind special 'flip-up' panels.

A rear Cougar spoiler is standard Eliminator equipment.

RUNNING GEAR

Steering: Recirculating ball

Front suspension: Unequal length wishbones with coil springs, telescopic shocks and anti-roll bar

Rear suspension: Semi-elliptical multi-leaf springs with staggered rear telescopic shocks

Brakes: Discs (front), drums (rear)

Wheels: Styled steel, 5 x 14 in.

Tires: F60-14 Goodyear Polyglas GT

DIMENSIONS

Length: 191.6 in.　　**Width:** 77.6 in.

Height: 52.8 in.　　**Wheelbase:** 111 in.

Track: 60 in. (front), 60 in. (rear)

Weight: 3,780 lbs.

Mercury **MONTCLAIR**

The Montclair Sun Valley was eye-catching when it first appeared in the mid-1950s. And with its chopped roof and custom paint, this customized Mercury continues to make a statement wherever it goes.

Chevrolet V8 engine
For practicality and power output this Mercury has a small-block Chevrolet V8 installed in place of the original Y-block engine.

Tuck-and-roll upholstery
Despite the engine and running gear this car has a number of period custom features, including the 1950s-style tuck-and-roll upholstery.

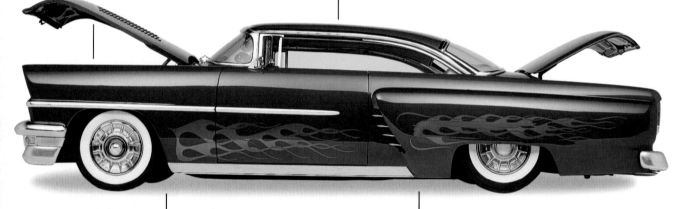

Modern running gear
A Camaro front subframe and suspension have been grafted onto the original chassis. The Salisbury rear axle was also taken from the same Camaro.

Smoothed body
Like most lead sleds the body has been smoothed out, with the headlights and taillights frenched into the body. The door handles and exterior badging have also been removed.

Air suspension
Air bags on the rear suspension give a smooth ride and also allow the car to be raised for driving or lowered for show purposes.

Modified grill

Although not obvious at first, the original bumper/grill has been reworked with additional chromed teeth.

Custom paint

As this car is driven regularly, the body has been coated in tough PPG blue acrylic urethane metallic paint. In true 1950s style, flames have been added below the beltline.

Specifications

1955 Mercury Montclair

ENGINE

Type: V8

Construction: Cast-iron block and heads

Valve gear: Two valves per cylinder operated by pushrods and rockers

Bore and stroke: 4 in. x 3.48 in.

Displacement: 350 c.i.

Compression ratio: 9.5:1

Induction system: Single Holley four-barrel carburetor

Maximum power: 210 bhp at 4,000 rpm

Maximum torque: 285 lb-ft at 2,800 rpm

Top speed: 120 mph

0–60 mph: 9.3 sec.

TRANSMISSION

Three-speed GM TurboHydramatic

BODY/CHASSIS

Separate chassis with two-door steel hardtop body

SPECIAL FEATURES

In popular lead sled style, even the radio antenna has been frenched into the bodywork.

This model even features a pair of fuzzy dice hanging from the rear-view mirror—a very period custom accessory.

RUNNING GEAR

Steering: Recirculating ball

Front suspension: Independent with unequal length wishbones, air bags, front stabilizer bar and telescopic shocks

Rear suspension: Live rear axle with airbags and telescopic shocks

Brakes: Power discs, 9.5-in. dia. (front), drums, 9-in. dia. (rear)

Wheels: Steel discs, 15-in. dia. (with 1957 Cadillac hub caps)

Tires: G78 x 15 Whitewalls

DIMENSIONS

Length: 198.6 in.   **Width:** 82.7 in.

Height: 51.8 in.   **Wheelbase:** 119 in.

Track: 62.5 in (front and rear)

Weight: 3,558 lbs.

Mercury SPORTSMAN

Mercury used the design genius of Bob Gregorie, who had created the look of the famous 1940 Lincoln Continental to make the Sportsman stand apart. He did it with extensive and stylish wood paneling.

V8 engine
It would not be until the 1954 model year that Mercury cars would receive standard overhead-valve V8 engines. The early post-war models used the existing, modest L-head sidevalve V8. The Sportsman managed just 100 bhp from a 239-cubic inch engine.

Drum brakes
Like every other car on sale in the U.S. at the time, the Sportsman has hydraulically-operated drum brakes. Ford introduced these for the 1939 model year.

Separate chassis
Like all Mercury cars of the time, the Sportsman is built on a separate steel chassis frame. One feature of the design is a very deep central tunnel, necessary to make room for the movement of the torque tube connected to the rear axle.

Wood trim
The wood trim on the Sportsman is nothing like the trim used on today's cars. The frame is maple or yellow birch, and each part dovetails to the next perfectly. The darker wood paneling is mahogany.

Split windshield

Along with all post-war U.S. auto manufacturers, Ford and Mercury had to make do with flat windshield glass. The only way the windshield could be angled backward was by having a central join.

Three-speed transmission

Mercury offered the Liquamatic automatic transmission before World War II, but it was dropped for the 1946 line. The only transmission was a three-speed manual with a column shifter.

Specifications

1946 Mercury Sportsman

ENGINE

Type: V8

Construction: Cast-iron block and heads

Valve gear: Two valves per cylinder operated in L-head cylinder heads by a block-mounted camshaft with solid lifters

Bore and stroke: 3.19 in. x 3.75 in.

Displacement: 239 c.i.

Compression ratio: 6.75:1

Induction system: Holley 94 two-barrel carburetor

Maximum power: 100 bhp at 3,800 rpm

Maximum torque: Not quoted

TRANSMISSION

Three-speed manual

BODY/CHASSIS

Separate steel channel-section chassis with two-door convertible body

SPECIAL FEATURES

Adding whitewalls and wood to the 1942 Mercury gave it its classic look.

With so much wood attached to the car's body, it makes sense to have a fire extinguisher on board the Sportsman.

RUNNING GEAR

Steering: Worm-and-sector

Front suspension: Solid axle with transverse semi-elliptic leaf spring and hydraulic lever-arm shock absorbers

Rear suspension: Live axle with transverse semi-elliptic leaf spring, angled trailing arms and hydraulic lever-arm shock absorbers

Brakes: Drums (front and rear)

Wheels: Pressed steel disc, 15 in. dia.

Tires: Crossply 6.50 x 15

DIMENSIONS

Length: 201.8 in.   **Width:** 73.1 in.

Height: Not quoted   **Wheelbase:** 118.0 in.

Track: 58.0 in. (front,) 60.0 in. (rear)

Weight: 3,407 lbs.

MG **METRO 6R4**

The Metro 6R4 is one of those unique supercars that was specifically created for racing in the now-defunct Group B rally championship. It was Leyland's last attempt to dominate world-class motorsports.

V6 engine

The engine is a 90-degree 3.0-liter quad-cam V6. The basic design was strong enough to be tweaked to produce more than 600 bhp in later, modified rallycross cars.

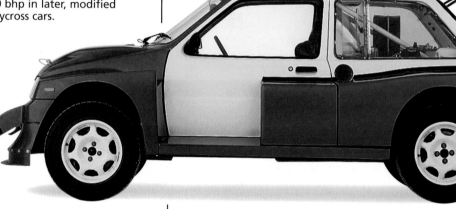

Built-in roll cage

The Metro 6R4 has an immensely strong structure, which is further strengthened by a full roll cage.

All-wheel drive

Power is fed to all four wheels through a five-speed transmission. The all-wheel drive has no fewer than three torque-splitting differentials. The rear differential is located within the engine oil pan.

Aerodynamic package

While the 6R4 was developed, a number of additional bits of bodywork were added. With the 'snowplow' front and tail styling, in addition to the roof-mounted rear spoiler, it earned itself the nickname '400-bhp shopping cart.'

Extended short wheelbase

Originally the 6R4 had an even shorter wheelbase. This made the car tricky to drive and thus it was extended as far as possible, giving very short front and rear overhangs.

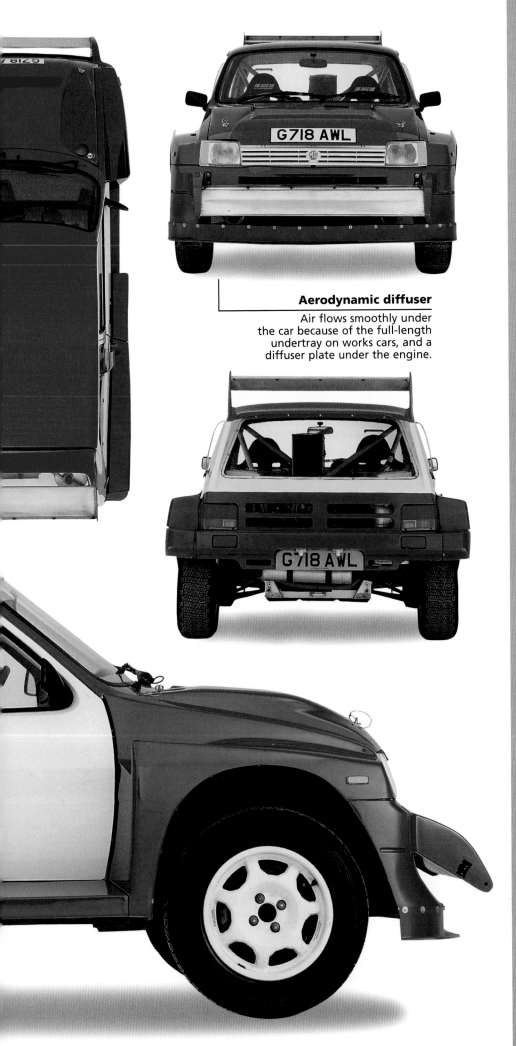

Aerodynamic diffuser

Air flows smoothly under the car because of the full-length undertray on works cars, and a diffuser plate under the engine.

Specifications

1985 MG Metro 6R4 Evolution*

ENGINE

Type: V6

Construction: Cast-alloy block and heads

Valve gear: Four valves per cylinder operated by two overhead camshafts per cylinder bank

Bore and stroke: 3.62 in. x 2.95 in.

Displacement: 2,991 cc

Compression ratio: 12.0:1

Induction system: Lucas electronic fuel injection

Maximum power: 410 bhp at 9,000 rpm

Maximum torque: 270 lb-ft at 6,500 rpm

Top speed: 140 mph

0–60 mph: 4.5 sec.

TRANSMISSION

Five-speed manual

BODY/CHASSIS

Chassis-less construction with multi-tubed underframe, suspension subframes and integral roll cage and carbonfiber and Kevlar body panels.

SPECIAL FEATURES

The huge side extensions contain the twin radiators to keep the engine cool.

Like most Group B cars, the whole rear panel can be removed for engine access.

RUNNING GEAR

Steering: Rack-and-pinion

Front suspension: Macpherson struts with lower wishbones, coil springs and anti-roll bar

Rear suspension: Macpherson struts with lower wishbones, coil springs and anti-roll bar

Brakes: Vented discs (front and rear)

Wheels: Magnesium alloy, 16-in. dia.

Tires: Michelin, 16-in. dia

DIMENSIONS

Length: 131.9 in.   **Width:** 74.0 in.

Height: 59.1 in.   **Wheelbase:** 94.1 in.

Track: 59.5 in. (front), 59.7 in. (rear)

Weight: 2,266 lbs.

*Details apply to 6R4 race version Evolution.

MG M-TYPE MIDGET

The M-Type Midget's lightweight fabric-covered bodywork, with its angled rakish windshield, was designed to make the car look fast and, thanks to its boat-tail rear, quite exotic compared with its rivals.

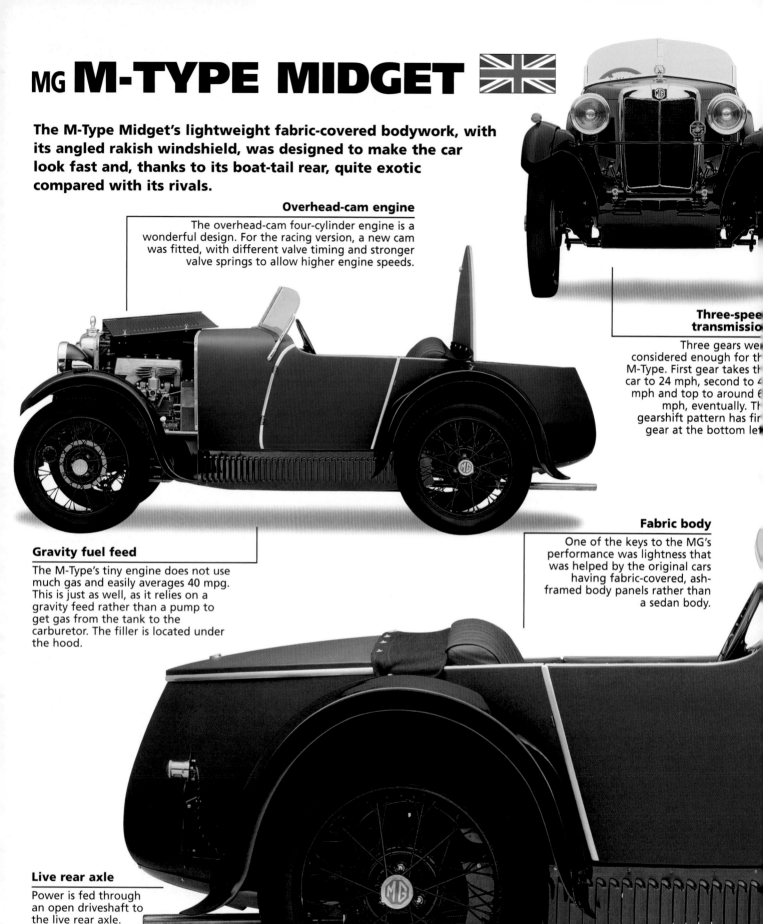

Overhead-cam engine
The overhead-cam four-cylinder engine is a wonderful design. For the racing version, a new cam was fitted, with different valve timing and stronger valve springs to allow higher engine speeds.

Three-speed transmission
Three gears were considered enough for the M-Type. First gear takes the car to 24 mph, second to 4 mph and top to around 6 mph, eventually. The gearshift pattern has first gear at the bottom left.

Gravity fuel feed
The M-Type's tiny engine does not use much gas and easily averages 40 mpg. This is just as well, as it relies on a gravity feed rather than a pump to get gas from the tank to the carburetor. The filler is located under the hood.

Fabric body
One of the keys to the MG's performance was lightness that was helped by the original cars having fabric-covered, ash-framed body panels rather than a sedan body.

Live rear axle
Power is fed through an open driveshaft to the live rear axle. Semi-elliptic leaf springs suspend and locate the axle, and work well, helped by the fact that the MG's track is so small.

Cable brakes

There are drum brakes on all four wheels, and because the MG is so tiny and light, the drums are also very small. To get even moderate braking, the cable system that connects them to the brake pedal has to be in good condition and perfectly adjusted.

Adjustable shocks

The Midget has adjustable shocks for all four wheels. These are of the Hartford friction type, in which the stiffness is adjusted simply by screwing the round friction plates tighter together.

Specifications
1929 MG M-Type Midget

ENGINE
Type: Inline four-cylinder
Construction: Cast-iron block and head
Valve gear: Two valves per cylinder operated by a single overhead camshaft
Bore and stroke: 2.13 in. x 3.27 in.
Displacement: 847 cc
Compression ratio: Not quoted
Induction system: Single carburetor
Maximum power: 20 bhp at 4,000 rpm
Maximum torque: Not quoted
Top speed: 64 mph
0–60 mph: 45.0 sec.

TRANSMISSION
Three-speed manual

BODY/CHASSIS
Separate ladder-type steel frame with fabric-covered two-door convertible body

SPECIAL FEATURES

Protruding from the top of the radiator is an ornate temperature gauge.

The V-angled two-piece windshield looks stylish and sporty.

RUNNING GEAR
Steering: Worm-and-wheel
Front suspension: Beam axle with semi-elliptic leaf springs and friction shock absorbers
Rear suspension: axle with semi-elliptic leaf springs and friction shock absorbers
Brakes: Drums (front and rear)
Wheels: Center-lock wire spoke, 27-in. dia.
Tires: Crossply, 4 x 27

DIMENSIONS
Length: 123.0 in.   **Width:** 50.0 in.
Height: 54.0 in.   **Wheelbase:** 78.0 in.
Track: 41.5 in. (front and rear)
Weight: 1,120 lbs.

MG TC

In its day, the MG TC was virtually unopposed in its class. Among small sports cars, it had the best combination of classic styling and affordability.

Folding windshield

All TCs had a standard folding windshield that provided a real wind-in-the-hair driving experience. Those who preferred not to wear goggles were able to keep the windshield in its upright position.

Split-window roof

The convertible top on the TC had a unique split rear window. Its top came in colors that matched the car's trim. They were originally only available in cream, red and green, but other colors were added as the TC grew in popularity.

Spare wheel

The spare wheel is mounted on the back of the fuel tank providing convenient access when required. Unlocking the center nut requires a mallet.

Chrome bumpers

No bumpers were fitted to UK-spec TCs, but in order to comply with legislation, U.S. export models had full-width chrome bumpers front and rear.

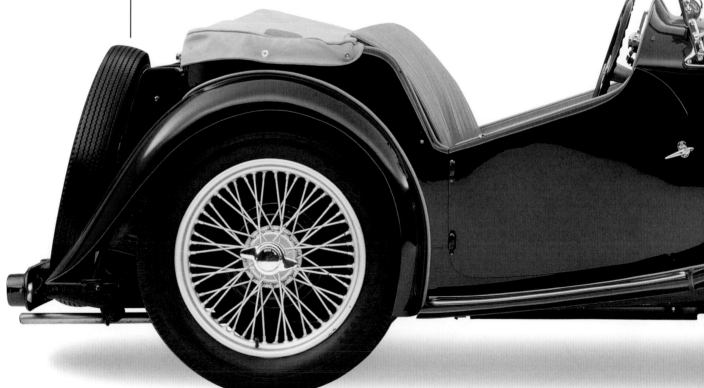

Single fog light

The single horn and fog light arrangement at the front is characteristic of all early MG T-types.

Rear lights

As well as bumpers, U.S.-spec models have special rear lights that contain built-in turn signals.

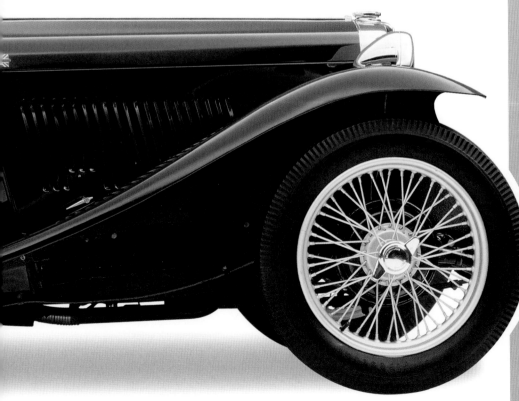

Specifications

1949 MG TC

ENGINE
Type: In-line four-cylinder
Construction: Cast-iron block and head
Valve gear: Two overhead valves per cylinder operated by pushrods
Bore and stroke: 2.62 in. x 3.54 in.
Displacement: 1,250 cc
Compression ratio: 7.25:1
Induction system: Single carburetor
Maximum power: 54 bhp at 5,200 rpm
Maximum torque: 64 lb-ft at 2,700 rpm
Top speed: 73 mph
0–60 mph: 21.2 sec.

TRANSMISSION
Four-speed synchromesh

BODY/CHASSIS
Separate steel frame with channel-section main sidemembers and tubular cross-bracing

SPECIAL FEATURES

The spare wheel is mounted on the back of the fuel tank.

All TCs had a windshield that could be folded flat.

RUNNING GEAR
Steering: Worm-and-peg
Front suspension: Beam axle with semi-elliptic leaf springs and lever-arm shock absorbers
Rear suspension: Live axle with semi-elliptic leaf springs and lever-arm shock absorbers
Brakes: Drums, 9-in. dia. (front and rear)
Wheels: Center-lock wire, 19-in. dia.
Tires: Crossply, 4.5 x 19 in.

DIMENSIONS
Length: 144.5 in. **Width:** 56.0 in.
Height: 53.2 in.   **Wheelbase:** 94.0 in.
Track: 45.0 in. (front and rear)
Weight: 1,845 lbs.

MGA

The MGA could hardly fail. It had all the ingredients of the older upright models that came before it—like the TA, TD and TF—but with a body which looked incredibly modern in the mid-1950s.

B-series engine
The MGA's predecessor had a 1,466-cc engine which was replaced for the MGA by the B-series engine, originally in 1,489-cc form.

Optional heater
There is little that is luxurious about the early MGA: even the crude Smiths heater was an option.

Optional four-wheel discs
Early MGAs have drum brakes all around, the Twin Cam has front discs, as did all MGAs from 1959. Toward the end of production you could order four-wheel Dunlop disc brakes if you specified the center lock wire wheels.

Optional axle ratio
If you wanted better acceleration from your MGA you could order a lower rear axle final drive ratio (4.55:1 compared with 4.10:1).

Alloy body panels
To help reduce weight, the hood, fenders, doors and trunk are all made of aluminum instead of heavy steel.

Live axle
Virtually all sports cars from the 1950s had live rear axles with semi-elliptic leaf springs. This arrangement worked well in the MGA.

No door handles
With car theft almost unheard of in the mid-1950s, it was possible to build a car with no external door handles. You simply put your hand through the sliding side window and opened the interior handle. It was also cheaper and gave a cleaner look to the door.

Wire or disc wheels
The MGA could be ordered with either center lock wire wheels or the more modern looking perforated steel discs.

Rack-and-pinion steering
Many 1950s British sports cars used advanced (for its time) rack-and-pinion steering.

Specifications
1959 MGA MkI

ENGINE
Type: In-line four cylinder
Construction: Cast-iron block and head
Valve gear: Two in-line valves per cylinder operated by single block-mounted camshaft via pushrods and rockers
Bore and stroke: 2.96 in. x 3.50 in.
Displacement: 1,588 cc
Compression ratio: 8.9:1
Induction system: Two SU H4 carburetors
Maximum power: 80 bhp at 5,600 rpm
Maximum torque: 95 lb-ft at 4,000 rpm
Top speed: 103 mph
0–60 mph: 13.7 sec.

TRANSMISSION
Four-speed manual

BODY/CHASSIS
Separate box-section chassis with steel and alloy two-seater roadster or coupe body

SPECIAL FEATURES

MkI MGAs have upright rear lights mounted on small fender plinths. The MkII is recognizable by its stylish horizontally-mounted rear taillights.

The MGA always relied on twin SU carburetors, giving the engine extra fuel to produce more power over the B-series-powered sedans.

Different grill
Early MGAs, like this one, have a sloping radiator grill, but for the last of the line, the MkII, the grill bars are inset almost vertically.

RUNNING GEAR
Steering: Rack-and-pinion
Front suspension: Double wishbones with coil springs and lever arm shocks
Rear suspension: Live axle with semi-elliptic leaf springs and lever arm shocks
Brakes: Discs front, drums rear
Wheels: Center lock wire spoke or steel discs, 16-in. dia.
Tires: 5.60 in. x 16 in., crossply

DIMENSIONS
Length: 156 in.   **Width:** 58 in.
Height: 50 in.   **Wheelbase:** 94 in.
Track: 47.5 in. (front), 48.2 in. (rear)
Weight: 1,985 lbs.

MGB 🇬🇧

There is no doubt that the MGB is what sports cars are supposed to be like. An open-topped, two-seater, front-engined, rear-wheel drive car is the way to travel.

Monocoque construction

Unlike all previous MG cars, the 'B' was designed around monocoque principles, using strong, double-skinned sills. This simplified the production process, reduced build costs and made the overall package more effective.

Leaf-sprung rear

Although MG experimented with an independently sprung rear end, the MGB has a live rear axle. It is suspended by semi-elliptic leaf springs and uses lever-arm shock absorbers.

Chrome bumpers

Early MGBs are colloquially known as 'chrome bumper' cars to distinguish them from the Federal-equipped 'rubber bumper' cars. Aesthetically, the original chrome finish is more pleasing and retains the familiar slatted grill of the older MGs.

Wind-up windows

Unlike all previous MG sports cars, which stuck with the old British custom of removable side windows or curtains, the MGB has glass windows that are opened and closed using a hand crank. Though this is a matter of course in U.S. built cars, it's considered a a luxury for MG owners.

Spacious cabin

By sports car standards, room inside the cockpit is very generous and the driver and passenger have no difficulty getting comfortable.

Specifications

1962 MGB Roadster

ENGINE

Type: In-line four-cylinder

Construction: Cast-iron block and head

Valve gear: Two valves per cylinder operated by a single camshaft via pushrods

Bore and stroke: 3.16 in. x 3.5 in.

Displacement: 1,796 cc

Compression ratio: 8.8:1

Induction system: Two SU carburetors

Maximum power: 95 bhp at 5,500 rpm

Maximum torque: 110 lb-ft at 3,500 rpm

TRANSMISSION

Four-speed manual (overdrive optional)

BODY/CHASSIS

Monocoque chassis with two-door steel open body

SPECIAL FEATURES

The early three-bearing MGB is recognizable by its 'pull' door handles.

The MGB was designed with chrome bumpers, but post-1974 cars have rubber bumpers to meet the U.S. safety regulations.

RUNNING GEAR

Steering: Rack-and-pinion

Front suspension: Wishbones with coil springs and lever-arm shock absorbers

Rear suspension: Live axle with semi-elliptic springs and lever-arm shock absorbers

Brakes: Discs (front), drums (rear)

Wheels: Steel, 14-in. dia.

Tires: 165/70 14

DIMENSIONS

Length: 153.2 in. **Width:** 59.9 in.

Height: 49.4 in. **Wheelbase:** 91 in.

Track: 49.2 in. (front), 49.2 in. (rear)

Weight: 2,080 lbs.

MGB GT V8

The MGB GT V8 should have been a greater success than it was. Yet this Rover V8-engined MG was the most satisfying to drive of all the 'B' family—beefy, relaxed and still reasonably sporty.

V8 engine

The installation of a slightly detuned all-alloy Rover V8 engine in the MGB GT bodyshell resulted in a well-balanced grand touring machine.

Overdrive transmission

The four-speed manual transmission came standard with a Laycock overdrive on top gear. This alters the ratio of the direct-drive (1:1) fourth gear to 0.82:1.

Classic body shape

The basic body shape of the GT was unchanged for the V8. This was not a bad thing, as the shape was timeless, thanks to its good proportions and practical flavor.

Comfortable interior

The roomy cabin of the 2+2 MGB is little altered, although it has smaller instruments and a speedometer calibrated to 140 mph. Standard equipment includes tinted windows, twin door mirrors and a heated rear window. The only option was inertia reel seatbelts.

Ideal weight distribution

By mounting the engine far back in the engine bay, a near-perfect 50:50 weight distribution is achieved.

Stiffened suspension

Although the suspension layout is identical to that of the (rather antiquated) MGB, the spring rates are adjusted at the rear to compensate for the extra torque.

ENGINE
Type: V8

Construction: Aluminum block and heads

Valve gear: Two valves per cylinder operated by a single camshaft

Bore and stroke: 3.50 in. x 2.80 in.

Displacement: 3,528 cc

Compression ratio: 8.25:1

Induction system: Two SU carburetors

Maximum power: 137 bhp at 5,000 rpm

Maximum torque: 193 lb-ft at 2,900 rpm

Top speed: 125 mph

0–60 mph: 8.6 sec

TRANSMISSION
Four-speed manual with overdrive

BODY/CHASSIS
Unitary monocoque construction with steel two-door coupe body

SPECIAL FEATURES

The all-alloy V8 weighs little more than the four-cylinder unit.

Unique wheels help distinguish the V8 from lesser-engined MGBs.

RUNNING GEAR
Steering: Rack-and-pinion

Front suspension: Double wishbones with coil springs, shock absorbers and anti-roll bar

Rear suspension: Live axle with semi-elliptic leaf springs and shock absorbers

Brakes: Discs (front), drums (rear)

Wheels: Alloy, 14-in. dia.

Tires: 175/70 HR14

DIMENSIONS
Length: 154.7 in.   **Width:** 60.0 in.

Height: 50.0 in.   **Wheelbase:** 91.0 in.

Track: 49.0 in. (front), 49.3 in. (rear)

Weight: 2,387 lbs.

Austin MINI Mk 1

The Mini changed the face of driving in Europe and became a popular low-budget car. Simple and cleverly engineered, it turned into one of the best-selling British cars ever made.

Transmission mounted under engine

One of the most revolutionary aspects of the Mini was the fact that the transmission is mounted under the engine's crankshaft, giving a very compact powertrain.

Subframe construction

To deal with vibration and to make the packaging more versatile, all of the major components—engine, steering, transmission and front suspension—are mounted together on the front subframe.

Tiny wheels

The 10 in. wheels on the Mini are the smallest of any car of its day (excluding bubble cars). The reason for such small wheels is that they intrude less on passenger space.

Boxy cabin

When he set about designing the Mini, engineer Alec Issigonis was obsessed by the need to save space. He established that the minimum area required for four passengers was a cube 104 in. long by 50 in. wide and 52 in. tall. This dictated the simple, boxy shape of the Mini, which is surprisingly roomy inside.

Useful boot

The boot may not be very large, but it can hold a lot thanks to the bottom-hinged tailgate.

Simple shape

The extremely simple profile of the Mini evolved entirely from engineering precepts. The man behind the Mini, Alec Issigonis, was anti-styling and resisted all attempts to make his car stylish. This is probably fortunate, as the Mini's shape is a timeless classic as a result.

Specifications
1959 Austin Seven

ENGINE

Type: In-line four-cylinder

Construction: Cast-iron block and head

Valve gear: Two valves per cylinder operated by a single camshaft

Bore and stroke: 2.48 in. x 2.68 in.

Displacement: 52 c.i.

Compression ratio: 8.3:1

Induction system: Single SU carburetor

Maximum power: 37 bhp at 5500 rpm

Maximum torque: 44 lb-ft at 2900 rpm

Top Speed: 75 mph

0–60 mph: 26.5 sec

TRANSMISSION

Four-speed manual

BODY/CHASSIS

Unitary monocoque construction with subframes and steel two-door sedan body

SPECIAL FEATURES

The rounded design of the Mk1's grille is its most distinctive feature.

RUNNING GEAR

Steering: Rack-and-pinion

Front suspension: Wishbones with rubber cone springs and telescopic shock absorbers

Rear suspension: Trailing arms with rubber cone springs and telescopic shock absorbers

Brakes: Drums (front and rear)

Wheels: Steel, 10 in. dia.

Tyres: 5.20 x 10

DIMENSIONS

Length: 120.3 in.

Width: 55.0 in.

Height: 53.0 in.

Wheelbase: 80.2 in.

Track: 48.2 in. (front), 46.2 in. (rear)

Weight: 1340 lbs.

Mini COOPER 🇬🇧

The Mini Cooper's amazing road holding comes from its wheel at each corner design and its light weight. It quickly became the best small sporting sedan in the world, at home on the race track as well as rally stage.

Transmission in sump

Placing the transmission below the engine meant that it had to share the engine's oil instead of the special high-pressure oil normally used for transmissions, but this was never a problem.

Sliding windows

Because the Mini was so narrow, and designed to be cheap, the windows were the cheaper sliding type so that the doors could be single skin and fitted with storage-useful pockets.

Disc brakes

All Coopers and Cooper Ss are fitted with front Lockhead disc brakes, the Cooper Ss with larger, 7.48-inch diameter, discs than the 7-inch discs fitted to the lesser-powered cars.

Small wheels

No other cars had been built with such tiny 10-inch diameter wheels as the Mini. The tires had to be made specially by Dunlop. In later years, after the Cooper went out of production, the Mini was equipped with taller wheels.

Hydrolastic suspension

In 1964 the rubber cone 'dry' suspension was replaced by the Hydrolastic type in which a pressurized fluid-filled hydraulic unit supplies the springing for each wheel. Each front unit is interconnected to the corresponding rear unit so that no separate shocks are needed.

Side radiator

To keep the car as short as possible there was no room for the radiator ahead of the engine and it is mounted to one side at right angles to the air stream, but it still functions adequately.

Rubber suspension

Early Coopers use special rubber cones instead of coil springs; compressing them had just the same effect but they take up much less space.

Exposed side seams

The seams where the body panels join together were deliberately exposed on the outside and made into a styling feature.

Twin fuel tanks

The popular misconception is that all Cooper S models had twin fuel tanks but in fact the right-hand tank was an option.

A-series engine

BMC's A-series engine may have been all cast iron, with a single block-mounted camshaft and two overhead valves per cylinder but it was an excellent design with considerable tuning potential.

Specifications
1964 970-cc Mini Cooper S

ENGINE

Type: In-line four cylinder
Construction: Cast-iron block and head
Valve gear: Two in-line valves per cylinder operated by single block-mounted camshaft, pushrods and rockers
Bore and stroke: 2.78 in. x 2.44 in.
Displacement: 970 cc
Compression ratio: 9.75:1
Induction system: Two SU HS2 carburetors
Maximum power: 65 bhp at 6,500 rpm
Maximum torque: 76 lb-ft at 3,500 rpm
Top speed: 97 mph
0–60 mph: 10.9 sec.

TRANSMISSION

Four-speed manual

BODY/CHASSIS

Steel monocoque two-door, four-seat sedan

SPECIAL FEATURES

The deliberately exposed seams on the bodywork became a Mini hallmark. External door hinges identify an early Mini.

To increase the Mini's carrying capacity it could be driven with the trunk lid half open, in which case the license plate folded down so it could still be seen.

RUNNING GEAR

Steering: Rack-and-pinion
Front suspension: Double wishbones with rubber cone springs and Girling telescopic shocks
Rear suspension: Longitudinal trailing arms, rubber cone springs and Girling telescopic shocks
Brakes: Discs (front), 7.48 in., drums (rear)
Wheels: Steel, 4.5 in. x 10 in.
Tires: Dunlop C41 5.20 x 10 or Dunlop SP41 145/10

DIMENSIONS

Length: 120 in.   **Width:** 55.5 in.
Wheelbase: 80.1 in.   **Height:** 53 in.
Track: 47.5 in. (front), 46.3 in. (rear)
Weight: 1,275 lbs.

Mitsubishi **LANCER EVO V**

The Evo V looks fantastic, but none of it is just cosmetic. All the features that make it look so stunning, such as the vast front air dam, big wheels, rear spoiler and hood scoops, are all there for performance.

Intercooled turbocharger

Mitsubishi uses its own turbocharger, which pumps in air at a high maximum boost of 16 psi. Such a high boost is partly made possible by the massive intercooler.

Twin-cam engine

In the U.S. market—in the Eclipse—the Evo's four-cylinder 16-valve twin-cam engine has 66 bhp less, at just 210 bhp, as well as 60 lb-ft of torque less than the Evo V's 274 lb-ft.

Tall wheels

The alloy wheels fitted to the Evo V are very tall, at 17 inches in diameter. One reason is to allow room for the extremely large disc brakes.

Multi-link rear

A complex multi-link rear suspension system with twin angled transverse links per side keeps the wheels on the road.

Electronic yaw control

The rear differential detects excessive under- or oversteer and varies the torque split to the two rear wheels to restore balance.

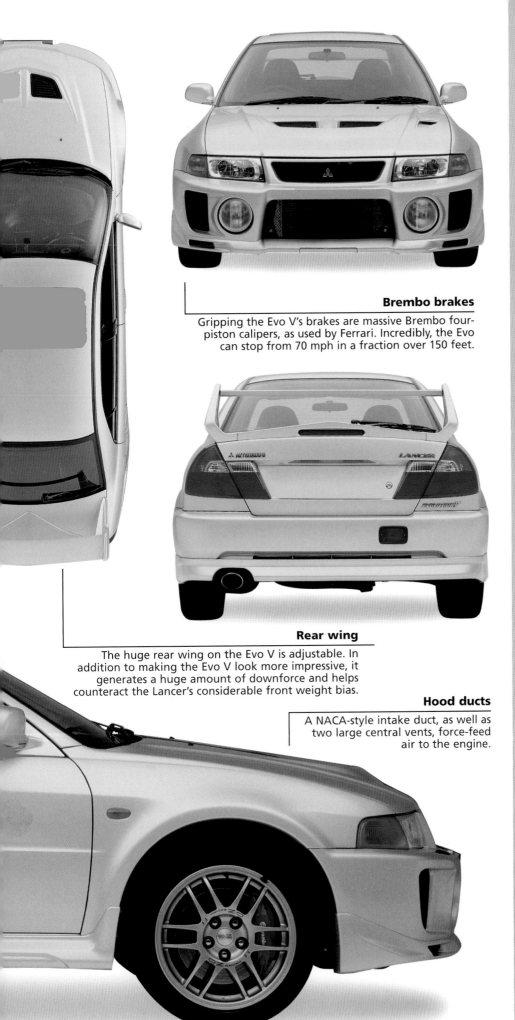

Brembo brakes

Gripping the Evo V's brakes are massive Brembo four-piston calipers, as used by Ferrari. Incredibly, the Evo can stop from 70 mph in a fraction over 150 feet.

Rear wing

The huge rear wing on the Evo V is adjustable. In addition to making the Evo V look more impressive, it generates a huge amount of downforce and helps counteract the Lancer's considerable front weight bias.

Hood ducts

A NACA-style intake duct, as well as two large central vents, force-feed air to the engine.

Specifications

1998 Mitsubishi Lancer Evo V

ENGINE

Type: In-line four-cylinder

Construction: Alloy block and head

Valve gear: Four valves per cylinder operated by twin overhead camshafts

Bore and stroke: 3.35 in. x 3.46 in.

Displacement: 1,997 cc

Compression ratio: 8.8:1

Induction system: Electronic fuel injection with intercooled turbocharger

Maximum power: 276 bhp at 6,500 rpm

Maximum torque: 274 lb-ft at 3,000 rpm

Top speed: 147 mph

0–60 mph: 4.7 sec.

TRANSMISSION

Five-speed manual

BODY/CHASSIS

Unitary monocoque construction with steel sedan body

SPECIAL FEATURES

Massive Brembo calipers are fitted to the Evo's vented disc brakes.

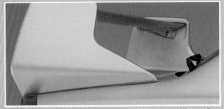

Rear wings usually play a cosmetic role, but the Evo's maximizes downforce.

RUNNING GEAR

Steering: Rack-and-pinion

Front suspension: MacPherson struts with lower wishbones, coil springs, telescopic shock absorbers and anti-roll bar

Rear suspension: Multi-link with coil springs, telescopic shock absorbers and anti-roll bar

Brakes: Vented discs, 12.6-in. dia. (front), 12-in. dia. (rear).

Wheels: Alloy, 7.5 x 17 in.

Tires: Bridgestone Potenza SO-1, 225/45 ZR17

DIMENSIONS

Length: 171.3 in. **Width:** 73.8 in.

Height: 55.9 in. **Wheelbase:** 98.8 in.

Track: 59.4 in. (front), 59.3 in. (rear)

Weight: 3,160 lbs.

Monteverdi 375 ✚

Although very elegant, the Monteverdi's classic Italian styling by Frua was already beginning to look dated by the late 1960s as the supercar world turned to more dramatic-looking mid-engined exotics.

Steel body

Although the 375S body was made by Italian craftsmen—there was no tradition of car building in Switzerland—the bodies were made of steel rather than alloy as might have been expected. The chassis were trucked from Switzerland to Italy to have the bodies fitted, first at Frua's factory and then at the Fissore company.

Chrysler engine

The standard 440-cubic inch Chrysler Magnum V8 in the 375S gave it impressive performance, but for those who wanted more, there was also the 400SS. This uses a more powerful 406 bhp version with twin four-barrel Carter carburetors giving the car a claimed top speed of 168 mph.

Automatic transmission

Although a manual option was available, most of the 375s built had Chrysler's TorqueFlite 727 three-speed automatic unit fitted.

De Dion rear axle

The rear was a very well thought out and designed system using a de Dion axle to connect the two wheel hubs together. The axle itself is well located, with trailing arms for longitudinal location, and a Watt linkage to stop lateral movement.

Opening rear windows

Although the 375S has a luxury leather interior with air conditioning as standard, the design still incorporates rear quarter windows which can open outward to help air flow through the cabin.

Separate chassis

The Monteverdi has a separate steel tubular chassis, onto which the body is welded. Extensive use of rubber bushings reduces vibrations and road shocks.

Frua styling

With no established Swiss stylists, Monteverdi selected the Italian company Frua to shape the look of the 375. The design bore a strong resemblance to other cars styled by the Italian firm, notably the Maserati Mistral and AC 428.

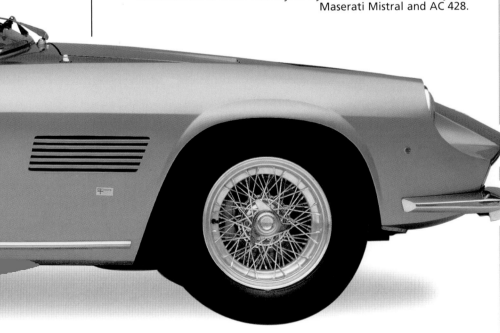

Specifications

1969 Monteverdi 375S

ENGINE

Type: V8

Construction: Cast-iron block and heads

Valve gear: Two valves per cylinder operated by a single camshaft with pushrods and rockers

Bore and stroke: 4.32 in. x 3.75 in.

Displacement: 7,206 cc

Compression ratio: 10.1:1

Induction system: Single four-barrel Carter AFB carburetor

Maximum power: 375 bhp at 4,600 rpm

Maximum torque: 481 lb-ft at 3,200 rpm

Top speed: 152 mph

0–60 mph: 5.9 sec.

TRANSMISSION

TorqueFlite 727 three-speed automatic

BODY/CHASSIS

Separate chassis of square-section steel tubes with steel two-door coupe body

SPECIAL FEATURES

The driver's side windshield wiper has a built-in air deflector.

The headlights on pre-1972 375s bear a strong resemblance to those of the Maserati Mistral.

RUNNING GEAR

Steering: Worm-and-roller

Front suspension: Double wishbones with coil springs, telescopic shock absorbers and anti-roll bar

Rear suspension: De Dion axle with trailing arms, Watt linkage, coil springs, telescopic shock absorbers and anti-roll bar

Brakes: Girling discs, 12-in. dia. (front), 11.8-in. dia. (rear)

Wheels: Campagnolo knock-on alloy, 7 x 15 in.

Tires: Michelin radial, 205/70 R15

DIMENSIONS

Length: 181.1 in. **Width:** 70.7 in.

Height: 48.4 in. **Wheelbase:** 98.8 in.

Track: 59.5 in. (front), 57.9 in. (rear)

Weight: 3,528 lbs.

Morgan **SUPER SPORTS**

Three-wheelers may have begun life as a low priced, simple solution to getting about, but Morgan refined the breed. Some reached speeds as high as 130 mph and became track legends.

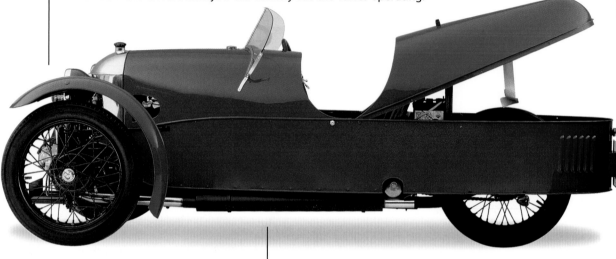

Exposed engine

Because of its extreme forward location and a desire for simplicity and easy servicing, the V-twin engine was left completely exposed up front. From the driver's seat you can actually see the valves operating.

Sliding-pillar suspension

Morgans have always been unique with their choice of front suspensions. It is a system of sliding stub axles, first used and patented in 1910 and still produced today at Malvern Link in its four-wheelers. For its day, it was an effective means of achieving independent wheel location.

Curious controls

In terms of its interior design, the Morgan owes more to the veteran era. There are only two pedals, one for the clutch and one for the rear brake. The throttle is applied by a small lever mounted on the steering wheel.

Lever-operated front brakes

The majority of 'ordinary' Morgans had only one brake, a 'band' brake mounted on the rear hub. As an option—but standard on the rapid Super Sports—front drum brakes were fitted. These are operated by cable and handbrake on the outside of the car.

Prop-and-chain drive

Drive is taken from the front engine to the rear wheel initially with a driveshaft to the transmission. Drive then goes to the wheel using a simple chain and sprocket.

Single rear wheel

In terms of stability, a single rear wheel is superior to a single front wheel. Because it has only three wheels, the design is simple (as no differential is necessary) and weight is kept down, allowing the Morgan to perform far better than its modest power output suggests.

Choice of rear-end treatment

Two different rear end styles were offered by Morgan for the Super Sports. The first was a rounded back, but equally popular was the so-called 'barrel back' design.

Specifications

1932 Morgan Super Sports

ENGINE

Type: V-twin

Construction: Cast-iron block and heads

Valve gear: Two valves per cylinder operated by a single camshaft via pushrods and rockers

Bore and stroke: 3.37 in. x 3.37 in.

Displacement: 990 cc

Compression ratio: 7.5:1

Induction system: Single Amal carburetor

Maximum power: 39 bhp at 4,200 rpm

Maximum torque: 50 lb-ft at 2,400 rpm

Top speed: 85 mph

0–60 mph: 14.0 sec.

TRANSMISSION

Three-speed manual

BODY/CHASSIS

Separate thin-tube chassis with doorless steel sports body

SPECIAL FEATURES

The rear body lifts up for easy access to the rear suspension and drivetrain.

The handbrake lever is mounted outside the body.

RUNNING GEAR

Steering: Burman

Front suspension: Sliding stub axles with coil springs and shock absorbers

Rear suspension: Pivoting fork with quarter-elliptic springs and shock absorbers

Brakes: Drums (front and rear)

Wheels: Wire, 18-in. dia.

Tires: 4.00 x 18

DIMENSIONS

Length: 124 in.   **Width:** 59.0 in.

Height: 40.0 in.   **Wheelbase:** 85.0 in.

Track: 49.5 in. (front)

Weight: 954 lbs.

Morris **1100/1300**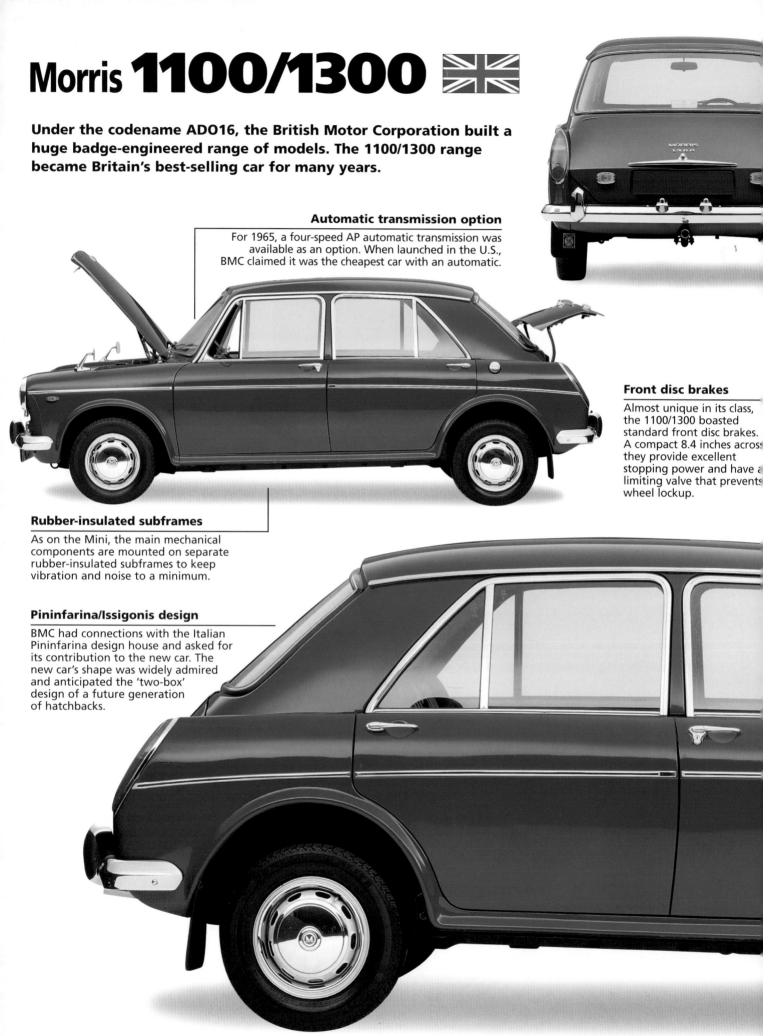

Under the codename ADO16, the British Motor Corporation built a huge badge-engineered range of models. The 1100/1300 range became Britain's best-selling car for many years.

Automatic transmission option

For 1965, a four-speed AP automatic transmission was available as an option. When launched in the U.S., BMC claimed it was the cheapest car with an automatic.

Front disc brakes

Almost unique in its class, the 1100/1300 boasted standard front disc brakes. A compact 8.4 inches across, they provide excellent stopping power and have a limiting valve that prevents wheel lockup.

Rubber-insulated subframes

As on the Mini, the main mechanical components are mounted on separate rubber-insulated subframes to keep vibration and noise to a minimum.

Pininfarina/Issigonis design

BMC had connections with the Italian Pininfarina design house and asked for its contribution to the new car. The new car's shape was widely admired and anticipated the 'two-box' design of a future generation of hatchbacks.

Masterful packaging

Thanks to Issigonis' input, the 1100/1300 shares the Mini's layout. The bored-out A-series engine is mounted transversely with the transmission in unit with the engine—a very compact arrangement. The lack of coil springs and shock absorbers also freed up more room inside, making it very spacious.

Sealed cooling

The water-cooling system is sealed for as little maintenance as possible, reflecting the setup of the sealed Hydrolastic suspension system.

Specifications

1966 Morris 1100/1300

ENGINE

Type: Inline four-cylinder

Construction: Cast-iron block and head

Valve gear: Two valves per cylinder operated by a single camshaft with pushrods and rockers

Bore and stroke: 2.82 in. x 3.25 in.

Displacement: 1,275 cc

Compression ratio: 8.8:1

Induction system: Single SU carburetor

Maximum power: 58 bhp at 5,250 rpm

Maximum torque: 67 lb-ft at 3,000 rpm

Top speed: 88 mph

0–60 mph: 17.3 sec.

TRANSMISSION

Four-speed manual

BODY/CHASSIS

Unitary monocoque construction with steel four-door sedan body

SPECIAL FEATURES

Mounting the gas tank under the rear seat helped maximize interior and trunk space. The gas cap is mounted on the left side.

Fins were toned down on most 1966 cars.

RUNNING GEAR

Steering: Rack-and-pinion

Front suspension: Wishbones with Hydrolastic shock absorbers and spring units

Rear suspension: Swinging trailing arms with Hydrolastic shock absorbers and spring units

Brakes: Discs (front), drums (rear)

Wheels: Steel, 12-in. dia.

Tires: 5.50 x 12

DIMENSIONS

Length: 146.7 in.   **Width:** 60.4 in.

Height: 52.7 in.   **Wheelbase:** 93.5 in.

Track: 51.5 in. (front), 50.9 in. (rear)

Weight: 1,860 lbs.

Morris MINOR 🇬🇧

The chubby styling of the Minor became very familiar on British roads as the population took to the charms of this competent little car. It offered a level of driving pleasure unseen before in its class.

Unibody constructio[n]

In 1948, just about every car ha[d] a separate chassis. The Min[or] was way ahead of its time [in] adopting unitary constructio[n.] The floor was produced in [a] single pressing, cutting costs a[nd] keeping weight down. It w[as] rigid, too, as proven by th[e] convertible which didn't nee[d] very much body reinforcemen[t]

Sidevalve engine

The first Minors used an outdated Morris sidevalve engine to keep costs down. Issigonis had developed new flat-four sidevalve engines, but these were shelved. A more satisfying Austin A30 overhead-valve engine arrived in 1952.

Correct proportions

One of the Minor's main selling points was that it looked right, even though Morris' boss called the prototype a 'poached egg.' One famous story relates how Issigonis, at the eleventh hour, sawed a prototype in half along its length, widening the shell by 4 inches until, in the charming words of an official press release, 'proportion was propitiated and harmony satisfied.'

Basic trim

The Minor was deliberately sparsely equipped. Only the driver's door has a lock, for example, and the rear windows are fixed in position. Inside, the dashboard is plain painted metal.

Low-set headlights

In an age when many cars still had separate headlights, the faired-in, very low-set lights were a startling detail. They give the body a smooth, air-formed look. They were raised after 1950.

Specifications

1950 Morris Minor MM

ENGINE

Type: In-line four-cylinder

Construction: Cast-iron block and head

Valve gear: Two side-mounted valves per cylinder

Bore and stroke: 2.24 in. x 3.54 in.

Displacement: 918 cc

Compression ratio: 6.7:1

Induction system: Single SU carburetor

Maximum power: 28 bhp at 4,400 rpm

Maximum torque: 39 lb-ft at 2,400 rpm

Top speed: 62 mph

0–60 mph: 52.0 sec.

TRANSMISSION

Four-speed manual

BODY/CHASSIS

Unitary monocoque construction with steel two-door sedan body

SPECIAL FEATURES

Trafficators, as they were called, were fitted on British cars, although the U.S market got flashing directional lights.

The split windshield reflects the era when curved glass was still a technical challenge to manufacture.

RUNNING GEAR

Steering: Rack-and-pinion

Front suspension: Wishbones with torsion bars and shock absorbers

Rear suspension: Live axle with semi-elliptic leaf springs and shock absorbers

Brakes: Drums (front and rear)

Wheels: Steel, 14-in. dia.

Tires: 5.00 x 14

DIMENSIONS

Length: 148.0 in.   **Width:** 61.0 in.

Height: 57.0in.   **Wheelbase:** 86.0 in.

Track: 50.5 in. (front), 50.5 in. (rear)

Weight: 1,745 lbs.

Nash **METROPOLITAN**

To answer the demands of a tiny but practical automobile, Nash introduced the Metropolitan. Its body was built by Fisher and Ludlow in Birmingham, England, and wrapped around an Austin rolling chassis complete with an Austin A40 engine.

B-series engine

The Metropolitan was first fitted with a 42-bhp, 1.2-liter four-cylinder engine. A forerunner of the famous B-series unit that later powered the MGA and MGB, the B-series remained in production until 1980.

Wishbone front suspension

Although it uses many Austin components, the wishbone front suspension follows typical Nash practice in having the coil springs mounted on the upper wishbone. The telescopic shock absorbers are mounted on the lower wishbone.

Three-speed transmission

The transmission is derived from the four-speed used in the Austin A40. The bottom gear is removed, so the Nash just uses the upper three ratios. This is possible because of the Nash's good power-to-weight ratio.

Large turning circle

The small, square-topped wheel cutouts limited how far the front wheels could turn, giving the Metropolitan a rather large turning circle for a car of its size.

No trunklid

Until 1959, the Metropolitan had no trunklid. Luggage had to be fed into the trunk from behind the seats.

Specifications

1957 Nash Metropolitan

ENGINE

Type: Inline four-cylinder

Construction: Cast-iron block and head

Valve gear: Two valves per cylinder operated by a single camshaft with pushrods and rockers

Bore and stroke: 2.87 in. x 3.50 in.

Displacement: 1,489 cc

Compression ratio: 7.2:1

Induction system: Single Zenith downdraft carburetor

Maximum power: 52 bhp at 4,500 rpm

Maximum torque: 69 lb-ft at 2,100 rpm

Top speed: 75 mph

0–60 mph: 24.1 sec.

TRANSMISSION

Three-speed manual

BODY/CHASSIS

Unitary monocoque construction with two-door convertible body

SPECIAL FEATURES

The tiny, 13-inch steel wheels are shod with whitewall tires.

The compact Metropolitan even has a miniaturized Continental kit.

RUNNING GEAR

Steering: Cam-and-peg

Front suspension: Double wishbones with coil springs and telescopic shock absorbers

Rear suspension: Live axle with semi-elliptic leaf springs and telescopic shock absorbers

Brakes: Drums (front and rear)

Wheels: Pressed steel, 13-in. dia.

Tires: 5.20 x 13

DIMENSIONS

Length: 149.5 in. **Width:** 61.5 in.

Height: 54.5 in. **Wheelbase:** 85.0 in.

Track: 45.3 in. (front), 44.8 in. (rear)

Weight: 1,885 lbs.

Nissan SKYLINE GTR

This car holds the record for the fastest lap by a production car at the famous Nürburgring circuit in Germany. The GT-R is a true performance machine for the keenest drivers.

Highly-tunable engine

The in-line six-cylinder engine is capable of delivering much more than it does in standard tune, since the GT-R's top speed is limited electronically to 135 mph. Most owners upgrade the engine's electronic management system to yield an extra 80 bhp.

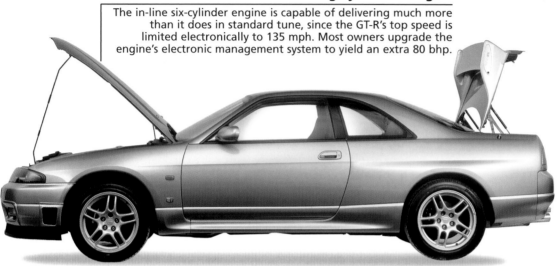

Active limited-slip differential

To prevent the rear tires from scrabbling under heavy acceleration, sensors on each rear wheel detect tire slip and automatically transfer more power to another wheel. Each wheel has its own multi-plate clutch so that the torque is infinitely variable between the wheels. Computer adjustments are made every 100th of a second.

Torque-split four-wheel drive

A computer-controlled four-wheel drive system provides optimum traction. Normally, 100 percent of drive is directed to the rear axle. Sensors analyze the car's traction and stability every 100th of a second. Up to 50 percent of the engine's torque can be directed to the front wheels.

Four-wheel steering

The Super HICAS four-wheel steering system has multiple sensors which detect steering input, turning rate, the car's speed, its yaw rate, and the lateral g-forces. It then calculates the amount of rear-wheel steer to be applied via an electric motor.

Adjustable rear spoiler

The body-colored rear spoiler mounted on the trunk lid is adjustable. It forms part of the GT-R body package, which also includes flared wheel arches, side skirts, an inset mesh grill and a deep front bumper/air dam.

Racing brakes

Behind the double five-spoke alloy wheels are very large vented disc brakes. They are 12.8 inch across at the front (with four-piston calipers made by Italian racing brake manufacturer Brembo). There is also a four-channel ABS anti-lock braking system.

Simple interior

The cockpit reflects the fact that the GT-R is based on a fairly standard sedan. Its plain black trim is only alleviated by attractive seats, carbon-fiber trim and alluring GT-R graphics.

Specifications

1998 Nissan Skyline GT-R

ENGINE

Type: In-line six-cylinder

Construction: Cast-iron cylinder block and aluminum cylinder head

Valve gear: Four valves per cylinder operated by double overhead camshafts

Bore and stroke: 3.38 in. x 2.91 in.

Displacement: 2,568 cc

Compression ratio: 8.5:1

Induction system: Sequential multi-point fuel injection

Maximum power: 277 bhp at 6,800 rpm

Maximum torque: 271 lb-ft at 4,400 rpm

Top speed: 155 mph

0–60 mph: 5.6 sec.

TRANSMISSION

Five-speed manual

BODY/CHASSIS

Integral with two-door steel and aluminum coupe body

SPECIAL FEATURES

The rear spoiler is adjustable for rake to give varying amounts of down force.

Ferrari-style circular tail lights evoke a thoroughbred, racing flavor.

RUNNING GEAR

Steering: Rack-and-pinion

Front suspension: Multi-link with coil springs, telescopic shocks, and anti-roll bar

Rear suspension: Multi-link with coil springs telescopic shocks, and anti-roll bar

Brakes: Vented discs, 12.8-in. dia. (front), 11.8-in. dia. (rear)

Wheels: Alloy, 17-in. dia.

Tires: 245/45 ZR17

DIMENSIONS

Length: 184 in.   **Width:** 70.1 in.

Height: 53.5 in.   **Wheelbase:** 107.1 in.

Track: 58.3 in. (front), 57.9 in. (rear)

Weight: 3,530 lbs.

NSU RO80

There are few cars designed in the 1960s which still look and feel modern. If only NSU had fully developed the rotary engine properly before production, it might have succeeded.

Power steering

With the Ro80 being so nose-heavy and designed for the luxury market, power assistance had to be included to make the steering lighter.

MacPherson strut suspension

The Ro80 was designed to be very comfortable and has MacPherson struts at the front. Much more unusually, it has them at the rear, too.

Rotary engine

Many manufacturers, including GM, evaluated the idea of rotary engines, but only NSU and Mazda put it into production. The Ro80's 995 cc is equivalent to a 1,990 cc conventional engine.

Inboard front discs

To reduce unsprung weight, the front discs are mounted inboard alongside the transmission.

Wider front track

The front track is wider than the rear as more weight is carried on the front. A wider track helped handling and roadholding.

Semi-automatic transmission

Although Mazda always used conventional transmissions with its rotary engines, NSU opted for a three-speed semi-automatic. This did little to help the dreadful fuel consumption.

Aerodynamic shape

The NSU's shape was developed in the wind tunnel at Stuttgart Technical University. The result was a wedge shape with a drag coefficient of 0.33.

Front heavy

Although the rotary engine is very compact, it is mounted ahead of the front axle line helping to give the Ro80 a front-heavy weight distribution of 63/37 front to rear.

Rear disc brakes

In the late-1960s rear drum brakes were common on most cars, but the Ro80 benefitted from four-wheel discs.

Specifications
1974 NSU Ro80

ENGINE
Type: Rotary twin
Construction: Alloy rotor housing
Valve gear: Single exhaust and inlet port per rotor covered and uncovered as the rotor passes
Compression ratio: 9.0:1
Induction system: Single Solex 32 DT ITS carburetor
Maximum power: 115 bhp at 5,500 rpm
Maximum torque: 121 lb-ft at 4,500 rpm
Top speed: 110 mph
0–60 mph: 13.4 sec

TRANSMISSION
Three-speed semi-automatic with torque converter

BODY/CHASSIS
Steel monocoque with four-door sedan body

SPECIAL FEATURES

Alloy wheels were not common on sedans in the 1960s and 1970s. The optional cast-alloy wheels on this car are typical of 1970s styling.

The origins of the Ro80 name are quite simple—'Ro' stands for rotary engine, 80 is the car's design number.

RUNNING GEAR
Steering: Rack-and-pinion
Front suspension: MacPherson struts, lower wishbones and anti-roll bar
Rear suspension: MacPherson struts and semi-trailing arms
Brakes: Four-wheel discs, 11.1 in. dia. (front), 10.7 in. dia. (rear)
Wheels: Steel or optional alloy, 5 in. x 14 in.
Tires: 175SR14

DIMENSIONS
Length: 190 in.   **Width:** 69.5 in.
Height: 55.5 in.   **Wheelbase:** 112.7 in.
Track: 58.5 in. (front), 56.5 in. (rear)
Weight: 2,695 lbs.

NSU **WANKEL SPIDER**

The world was probably not ready for the Wankel engine when NSU launched its Spider in 1964, but there is no doubting the technical genius that lay behind it. The technology continues with Mazda to this day.

Convertible roof

Whereas the conventionally engined Sport Prinz was sold in coupe form, the Wankel Spider was made only as a roadster. The soft-top stowed in the rear deck. Alternatively, a detachable hardtop was available.

Rotary engine

The simplicity of Felix Wankel's idea for a rotary engine did not receive commercial success. With only one rotating piston and a capacity of 497 cc, it develops an impressive 64 bhp with turbine-like smoothness.

Front-mounted radiator

Unlike the Sport Prinz, which has a rear-mounted radiator, the cooling for the Wankel engine comes from a radiator installed in the nose. In turn, that meant that the spare wheel had to be repositioned in the tail.

Bertone styling

While the original NSU Prinz sedan was nothing much to look at, the Spider was a design jewel. Styled by Bertone's Franco Scaglione (better known for his Alfa Romeo designs), it looked right from every angle, which is the best judge of a car's overall design effectiveness.

Front disc brakes

Priced just under $3,000, the Spider was an expensive little car. The front disc brakes did little to justify the price.

Low center of gravity

Because the engine is so compact, the center of gravity over the rear is kept very low. This has beneficial effects on handling and stability. The transmission is mounted in line with the engine and transaxle.

Specifications

1967 NSU Wankel Spider

ENGINE

Type: Single-rotor Wankel

Construction: Cast-iron cylinder block

Valve gear: Circumferential porting

Bore and stroke: N/A

Displacement: 497 cc

Compression ratio: 8.6:1

Induction system: Single Solex sidedraft carburetor

Maximum power: 50 bhp at 5,000 rpm

Maximum torque: 54 lb ft at 3,000 rpm

Top speed: 98 mph

0–60 mph: 15.0 sec.

TRANSMISSION

Four-speed manual

BODY/CHASSIS

Unitary monocoque construction with steel two-door roadster body

SPECIAL FEATURES

Vents are positioned under the rear fender to assist engine cooling.

The rear deck lifts backward for access to the engine.

RUNNING GEAR

Steering: Rack-and-pinion

Front suspension: Wishbones with anti-roll bar, coil springs and shocks

Rear suspension: Semi-trailing arms with coil springs and shocks

Brakes: Discs (front), drums (rear)

Wheels: Steel, 12-in. dia.

Tires: 5.00 x 12

DIMENSIONS

Length: 141.0 in.　　**Width:** 60.0 in.

Height: 49.5 in.　　**Wheelbase:** 79.5 in.

Track: 49.0 in. (front), 48.3 in. (rear)

Weight: 1,543 lbs.

Oldsmobile STARFIRE

An Oldsmobile flagship, the Starfire offered all the luxury and performance of the bigger 98 series in a more compact and sporty package.

More powerful engine

For 1961, Oldsmobile enlarged the 371-cubic inch V8 to 394 cubic inches. For the Starfire, this included an improved induction system and a hotter camshaft. To achieve the ultimate performance from the 394, the Starfire utilized the Skyrocket's four barrel carburetor and high-compression pistons.

Style by skegs

Oldsmobiles shared a corporate styling quirk that was used by only one other GM division—the skeg. Skegs are sort of upside-down tailfins, which protrude from the bottom of the rear quarter panels.

Stiffer chassis

In order to boost torsional stiffness, Oldsmobile created a new frame by adding sturdier sections to the front and back of the side rails. To prevent the excessive chassis flex that many larger American cars suffered from, four steel members were triangulated to counteract torsional and bending movement.

Two pipes are nice

Starfires came standard with a dual-exhaust system. Not only functional in increasing horsepower, they also signified the car's presence on the road.

Room for four

As a range of small, sporty pretenders assaulted the U.S.-car market, the Starfire wore its full-size credentials with pride. Just because it was a big car didn't mean it was slow. As sales of other big sportsters like the Chrysler 300 and the Thunderbird showed, car buyers couldn't get enough.

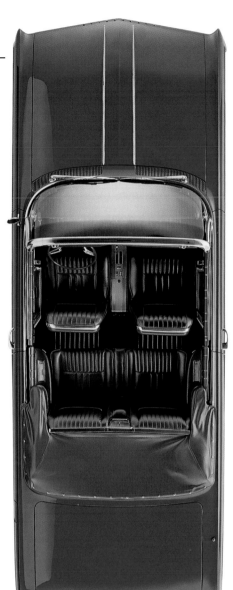

Lavish interior

The Starfire had one of the most luxurious interiors in the Oldsmobile lineup. Bucket seats with power adjustment and a console were standard, as was leather upholstery and a tachometer.

Specifications
1961 Oldsmobile Starfire

ENGINE
Type: V8

Construction: Cast-iron block and head

Valve gear: Two valves per cylinder operated by a single camshaft with hydraulic valve lifters

Bore and stroke: 4.125 in. x 3.688 in.

Displacement: 394 c.i.

Compression ratio: 10.25:1

Induction system: Rochester 4GC four-barrel carburetor

Maximum power: 330 bhp at 4,600 rpm

Maximum torque: 440 lb-ft at 2,800 rpm

TRANSMISSION
Hydramatic three-speed automatic

BODY/CHASSIS
Separate chassis with steel two-door convertible body

SPECIAL FEATURES

Skegs were a prominent feature of the 1961 Starfire.

The Starfire was fitted with Oldsmobile's most powerful and highest-compression V8.

RUNNING GEAR
Steering: Recirculating-ball

Front suspension: Unequal-length upper and lower A-arms with coil springs and telescopic shock absorbers

Rear suspension: Live axle with control arms, coil springs and telescopic shock absorbers

Brakes: Drums (front and rear)

Wheels: Steel, 14-in. dia.

Tires: 8.50 x 14

DIMENSIONS
Length: 212.0 in.   **Width:** 77.0 in.

Height: 55.0 in.   **Wheelbase:** 123.0 in.

Track: 61.0 in. (front and rear)

Weight: 4,305 lbs.

379

Oldsmobile 4-4-2 W30

The 4-4-2 was one of the best muscle cars of the 1960s. It has incredible performance and, unlike many of its rivals, it also has the agility and braking to match the speed.

Custom paint

The bodywork has been sprayed with a base coat of Infinity White paint, followed by a clear coat to give a deep, high gloss finish.

4-4-2 badging

By 1968 the 4-4-2 nameplate had become familiar and sought-after property. Badging in the grill announced that you were driving something special.

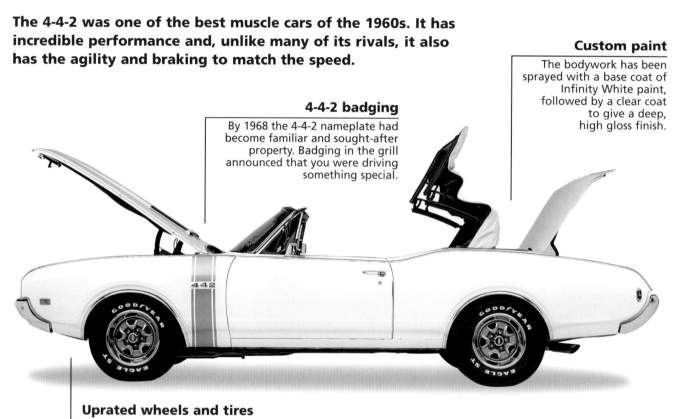

Uprated wheels and tires

The 1968 4-4-2 had 14-inch diameter wheels, but the owner of this car has chosen to upgrade to 15-inch Super Stock II rims, shod with Goodyear Eagle ST tires.

Improved cabin

As well as 1970 Gold Madrid interior, this particular car features full GM and AutoGauge instruments and a 'Rallye' steering wheel.

Heavy-duty suspension

The rear end has been beefed up by replacing the stock coil springs with heavy-duty springs from a station wagon. Modern polyurethane bushings and 1 7/8-inch thick front and rear anti-roll bars have also been added to tighten the suspension further.

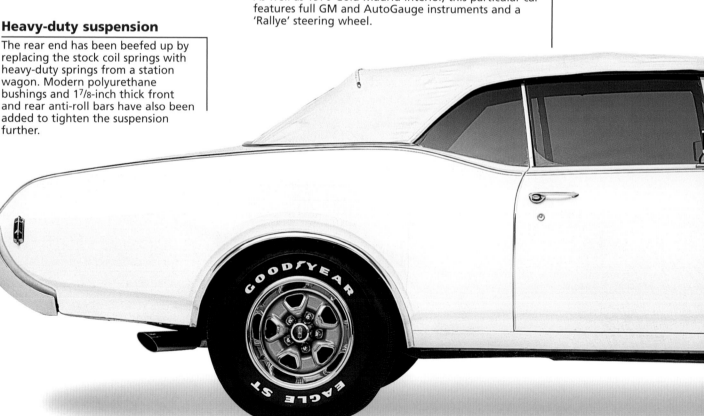

Specifications

Oldsmobile 4-4-2 Convertible

ENGINE

Type: V8

Construction: Cast-iron cylinder block and cylinder heads

Valve gear: Two valves per cylinder operated by a single camshaft

Bore and stroke: 4.12 in. x 4.25 in.

Displacement: 455 c.i.

Compression ratio: 10.5:1

Induction system: Four-barrel carburetor

Maximum power: 410 bhp at 5,500 rpm

Maximum torque: 517 lb-ft at 3,500 rpm

Top speed: 154 mph

0–60 mph: 6.8 sec.

TRANSMISSION

Turbo HydraMatic 350 three-speed automatic

BODY/CHASSIS

Separate chassis with two-door convertible steel body

SPECIAL FEATURES

The interior has been taken from a 1970 Oldsmobile and features Gold Madrid vinyl upholstery.

On this modified car, the exhaust tips exit behind the rear tires rather than out of the back as on the standard 4-4-2s.

RUNNING GEAR

Steering: Recirculating ball

Front suspension: Wishbones with coil springs, shocks, and anti-roll bar

Rear suspension: Rigid axle with coil springs, shocks, and anti-roll bar

Brakes: Discs front, drums rear

Wheels: Super Stock II, 15-in. dia.

Tires: Goodyear Eagle ST

DIMENSIONS

Length: 201.6 in. **Width:** 76.2 in.

Height: 52.8 in. **Wheelbase:** 112 in.

Track: 59.1 in. (front), 59.1 in. (rear)

Curb weight: 3,890 lbs.

Sharp steering

To improve handling, the owner installed a quick-ratio steering box. This means the wheel has to be turned less when cornering.

Big 455 V8

Although the 455 V8 engine was not offered in the 1968 4-4-2, it was available in a special edition called the Hurst/Olds. It became standard for all 4-4-2 models in 1970.

Oldsmobile 88

Between 1954 and 1957, Oldsmobile set a new production record, manufacturing some 583,000 cars in 1955 alone. Here's an example of a modified 1956.

Pre-war transmission

The owner has opted to fit a vintage-style transmission from a 1937 La Salle—a prewar 'junior' Cadillac.

J2 power

This car has been fitted with a 1957 371-cubic inch engine and features the J-2 option with three two-barrel carburetors. The engine has been tuned to deliver 312 bhp.

Lowered suspension

The suspension on this car has been lowered. At the front end, 1957 coil springs were added and cut, while lowering blocks have been mounted on the rear leaf springs.

Chrome wheels

The full chrome 7 inch x 15 inch wheels are shod with Remington tires front and rear.

Hardtop coupe style

Undoubtedly the most elegant of all the Oldsmobile 88 body variations, the Holiday hardtop coupe was also the most popular.

Thunderbird paint

Coating the body in 1990 Thunderbird Bright Red enamel paint produces a strikingly different effect and is well suited to the handsome lines on this 1956 88.

Wraparound windows

For its time, the 88 was a styling sensation, featuring sleek lines and fully wraparound glass both front and rear. The so-called Panoramic wraparound treatment was pioneered by the 1953 Oldsmobile Ninety-Eight Fiesta.

Specifications
1956 Oldsmobile 88 Holiday hardtop coupe

ENGINE

Type: V8

Construction: Cast-iron cylinder block and cylinder heads

Valve gear: Two valves per cylinder operated by single camshaft via pushrods and rockers

Bore and stroke: 4.0 in. x 3.69 in.

Displacement: 371 c.i.

Compression ratio: 8.4:1

Induction system: Three two-barrel carburetors

Maximum power: 312 bhp at 4,600 rpm

Maximum torque: 410 lb-ft at 2,800 rpm

Top speed: 121 mph

0–60 mph: 8.7 sec.

TRANSMISSION

1937 La Salle three-speed manual

BODY/CHASSIS

Steel chassis with two-door hardtop coupe body

SPECIAL FEATURES

The grill of the 1956 Oldsmobile was unique to that year, with a big divider and horizontal bars.

Outer space was a popular theme among stylists in the 1950s which is evident on this 88's taillights.

RUNNING GEAR

Steering: Recirculating ball

Front suspension: Independent with coil springs

Rear suspension: Live axle with semi-elliptic leaf springs

Brakes: Drums, front and rear

Wheels: Pressed steel, 15-in. dia.

Tires: Remington G-78 (front), L-78 (rear)

DIMENSIONS

Length: 203.4 in.

Width: 77 in.

Height: 60 in.

Wheelbase: 122 in.

Track: 59 in. (front), 58 in. (rear)

Curb weight: 3,771 lbs.

Oldsmobile **TORONADO**

Front-wheel drive was one thing, but an innovative engine/transmission layout freed up a lot of space inside and allowed engineers to deliver class-leading handling.

Concealed headlights

In all but 1970 models, the quad headlights are hidden away in pods. These swing up at the press of a button, increasing the sense of drama around the car.

Split transmission

For packaging reasons, the transmission is not an all-in-one unit. Instead, there is a torque converter mounted behind the engine with a two-inch Morse chain running to the Turbohydramatic three-speed.

Beam rear axle

In contrast with the innovative front end, the rear is conventional. The beam axle is suspended on rudimentary single-leaf, semi-elliptic springs. Two sets of shock absorbers are fitted, one pair mounted horizontally.

Bold styling

The Toronado combines European and American styling influences. Its designer, David North, created a clean and dramatic shape dominated by swoopy rear pillars, smooth flanks and heavy chrome bumpers.

Specifications

1966 Oldsmobile Toronado

ENGINE
Type: V8

Construction: Cast-iron block and heads

Valve gear: Two valves per cylinder operated by a single camshaft with pushrods and rockers

Bore and stroke: 4.13 in. x 3.98 in.

Displacement: 425 c.i.

Compression ratio: 10.5:1

Induction system: Single four-barrel carburetor

Maximum power: 385 bhp at 4,800 rpm

Maximum torque: 475 lb-ft at 3,200 rpm

TRANSMISSION
Turbohydramatic three-speed automatic

BODY/CHASSIS
Separate chassis with steel two-door coupe body

SPECIAL FEATURES

Cornering lights on the front fenders were an option on 1967 Toronados.

The heavily chromed rear bumper has cutouts for twin exhaust pipes.

RUNNING GEAR
Steering: Recirculating ball

Front suspension: Wishbones with longitudinal torsion bars, shock absorbers and anti-roll bar

Rear suspension: Beam axle with semi-elliptic springs and shock absorbers

Brakes: Drums, front and rear

Wheels: Steel 15-in. dia.

Tires: 8.85 x 15

DIMENSIONS
Length: 211.0 in. **Width:** 78.5 in.

Height: 52.8 in. **Wheelbase:** 119.0 in.

Track: 63.5 in. (front), 63.0 in. (rear)

Weight: 4,655 lbs.

Big cabin
Enormous doors open wide to provide access to a very spacious six-passenger interior. A long, 119-inch wheelbase coupled with the compact drivetrain gives ample room for passengers.

Front-wheel drive
In 1966, front-wheel drive cars were unique to the U.S market. The Toronado was easily the world's biggest example.

Opel GT

Opel had no real intention of making the GT when it first appeared at the 1965 Frankfurt Motor Show, but public reaction soon changed that thinking.

2+2 cabin

Although described as a four-seater, there is really only room for two passengers sitting on high-back bucket seats. In the rear, a simple platform can be used for passengers but is more useful for luggage.

Choice of engines

Most GTs had a 1,897-cc overhead-camshaft powerplant. This gave 50 percent more power than the smaller 1.1-liter unit offered as an option in early cars.

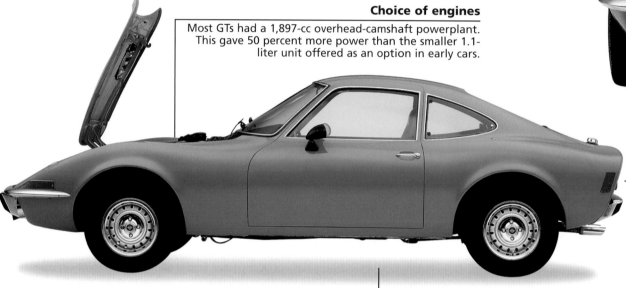

Cut-off tail

Echoing the style of the Corvette, the GT's tail is sharply cut off, partly for aerodynamic reasons and partly for style. The kicked-up, built-in spoiler certainly helps airflow. Notice that there is no trunk lid.

Kadett platform

The GT is essentially a shortened Kadett sedan. This was done in the interest of economy, although the engine and cockpit were moved back by about a foot to improve weight distribution and handling.

American styling

General Motors stylist Clare MacKichan worked on the GT. It therefore comes as little surprise that the car bears many Corvette styling cues.

Concealed headlights

The Corvette-inspired shark nose was given an even more dramatic profile by concealing the headlights under vacuum-operated covers. They are activated by a lever on the transmission tunnel.

French-built bodywork

The steel bodies were built in France by Chausson (based near Paris) and then trimmed by Brissoneau & Lotz before being dispatched to the Opel factory in Bochum, Germany, to be mated with the engine and running gear.

Specifications

1969 Opel GT 1900

ENGINE

Type: In-line four-cylinder

Construction: Cast-iron block and aluminum head

Valve gear: Two valves per cylinder operated by a single overhead camshaft

Bore and stroke: 3.66 in. x 2.75 in.

Displacement: 1,897 cc

Compression ratio: 9.0:1

Induction system: Single Solex two-barrel carburetor

Maximum power: 102 bhp at 5,200 rpm

Maximum torque: 121 lb-ft at 3,600 rpm

Top speed: 110 mph

0–60 mph: 10.1 sec.

TRANSMISSION

Four-speed manual or three-speed automatic

BODY/CHASSIS

Integral chassis with steel two-door coupe body

SPECIAL FEATURES

The pop-up headlights rotate 180 degrees to lie flat when not in use.

Opel GTs have standard 13-inch steel wheels. This car has been fitted with modern radial tires.

RUNNING GEAR

Steering: Rack-and-pinion

Front suspension: Unequal length wishbones with leaf spring and shock absorbers

Rear suspension: Live axle with coil springs, radius arms, Panhard rod and shock absorbers

Brakes: Discs (front), drums (rear)

Wheels: Steel, 13-in. dia.

Tires: 165 HR13

DIMENSIONS

Length: 161.9 in.   **Width:** 62.2 in.

Height: 48.2 in.   **Wheelbase:** 95.7 in.

Track: 49.4 in. (front), 50.6 in. (rear)

Weight: 2,100 lbs.

Packard CARIBBEAN

With two-tone paintwork, lots of chrome and wire wheels, the Caribbean was an impressive showpiece. It was ideally suited for wealthier Americans to cruise around in on Sunday afternoon drives.

Power top

For the price Packard charged, Caribbean buyers were not expected to have to lower the convertible top manually an there was a hydraulically powered system that could raise lower the roof completely in around 30 seconds. When lowered, the top disappeared completely.

Inline eight cylinder

Prestige and smooth running apart, there were clear disadvantages to the straight-eight design. The design was inherently heavier and larger than a V8. The length of the crankshaft also kept engine speeds down. The 1954 engine was the final flowering of the straight-eight concept and has an alloy head and one of the highest compression ratios of any U.S. engine at the time.

Live rear axl

Packard used a live axle that is both locate and suspended by semi-elliptic leaf spring There are telescopic shock absorbers and a anti-roll bar. Packard was working on sophisticated system of torsion-bar sel leveling suspension but this would not debu until the following yea

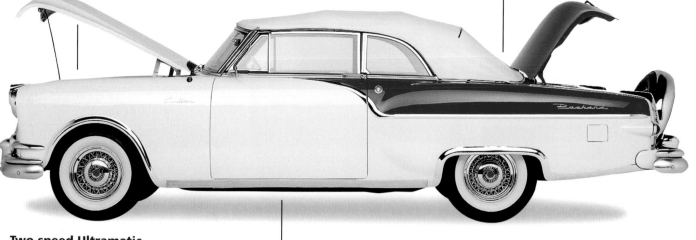

Two-speed Ultramatic

The idea of a two-speed automatic transmission may sound frustrating, but Packard's Ultramatic with torque converter is extremely smooth. It shifts into high gear at speeds ranging from 15 mph to 50 mph depending on how hard the driver accelerates.

Power steering

Although the steering gear on the Caribbean is very low-geared and needs a full 4.4 turns to get from lock to lock, it still has power assistance, although the system chosen is slow to self-center after a turn.

Specifications

1954 Packard Caribbean

ENGINE

Type: Inline eight cylinder

Construction: Cast-iron block and alloy head

Valve gear: Two inline side valves per cylinder operated upwards by a single block-mounted camshaft

Bore and stroke: 3.56 in. x 4.50 in.

Displacement: 359 c.i.

Compression ratio: 8.7:1

Induction system: Single Carter WCFB four-barrel carburetor

Maximum power: 212 bhp at 4,000 rpm

Maximum torque: 310 lb-ft at 2,000 rpm

TRANSMISSION

Two-speed Ultramatic automatic

BODY/CHASSIS

Separate box-section steel chassis frame with two-door convertible body

SPECIAL FEATURES

Chrome-plated flat-top rear wheel arches are a feature unique to the 1954 Caribbean.

The spare wheel is neatly incorporated into the rear bodywork and was color-coded, too.

RUNNING GEAR

Steering: Spiral-bevel

Front suspension: A-arms with coil springs and telescopic shock absorbers

Rear suspension: Live axle with semi-elliptic leaf springs, telescopic shock absorbers and anti-roll bar

Brakes: Drums front and rear, 12.0-in. dia. (front and rear)

Wheels: Wire spoke, 15-in. dia.

Tires: 8.00 x 15

DIMENSIONS

Length: 211.5 in.   **Width:** 77.8 in.

Height: 64.0 in.   **Wheelbase:** 122.0 in.

Track: 60.0/60/8 front and rear

Weight: 4,400 lbs.

Peugeot **504 CABRIOLET**

Smooth and comfortable, the handsome Pininfarina-styled 504 Cabriolet has a sophisticated rather than sporty image. It was a long-lived model with few direct rivals, though rust has depleted its numbers dramatically.

Dependable four-cylinder

Most 504s have Peugeot's rugged in-line four-cylinder engine fitted. It is reliable and has endured, but it lacks aggressive character: it is a cruiser rather than a sprinter.

Refined suspension

Few open-top cars ride as well as the 504 Cabriolet, which mixes firm damping with soft springs. Road noise is minimal and the car is remarkably free of cowl shake, even by today's standards.

Pininfarina badging

These badges in front of the rear wheel cutouts indicate that the 504 was built as well as styled by Pininfarina at the company's factory in Turin, alongside the fixed-head coupe version.

Excellent top

The 504's top looks handsome when up, and, perhaps more important, it folds neatly out of sight, leaving a clean side profile.

Smooth, elegant profile

The timeless, good-looking shape of the 504 was penned by Pininfarina in the late 1960s. There is an individuality about that firm's designs of the time—you can see styling hints of the Fiat Dino and 124 Spider.

Left-hand drive only

The 504 Cabriolet left the factory with the steering wheel on the left-hand side only, although a few models, like this one, were converted to right hand drive for the British market by a specialist company. These RHD exports ceased in 1974.

Comfortable interior

The 504 has big sedan style seats with soft cushions that hug the torso and make for a comfortable ride.

Specifications
Peugeot 504 Cabriolet

ENGINE
Type: In-line four-cylinder
Construction: Iron block and alloy head
Valve gear: Two valves per cylinder operated by a single camshaft via pushrods and rockers
Bore and stroke: 3.46 in. x 3.19 in.
Displacement: 1,971 cc
Compression ratio: 8.3:1
Induction system: Kügelfischer mechanical fuel injection
Maximum power: 110 bhp at 5,600 rpm
Maximum torque: 131 lb-ft at 3,000 rpm
Top speed: 111 mph
0–60 mph: 12.0 sec.

TRANSMISSION
Five-speed manual or four-speed automatic

BODY/CHASSIS
Steel monocoque two-door convertible

SPECIAL FEATURES

Mark 1 models are distinguished by their four-light front end design.

Pronounced cowl scoops gather air for the ventilation system.

RUNNING GEAR
Steering: Rack-and-pinion
Front suspension: MacPherson struts with coil springs, telescopic shock absorbers and anti-roll bar
Rear suspension: Semi-trailing arms, coil springs, telescopic shock absorbers and anti-roll bar
Brakes: Discs, 10.75-in. dia. (front and rear)
Wheels: Steel, 4.35 x 14 in.
Tires: Michelin XAS, 175/70 HR14

DIMENSIONS
Length: 172.0 in. **Width:** 67.0 in.
Height: 55.0 in. **Wheelbase:** 100.4 in.
Track: 58.7 in. (front), 56.3 in. (rear)
Weight: 2,685 lbs.

Plymouth **BARRACUDA**

The Barracuda, with the Mustang, is in many ways the quintessential pony car. It offered the buyer a practical car that could be driven every day, yet had great performance potential – especially with the 6276cc (383ci) engine.

Engine options

In 1967, buyers could choose either the base 145 bhp, 225 c.i. slant-six engine or the 273 c.i. or 383 c.i. V8. The following year, Plymouth offered another V8, the 340 c.i., to fill the gap between the earlier engines.

Transmission choices

Barracudas may have come as standard with a three-speed manual, but the options list also included a four-speed manual, as well as a TorqueFlite three-speed automatic transmission.

Restyled rear window

Although the first-generation Barracuda sported a distinctive wraparound rear window, the styling cue could not entirely disguise its Valiant origins. New bodystyles for 1967 included a convertible and a hardtop.

Stretched chassis

For 1967, the Barracuda's wheelbase was stretched by 2 in. and the car grew by about 4 in. overall. It still remained in proportion, however, and the motoring press universally applauded its modest, yet distinctive, good looks.

Sporty options

Buyers could specify a range of options to give the car a sporty feel, from cosmetic items – such as bucket seats, consoles and stripes – to real performance hardware – like a Sure-Grip differential or the 383 c.i. V8 engine.

Specifications

1967 Plymouth Barracuda

ENGINE

Type: V8

Construction: Cast-iron block and heads

Valve gear: Two valves per cylinder operated by a single camshaft

Bore and stroke: 4.25 in. x 3.38 in.

Displacement: 383 c.i.

Compression ratio: 10.0:1

Induction system: Carter four-barrel carburetor

Maximum power: 280 bhp at 4200 rpm

Maximum torque: 400 lb-ft at 2400 rpm

Top speed: 120 mph

0–60mph: 7.0 sec

TRANSMISSION

Three-speed manual/four-speed manual or three-speed auto

BODY/CHASSIS

Unitary construction with steel body panels

SPECIAL FEATURES

The rear seats fold down to create cavernous luggage space.

 The race inspired style of the fuel- filler cap is unique to the Barracuda.

RUNNING GEAR

Steering: Worm-and-roller

Front suspension: A-arms with torsion bars and telescopic shock absorbers

Rear suspension: Live axle with semi-elliptic leaf springs and telescopic shock absorbers

Brakes: Drums (front and rear)

Wheels: Steel, 14 in. dia.

Tyres: Firestone wide ovals, D70 x 14 in.

DIMENSIONS

Length: 192.8 in.

Width: 69.6 in.

Height: 52.7 in.

Wheelbase: 108.0 in.

Track: 57.4 in. (front), 55.6 in. (rear)

Weight: 2940 lbs.

Plymouth FURY

Living up to its name, the Fury was a full-size coupe that could outperform and outhandle many contemporary sports cars. This was due to fairly advanced engineering by 1957 Detroit standards.

Torsion-bar front suspension

The Fury was available with a suspension unlike GM's or Ford's. Torsion-bar springing was first applied to the 1957 DeSoto. This 1958 Fury uses the same system.

Golden Commando power

While the Fury stopped short of the one-horsepower-per-cubic-inch claim of its DeSoto and Chrysler stablemates, it was not far off. For 1958, the 350-cubic inch motor pumped out 305 bhp or, with fuel injection, 315 bhp.

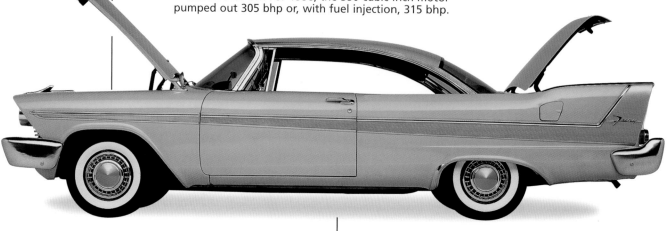

Long, low and lean

The long, wide stance of the Fury is not just due to style. It significantly lowers the center of gravity, making the Fury one of the best-handling cars of its day.

Slimline roofline

The arching shape of the coupe roofline is one of the best styling features. It enhances the sporty feel of the car and, together with the wraparound front and rear windows, contributes toward excellent all-around visibility.

Tailfins

1957 was the biggest year yet for tailfins, and Virgil Exner's contribution made the Fury one of the year's tailfin stars. Although they were claimed to add directional stability at speed, the real reason for their existence is, of course, cosmetic.

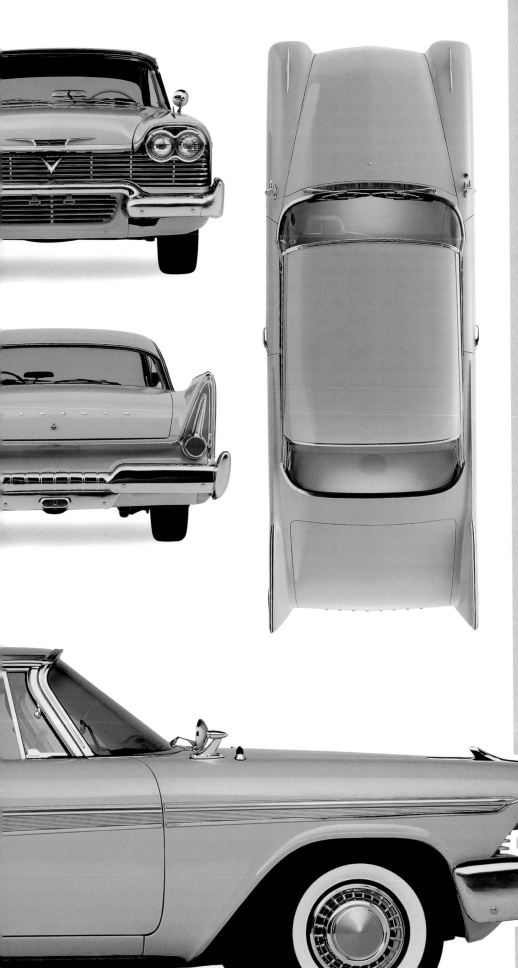

Specifications

1958 Plymouth Fury

ENGINE

Type: V8

Construction: Cast-iron block and heads

Valve gear: Two valves per cylinder operated via pushrods and rockers

Bore and stroke: 4.06 in. x 3.38 in.

Displacement: 350 c.i.

Compression ratio: 10.0:1

Induction system: Dual Carter carburetors

Maximum power: 305 bhp at 5,000 rpm

Maximum torque: 370 lb-ft at 3,600 rpm

Top speed: 122 mph

0–60 mph: 8.0 sec.

TRANSMISSION

Three-speed automatic

BODY/CHASSIS

Separate chassis with two-door coupe body

SPECIAL FEATURES

The 'V' emblem on the grill signifies that a V8 engine is fitted.

The quad-headlight treatment was new for the 1958 model year.

RUNNING GEAR

Steering: Rack-and-pinion

Front suspension: Independent by upper and lower wishbones with longitudinal torsion bars and shock absorbers

Rear suspension: Live axle with semi-elliptic leaf springs and shock absorbers

Brakes: Drums (front and rear)

Wheels: Steel, 14-in. dia.

Tires: 8.00 x 14

DIMENSIONS

Length: 206.0 in.   **Width:** 78.0 in.

Height: 57.0 in.   **Wheelbase:** 118.0 in.

Track: 60.9 in. (front), 59.6 in. (rear)

Weight: 3,510 lbs.

Plymouth HEMI 'CUDA

Lime Light green was only one of the factory optioned 'High Impact' colors available for the 1970 'Cuda. If you have an engine as powerful as this one, why not have a paint scheme that's equally outrageous?

Hemi V8

The Hemi V8 was so called because of its hemispherical combustion chambers. These promote more efficient combustion of the air/fuel mixture. It was one of the most powerful engines ever put in any muscle car.

Low ratio back axle

The lowest standard axle ratio available was 4.10:1. This car has an even lower 4.56:1 ratio axle for more urgent acceleration.

Torsion bar front suspension

The 'Cuda uses double wishbone front suspension sprung by longitudinally-mounted torsion bars. Adjustable Koni shock absorbers are used on this car.

Drag racing tires and wheels

For looks and performance, huge 14-inch wide Weld Racing Pro-Star alloy wheels and super-sticky Mickey Thompson tires have been added to this wild Hemi 'Cuda.

Hardtop body

This, like most Hemi 'Cudas, has a two-door hardtop body. There were only 14 Hemi convertibles made in 1970.

Hood-retaining pins

These race-style hood-retaining pins were actually factory fitted with the shaker hood which came as standard equipment on the Hemi 'Cuda.

Custom tail pipes

Even with the free-flow system fitted to this car, the owner has managed to retain the neat feature of having the twin tail pipes exiting through the rear valance.

Limited-slip differential

The 'Cuda has a Chrysler 'Sure-Grip' limited-slip differential as standard equipment.

Specifications
1971 Plymouth Hemi 'Cuda

ENGINE
Type: V8

Construction: Cast-iron block and heads

Valve gear: Two valves per cylinder actuated by a single camshaft via mechanical lifters and pushrods

Bore and stroke: 4.25 in. x 3.75 in.

Displacement: 432 c.i.

Compression ratio: 10.25:1

Induction system: Twin Carter AFB four-barrel carburetors

Maximum power: 620 bhp at 6,500 rpm

Maximum torque: 655 lb-ft at 5,100 rpm

Top speed: 137 mph

0–60 mph: 4.3 sec.

TRANSMISSION
Chrysler A-833 four-speed manual

BODY/CHASSIS
Steel monocoque two-door coupe body

SPECIAL FEATURES

This Hemi 'Cuda has the popular shaker hood. The Shaker was often a different color from the bodywork.

The most obvious change from stock on this car is the enormous rear wheels and tires.

RUNNING GEAR
Steering: Recirculating ball

Front suspension: Double wishbones with longitudinal torsion bars, Koni adjustable telescopic shock absorbers and anti-roll bar

Rear suspension: Live axle with semi-elliptic leaf springs, Koni adjustable shock absorbers

Brakes: Discs (front), drums (rear)

Wheels: Weld Racing Pro-Star, 15 x 7 (front), 15 x 14 (rear)

Tires: P225/70R-15 General (front), 18.5-31 Mickey Thompson (rear)

DIMENSIONS
Length: 186.7 in. **Width:** 74.9 in.

Height: 50.9 in. **Wheelbase:** 108 in.

Track: 59.7 in. (front), 60.7 in. (rear)

Weight: 3,945 lbs.

397

Plymouth **ROAD RUNNER**

The Road Runner was so successful that it inspired rival manufacturers to offer budget muscle cars of their own. Anyone who drove a Road Runner was soon mesmerized by its incredible performance.

Torsion-bar front suspension

A typical 1960s Chrysler feature is a torsion-bar front suspension. Twin longitudinal bars provide springing for the front wishbones and give a smoother ride than coil setups. Road Runners have bigger front bars in an attempt to improve handling.

Big-block V8

Inexpensive to build, yet with a few simple tweaks mightily effective, the 383 V8 was the ideal engine for Plymouth's budget muscle-car. Packing 335 bhp and a monster 425 lb-ft of torque, even in stock trim it was a street terror.

Drum brakes

Most muscle cars are about going fast in a straight line and little else. Stopping the Road Runner could be quite entertaining, with the standard four-wheel drums, so ordering front discs was a wise option.

Hardtop styling

When introduced, the Road Runner was only available in one body-style—a pillared coupe. A hardtop version appeared mid year and a convertible was introduced in 1969.

Four-speed transmission

An essential performance ingredient on any real street racer is a manual transmission, and the Road Runner has a standard four-on-the-floor. A TorqueFlite automatic was optional.

Steel wheels

In keeping with its frugal image, the Road Runner came with standard 14-inch steel wheels and center hub caps. However, 14-inch Magnum 500 rims were a popular upgrade.

Specifications

1968 Plymouth Road Runner

ENGINE

Type: V8

Construction: Cast-iron block and heads

Valve gear: Two valves per cylinder operated by a single camshaft

Bore and stroke: 4.25 in. x 3.38 in.

Displacement: 383 c.i.

Compression ratio: 10.0:1

Induction system: Carter AFB four-barrel downdraft carburetor

Maximum power: 335 bhp at 5,200 rpm

Maximum torque: 425 lb-ft at 3,400 rpm

Top speed: 130 mph

0–60 mph: 6.7 sec.

TRANSMISSION

Four-speed manual

BODY/CHASSIS

Unitary steel construction with stamped steel body panels

SPECIAL FEATURES

To extract the most power out of the engine, Road Runners were equipped with standard dual exhaust.

The flat black hood center gave this potent Plymouth a very aggressive look.

RUNNING GEAR

Steering: Recirculating-ball

Front suspension: Unequal-length A-arms with torsion bars, telescopic shock absorbers and anti-roll bar

Rear suspension: Live axle with semi-elliptic leaf springs and telescopic shock absorbers

Brakes: Drums (front and rear)

Wheels: Pressed steel, 14-in. dia.

Tires: F70-14

DIMENSIONS

Length: 202.7 in. **Width:** 81.7 in.

Height: 56.3 in. **Wheelbase:** 116.0 in.

Track: 59.5 in. (front and rear).

Weight: 3,400 lbs.

Plymouth SUPERBIRD

The Superbird could achieve over 200 mph on the race track using the vital downforce generated by the huge rear wing. Even the tamer street version could easily reach 140 mph.

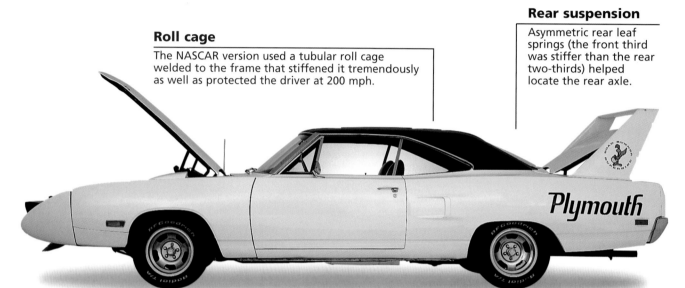

Roll cage
The NASCAR version used a tubular roll cage welded to the frame that stiffened it tremendously as well as protected the driver at 200 mph.

Rear suspension
Asymmetric rear leaf springs (the front third was stiffer than the rear two-thirds) helped locate the rear axle.

Four-speed transmission
Heavy-duty four-speed Chrysler model 883 was the strongest transmission available at the time.

Standard steel wheels
Steel wheels are still standard in NASCAR—wider 9.5 inch x 15 inch are used now, 15 inch x 7 inch when the Superbird ran. All NASCAR tires then were bias ply with inner tubes.

Live rear axle
Dana-built rear axle was originally intended for a medium-duty truck. Even in drag racing, the mighty Hemi could break it.

High-mounted rear wing
The rear wing provided downforce at the rear. Its angle was adjustable—too much and the increased force would shred the tires.

Front suspension

Front torsion bars resulted in better front suspension than competitors.

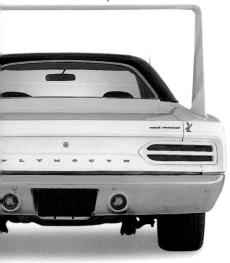

Cowl induction

Carburetor intake air was picked up from the high-pressure area at the base of the windshield—called cowl induction.

Aerodynamic nose

The nose was designed to lower drag and increase top speed while adding downforce—it actually put more weight on the front as speed increased.

Specifications
1970 Plymouth Superbird

ENGINE

Type: Hemi V8
Construction: Cast-iron block and heads; hemispherical combustion chambers
Valve gear: Two valves per cylinder operated by single block-mounted camshaft
Bore and stroke: 4.25 in. x 3.74 in.
Displacement: 426 c.i.
Compression ratio: 12:1
Induction system: Two four-barrel carbs, aluminum manifold
Maximum power: 425 bhp at 5,000 rpm
Maximum torque: 490 lb-ft at 4,000 rpm
Top speed: 140 mph
0–60 mph: 6.1 sec.

TRANSMISSION

Torqueflite three-speed auto plus torque converter or Mopar 883 four-speed manual

BODY/CHASSIS

Steel channel chassis welded to body with bolted front subframe

SPECIAL FEATURES

Front spoiler overcomes front-end lift.

The rear wing's height means it operates in less-disturbed airflow.

RUNNING GEAR

Steering: Recirculating ball steering, power-assisted on road cars
Front suspension: Double wishbones with torsion bars and telescopic shocks
Rear suspension: Live axle with asymmetric leaf springs and telescopic shocks
Brakes: Vented discs 11 in. dia. (front), drums 11 in. dia. (rear)
Wheels: Steel disc, 7 in. x 15 in.
Tires: Goodyear 7.00/15

DIMENSIONS

Length: 218 in.   **Width:** 76.4 in.
Wheelbase: 116 in.
Height: 1159.4 in. (including rear wing)
Track: 59.7 in. (front), 58.7 in. (rear)
Weight: 3,841 lbs.   **401**

Pontiac CHIEFTAIN

It took until 1949 before Pontiac offered its first new post-war cars. Longer, lower and wider than pre-war models, with cleaner, more integrated styling, they were also offered with more luxury features.

Side-valve, in-line eight

Although rival Oldsmobile® got a V8 for 1949, Pontiac stuck with its tried and tested L-head six and eight engines. Steady improvement, however, saw the power increase every year during the early 1950s as the horsepower race intensified. In 1949, it put out 104/106 bhp, but by 1954 it was up to 127.

Whitewall tires

Classy whitewall tires became increasingly popular on medium-priced cars during the 1940s. In 1952, due to the conflict in Korea, supplies of whitewalls were restricted along with supplies of copper, used on bumpers and chrome trim.

Power convertible top

Deluxe Chieftain convertibles came with a mohair-lined, power-operated top and a small glass rear window. Plexiglas windows did not become popular until the late 1950s.

Sealed beam headlights

GM had pioneered sealed beam lights in the late 1930s and these were still standard for 1949. Three years later, the famous Autotronic Eye arrived. This system dimmed the headlights automatically at oncoming traffic.

Drum brakes

Drum brakes were the industry standard in 1949. The Chieftain's were hydraulically operated and could stop the car in just over over 200 feet from 60 mph—more than adequate by contemporary standards.

Specifications
1950 Pontiac Chieftain

ENGINE
Type: In-line eight-cylinder

Construction: Cast-iron block and head

Valve gear: Two side-mounted valves per cylinder driven by a single, block-mounted camshaft with solid lifters

Bore and stroke: 3.25 in. x 3.75 in.

Displacement: 248.9 c.i.

Compression ratio: 6.5:1

Induction system: Single Carter WCD two-barrel carburetor

Maximum power: 104 bhp at 3,800 rpm

Maximum torque: 188 lb-ft at 2,000 rpm

Top speed: 86 mph

0–60 mph: 19.0 sec.

TRANSMISSION
Four-speed Hydramatic automatic

BODY/CHASSIS
Separate steel chassis with two-door convertible body

SPECIAL FEATURES

The Pontiac Indian Chief hood ornament illuminates when the headlights come on.

Rear fender skirts were dealer-installed options in 1949.

RUNNING GEAR
Steering: Worm-and-sector

Front suspension: Double wishbones with coil springs and telescopic shock absorbers

Rear suspension: Live axle with semi-elliptic leaf springs and telescopic shock absorbers

Brakes: Drums (front and rear)

Wheels: Stamped steel, 15-in. dia.

Tires: 7.10 x 15

DIMENSIONS
Length: 202.5 in. **Width:** 75.8 in.

Height: 63.3 in. **Wheelbase:** 120.0 in.

Track: 58.0 in. (front), 59.0 in. (rear)

Weight: 3,670 lbs.

Pontiac GTO

Pontiac set an all-time production record with the 1966 GTO, thanks to the car's combination of outstanding performance, eye-catching looks and attractive pricing.

Ram Air kit

The standard bonnet scoop was purely for decoration, but a dealer-installed Ram Air kit was also available. Quoted horsepower remained unchanged, but fresh air induction would probably add a few additional bhp.

Big-block V8

In 1966, the GTO could be ordered with the 389 c.i. engine in two different states of tune. This car is one of 19,045 ordered with the optional Tri-Power set up, which boosted power output to 360bhp.

Power convertible top

The GTO, if ordered in convertible form, was available with a power top.

Coil-sprung suspension

Like the other General Motors "A"-body intermediates of the time, the GTO has coil springs front and rear. This results in a much smoother ride than rival Ford and Chrysler muscle cars.

Four-speed transmission

In order to extract maximum performance from the big-block V8, a four-speed manual was the hot ticket, although a TurboHydramatic automatic was offered.

Promotional licence plate

GTOs quickly became known on the streets and at the race tracks for their unbelievable performance. One of Pontiac's campaign slogans compared the car's power with that of a tiger, hence the "growling" licence plate.

Restyled body

Still Tempest-based, the GTO grew dimensionally larger for 1966 with a longer body and more flowing lines. It was offered in pillared coupe, hardtop and convertible forms. The hardtop was by far the most popular model.

fluted taillights

Although base model Tempests and Le Mans have simple rear lights, the GTO has a unique tail end treatment with fluted taillight lenses. These are unique to this model year, as the rear end was revised for 1967.

Optional axle gearing

Since the GTO was after all a muscle car, it had to have considerable torque to get it out ahead of the competition. Naturally, Pontiac offered it with a variety of rear axle ratios, ranging from econo-wise 3.08:1 gears to the tire-frying 4.33:1s.

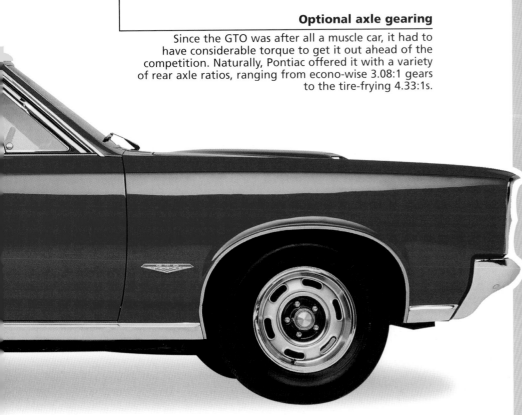

Specifications

1966 Pontiac GTO

ENGINE

Type: V8

Construction: Cast-iron block and heads

Valve gear: Two valves per cylinder operated by a single camshaft with pushrods and rockers

Bore and stroke: 4.06 in. x 3.75 in.

Displacement: 389 c.i.

Compression ratio: 10.75:1

Induction system: Three Rochester two-barrel carburetors

Maximum power: 360 bhp at 5200 rpm

Maximum torque: 424 lb-ft at 3600 rpm

Top speed: 125 mph

0–60mph: 6.2 sec

TRANSMISSION

Muncie M21 four-speed manual

BODY/CHASSIS

Steel perimeter chassis with separate steel convertible two-door body

SPECIAL FEATURES

Its sinister look is attributed to the vertical headlights and split front grill.

RUNNING GEAR

Steering: Recirculating ball

Front suspension: Unequal length wishbones with coil springs, telescopic shock absorbers and anti-roll bar

Rear suspension: Live axle with coil springs and lower control arms

Brakes: Drums (front and rear)

Wheels: Steel Rally I, 14 in. dia.

Tyres: Uniroyal 155/F70 14

DIMENSIONS

Length: 199.0 in.

Width: 79.8 in.

Height: 54.8 in.

Wheelbase: 116.0 in.

Track: 53.8 in. (front), 50.1 in. (rear)

Weight: 3555 lbs.

Pontiac **TORPEDO EIGHT**

The Custom Torpedo might lack the dramatic flowing lines of the fastback Streamliner Torpedoes but it still showed the way of things to come in body design, marking an end to separate headlights.

In-line eight-cylinder

Sidevalve engines seem very old-fashioned now, particularly in-line, eight-cylinder units, but they did have their advantages. At moderate engine speeds they run very smoothly and with a long stroke produce large amounts of torque.

Sealed beam headlights

In 1940, General Motors pioneered the sealed beam-type headlight in which the glass, reflector and bulb came as one unit and were replaced together instead of changing a separate bulb. They were regarded as a great advancement giving more light than standard headlights during the 1940s.

Integrated headlights

It was only a few years before the Torpedo that Pontiac had separate headlights mounted on the fenders, so the evolution of faired-in headlights built right into the fenders came very quickly.

Separate chassis

The chassis is of the perimeter type with two main outer box-section sidemembers and a central X-brace. The body is held on to the chassis by rubber mounts.

Rectangular grill

The switch to an almost rectangular radiator grill for 1941 was a sign of things to come as the old-fashioned upright grills gave way to lower, wider ones through the 1950s and 1960s.

Live rear axle

Like virtually all contemporary American cars the Torpedo uses a live rear axle. Pontiac gave it a name—'Duflex'—and promoted its telescopic shocks that reduced sway.

Specifications

1941 Pontiac Torpedo Eight

ENGINE

Type: In-line eight-cylinder

Construction: Cast-iron block and head

Valve gear: Two in-line side valves per cylinder operated by a single block-mounted camshaft

Bore and stroke: 3.25 in. x 3.75 in.

Displacement: 249 c.i.

Compression ratio: 6.5:1

Induction system: Single, twin-choke, Carter carburetor

Maximum power: 103 bhp at 3,500 rpm

Maximum torque: 190 lb-ft at 2,000 rpm

Top speed: 88 mph

0–60 mph: 18.9 sec

TRANSMISSION

Three-speed manual

BODY/CHASSIS

Separate box-section steel chassis frame with central X-brace and steel two-door coupe body

SPECIAL FEATURES

Pontiac's distinctive Indian's head mascot adorns the hood of this Torpedo.

Some critics termed the rectangular radiator grill the 'tombstone' grill.

RUNNING GEAR

Steering: Worm-and-sector

Front suspension: Double wishbones with coil springs and telescopic shocks

Rear suspension: Live axle with semi-elliptic leaf springs and telescopic shock absorbers

Brakes: Hydraulically-operated drums

Wheels: Pressed steel disc, 16-in. dia.

Tires: 6.0 x 16

DIMENSIONS

Length: 201.0 in   **Width:** 64.5 in.

Height: 65.0 in.   **Wheelbase:** 122.0 in.

Track: 58.0 in. (front), 61.5 in. (rear)

Weight: 3,325 lbs.

Pontiac TRANS AM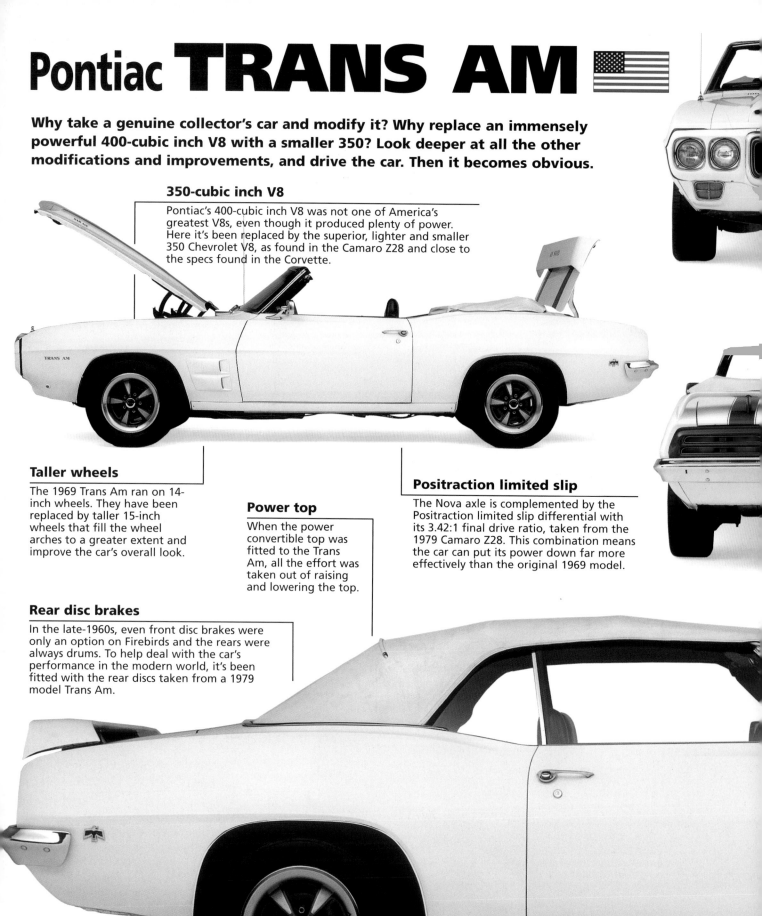

Why take a genuine collector's car and modify it? Why replace an immensely powerful 400-cubic inch V8 with a smaller 350? Look deeper at all the other modifications and improvements, and drive the car. Then it becomes obvious.

350-cubic inch V8

Pontiac's 400-cubic inch V8 was not one of America's greatest V8s, even though it produced plenty of power. Here it's been replaced by the superior, lighter and smaller 350 Chevrolet V8, as found in the Camaro Z28 and close to the specs found in the Corvette.

Taller wheels

The 1969 Trans Am ran on 14-inch wheels. They have been replaced by taller 15-inch wheels that fill the wheel arches to a greater extent and improve the car's overall look.

Power top

When the power convertible top was fitted to the Trans Am, all the effort was taken out of raising and lowering the top.

Positraction limited slip

The Nova axle is complemented by the Positraction limited slip differential with its 3.42:1 final drive ratio, taken from the 1979 Camaro Z28. This combination means the car can put its power down far more effectively than the original 1969 model.

Rear disc brakes

In the late-1960s, even front disc brakes were only an option on Firebirds and the rears were always drums. To help deal with the car's performance in the modern world, it's been fitted with the rear discs taken from a 1979 model Trans Am.

Hood scoops

The two hood scoops look impressive, but their function was to force air to the intake of the appropriately named Ram Air engine.

Rear spoiler

Part of the Trans Am package on the early Firebirds was the rear spoiler. It wasn't huge, but it was big enough to provide some downforce and, just as important, to make the car stand out from other Firebirds.

Chevy Nova rear end

Chevrolet produced Novas for Police Departments across the country. They have a heavy-duty rear suspension designed to cope with lots of power and sustained chases and abuse. This suspension has been incorporated into this Trans Am.

Specifications
1969 Modified Pontiac Trans Am

ENGINE

Type: Chevrolet small-block V8

Construction: Cast-iron block and heads

Valve gear: Two valves per cylinder operated by single block-mounted camshaft via pushrods, rockers and hydraulic tappets

Bore and stroke: 4 in. x 3.48 in.

Displacement: 350 c.i.

Compression ratio: 10:1

Induction system: Throttle body electronic fuel injection

Maximum power: 250 bhp at 5,000 rpm

Maximum torque: 295 lb-ft at 3,650 rpm

TRANSMISSION

1989 700R4 automatic transmission with overdrive

BODY/CHASSIS

Semi-unitary body/chassis with two-door convertible body

SPECIAL FEATURES

Rear disc brakes installed on this car come from a 1979 model Trans Am.

Fuel injection on IROC Z28 engine gives cleaner emissions and smoother pick-up.

RUNNING GEAR

Steering: Recirculating ball

Front suspension: Double wishbones with coil springs, telescopic shocks and anti-roll bar

Rear suspension: Live axle from 1979 Chevrolet Nova Police specification with semi-elliptic leaf springs and telescopic shocks

Brakes: Discs (front), with discs from a 1979 model Trans Am (rear)

Wheels: Steel 15 in. x 6 in.

Tires: BF Goodrich 235/60R15

DIMENSIONS

Length: 191.1 in.   **Width:** 173.9 in.

Height: 49.6 in.   **Wheelbase:** 108.1 in.

Track: 60 in. (front and rear)

Weight: 3,649 lbs.

Pontiac GRAND PRIX

Occupying a place at the top of the Pontiac lineup, the Grand Prix encapsulated all the qualities of the marque: a wide, low stance; strong V8 power; luxurious trim and a performance edge.

Full-size V8

A 350 bhp, 400-cubic inch V8 was the standard Grand Prix engine in 1967. A larger 428-cubic inch HO (High Output) V8 was optional with as much as 375 bhp.

Convertible body

1967 was the only model year that the Grand Prix was offered as a convertible. This model is one of the more common hardtops.

Wasp-waist styling

A prominent downward-sliding body accent starts in the door and runs to the rear fender. This gives an impression of a slim midriff and chunky rear. The covers on the rear wheels are optional.

Wedge-shaped fender tips

The front fenders jut forward with a strong wedge-shaped thrust mirroring the ridge along the hood that splits the grill in two pieces. It might not be very aerodynamic but it set a style that evolved through the 1970s.

Hooded headlights

In contrast to the 1966 Pontiac lineup and the rest of the 1967 Pontiac range that feature stacked quad headlights, the 1967 Grand Prix has concealed headlights. This clean look has the parking lights hidden behind vacuum-operated headlight doors concealed in the grill.

Automatic or manual transmission

The majority of 1967 Grand Prix cars had TurboHydramatic three-speed automatic trans-missions that were smooth-shifting and reliable. Fully synchronized four-speeds were offered as well, but only 760 cars were ordered with them.

1967 Pontiac Grand Prix

ENGINE

Type: V8

Construction: Cast-iron block and heads

Valve gear: Two valves per cylinder operated by a single camshaft with pushrods and rocker arms

Bore and stroke: 4.125 in. x 3.75 in.

Displacement: 400 c.i.

Compression ratio: 10.5:1

Induction system: Single Carter four-barrel carburetor

Maximum power: 350 bhp at 5,000 rpm

Maximum torque: 440 lb-ft at 3,200 rpm

Top speed: 110 mph

0–60 mph: 9.4 sec.

TRANSMISSION

TH400 automatic or four speed manual

BODY/CHASSIS

Separate chassis with steel two-door coupe body

SPECIAL FEATURES

The split front grill was a Pontiac trademark in the mid 1960s.

The concealed headlights make the Grand Prix instantly identifiable.

RUNNING GEAR

Steering: Recirculating ball

Front suspension: A-arms with coil springs and shock absorbers

Rear suspension: Live axle with coil springs and shock absorbers

Brakes: Drums (front and rear)

Wheels: Steel, 14-in. dia.

Tires: 8.55 x 14

DIMENSIONS

Length: 215.6 in.   **Width:** 79.4 in.

Height: 54.2 in.   **Wheelbase:** 121.0 in.

Track: 63.0 in. (front), 64.0 in. (rear)

Weight: 4,005 lbs.

Porsche 356

From its introduction in 1948, the 356 was improved annually. It matured from a crude little tourer to a sophisticated and competitive sports car.

Karmann-built bodywork

This car has the rare Karmann Hardtop bodywork. Introduced for the 1961 model year, it was built for only one year. It is basically a cabriolet with a welded-on hard top.

Choice of engines

The air-cooled flat-four engine comes in 1,100-, 1,300-, 1,500- and 1,600-cc versions and produces between 40 and 95 bhp in pushrod form. The quad-cam Carrera unit is highly specialized and is developed from racing practice.

Beetle-derived suspension

Although derived from the Volkswagen Beetle, the swing axle rear suspension has few components in common, particularly on later cars. Springing is by torsion bars with telescopic shock absorbers.

Worm and peg

he worm-and-peg steering was a
W item, and was improved by a
steering damper from the type A
onward. On the 365C a ZF
steering box was used.

nchromesh transmission

ly cars have 'crash' non-synchromesh
nsmissions, but a full synchro transmission
later cars is noted for its precision and
gineered' feel despite its lengthy linkage.

Drum brakes all around

Twin leading shoe hydraulic
brakes are found on all
356s up until the C model
of 1963, which features
four-wheel discs.

Specifications

1961 Porsche 356B 1600S

ENGINE

Type: Flat-four

Construction: Alloy block and heads

Valve gear: Two valves per cylinder
operated by a single camshaft via pushrods
and rockers

Bore and stroke: 3.25 in. x 2.91 in.

Displacement: 1,582 cc

Compression ratio: 8.5:1

Induction system: Two Zenith carburetors

Maximum power: 75 bhp at 5,000 rpm

Maximum torque: 85 lb-ft at 3,700 rpm

TRANSMISSION

Four-speed manual

BODY/CHASSIS

Steel platform chassis with steel Karmann
bodywork and welded-on hard top

SPECIAL FEATURES

**These sport mirrors are most often
seen on later 356B and C models.**

**By 1965, amber rear turn signals were
fitted on European-specification cars.**

RUNNING GEAR

Steering: Worm-and-peg

Front suspension: Torsion bars with
trailing arms, telescopic shock absorbers
and anti-roll bar

Rear suspension: Swing axles with torsion
bars and telescopic shock absorbers

Brakes: Hydraulic drums (front
and rear)

Wheels: Steel discs, 4.50 x 15 in.

Tires: Radials, 165 x 15

DIMENSIONS

Length: 155.5 in.   **Width:** 65.7 in.

Height: 50.7 in.   **Wheelbase:** 82.6 in.

Track: 51.5 in. (front and rear)

Weight: 2,059 lbs.

Porsche 911

Looking at the latest Porsche 911, it is easy to see that, even after more than 35 years, the famous German sports car builder has applied the theory of 'evolution, not revolution' to the 911.

Five-speed transmission

The five-speed transmission uses a dog-leg first gear, which was criticized in magazines, because road testers found it too easy to shift from first to fourth and completely miss second gear.

Air-cooled flat six

Porsche launched the 911 with a 2.0-liter version of its new horizontally opposed, six-cylinder engine. With two triple-choke Solex carburetors it produces 145 bhp.

Torsion-bar front suspension

The 911's MacPherson strut front suspension uses lower wishbones and is sprung by space-saving longitudinal torsion bars.

Unitary construction

The 911's monocoque gets its strength from a stiffened floorpan, large box-section sills and a stressed roof panel. Extra box sections support the engine and rear suspension, and the front is kept stiff by the assembly of sheet metal, especially the sculpted inner fenders and the crossmember supporting the gas tank.

Four-wheel discs

The original 911 uses four-wheel, solid disc brakes. To deal with the rear weight bias, the rear pair has a slightly larger diameter (11.2-inch) than at the front (11.1-inch)

Rear weight bias

The original 911 has a weight distribution of 43/57 percent front/rear. With the car's short wheelbase, this made handling tricky at high speeds.

Specifications

1965 Porsche 911

ENGINE

Type: Horizontally-opposed six-cylinder

Construction: Alloy block and heads

Valve gear: Two valves per cylinder operated by one camshaft per cylinder bank

Bore and stroke: 3.15 in. x 2.60 in.

Displacement: 1,991 cc

Compression ratio: 9.0:1

Induction system: Two triple-choke Solex carburetors

Maximum power: 145 bhp at 6,100 rpm

Maximum torque: 143 lb-ft at 4,200 rpm

Top speed: 132 mph

0–60 mph: 9.0 sec.

TRANSMISSION

Five-speed manual

BODY/CHASSIS

Unitary monocoque construction with steel two-door coupe body

SPECIAL FEATURES

The slatted front is a horn grill rather than an engine air intake.

This car has been fitted with later 4.5-inch, Fuchs alloy wheels, which were introduced in 1967.

RUNNING GEAR

Steering: Rack-and-pinion

Front suspension: MacPherson struts with lower wishbones, longitudinal torsion bars, telescopic shock absorbers and anti-roll bar

Rear suspension: Semi-trailing arms with transverse torsion bars and telescopic shock absorbers

Brakes: Discs (front and rear)

Wheels: Alloy, 4.5J x 15

Tires: Dunlop SP, 165/70 HR15

DIMENSIONS

Length: 164.5 in. **Width:** 63.6 in.

Height: 52.0 in. **Wheelbase:** 87.0 in.

Track: 54.1 in. (front), 51.8 in. (rear)

Weight: 2,360 lbs.

Porsche **911 TURBO**

The addition of a turbocharger transformed the acclaimed 911 Carrera into a firecracker on wheels. The extra power was accompanied by a host of improvements derived from Porsche's racing program.

KKK turbocharger

In 1974, turbocharging had only really been tried by Chevrolet and BMW. Porsche knew that turbocharging had a strong appeal because of its successful turbocharged racing program. The roadgoing 911 Turbo uses a single KKK Type 3 turbocharger with a maximum 0.8 bar (about12 PSI) of boost.

Wide wheels and tires

The wider cast-alloy wheels are a standard seven inches at the front and eight inches at the back. The standard tire specification was Pirelli Cinturato 205s up front and 215s at the rear, but wider, lower-profile 225/50 rear tires could be fitted as an option.

Stronger transmission

Although it still had only four speeds, the transmission was redesigned with longer ratios to take advantage of the higher possible speeds. The case casting was stronger and the synchromesh more resilient. Buyers were offered alternative final drivesets.

Luxury specification

The pricey Turbo was Porsche's top model. In the U.S., the Turbo came with standard air conditioning, leather upholstery, radio and power windows. A sliding sunroof was optional, but there was no targa roof option as with other 911 models.

Bulging arches

To cover the huge wheels and tires, the normally flush front arches have a notable flare in them. At the rear, the arches have gargantuan proportions.

'Whale tail' spoiler

Porsche's 'whale tail' rear spoiler was born on the 911 Turbo. It has two functions: The spoiler houses the turbo's intercooler and it also aids in high-speed downforce.

Specifications

1976 Porsche 911 Turbo

ENGINE

Type: Horizontally opposed "flat" six-cylinder

Construction: Aluminum block and heads

Valve gear: Two valves per cylinder operated by a single chain-driven overhead camshaft per bank of cylinders

Bore and stroke: 3.74 in. x 2.77 in.

Displacement: 2,993 cc

Compression ratio: 6.5:1

Induction system: Bosch (K-jetronic) KKK turbo, intercooler fuel injection

Maximum power: 234 bhp at 5,500 rpm

Maximum torque: 245 lb-ft at 4,000 rpm

Top speed: 156 mph

0–60 mph: 4.9 sec.

TRANSMISSION

Four-speed manual

BODY/CHASSIS

Steel monocoque (unibody)

SPECIAL FEATURES

The deep-set front chin spoiler is unique to the 911 Turbo.

The 'whale tail' spoiler houses the Turbocharger's intercooler.

RUNNING GEAR

Steering: Rack-and-pinion

Front suspension: MacPherson struts, transverse lower A-arms, longitudinal torsion bars, anti-roll bar

Rear suspension: Semi-trailing arms with transverse torsion bars, shock absorbers and anti-roll bar

Brakes: Vented discs (front and rear)

Wheels: Alloy, 15-in. dia.

Tires: 215/60 VR15

DIMENSIONS

Length: 168.9 in. **Width:** 69.9 in.

Height: 52.0 in. **Wheelbase:** 89.4 in.

Track: 56.3 in. (front), 59.1 in. (rear)

Weight: 2,514 lbs.

Porsche 912

For many, the Porsche 911 is simply too expensive. The four-cylinder 912 has always been much more affordable but has just the same street presence.

911 interior
It is difficult to tell that it's not a 911 when you're inside the 912. It has exactly the same trim as the basic 911.

356 engine
The pushrod flat-four engine taken from the 356 Super 90 is all alloy and with two twin-choke Solex carburetors it produces 102 bhp at 5,800 rpm.

Trailing arms
Whereas the 356 used swing-axle rear suspension, the 911 and 912 use triangulated semi-trailing arms to reduce much of the sudden snap oversteer of the earlier model.

Five-speed transmission
Until 1967 a five-speed transmission was optional. First and fifth gears were the same ratios as the four-speed unit but the intermediate gears were closer together.

911 styling
The classic 911 shape was penned by Ferdinand 'Butzi' Porsche, son of Dr. Ferry Porsche who had started the company with the 356 in 1948. The 912's body was exactly the same as its more expensive brother.

Front luggage compartment

With the engine in the back, the luggage compartment is located up front. Longitudinal torsion bars give more space than the transverse bars of the previous 356.

Rear-mounted engine

The flat four, being all alloy, is more than 100 lbs. lighter than the flat six fitted to the 911. This improves the strong rear weight bias.

Specifications
1967 Porsche 912

ENGINE
Type: Flat four-cylinder
Construction: Alloy block and heads
Valve gear: Two valves per cylinder operated by a single camshaft
Bore and stroke: 3.25 in. x 2.91 in.
Displacement: 1,582 cc
Compression ratio: 9.3:1
Induction system: Two twin-choke Solex carburetors
Maximum power: 102 bhp at 5,800 rpm
Maximum torque: 90 lb-ft at 3,500 rpm
Top speed: 119 mph
0–60 mph: 11.6 sec.

TRANSMISSION
Four- or five-speed manual

BODY/CHASSIS
Unitary monocoque construction with steel two-door coupe body

SPECIAL FEATURES

Apart from the 912's badge, there is little to differentiate it from the more expensive 911.

The 912 was fitted with these 15-inch chromed steel wheels as standard.

RUNNING GEAR
Steering: Rack-and-pinion
Front suspension: MacPherson struts with lower wishbones, torsion bars, telescopic shock absorbers and anti-roll bar
Rear suspension: Trailing arms with transverse torsion bars and telescopic shock absorbers
Brakes: Discs (front and rear)
Wheels: Steel 4.5 x 15 in.
Tires: Goodyear Highspeed, 165 x 15 in.

DIMENSIONS
Length: 163.9 in.   **Width:** 63.4 in.
Height: 52.0 in.   **Wheelbase:** 87.0 in.
Track: 52.6 in. (front), 51.8 in. (rear)
Weight: 2,100 lbs.

Porsche 914/6

Porsche's first mid-engined production sports car was produced years before the current Boxster, but despite its great dynamic abilities, off-beat looks and a high price caused its downfall after only three years.

Pop-up lights

Gugelot, the 914/6's stylists, wanted an uncluttered and rectangular look, and dispensed with exposed headlights, opting instead for two round lights in pop-up pods.

Flat-six engine

Because the 914/6 was meant to be the affordable Porsche, it couldn't have the same power as the more expensive 911. So it uses the 125-bhp 2-liter.

Fiberglass roof

The 914/6 was designed as a targa top, and the lightweight fiberglass roof panel can be unclipped and lifted clear. It then stows under the rear compartment.

Magnesium wheels

All 914/6s have five-lug rather than four-lug wheels. Just a few cars have the desirable Mahle diecast magnesium wheels, although more were made with Fuchs five-spoke aluminum alloys. Either way, the wheels house excellent vented disc brakes.

Fixed passenger seat

With no room behind, there was no need for a movable passenger seat. Instead, there's a movable footrest in the footwell. Eventually, however, a movable seat was introduced for the 1972 model year.

Rear-mounted transmission

The only drawback to setting the transmission behind the mid-mounted engine is that this requires a long gear linkage—never as precise or good to use as the shorter one in the 911.

Specifications

1970 Porsche 914/6

ENGINE

Type: Flat six-cylinder

Construction: Alloy crankcase with separate Biral (cast iron with alloy cooling fins) cylinder barrels and alloy cam carriers and cylinder heads

Valve gear: Two valves per cylinder operated by a single chain-driven overhead camshaft per bank of cylinders

Bore and stroke: 3.15 in. x 2.60 in.

Displacement: 1,991 cc

Compression ratio: 8.6:1

Induction system: Two Weber triple-choke downdraft carburetors

Maximum power: 125 bhp at 5,800 rpm

Maximum torque: 131 lb-ft at 4,200 rpm

Top speed: 123 mph

0–60 mph: 8.7 sec.

TRANSMISSION

Five-speed manual

BODY/CHASSIS

Unitary monocoque construction with steel targa top convertible two-seater body

SPECIAL FEATURES

Most 914/6s wore Fuchs five-spoke aluminum wheels.

Under-bumper driving lights supplement the pop-up headlights.

RUNNING GEAR

Steering: Rack-and-pinion

Front suspension: Struts with lower wishbones and longitudinal torsion bars

Rear suspension: Semi-trailing arms with coil springs and telescopic shock absorbers

Brakes: Vented discs (front), Solid discs rear

Wheels: 5.5 x 14 in.

Tires: 185 HR 14

DIMENSIONS

Length: 156.9 in.   **Width:** 65.0 in.

Height: 48.0 in.   **Wheelbase:** 96.4 in.

Track: 53.6 in. (front), 54.4 in. (rear)

Weight: 2,195 lbs.

Porsche 959

Porsche deliberately made the 959 look as much like a 911 as possible—to help the 911's image and to show what the company had in store for their oldest and greatest model.

Front-mounted cooling system

The engine is in the rear but the radiator is at the front. The two side vents feed air to the twin engine oil coolers at the rear.

Adjustable shocks

The 959's eight shocks are adjustable to hard, medium or soft settings.

Rear wing

The rear wing helps generate the enormous downforce necessary to keep the 959 on the road at speeds over 190 mph.

Four-wheel drive

The 959 has four-wheel drive with six-speed gearbox and adjustable center and rear differentials. The normal torque split is slightly biased towards the rear wheels but varies according to wheel grip.

Double wishbone suspension

Double wishbone suspension is used all around, with two coil spring/shock units at each corner for extra wheel control.

Alloy and composite construction

Doors and hood are alloy and the other panels are a mix of fiberglass and Kevlar combining great strength and lightness.

Rear turbo vents

The twin turbos used on the 959 operate in sequence. The heat generated is expelled through these vents.

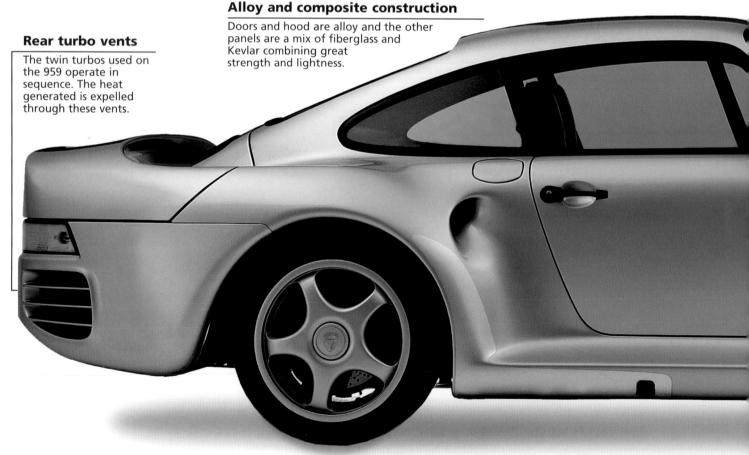

Specifications
1988 Porsche 959

ENGINE
Type: Flat-six
Construction: Alloy block and heads with alloy cylinder barrels and Nikasil coated bores
Valve gear: Four valves per cylinder operated by twin chain drive camshafts per bank of cylinders
Bore and stroke: 3.74 in. x 2.64 in.
Displacement: 2,851 cc
Compression ratio: 8.3:1
Induction system: Bosch Motronic fuel injection with twin intercooled KKK turbochargers
Maximum power: 450 bhp at 6,500 rpm
Maximum torque: 370 lb-ft at 5,500 rpm

TRANSMISSION
Type: Six-speed manual with four-wheel drive and adjustable center and rear diff.

BODY/CHASSIS
Alloy and composite paneled two-door, two-seat coupe with Porsche 911-based center monocoque section

SPECIAL FEATURES

Only one turbo operates below 4,500 rpm; above that the second engages, generating another 150 bhp.

Large vents above the rear wheels feed air to the intercoolers for the twin turbochargers.

RUNNING GEAR
Steering: Rack-and-pinion
Front suspension: Twin wishbones with twin coil spring/shock units
Rear suspension: Twin wishbones with twin coil spring/shock units; electronic ride control
Brakes: Vented discs with ABS, 12.7 in. dia. (front), and 12 in. dia. (rear)
Wheels: Alloy 17 in.
Tires: 235/45 VR17 (front), 255/45 VR17 (rear)

DIMENSIONS
Length: 168 in. **Width:** 72.5 in.
Height: 50.4 in. **Wheelbase:** 89.5 in.
Track: 59.2 in. (front), 61 in. (rear)
Weight: 3,199 lbs.

rsche 911 rear lights
Despite the family resemblance, the only recognizable standard 911 production parts are the rear light clusters.

Variable ride height
At over 100 mph, the ride height was automatically lowered to 4.75 inches for increased stability. Over rough ground, the ride height could be increased to 6 or even 7 inches.

Porsche 935

The 935 was used by a host of private teams for very good reasons. It was fast, reliable, and extremely strong. With a 935 you could almost guarantee a finish.

Alloy roll cage

The alloy roll cage performs two functions—protecting the driver and making the whole structure stiffer.

Plexiglass windows

To keep weight down, Plexiglass is used for the side windows. Porsche actually made the 935 lighter than the regulations allowed so they could put weight back in the form of ballast where it is most needed—in the front.

Flat-six engine

Group 5 regulations stipulate that the engines used are based on those of a production car. To begin with the 935's was very similar, but was stronger, had slightly smaller displacement, and later had four valves per cylinder.

Front MacPherson struts

Because the regulations required that the same form of suspension was used in Group 5 cars as on the production cars, Porsche uses MacPherson struts. But at the rear, titanium springs are used.

Intercooler vents

After the intercooler in the tail was banned Porsche was forced to fit two smaller intercoolers, one on each side ahead of the rear wheels where air is fed to them through vents behind the doors.

Porsche 911 center section

The only significant part of the structure of the production 911 which is retained is the center section and floorpan.

Single turbo

Initially, the 935 used a single large KKK turbo mounted right at the tail of the car behind the engine, whose compression ratio was lowered to 6.5:1.

Fiberglass and polyurethane bodywork

The body contributes nothing to the 935's strength. Its detachable panels can be made in fiberglass or a lightweight polyurethane foam sandwich material.

Porsche 917 brakes

Brakes from the production 911 Turbo on which the 935 is loosely based would not have coped. The 935 uses the enormous vented discs and four-pot calipers used Porsche 917 racing cars.

Front oil cooler

With dry-sump racing engines, there's no oil pan for the oil to sit in. It's pumped around from a separate tank, in this case in the 935's nose. It's placed there, along with an oil cooler, to help weight distribution.

Specifications
1976 Porsche 935

ENGINE

Type: Flat-six

Construction: Alloy crankcase, cylinder barrels and heads

Valve gear: Two valves per cylinder operated by single chain-driven overhead cam per bank of cylinders

Bore and stroke: 3.66 in. x 2.75 in.

Displacement: 2,856 cc

Compression ratio: 6.5:1

Induction system: Bosch mechanical fuel injection with intercooled KKK turbocharger

Maximum power: 590 bhp at 7,900 rpm

Maximum torque: 434 lb-ft at 7,900 rpm

Top speed: 200 mph

0–60 mph: 3.1 sec.

TRANSMISSION

Four-speed manual

BODY/CHASSIS

Strengthened Porsche 911 floorpan with alloy roll cage and fiberglass/polyurethane foam body panels

SPECIAL FEATURES

The titanium coil springs are lighter than the 911's steel torsion bars, and easier to tune and change for racing.

Large rear spoiler helps increase the downforce of high-speed stability of this 190-plus mph car.

RUNNING GEAR

Steering: Rack-and-pinion

Front suspension: MacPherson struts with lower wishbones and anti-roll bar

Rear suspension: Semi-trailing arms, coil springs, telescopic shocks and anti-roll bar

Brakes: Vented discs, 11.8 in. dia.

Wheels: Alloy, 11 in. x 16 in. (front), 15 in. x 19 in. (rear)

Tires: Dunlop racing

DIMENSIONS

Length: 183.3 in.　　**Width:** 78.7 in.

Height: 50 in.　　**Wheelbase:** 89.4 in.

Track: 59.1 in. (front), 61.4 in. (rear)

Weight: 2,139 lbs.

Porsche **993 TURBO**

Wide and low, with huge flared rear wheel arches and distinctive sloping headlamps, the 993 Turbo is still instantly recognizable as a descendant of the very first 911 from the early 1960s.

Twin turbos

The flat-six-engine design lent itself to having one turbocharger for each bank of cylinders. Porsche used small German-made KKK K-16 turbos. Each one could thus be placed as close as possible to an exhaust manifold, quickening its response time and virtually eliminating lag.

Integrated bumpers

At the same time that Porsche changed the front headlamp design, it merged the bodywork and bumpers together into one smooth shape.

Alloy wheels

Alloy wheels have long been fitted to Porsche Turbos—they just keep getting bigger and bigger. Turbo 993s have massive 18-inch diameter alloys. They are this large for a couple of reasons: to accommodate brake discs that are greater than a foot in diameter and to carry very wide low-profile tires.

Four-wheel drive

Porsche applied four-wheel drive to the Carrera 4 in 1989 and then modified it for the second-generation model, with a wider variable torque split. It was this system, with its center viscous coupling and rear limited-slip differential that is applied to the 993 Turbo. Drive would normally be automatically applied to the rear wheels until the car's sensors detect that torque needs to be fed to the front wheels as well.

Rear-heavy

Despite being four-wheel drive and having the additional weight of two front drive-shafts, extended propshaft and front differential, the weight distribution of the 993 Turbo is still heavily rear-biased, with 55 percent of the weight at the back.

Specifications

1997 Porsche 993 Turbo

ENGINE

Type: Flat six

Construction: Alloy block and heads

Valve gear: Two valves per cylinder operated by a single overhead cam per bank of cylinders

Bore and stroke: 4.0 in. x 3.05 in.

Displacement: 3,600 cc

Compression ratio: 8.0:1

Induction system: Bosch electronic fuel injection with twin KKK turbochargers

Maximum power: 400 bhp at 5,750 rpm

Max torque: 400 lb-ft at 4,500 rpm

Top speed: 180 mph

0–60 mph: 3.8 sec.

TRANSMISSION

Six-speed manual with permanent four-wheel drive

BODY/CHASSIS

Unitary monocoque construction with steel two-door coupe body

SPECIAL FEATURES

The large alloy wheels house the massive vented disc brakes.

The huge rear spoiler produces downforce and aids straight-line stability.

RUNNING GEAR

Steering: Rack-and-pinion

Front suspension: MacPherson struts with lower wishbones and anti-roll bar

Rear suspension: Double wishbones with coil springs, telescopic shock absorbers and anti-roll bar

Brakes: Vented discs, 12.7-in. dia. (front and rear)

Wheels: Cast alloy, 8 in. x 18 in. (front), 10 in. x 18 in. rear

Tires: 225/40 ZR18 (front), 285/30 ZR18 (rear)

DIMENSIONS

Length: 167.7 in.   **Width:** 70.7 in.

Height: 51.8 in.   **Wheelbase:** 89.4 in.

Track: 55.5 in. (front), 59.3 in. (rear)

Weight: 3,307 lbs.

Land Rover **RANGE ROVER**

The surprising thing about the Range Rover is not that it was voted the best 4x4 in the world by numerous magazines, but that it was still winning such awards more than 20 years after it was launched.

V8 engine

A detuned (low-compression) version of the perennial Rover/Buick V8 engine powers the Range Rover. Its lightness allows excellent weight distribution and its power and torque are perfect for its intended role.

Live floating axles

Both axles are live and floating, mainly for reasons of ground-clearance and simplicity. Coil springs are fitted front and rear, with Woodhead shocks up front and a Boge Hydromat self-leveling damper strut at the rear. This is because, although the Range Rover has perfect 50:50 weight distribution, the rear end, in some cases, sagged under heavy loads.

Permanent four-wheel drive

Unlike the Land Rover, the four-wheel drive system is permanently engaged, with a special Salisbury differential eliminating windup. The two-speed transfer gear shares the same casing as the main transmission, with a large difference between high and low speeds (2.83 to 1).

Luxurious feel

Compared to the 4x4 standards of its day, this was a very luxurious truck. Although the first Range Rovers had PVC trim and rubber floormats, the seats were well padded and there was an attractive, well-laid-out dash. As the years passed, the Range Rover grew steadily more luxurious, gaining leather upholstery, wood trim, air conditioning, air suspension and so on.

Excellent ground clearance

The lowest point on the Range Rover sits 7 inches above the ground, well out of the way of rocks and ruts. Most of the vulnerable components, such as the transmission and fuel tank, are situated well within the chassis frame for protection. The suspension itself is fairly soft, with up to 8 inches of travel.

Specifications

1970 Land Rover Range Rover

ENGINE

Type: V8

Construction: Aluminum block and heads

Valve gear: Two valves per cylinder operated by a single camshaft with pushrods and rockers

Bore and stroke: 3.50 in. x 2.80 in.

Displacement: 3,528 cc

Compression ratio: 8.5:1

Induction system: Two Zenith-Stromberg carburetors

Maximum power: 130 bhp at 5,000 rpm

Maximum torque: 205 lb-ft at 3,000 rpm

Top speed: 99 mph

0–60 mph: 12.9 sec.

TRANSMISSION

Four-speed manual driving all four wheels

BODY/CHASSIS

Separate chassis with steel and aluminum two-door station wagon body

SPECIAL FEATURES

Early Range Rovers came with a simple four-speed transmission as standard.

The V8 engine was detuned to optimize off-road performance.

RUNNING GEAR

Steering: Recirculating-ball

Front suspension: Live axle with leading arms, Panhard rod, coil springs and shock absorbers

Rear suspension: Live axle with A-bracket, radius arms, self-leveling strut, coil springs and shock absorbers

Brakes: Discs (front and rear)

Wheels: Steel, 16-in. dia.

Tires: 205 x 16

DIMENSIONS

Length: 176.0 in.   **Width:** 70.0 in.

Height: 70.0 in.   **Wheelbase:** 100.0 in.

Track: 58.5 in. (front and rear)

Weight: 3,864 lbs.

Renault 8 GORDINI ▌▐

After the curves of the Dauphine, Renault wanted a contrast—a shape that would shock and get noticed by looking as box-like and deliberately unstyled as possible. The concept worked.

Tuned pushrod engine

One of Gordini's tuning tricks was to have the spark split by a forked tunnel. This has the effect of spreading the flame and improving combustion. It helps in producing 103 bhp from a pushrod 1,255-cc engine.

Lower ride height

The Gordini version is lowered by 1.5 inches all around, as well as having stiffer springs and extra rear shocks. The rear wheels have a negative camber so that even under hard cornering they will not tuck under and lose traction.

Two fuel tanks

The original Renault 8 had a small fuel tank mounted at the back, so to improve the range of the thirstier Gordini, an extra fuel tank was mounted in the front trunk. The two tanks are entirely separate, with a switch mounted on the cockpit floor to change from one to the other.

One color only

The Renault 8 Gordini came in just one color—French Racing Blue. In France, the cars also came with the distinctive white stripes as standard, although for foreign markets the stripes were made from tape which could be removed if the owner chose to do so.

Wishbone front suspension

Double pressed-steel wishbones are used at the front, with a co-axial coil spring/shock unit operating vertically between the two wishbones, plus a thick anti-roll bar.

Specifications

1967 Renault R8 Gordini

ENGINE

Type: Inline four-cylinder

Construction: Cast-iron block and alloy head

Valve gear: Two valves per cylinder operated by a single block-mounted camshaft with pushrods and rockers

Bore and stroke: 74.5 mm x 72.0 mm

Displacement: 1,255 cc

Compression ratio: 10.5:1

Induction system: Two sidedraft Weber 40 DCOE carburetors

Maximum power: 103 bhp at 6,750 rpm

Maximum torque: 86 lb-ft at 5,000 rpm

Top speed: 112 mph

0–60 mph: 10.9 sec.

TRANSMISSION

Five-speed manual

BODY/CHASSIS

Unitary monocoque construction with steel sedan body

SPECIAL FEATURES

A small fuel tank is mounted behind the engine.

The 1300 version has two extra large Halogen driving lights.

RUNNING GEAR

Steering: Rack-and-pinion

Front suspension: Double wishbones with coil springs, telescopic shock absorbers and anti-roll bar

Rear suspension: Swing axles with radius arms and coil springs/twin telescopic shock absorbers per side

Brakes: Discs, 10.30-in. dia. (front and rear)

Wheels: Pressed-steel disc, 5.3 x 15 in.

Tires: Dunlop SP radial, 135-380 mm

DIMENSIONS

Length: 157.0 in. **Width:** 58.0 in.

Height: 53.0 in. **Wheelbase:** 89.0 in.

Track: 49.0 in. (front), 48.0 in. (rear)

Weight: 1,885 lbs.

Renault 16

The Renault 16 remained in production for 15 years and won a big following for its innovative features and unrivaled practicality.

Hatchback body

Back in 1964, most cars had a three-box shape (that is, with the trunk sticking out at the back), but Renault applied some logic and turned the trunk into a bigger area accessed by a large tailgate. Pundits at the time were not sure what to call it: was it a sedan or a station wagon? But the 16 launched a genre that we now know as the hatchback.

Front-wheel drive

In 1964, the benefits of front-wheel drive were just beginning to be appreciated. The Renault 16 led the way, showing its superior traction on bad surfaces and demonstrating its greater interior space.

Adaptable cabin

An attractive aspect of the 16 was its practical and extremely spacious interior. Front-wheel drive means that the floor is flat and a column gearshift provided greater space to move around up front. Rear seat legroom was unrivaled at the time. The rear seats can also fold down for increased carrying capacity.

Front disc brakes

Again, the 16 was ahead of its time in terms of braking. Few family cars could boast front disc brakes in 1964 and the 16 gained a reputation as a safe-braking and safe-handling car.

Specifications

1973 Renault 16 TS

ENGINE

Type: In-line four-cylinder

Construction: Aluminum block and head

Valve gear: Two valves per cylinder operated by a single camshaft via pushrods and rockers

Bore and stroke: 3.03 in. x 3.31 in.

Displacement: 1,565 cc

Compression ratio: 8.6:1

Induction system: Single Solex carburetor

Maximum power: 70 bhp at 5,200 rpm

Maximum torque: 86 lb-ft at 2,500 rpm

Top speed: 93 mph

0–60 mph: 16.2 sec.

TRANSMISSION

Four-speed manual or three-speed automatic

BODY/CHASSIS

Unitary construction with steel five-door hatchback body

SPECIAL FEATURES

To save yet more space, the spare tire is mounted in the engine bay.

A discreet tailgate spoiler is standard on the TX model.

RUNNING GEAR

Steering: Rack-and-pinion

Front suspension: Wishbones with torsion bars, anti-roll bar and shock absorbers

Rear suspension: Trailing arms with torsion bars, anti-roll bar and shock absorbers

Brakes: Discs (front), drums (rear)

Wheels: Steel, 14-in. dia.

Tires: 5 x 14 in.

DIMENSIONS

Length: 166.8 in. **Width:** 65 in.

Height: 57 in. **Wheelbase:** 106 in.

Track: 52.6 in. (front), 50.3 in. (rear)

Weight: 2,260 lbs.

Independent suspension

By 1960s standards, the Renault 16 was advanced in that it uses independent suspension all around. It has torsion bars front and rear, with wishbones up front and trailing arms at the rear. This system provides very generous suspension travel, allowing the springs to absorb potholes with ease.

Renault SPORT SPIDER

Despite huge success in Formula One racing, Renault needed a street car to show its racing heritage. One answer was the Sport Spider, a state-of-the-art sports car that is fast, advanced and equally at home on the road or track.

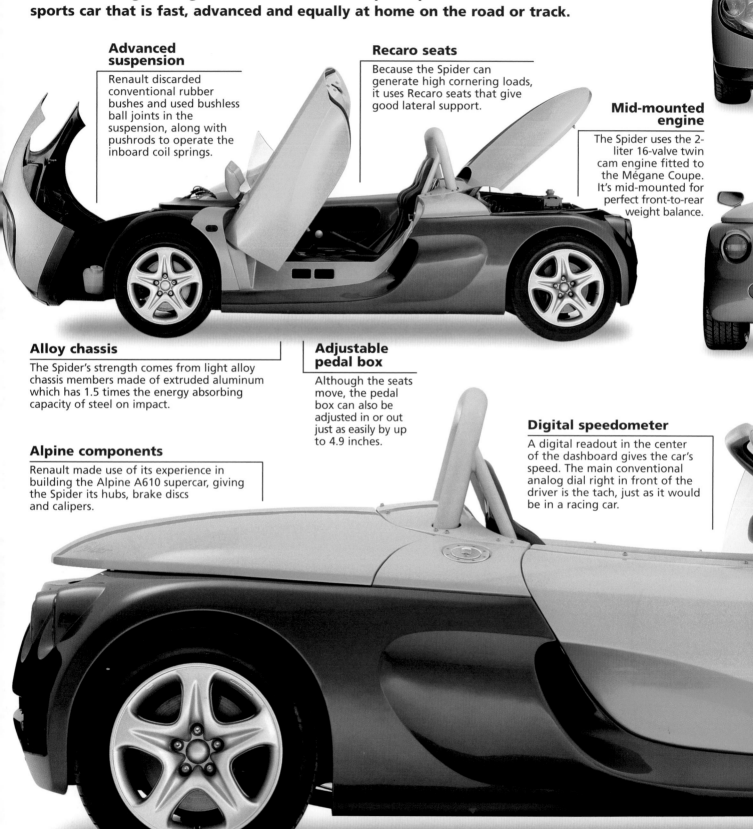

Advanced suspension

Renault discarded conventional rubber bushes and used bushless ball joints in the suspension, along with pushrods to operate the inboard coil springs.

Recaro seats

Because the Spider can generate high cornering loads, it uses Recaro seats that give good lateral support.

Mid-mounted engine

The Spider uses the 2-liter 16-valve twin cam engine fitted to the Mégane Coupe. It's mid-mounted for perfect front-to-rear weight balance.

Alloy chassis

The Spider's strength comes from light alloy chassis members made of extruded aluminum which has 1.5 times the energy absorbing capacity of steel on impact.

Alpine components

Renault made use of its experience in building the Alpine A610 supercar, giving the Spider its hubs, brake discs and calipers.

Adjustable pedal box

Although the seats move, the pedal box can also be adjusted in or out just as easily by up to 4.9 inches.

Digital speedometer

A digital readout in the center of the dashboard gives the car's speed. The main conventional analog dial right in front of the driver is the tach, just as it would be in a racing car.

Fixed windshield

...ly Sport Spiders were produced with a deflector to send the slipstream up over the driver and passenger. It was not a total success and a conventional windshield was introduced for colder climates.

Composite bodywork

Because the Spider's bodywork plays no structural role, the panels can be made in a lightweight composite material which will never rust, corrode or degenerate.

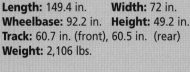

1997 Renault Sport Spider

ENGINE

Type: In-line four
Construction: Cast-iron block and light alloy cylinder head
Valve gear: Four valves per cylinder operated by twin overhead camshafts
Bore and stroke: 3.25 in. x 3.66 in.
Displacement: 1,998 cc
Compression ratio: 9.8:1
Induction system: Electronic fuel injection
Maximum power: 150 bhp at 6,000 rpm
Maximum torque: 140 lb-ft at 4,500 rpm

TRANSMISSION

Five-speed manual

BODY/CHASSIS

Extruded and welded alloy frame with fiberglass, two-door, two-seat convertible body

SPECIAL FEATURES

The aluminum chassis is extremely light, at only 176 lbs. This helps give excellent performance from the 16-valve engine.

Renault put the big circular tachometer right ahead of the driver, with a digital speedometer off to the side.

RUNNING GEAR

Steering: Rack-and-pinion
Front suspension: Double wishbones with horizontally mounted inboard coil spring/shocks and anti-roll bar
Rear suspension: Double wishbones with longitudinally mounted coil/spring shocks and anti-roll bar
Brakes: Vented discs, 11.8 in. dia. (front and rear)
Wheels: Alloy 8 in. x 16 in. (front), 9 in. x 16 in. (rear)
Tires: 205/60 VR16 (front), 225/50 VR16 (rear)

DIMENSIONS

Length: 149.4 in. **Width:** 72 in.
Wheelbase: 92.2 in. **Height:** 49.2 in.
Track: 60.7 in. (front), 60.5 in. (rear)
Weight: 2,106 lbs.

Renault 5 TURBO 2

The mid-engined Renault 5 Turbo was designed to achieve two goals—to be a competitive World Championship rally car and to raise the profile of Renault's rather ordinary roadgoing models.

Turbocharged engine

Even the road cars have an excellent power output—160 bhp from just 1,397 cc—due to an intercooled Garrett turbocharger operating in conjunction with Bosch fuel injection.

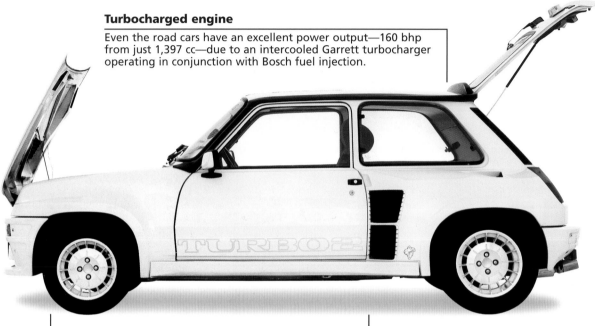

Front radiator

Although the engine is mounted behind the cabin, the radiator is at the front in the usual Renault 5 location; an electric fan assists cooling.

Intercooler vent

The vent on the left-hand side ahead of the rear wheel arch allows air to pass to the intercooler, which is mounted alongside the four-cylinder engine.

Rear-mounted transmission

In the standard Renault 5 the transmission is located ahead of the engine at the front of the car. In the mid-engined Turbo the whole package is rotated 180 degrees and moved back so that the transmission is toward the rear.

Wishbone rear suspension

The rear suspension is a double unequal-length wishbone system with long coil spring/shock absorber units mounted on top of spring-mounted turrets. These are connected by a bar in the engine bay to provide greater chassis stiffness.

Vented disc brakes

Braking on the Turbo is superb, as large vented discs are used all around. Both front and rear discs have a diameter of 10.2 inches.

Specifications

1984 Renault 5 Turbo 2

ENGINE

Type: In-line four-cylinder

Construction: Cast-iron block with wet cylinder liners and alloy cylinder head

Valve gear: Two valves per cylinder operated by pushrods and rockers

Bore and stroke: 3.0 in. x 3.03 in.

Displacement: 1,397 cc

Compression ratio: 7.0:1

Induction system: Bosch K-Jetronic fuel injection with single intercooled Garrett T3 turbocharger

Maximum power: 160 bhp at 6,000 rpm

Maximum torque: 158 lb-ft at 3,500 rpm

Top speed: 124 mph

0–60 mph: 7.7 sec.

TRANSMISSION

Five-speed manual

BODY/CHASSIS

Steel monocoque with fiberglass, alloy and steel two-door body

SPECIAL FEATURES

Huge vents behind the doors feed air into the twin intercoolers.

At 7.5 inches wide, the rear wheels are larger than those at the front.

RUNNING GEAR

Steering: Rack-and-pinion

Front suspension: Double wishbones with longitudinal torsion bars, telescopic shock absorbers and anti-roll bar

Rear suspension: Double wishbones with coil springs, telescopic shock absorbers and anti-roll bar

Brakes: Vented discs, 10.2-in. dia (front and rear)

Wheels: Cast-alloy, 5 x 13 in. (front), 7.5 x 13 in. (rear)

Tires: Michelin, 190/55 HR13 (front), 220/55 HR14 (rear)

DIMENSIONS

Length: 144.3 in.   **Width:** 69.0 in.

Height: 52.1 in.   **Wheelbase:** 95.7 in.

Track: 53.0 in. (front), 58.0 in. (rear)

Weight: 2,138 lbs.

Renault ALPINE A110 🇫🇷

The A110 was an outstanding car. From the start of its production in 1963, steady improvements ensured that it remained competitive on the world rally stage for more than 10 years.

Four-cylinder engine

All A110s were powered by versions of the four-cylinder engines used in production Renaults like the R8, R12 and R16. The overhead-valve unit which powers the 1600S is all-alloy and is taken from the R16.

Front fuel tank

The rear-mounted engine dictated that the fuel tank had to be positioned at the front of the car and was accessed through the hood.

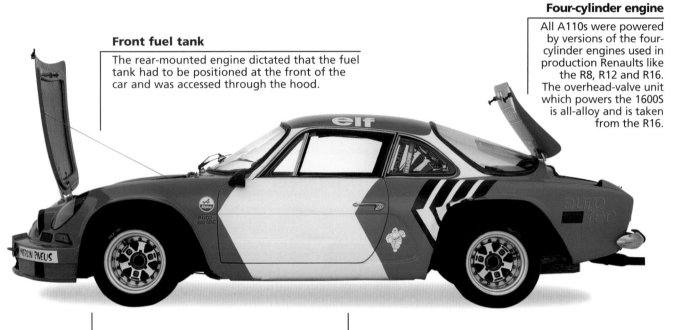

Disc brakes

With four-wheel disc brakes, the A110's stopping power was tremendous.

Fiberglass body

Because it was a limited production car and intended for competition, the body is constructed from fiberglass instead of steel.

Rear weight bias

With a rear-mounted engine and transmission, the A110 has a substantial rear weight bias that resulted in surprisingly light steering.

Specifications
1973 Alpine A110 1600S

ENGINE
Type: In-line four-cylinder Renault

Construction: Light alloy block and head with cast-iron wet liners

Valve gear: Two inclined valves per cylinder operated by a single block-mounted camshaft via pushrods and rockers

Bore and stroke: 3.07 in. x 3.30 in.

Displacement: 1,605 cc

Compression ratio: 10.25:1

Induction system: Two sidedraft Weber 45 DCOE carburetors

Maximum power: 138 bhp at 6,000 rpm

Maximum torque: 106 lb-ft at 5,000 rpm

Top speed: 127 mph

0–60 mph: 6.3 sec.

TRANSMISSION
Five-speed manual Renault

BODY/CHASSIS
Single tube backbone chassis with separate fiberglass two-door coupe body

SPECIAL FEATURES

The A110's single spine-type chassis is light and strong.

A front-mounted fuel tank doesn't leave too much space for luggage.

RUNNING GEAR
Steering: Rack-and-pinion

Front suspension: Double unequal-length wishbones, coil springs, telescopic shocks and anti-roll bar

Rear suspension: Swing axles with double coil springs/shock units per side

Brakes: Four-wheel discs, 10.2 in. dia.

Wheels: Alloy, 5.5 in. x 13 in.

Tires: Michelin or Dunlop radials, 185/70 VR13

DIMENSIONS
Length: 151.6 in. **Width:** 59.8 in.

Height: 44.5 in. **Wheelbase:** 82.7 in.

Track: 53.5 in. (front), 53.5 in. (rear)

Curb weight: 1,566 lbs.

Wishbone front suspension
The front suspension was an effective system of upper and lower unequal-length wishbones with concentric coil spring/shock units and an anti-roll bar.

Dual shock absorbers
Whether fitted with swing axles or double wishbone rear suspension, there are two coil/shock units on each side.

Renault DAUPHINE

One of the Dauphine's greatest strengths was its style. Nothing in its class could match its smart, rounded and aerodynamic appearance. Despite problems with build quality, it reestablished the Renault name.

Sliding side windows

Although the front windows wind up and down in the usual way, the rear side windows are of the simpler sliding type to keep manufacturing costs down

Four-cylinder engine

In standard form, the 845-cc four-cylinder engine was in a deliberately low state of tune to ensure a long and reliable life. There was much more torque than power from the long-stroke engine.

Supercharged option

Many Dauphines were sold in the U.S. As an option, the Judson Research and Manufacturing Co. of Conshokocken, England offered a supercharger kit for just $165. It virtually halved the 0-60 time to 15.5 seconds.

Magnetic clutch

Dauphine drivers had the option of the Ferlec magnetic clutch to turn the car into a semi-automatic. When the shifter is moved, the magnetic system automatically comes into operation to disengage the clutch.

Wishbone front suspension

The front suspension was quite advanced, consisting of double wishbones with concentric springs and telescopic shocks. It is mounted on a subframe bolted to the body.

Rear radiator

So that the Dauphine could have trunk space under the front cover with decent capacity, the radiator is located in the rear, inside the engine bay.

Specifications

1957 Renault Dauphine

ENGINE

Type: Inline four-cylinder

Construction: Cast-iron block and alloy cylinder head

Valve gear: Two valves per cylinder operated by a single block-mounted camshaft with pushrods and rockers

Bore and stroke: 2.28 in. x 3.15 in.

Displacement: 845 cc

Compression ratio: 7.25:1

Induction system: Single Solex carburetor

Maximum power: 30 bhp at 4,200 rpm

Maximum torque: 48 lb-ft at 2,000 rpm

Top speed: 71 mph

0–60 mph: 31.6 sec.

TRANSMISSION

Three-speed manual

BODY/CHASSIS

Unitary monocoque construction with four door sedan body

SPECIAL FEATURES

The spare tire is carried under the front cover. Access is gained through a panel hidden under the license plate.

Air for the rear-mounted radiator enters through grills in front sections of the rear wheels.

RUNNING GEAR

Steering: Rack-and-pinion

Front suspension: Double wishbones with coil springs and telescopic shock absorbers

Rear suspension: Swing axles with coil springs and telescopic shock absorbers

Brakes: Drums, 8.9-in. dia. (front and rear)

Wheels: Pressed-steel disc, 15-in. dia.

Tires: 5.20 x 15

DIMENSIONS

Length: 155.0 in.   **Width:** 60.0 in.

Height: 57.0 in.   **Wheelbase:** 89.5 in.

Track: 49.5 in. (front), 48.0 in. (rear)

Weight: 1,360 lbs.

Riley **RM ROADSTER** 🇬🇧

Designed by the company's own stylist, the 2.5-liter Riley looked its best as a four-door sedan, whereas the two-door RMC was designed to win buyers here in the U.S.

Twin-cam engine

Although the 2.5-liter four-cylinder is a twin-cam engine, its layout is designed simply to give a good combustion chamber shape, not high revs. The long-stroke design helps give an impressive amount of torque at only 3,000 rpm.

Rack-and-pinion steering

With its 1940s model, Riley became the first British manufacturer to go into production with a combination of double A-arm front suspension and rack-and-pinion steering, setting the standard for years to come.

Mohair hood

The Roadster was an expensive car, and Riley made sure the quality of the convertible top was high. There is no power operation, but the headliner is made from mohair and fully lined.

Drum brakes

The Riley's Girling hydro-mechanical brake system sounds antiquated, with just the front drums having hydraulic operation and a mechanical linkage for the rear drums. It works surprisingly well, though, because most of the braking force is taken by the front wheels.

V-shaped windshield

The RMC Roadster has a flat windshield because an integral part of that car's design was a windshield that folded flat. In theory, this would increase the car's top speed.

Wood-framed bodywork

Riley used very traditional methods for making their car bodies, relying on an ash wood frame over which steel panels could be fastened. It means the bodies play very little part in the overall structural stiffness of the cars.

Specifications

1950 Riley RMC Roadster

ENGINE

Type: In-line four-cylinder

Construction: Cast-iron block and head

Valve gear: Two valves per cylinder operated by two block-mounted camshafts with pushrods and rockers

Bore and stroke: 3.17 in. x 4.72 in.

Displacement: 2,443 cc

Compression ratio: 6.8:1

Induction system: Two SU carburetors

Maximum power: 100 bhp at 4,500 rpm

Maximum torque: 134 lb-ft at 3,000 rpm

Top speed: 98 mph

0–60 mph: 19.0 sec.

TRANSMISSION

Four-speed manual

BODY/CHASSIS

Separate steel box-section perimeter chassis frame with wood-framed steel body.

SPECIAL FEATURES

The unusual stalked rear lights make the rear of the RMC easily recognizable.

The distinctive sweep on the top of the grill is a feature of all Rileys.

RUNNING GEAR

Steering: Rack-and-pinion

Front suspension: Double A-arms with longitudinal torsion bars and telescopic shock absorbers

Rear suspension: Live axle with semi-elliptic leaf springs and hydraulic shock absorbers

Brakes: Drums, 12.0-inch dia. (front and rear)

Wheels: Pressed steel disc, 6 x 16 in.

Tires: Crossply, 6.00 x 16

DIMENSIONS

Length: 186.0 in.   **Width:** 63.5 in.

Height: 55.0 in.   **Wheelbase:** 119.0 in.

Track: 52.3 in. (front and rear)

Weight: 3,052 lbs.

Rolls-Royce **CAMARGUE** 🇬🇧

Opulent and ultra-expensive—the Camargue certainly made a statement about its owner. Each Camargue took six months to build, leaving the factory at a rate never higher than one per week.

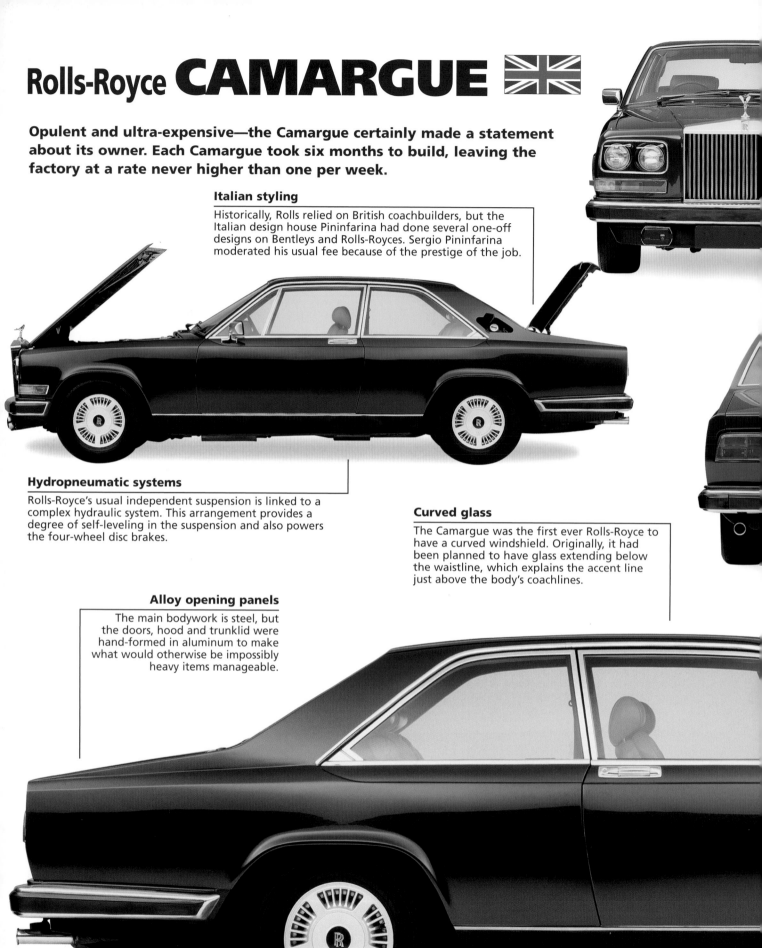

Italian styling

Historically, Rolls relied on British coachbuilders, but the Italian design house Pininfarina had done several one-off designs on Bentleys and Rolls-Royces. Sergio Pininfarina moderated his usual fee because of the prestige of the job.

Hydropneumatic systems

Rolls-Royce's usual independent suspension is linked to a complex hydraulic system. This arrangement provides a degree of self-leveling in the suspension and also powers the four-wheel disc brakes.

Curved glass

The Camargue was the first ever Rolls-Royce to have a curved windshield. Originally, it had been planned to have glass extending below the waistline, which explains the accent line just above the body's coachlines.

Alloy opening panels

The main bodywork is steel, but the doors, hood and trunklid were hand-formed in aluminum to make what would otherwise be impossibly heavy items manageable.

Height of opulence

The luxurious interior has leather upholstery, split-level air conditioning, cigar lighters in the front and rear and folding trays.

Imposing grill

All Rolls-Royces have an impressive front grill, but the Camargue's is unusual in two respects. First, it is angled forward slightly at the top, and second, it is the widest grill ever to appear on a Rolls-Royce.

Split-level air conditioning

The star technical attraction of the Camargue was its amazing and effective split-level air conditioning system, which cost nearly 10 percent of the value of the car and had the cooling capacity of 30 domestic refrigerators.

Specifications

1980 Rolls-Royce Camargue

ENGINE

Type: V8

Construction: Aluminum block and heads

Valve gear: Two valves per cylinder operated by a single camshaft via pushrods and rockers

Bore and stroke: 4.10 in. x 3.90 in.

Displacement: 6,750 cc

Compression ratio: 7.3:1

Induction system: Twin SU sidedraft carburetors

Maximum power: 220 bhp at 4,000 rpm (est.)

Maximum torque: 330 lb-ft at 2,500 rpm (est.)

Top speed: 130 mph

0–60 mph: 9.7 sec.

TRANSMISSION

Three-speed automatic

BODY/CHASSIS

Unitary monocoque construction with subframes and steel two-door coupe body

SPECIAL FEATURES

The four headlights have their own individual wipers and washers.

On the Camargue, the traditional 'Flying Lady' mascot adorns the widest-ever Rolls-Royce grill.

RUNNING GEAR

Steering: Rack-and-pinion

Front suspension: Wishbones with coil springs, self-leveling, telescopic shock absorbers and anti-roll bar

Rear suspension: Semi-trailing arms with coil springs, self-leveling, telescopic shock absorbers and anti-roll bar

Brakes: Vented discs (front), solid discs (rear)

Wheels: Steel or alloy, 15-in. dia.

Tires: HR70 x 15

DIMENSIONS

Length: 203.5 in. **Width:** 75.6 in.

Height: 57.9 in. **Wheelbase:** 120.1 in.

Track: 60.0 in. (front), 59.6 in. (rear)

Weight: 5,175 lbs.

Rolls-Royce **PHANTOM I**

The Phantom I chassis could carry a variety of coachbuilt bodies depending on customer requirements. The most attractive of all are those built at the Rolls' factory in Springfield, Massachusetts.

Overhead-valve engine

Based on the 40/50 engine, but with overhead valves, pushrods and a single block-mounted camshaft, the long-stroke, 7.7-liter six boasts phenomenal torque (320 lb-ft) for its day.

Twin ignition system

Because ignition systems were not that reliable in the 1920s, Rolls-Royce used a twin-spark system with two spark plugs for each cylinder; a magneto fired one set and a coil was used for the others. This all changed for the Phantom II. Rolls-Royce felt confident enough to use just one set of plugs.

Solid front axle

Rolls-Royce continued to use a solid front axle with the wheels turning on kingpins. The whole setup is supported and located by semi-elliptic leaf springs.

Nickel plating

To make the finish as durable as possible, Rolls-Royce did not rely on electroplating and chroming but used extremely thin sheets of nickel (0.006 inches thick) which were cut and soldered to the metal.

Drum brakes
It was not until 1924 that Rolls-Royce relied on front brakes. The Phantom I has mechanically operated drums front and rear with a servo driven by the transmission.

Live rear axle
Unlike the Ghost, the Phantom I has cantilever leaf springs for the live axle.

Spirit of Ecstasy
The famous 'Spirit of Ecstasy' radiator mascot was modeled by Charles Sykes.

Specifications

1927 Rolls-Royce Phantom I

ENGINE
Type: In-line six-cylinder

Construction: Cast-iron block and head

Valve gear: Two valves per cylinder operated by a single block-mounted camshaft

Bore and stroke: 4.25 in. x 5.50 in.

Displacement: 7,668 cc

Compression ratio: 4.5:1

Induction system: Single Rolls-Royce twin-jet carburetor

Maximum power: 107 bhp at 2,500 rpm

Maximum torque: 320 lb-ft at 1,200 rpm

Top speed: 80 mph

0–60 mph: 24.0 sec.

TRANSMISSION
Four-speed manual

BODY/CHASSIS
Separate ladder-type channel section chassis with customer's choice of bodywork

SPECIAL FEATURES

A spotlight carried on the A-pillar was to help the driver read signs at night.

There was ample storage space in the Phantom's capacious trunk.

RUNNING GEAR
Steering: Worm-and-nut

Front suspension: Solid axle with semi-elliptic leaf springs and friction shock absorbers

Rear suspension: Live axle with cantilever leaf springs and friction shock absorbers

Brakes: Drums (front and rear)

Wheels: Wire spoke, 21-in. dia.

Tires: 7.00 x 21

DIMENSIONS
Length: 190.3 in. **Width:** 72.0 in.

Height: 60.0 in. **Wheelbase:** 143.3 in

Track: 57.0 in. (front), 56.0 (rear)

Weight: 4,725 lbs.

447

Rolls-Royce SILVER GHOST

For a Rolls-Royce, the Silver Ghost was amazingly versatile. It could carry stately formal bodywork in near silence, beat all comers in demanding Alpine Trials competitions and even perform as an armored car in World War I.

Side-valve engine

There are different types of side-valve engines. The Silver Ghost's is an L-head—the valves are along one side of the engine with their heads upward operating in the combustion chambers above them.

Alpine Eagle bodywork

Silver Ghosts carry a diverse range of bodies. This is the open Alpine Eagle style as used in the 1913 Alpine Trial.

Solid axle

Like all cars of its era, the Silver Ghost has a solid front axle. In this case, it is an 'I' section beam mounted on semi-elliptic leaf springs.

Cantilever rear springs

Rolls-Royce changed the rear suspension design several times, settling on a system of cantilevered semi-elliptic rear springs.

Alloy pistons

Although heavy iron pistons were common before World War I, Rolls-Royce used lighter alloy pistons, which eased the stress on the crankshaft and its bearings.

Four-speed transmission

The Ghost's engine has a huge torque output, but the Alpine Eagle model has a four-speed transmission. This way, owners would not be embarrassed by steep mountain passes as they could be with the previous three-speed model.

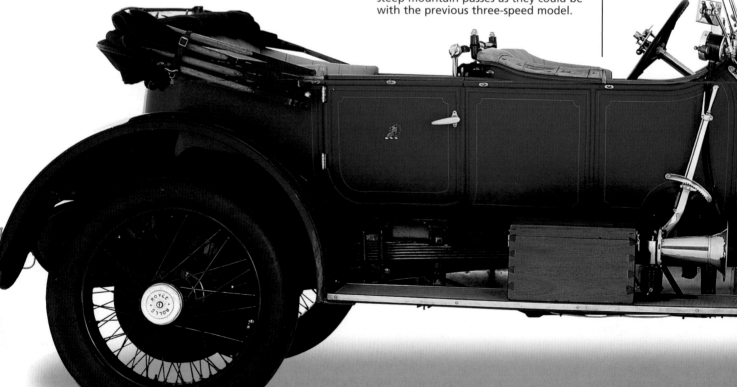

No front brakes

For most of its life, the Silver Ghost had no front brakes, even when some rivals like Hispano-Suiza had switched to four-wheel brakes.

Solid nickel plating

It is no wonder the finish on Rolls-Royces is durable. Nickel plate was applied in thin layers which were soldered to the metal underneath.

Specifications
1913 Rolls-Royce Silver Ghost Alpine Eagle

ENGINE

Type: In-line six-cylinder side-valve
Construction: Cast-iron monoblock with alloy crankcase and pistons
Valve gear: Two side valves per cylinder operated by single gear-driven camshaft
Bore and stroke: 4.49 in. x 4.76 in.
Displacement: 7,428 cc
Compression ratio: 3.5:1
Induction system: Single Rolls-Royce twin-jet carburetor
Maximum power: 75 bhp at 1,800 rpm
Maximum torque: Not quoted
Top speed: 82 mph
0–60 mph: Not quoted

TRANSMISSION

Separate four-speed gearbox

BODY/CHASSIS

Ladder-type steel frame with crossmembers and customer's choice of coachbuilt bodywork

SPECIAL FEATURES

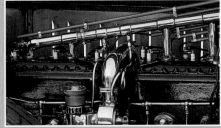

There are two sets of spark plugs. One set runs off a trembler coil system, the other by magneto.

Spirit of Ecstasy mascot was modeled after motoring pioneer Lord Montagu's secretary, Eleanor Thornton.

RUNNING GEAR

Steering: Worm and nut
Front suspension: Beam axle with semi-elliptic leaf springs
Rear suspension: Live axle with cantilevered semi-elliptic leaf springs
Brakes: Rear drums only, rod operated
Wheels: 35-in. wire spoked
Tires: Dunlop grooved square tread beaded edge 895 x 195

DIMENSIONS

Length: 192 in.　　**Width:** 162.5 in.
Height: 161 in.　　**Wheelbase:** 143.5 in.
Track: 56 in. (front and rear)
Weight: 2,856 lbs. (chassis only)

Rover **P5B COUPE** 🇬🇧

Installing a V8 engine into the P5 transformed it from a stuffy sedan into a powerful and refined luxury cruiser. Though still considered small, especially for a four door, it proved to be popular in many other markets.

Buick V8

The V8 engine under the P5B's hood really made the car fast. Because it was made from a light alloy, the engine weighed about the same as the Rover 2.0-liter four-cylinder engine. The U.S. engine was so effective that it powered successive generations of Rover sedans, and is still used today.

Front disc brakes

The P5B uses front disc brakes to stop its considerable weight at high speeds.

Front subframe

A separate box-section steel subframe carries the engine and suspension. This whole unit can be dropped out for easy servicing, by simply detaching six rubber bushings.

Sumptuous interior

The leather-trimmed seats in the P5B are deeply padded and very comfortable. Cabin ambience is created by plush carpeting, extensive wood veneer trim, chrome detailing and surprisingly modern-looking instruments set right in front of the driver.

Coupe shape

Two inches lower than the P5B sedans, the Coupe has steeper front and rear pillars. It was originally intended to have been a pillarless design, but wind noise and torsional rigidity problems prevented this design.

Power steering

Although optional on the original P5, power steering was a standard item on the V8-engined P5B. This helps when maneuvering the hefty barge at low speeds.

Laminated torsion bars

Rover's choice of laminated torsion bars was very unusual. The advantage of using them was to save valuable space underneath.

1968 Rover 3.5-liter P5B Coupe

ENGINE

Type: V8

Construction: Aluminum block and heads

Valve gear: Two valves per cylinder operated by a single camshaft via pushrods and rockers

Bore and stroke: 3.50 in. x 2.79 in.

Displacement: 3,528 cc

Compression ratio: 10.5:1

Induction system: Two SU carburetors

Maximum power: 161 bhp at 5,200 rpm

Maximum torque: 210 lb-ft at 2,600 rpm

Top speed: 110 mph

0–60 mph: 12.4 sec.

TRANSMISSION

Three-speed automatic

BODY/CHASSIS

Integral chassis with four-door steel coupe body

SPECIAL FEATURES

A fold-out wood veneer armrest with glass holders adds a touch of class.

Side marker lights are set in small housings at the edge of the fenders.

RUNNING GEAR

Steering: Worm-and-nut

Front suspension: Wishbones with radius links, torsion bars, telescopic shock absorbers and anti-roll bar

Rear suspension: Rigid axle with semi-elliptic leaf springs and telescopic shock absorbers

Brakes: Discs (front), drums (rear)

Wheels: Steel, 15-in. dia

Tires: 6.70 x 15

DIMENSIONS

Length: 186.5 in. **Width:** 70.0 in.

Height: 57.3 in. **Wheelbase:** 110.5 in.

Track: 55.3 in. (front), 56.0 in. (rear)

Weight: 3,479 lbs.

Rover P6 🇬🇧

Only 2,043 of these North American-specification 3500s were built. With its aggressive hood scoops and generous standard equipment, it is one of the most valuable variants.

Hood scoops

Only the North American-specification 3500 had these distinctive hood scoops. The center scoop is for ram air and the outer pair are for engine-bay cooling.

All-alloy V8

Rover's all-alloy 184-bhp V8 was originally a Buick design. Rover modified it to deal with the higher speeds expected from a V8 powered 4-door.

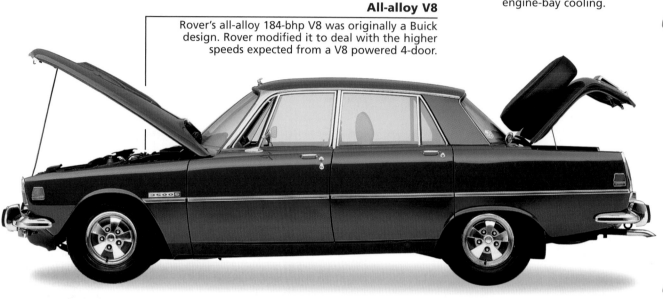

Deck lid-mounted spare wheel

On European-specification cars, the deck lid-mounted spare was an option. On cars destined for North America they came as standard equipment. It freed up a good deal of luggage space.

High equipment levels

The North American-spec 3500 has higher levels of standard equipment than European-spec models. The list includes side-impact protection beams, side marker lamps and reflectors, an ice-warning system and wrap-around bumpers.

Four-wheel disc brakes

The P6 was unusual for a 1960s sedan in having four-wheel disc brakes. There is a vacuum brake booster, and the rear discs are mounted inboard on the final-drive casing.

Bolt-on panels

All the P6's body panels are bolt-on and, apart from the roof panel, unstressed. The extremely rigid steel monocoque skeleton takes all the load. Bolt-on panels reduce the cost of body repairs.

Specifications
1970 Rover 3500

ENGINE
Type: V8

Construction: Alloy block and heads

Valve gear: Two valves per cylinder operated by a single camshaft

Bore and stroke: 3.50 in. x 2.80 in.

Displacement: 3,528 cc

Compression ratio: 10.5:1

Induction system: Two SU carburetors

Maximum power: 184 bhp at 5,200 rpm

Maximum torque: 226 lb-ft at 3,000 rpm

Top speed: 108 mph

0–60 mph: 11.5 sec.

TRANSMISSION
Three-speed automatic

BODY/CHASSIS
Unitary monocoque construction with bolt-on steel panels

SPECIAL FEATURES

These distinctive wheels identify the car as the 3500S model.

The box on the grill is the Ice-alert ice warning sensor.

RUNNING GEAR
Steering: Recirculating-ball

Front suspension: Leading top links, lower wishbones, coil springs, telescopic shock absorbers and anti-roll bar

Rear suspension: De Dion sliding tube located by Watt linkage and driveshafts, coil springs and telescopic shock absorbers

Brakes: Discs (front and rear)

Wheels: Steel, 5J x 14

Tires: 165SR-14

DIMENSIONS
Length: 181.0 in. **Width:** 66.0 in.

Height: 56.3 in. **Wheelbase:** 103.4 in.

Track: 53.4 in. (front), 51.8 in. (rear)

Weight: 3,200 lbs.

Saab 96

On rallies where the tracks had loose surfaces or were covered in ice and snow, the front-wheel drive 96 could leave much more powerful competitors in its wake.

Freewheel transmission

Because conventional two-strokes give no lubrication on the overrun, the Saab has a freewheel transmission that disengages the engine from the wheels when the accelerator is released. It also allows clutchless gear shift

Two-stroke engine

Like the 92 and 93 before it, the 96 uses a three-cylinder, two-stroke engine. It displaces 841 cc, a size first seen in the 95 station wagon in 1959.

Disc brakes

The 850 GT's front disc brakes stop the car with ease. This is a must since the freewheel transmission gives no engine braking.

Aerodynamic body

Saab's aircraft background meant that it was one of the first manufacturers to make use of a wind tunnel in designing its cars.

Front-wheel drive

The Saab's biggest advantage in rallying was its sure-footed front-drive handling, helped by the weight of the engine over the driven wheels.

Increased luggage space

A redesigned rear fender line improved luggage space over the earlier 93 model. The spare wheel is stored underneath in a separate compartment.

U-beam rear axle

The coil-sprung rear suspension uses a shallow U-beam dead axle that helps keep the rear end from lifting under heavy braking.

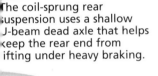

Specifications

1963 Saab 850 GT

ENGINE
Type: In-line three-cylinder
Construction: Cast-iron block
Valve gear: Two-stroke, open ports and reverse-flow
Bore and stroke: 2.70 in. x 2.80 in.
Displacement: 841 cc
Compression ratio: 9.0:1
Induction system: Three Solex carburetors
Maximum power: 57 bhp at 5,000 rpm
Maximum torque: 68 lb-ft at 3,500 rpm
Top speed: 87 mph
0–60 mph: 21.2 sec.

TRANSMISSION
Four-speed manual with freewheel

BODY/CHASSIS
Unitary monocoque construction with steel two-door sedan body

SPECIAL FEATURES

A discreet vent on the C-pillar gives much-needed cabin ventilation.

The bluff front end gives the car its 'bullnose' nickname.

RUNNING GEAR
Steering: Rack-and-pinion
Front suspension: Double wishbones with coil springs and telescopic shock absorbers
Rear suspension: Beam axle with coil springs and telescopic shock absorbers
Brakes: Discs (front), drums (rear)
Wheels: Steel, 15-in. dia.
Tires: 155 x 15

DIMENSIONS
Length: 159.0 in.   **Width:** 62.0 in.
Height: 58.0 in.   **Wheelbase:** 98.0 in.
Track: 48.0 in. (front and rear)
Weight: 1,860 lbs.

Saab 99 TURBO

Although the 99 first appeared in 1968, Saab managed to make the 99 Turbo look impressive by adding special wheels and making the cars exclusively red or black.

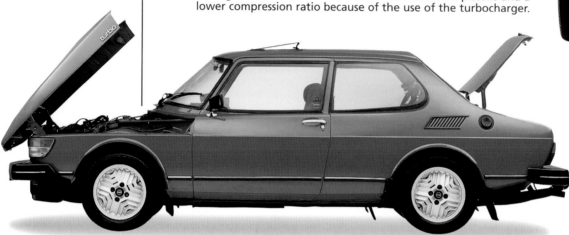

Four-cylinder engine

Saab worked wonders on the British-designed slant-four engine and made it tough and reliable. These models have different pistons and a lower compression ratio because of the use of the turbocharger.

Front spoiler

The ordinary 99 had excellent ground clearance—useful in Swedish winters. Although the Turbo wasn't lowered for its performance role, it was given a deep front spoiler to prevent excess air from getting under the car at speed.

No rocker panels

Part of the strength of a conventional modern monocoque design is in the door sills. The Saab did without and still proved to be extremely strong. The doors come right down to the bottom of the car and there are no sills to step over as you get in.

Special wheels

One way the Turbo was made to stand out from the lesser 99s was by fitting special 'Inca' alloy wheels. Rally versions used eight-spoke Minilite alloy wheels.

Rack-and-pinion steering

All the 99s use rack-and-pinion steering. Surprisingly for such a heavy front-wheel drive car there is no power assistance. The steering wheel is therefore unusually large to give enough leverage.

Front-hinging hood

Extending all the way to the cowl, the hood can be slid forwards and then hinged forward at the front for access to the engine.

Specifications
1978 Saab 99 Turbo

ENGINE

Type: In-line four-cylinder

Construction: Cast-iron block and alloy head

Valve gear: Two valves per cylinder operated by a single chain-driven overhead camshaft

Bore and stroke: 3.54 in. x 3.07 in.

Displacement: 1,985 cc

Compression ratio: 7.2:1

Induction system: Bosch fuel injection with Garrett T3 turbocharger

Maximum power: 145 bhp at 5,000 rpm

Maximum torque: 174 lb-ft at 3,000 rpm

Top speed: 120 mph

0–60 mph: 9.1 sec.

TRANSMISSION

Four-speed manual

BODY/CHASSIS

Unitary construction steel monocoque two-door sedan or three-door hatchback body

SPECIAL FEATURES

Vents on the rear quarter panels are a feature of all 99s.

Big black bumpers are fitted to all later 99s; early cars use chrome bumpers.

RUNNING GEAR

Steering: Rack-and-pinion

Front suspension: Double wishbones with coil springs, telescopic shock absorbers and anti-roll bar

Rear suspension: Beam axle with coil springs, Panhard rod, trailing arms and telescopic shock absorbers

Brakes: Discs (front and rear)

Wheels: Alloy, 5.5 x 15 in.

Tires: Pirelli P6, 175/70 HR15

DIMENSIONS

Length: 178.3 in.   **Width:** 66.5 in.

Height: 56.7 in.   **Wheelbase:** 97.5 in.

Track: 55.1 in. (front), 55.9 in. (rear)

Weight: 2,715 lbs.

Shelby MUSTANG GT350

Ford's Mustang was selling well, but it lacked the high-performance image of the Corvette. So Ford asked Carroll Shelby to develop the GT350, which beat the Corvette on the race track and outperformed it on the road.

Improved front suspension

The standard Mustang front suspension was improved for the GT350 with stiffer springs, revalved Koni shocks and relocated control arms.

High performance 289 V8

Shelby modified Ford's 'Hi-Po' version of the small-block V8 with 10.5:1 compression ratio, improved valve timing and better breathing. This gave 306 bhp at 6,000 rpm.

Rear-exiting exhaust system

The original GT350s had side-exiting exhausts which were noisy and not permitted in some states. 1966 models were given a conventional rear-exiting exhaust system.

Rear drum brakes

The GT350's extra performance dictated the use of Kelsey-Hayes front discs, but drums were retained at the rear.

Optional Cragar alloy wheels

Conventional steel wheels were standard wear on the GT350, but many owners opted for the lighter Cragar alloys approved by Shelby.

Functional side scoops

The 1966 GT350 had side scoops which fed air to the rear brakes, distinguishing it from the standard fastback Mustang.

Acrylic rear quarter windows

On the 1966 models the standard Mustang fastback louvers were replaced by acrylic windows to make the car lighter.

Specifications
1966 Shelby Mustang GT350

ENGINE
Type: V8

Construction: Cast-iron block and heads, aluminum intake manifold, tubular steel exhaust manifolds

Valve gear: Two valves per cylinder operated by single block-mounted camshaft via pushrods and rockers

Bore and stroke: 4.02 in. x 2.87 in.

Displacement: 289 c.i.

Compression ratio: 10.5:1

Induction system: Holley four-barrel carburetor

Maximum power: 306 bhp at 6,000 rpm

Maximum torque: 329 lb-ft at 4,200 rpm

TRANSMISSION
Borg Warner T-10 four-speed with close-ratio gears and aluminum case

BODY/CHASSIS
Standard steel Mustang fastback body with Shelby grill; fiberglass hood, removed rear seat, Mustang monocoque with subframes

SPECIAL FEATURES

Goodyear tires were the performance rubber to have on your 1960s muscle car.

Shelby Mustang ID plate is mounted on left fenderwell.

RUNNING GEAR
Front suspension: Wishbones, coil springs, Koni shocks and anti-roll bar

Rear suspension: Live axle with semi-elliptic leaf springs, Koni shocks and traction control arms

Brakes: Kelsey-Hayes disc brakes 11.3 in. dia. (front), drums (rear)

Wheels: Steel 6 in. x 14 in. or magnesium alloy 7 in. x 14 in.

Tires: Goodyear crossply Blue Dot 775-14

DIMENSIONS
Length: 181.6 in. **Width:** 68.2 in.

Height: 55 in. **Wheelbase:** 108 in.

Track: 56.5 in. (front), 57 in. (rear)

Weight: 2,792 lbs.

Custom fuel cap

The 1966-model GT350s were given their very own fuel cap in the middle of the rear of the car, carrying the Cobra logo.

Limited slip differential

Early Shelbys were fitted with the Detroit Locker limited slip differential to improve cornering traction and eliminate wheelspin.

Singer CHAMOIS

No other major British car maker used a rear-engined layout, but the Singer Chamois was a triumph of engineering over a flawed layout. In the Rootes Group hierarchy, Singer was definitely the superior brand.

Superior chrome

Compared to the Hillman Imp, the Chamois was a superior machine, at least in marketing terms. It came with various trim levels, such as double chrome flashes down the sides, chrome strips on the engine lid and a dummy front grill.

Luxury interior

The Chamois' cabin is also more luxurious than the Imp's. Superior features include extra instruments, a padded fascia, door panels and a standard heater.

Swing-axle suspension

All-independent suspension is another strong technical feature. Swing axles are employed at the front with more conventional semi-trailing arms at the rear.

Opening rear window

The sedan has a rear window that hinges upward for access to the rear speaker shelf, and the rear seat can be folded down to provide a luggage platform. The coupe, on the other hand, has a fixed back window.

Although it was one of the most affordable cars on the market, the Chamois was fitted with an advanced powerplant. It was derived from a Coventry/Climax racing engine that had an overhead camshaft and aluminum construction.

Specifications

1965 Singer Chamois

ENGINE

Type: Inline four-cylinder

Construction: Aluminum block and head

Valve gear: Two valves per cylinder operated by a single overhead camshaft

Bore and stroke: 2.70 in. x 2.40 in.

Displacement: 875 cc

Compression ratio: 10.0:1

Induction system: Single Solex carburetor

Maximum power: 39 bhp at 5,000 rpm

Maximum torque: 52 lb-ft at 2,800 rpm

Top speed: 84 mph

0–60 mph: 22.9 sec.

TRANSMISSION

Four-speed manual

BODY/CHASSIS

Unitary monocoque construction with steel two-door sedan body

SPECIAL FEATURES

The tiny, rear-mounted, aluminum engine is surprisingly responsive.

The petite round rear lights are in keeping with the Chamois' cute looks.

RUNNING GEAR

Steering: Rack-and-pinion

Front suspension: Swing axles with coil springs and shock absorbers

Rear suspension: Semi-trailing arms with coil springs and shock absorbers

Brakes: Drums (front and rear)

Wheels: Steel, 12-in. dia.

Tires: 155 x 12

DIMENSIONS

Length: 141.0 in.   **Width:** 60.3 in.

Height: 54.5 in.   **Wheelbase:** 82.0 in.

Track: 49.1 in. (front), 47.9 in. (rear)

Weight: 1,530 lbs.

Skoda FELICIA

Skodas were always tough little cars, designed to cope with very poor roads. The Felicia was a rare attempt to inject some fun and allure into the marque, a factor that makes it desirable today.

Four-seater cabin

Despite its compact dimensions, the Felicia is a full four-seater with relatively generous space. The trunk is also a good size.

Choice of engine sizes

When launched, the Felicia had a 50-bhp, 1,089-cc engine. From 1961, you could also buy a Felicia Super with a 53-bhp, 1,221-cc unit that was advantageous mainly for its torquey pulling power.

Fender bulge

One of the strongest features of the body design is a bold, extended arch over each front wheel. Its character is emphasized by a chrome strip running above it.

Convertible top

Unique to the Felicia in Skoda's range was its convertible roof, which folds away elegantly behind the seats. Alternatively, you could opt to fit a removable fiberglass hardtop for an extra $150. This had the distinction of being designed by Ghia.

Restyled front end

Compared to the Octavia sedan, the Felicia looks sleeker, thanks to a restyled front end. Whereas the sedan had an old-fashioned split grill, the Felicia is much more modern with its single oval grill and attractive mesh.

Tailfins

Even the Czechs were influenced by the tailfin craze. The Felicia has small fins tacked onto what is otherwise a very curvaceous bodystyle.

Specifications

1959 Skoda Felicia

ENGINE

Type: Inline four-cylinder

Construction: Cast-iron block and head

Valve gear: Two valves per cylinder operated by a single camshaft via pushrods and rockers

Bore and stroke: 2.68 in. x 2.95 in.

Displacement: 1,089 cc

Compression ratio: 8.4:1

Induction system: Two downdraft carburetors

Maximum power: 53 bhp at 5,000 rpm

Maximum torque: 55 lb-ft at 3,500 rpm

Top speed: 83 mph

0–60 mph: 24.5 sec

TRANSMISSION

Four-speed manual

BODY/CHASSIS

Separate backbone chassis with steel two-door convertible body

SPECIAL FEATURES

All Felicia models were built as convertibles.

Fins and dagger-shaped taillights mirror Detroit cars of the period.

RUNNING GEAR

Steering: Worm-and-nut

Front suspension: Double wishbones with coil springs and shock absorbers

Rear suspension: Swing axles with semi-elliptic leaf spring and shock absorbers

Brakes: Drums (front and rear)

Wheels: Steel disc, 15-in. dia.

Tires: 5.50 x 15

DIMENSIONS

Length: 159.0 in.   **Width:** 63.0 in.

Height: 54.0 in.   **Wheelbase:** 94.5 in.

Track: 47.6 in. (front), 49.2 in. (rear)

Weight: 2,009 lbs.

Studebaker GOLDEN HAWK

After the Ford Thunderbird had been restyled, the Golden Hawk emerged as just about the best-looking two-door coupe on the market in 1958. And it had the performance to match its styling.

Auto anti-creep

Another option offered by Studebaker was an anti-creep device for the optional automatic transmission. As its name suggests, this stops the car from creeping forward without the driver needing to keep his foot on the brake at the lights or stop signs.

V8 engine

Studebaker developed a V8 engine before Packard (which took over the company in 1954) and so continued to use its own V8. The biggest version, the 289-cubic inch unit, was supercharged for the 1957 Golden Hawk.

Power windows

For the first time with the 1958 models, Studebaker made power front windows available. It was $102 option and, curiously, power seats cost less than half that price.

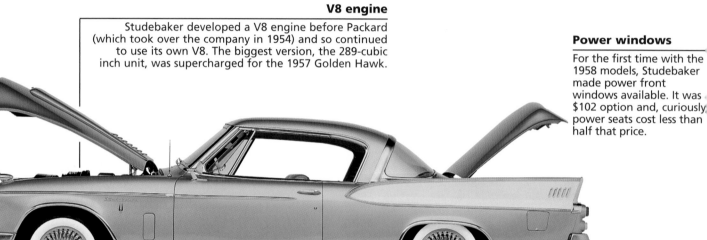

Power brakes

Disc brakes were still a rarity in the late 1950s, and so Studebaker used large drums all around. They were given finned casings to help dissipate heat and maintain braking efficiency. At this time, Studebaker charged $38 for power-assisted brakes.

Wraparound rear window

One of the keys to the Golden Hawk's good looks is the wraparound rear window, which permitted the front and rear roof pillars to be set at almost the same angle.

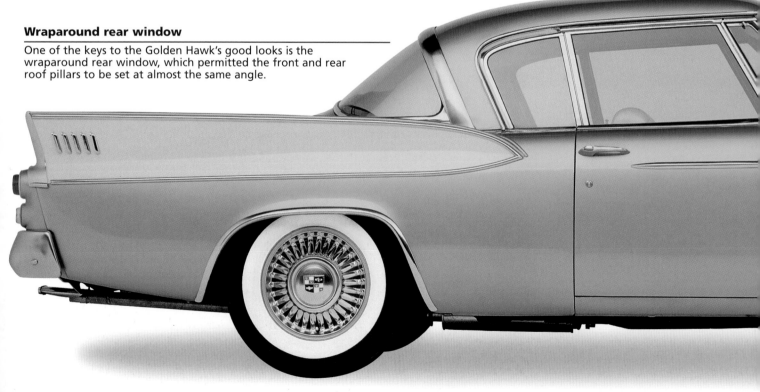

Wishbone suspension

Studebaker used independent double-wishbone front suspension but, unusually, angled both wishbones back in the chassis. Most other manufacturers had the inboard ends of the wishbones parallel to the wheels.

Specifications

1958 Studebaker Golden Hawk

ENGINE

Type: V8

Construction: Cast-iron block and heads

Valve gear: Two overhead valves per cylinder operated by a single centrally-mounted camshaft with pushrods, rockers and solid valve lifters

Bore and stroke: 3.56 in. x 3.63 in.

Displacement: 289 c.i.

Compression ratio: 7.8:1

Induction system: Single Stromberg two-barrel WW carburetor with supercharger

Maximum power: 275 bhp at 4,800 rpm

Maximum torque: Not quoted

TRANSMISSION

Three-speed Flightomatic

BODY/CHASSIS

Separate steel ladder frame with steel two-door coupe bodywork

SPECIAL FEATURES

The distinctive fins on the Hawks were originally made in fiberglass and later in steel.

A machined aluminum dash was quite a novelty on a 1958 Detroit car.

RUNNING GEAR

Steering: Recirculating ball

Front suspension: Double wishbones with coil springs, telescopic shock absorbers and anti-roll bar

Rear suspension: Live axle with semi-elliptic leaf springs and telescopic shock absorbers

Brakes: Finned drums (front and rear)

Wheels: Pressed steel disc, 14-in. dia.

Tires: 8.00 x 14

DIMENSIONS

Length: 204.0 in.   **Width:** 71.3 in.

Height: 55.5 in.   **Wheelbase:** 120.5 in.

Track: 57.1 in. (front), 56.1 in. (rear)

Weight: 3,470 lbs.

Sunbeam ALPINE

The Alpine went through five incarnations during its nine-year life span. The car shown here is the last and, to many, the best, thanks to the more subtle styling and bigger, stronger five-bearing engine.

Five-bearing engine
The Series V was the only Alpine to get the five-bearing 1,725-cc version of Rootes' four-cylinder pushrod engine. With twin Stromberg carburetors and a 9.2:1 compression ratio it makes 92 bhp.

Subtle fin
The Series I, II and Alpines had very larg rear fins. These wer rounded off for th Series IV to keep u with contemporar styling fashion

Unitary construction
Unlike the separate-chassis Sunbeam Alpine of the mid-1950s, the new Alpine uses more modern unitary construction. To ensure maximum torsional rigidity, the structure is stiffened with longitudinal and transverse box sections and a very stiff cruciform member.

Soft or hard top
From the Series III model, the Alpine was available with a normal soft top. GT versions, however, had a standard hard top which made the car marginally heavier. The Series III GT actually produced less power than its soft-top counterpart due to a more restrictive but quieter cast-iron exhaust manifold.

Wishbone suspension

The Alpine uses the classic sports car setup of double-wishbone front suspension with coil springs and telescopic shock absorbers.

Overdrive transmission

The four-speed manual transmission has optional overdrive that operates in third and fourth gear.

Disc brakes

Front disc brakes were standard from the start of production and were combined with rear drum brakes.

Specifications

1967 Sunbeam Alpine Series V

ENGINE

Type: In-line four cylinder

Construction: Cast-iron block and head

Valve gear: Two valves per cylinder operated by a single camshaft via pushrods and rockers

Bore and stroke: 3.21 in. x 3.25 in.

Displacement: 1,725 cc

Compression ratio: 9.2:1

Induction system: Twin Stromberg 150CD carburetors

Maximum power: 92 bhp at 5,500 rpm

Maximum torque: 110 lb-ft at 3,700 rpm

Top speed: 100 mph

0–60 mph: 13.6 sec.

TRANSMISSION

Four-speed manual with overdrive

BODY/CHASSIS

Unitary monocoque construction with steel two-door open body

SPECIAL FEATURES

Even the later, more subtle cars are fitted with plenty of chrome.

Smart center-lock wire wheels were a popular option with buyers.

RUNNING GEAR

Steering: Recirculating ball

Front suspension: Double wishbones with coil springs, telescopic shock absorbers and anti-roll bar

Rear suspension: Live axle with semi-elliptic leaf springs and telescopic shock absorbers

Brakes: Discs (front), drums (rear)

Wheels: Wire, 4.5 x 13 in.

Tires: Dunlop RS5, 5.90-13

DIMENSIONS

Length: 156.0 in.   **Width:** 60.5 in.

Height: 51.5 in.   **Wheelbase:** 86.0 in.

Track: 51.8 in. (front), 48.5 in. (rear)

Weight: 2,246 lbs.

Talbot **SUNBEAM-LOTUS**

A Lotus engine, modified suspension, racing transmission and unique cosmetic appeal, as well as a distinguished competition pedigree, a Lotus badge and considerable rarity, make the Sunbeam-Lotus a classic.

Lotus engine

The very heart of the Sunbeam-Lotus was its engine. The 2.2-liter unit was a modified version of that used in the Lotus Elite—it boasted probably the most advanced specification of any roadgoing four-cylinder engine then being produced.

Five-speed transmission

Unlike all other members of the Sunbeam family, which had a four-speed transmission, the Lotus has a close-ratio ZF five-speed. The transmission and a higher axle ratio allowed much higher cruising speeds.

Unique color scheme

The Sunbeam-Lotus had a distinctive paint finish. Early cars have a black main body color with a wide silver stripe at waist level. Later cars like this one had a light metallic main body color with a black stripe.

Lowered suspension

Although the suspension is lowered and the spring and shock rates are stiffer, the suspension is basically shared with the unmodified Sunbeams. That means a live rear axle located by four links, and front struts and coils with an anti-roll bar.

Standard interior

The Sunbeam-Lotus was based on the top-of-the-range GLS model. This means it is well equipped, but it also means that it doesn't feel as special as the rest of the car: for instance, there is no Lotus badging on the interior. Equipment includes special rally-style front seats with headrests, tinted glass, brushed nylon trim and a split/fold rear seat.

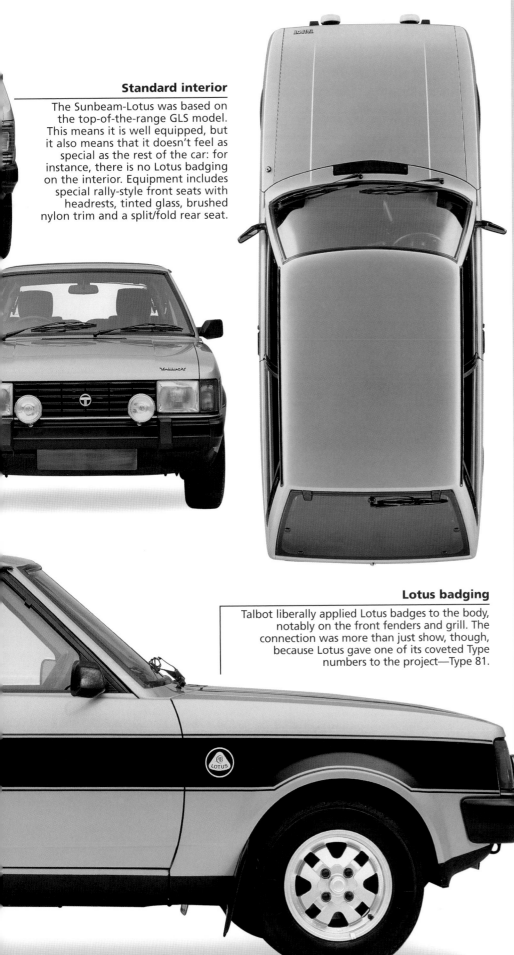

Lotus badging

Talbot liberally applied Lotus badges to the body, notably on the front fenders and grill. The connection was more than just show, though, because Lotus gave one of its coveted Type numbers to the project—Type 81.

Specifications
Talbot Sunbeam-Lotus

ENGINE

Type: In-line four-cylinder

Construction: Aluminum cylinder block and head

Valve gear: Four valves per cylinder operated by belt-driven double overhead camshafts

Bore and stroke: 3.75 in. x 3.0 in.

Displacement: 2,174 cc

Compression ratio: 9.44:1

Induction system: Two twin-barrel carburetors

Maximum power: 150 bhp at 5,750 rpm

Maximum torque: 150 lb-ft at 4,500 rpm

Top speed: 121 mph

0–60 mph: 7.4 sec.

TRANSMISSION

ZF five-speed manual

BODY/CHASSIS

Unitary monocoque construction with three-door steel hatchback body

SPECIAL FEATURES

The Sunbeam-Lotus was unique in the range in having special Lotus-designed double four-spoke alloy wheels.

The engine is based on a GM block and was designed by Lotus.

RUNNING GEAR

Steering: Rack-and-pinion

Front suspension: MacPherson struts with coil springs, shock absorbers and anti-roll bar

Rear suspension: Live axle with trailing arms, coil springs and shock absorbers

Brakes: Discs (front), drums (rear)

Wheels: Alloy, 6 x 13 in.

Tires: 185/70 HR13

DIMENSIONS

Length: 151.2 in.   **Width:** 63.1 in.

Height: 55.3 in.   **Wheelbase:** 95.0 in.

Track: 51.75 in. (front), 51.25 in. (rear)

Weight: 2,116 lbs.

Tatra **T2-603**

Tatra used the rear-mounted engine design for all of its passenger cars. The most successful model was the distinctive-looking 603. It stayed in production for 20 years.

Spacious interior

Early T603s can seat six passengers with ample head and legroom. Later T2-603 models are five seaters but still have cavernous interiors.

V8 engine

The 603's 2.5-liter, V8 engine was one of the lightest in the world for its capacity and power when it appeared in 1955—it weighs just 398 lbs.

Aerodynamic styling

The 603's smooth, wind-cheating shape with its near-flat underside, shows the car's performance potential—105 mph on 105 bhp from such a large sedan is remarkable for this period. Note the split rear window: originally the 603 would have had a fin like the earlier T77 and T87 models.

Disc brakes

Early 603 models had drum brakes, but from the mid-1960s, Dunlop discs—as found on the MKII Jaguar—were fitted as standard.

Spare tire

The spare tire is stored in a special compartment at the front of the car, separate from the luggage area.

Specifications

Tatra T2-603

ENGINE

Type: V8

Construction: Alloy block and head

Valve gear: Two valves per cylinder operated by a single camshaft

Bore and stroke: 3.00 in. x 2 .75 in.

Displacement: 2,472 cc

Compression ratio: 8.2:1

Induction system: Twin Jikov carburetors

Maximum power: 105 bhp at 5,000 rpm

Maximum torque: 123 lb-ft at 4,000 rpm

Top speed: 99 mph

0–60 mph: Not quoted

TRANSMISSION

Four-speed manual

BODY/CHASSIS

Unitary monocoque construction with steel four-door sedan body

SPECIAL FEATURES

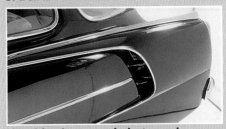

The side air scoops help to cool the rear-mounted V8 engine.

The quad headlight front end is a hallmark of later T2-603 models.

RUNNING GEAR

Steering: Rack-and-pinion

Front suspension: Trailing arms, with coil springs, telescopic shock absorbers and anti-roll bar

Rear suspension: Swing axles with coil springs and telescopic shock absorbers

Brakes: Discs (front and rear)

Wheels: Steel disc, 15-in. dia.

Tires: Crossply, 6.70 x 15

DIMENSIONS

Length: 196.7 in. **Width:** 74.6 in.

Height: 61.2 in. **Wheelbase:** 105.3 in.

Track: 58.5 in. (front) 55.1 in (rear)

Weight: 3,241lbs.

Triumph DOLOMITE SPRINT

A trademark black vinyl roof masked just how tall and upright the old Dolomite bodyshell was. However, in Sprint form the Dolomite had one of the most powerful 2.0-liter engines in production—with performance to match.

16-valve engine

Sprints have, what was for the time, a very modern 16-valve engine in which four valves per cylinder allow more valve area per piston. There is only one camshaft, but the long rockers pivot on a second shaft.

Uprated radiator

The extra power generated by the 16-valve engine required an uprated radiator. This uses a viscous-coupled cooling fan, which is driven off the engine.

TR6 rear brakes

Although Triumph did not go as far as fitting discs on the rear brakes, it did uprate them by fitting the larger drums from the TR6. On the Sprint they incorporate a brake balance unit.

Unique alloy wheels

One feature unique to the Sprint is the painted black and silver alloy wheels. Until the launch of the Sprint, no British manufacturer had fitted alloy wheels as a standard feature on a mass-production model.

Vinyl roof

With so few changes to the bodywork, Triumph wanted some way of distinguishing the Sprint from the ordinary Dolomite. It chose what was then a popular feature—a black vinyl roof.

Overdrive transmission

The earliest Sprints were only available with a four-speed manual transmission, although a three-speed automatic was added a few months after launch. From 1975, however, a Laycock overdrive became standard, operating on third and fourth gears, effectively giving a six-speed transmission.

Wishbone suspension

As usual with Triumphs, the front suspension is a double wishbone arrangement, but with a concentric coil spring shock unit working on the top wishbone. This is a legacy of the previous front-drive design which could not accommodate a bottom-mounted spring.

Specifications
1975 Triumph Dolomite Sprint

ENGINE

Type: In-line slant four

Construction: Cast-iron block and alloy head

Valve gear: Four valves per cylinder operated by a single chain-driven overhead camshaft

Bore and stroke: 3.54 in. x 3.07 in.

Displacement: 1,998 cc

Compression ratio: 9.5:1

Induction system: Two SU carburetors

Maximum power: 127 bhp at 5,700 rpm

Maximum torque: 122 lb-ft at 4,500 rpm

Top speed: 115 mph

0–60 mph: 8.8 sec.

TRANSMISSION

Four-speed manual with overdrive on third and fourth gears

BODY/CHASSIS

Unitary construction steel monocoque with four-door sedan body

SPECIAL FEATURES

Though late compared to other global auto builders, the Sprint was the first Triumph production car to feature alloy wheels.

The Sprint is distinguished from basic Dolomites by its distinctive rear badge.

RUNNING GEAR

Steering: Rack-and-pinion

Front suspension: Double wishbones with coil springs, telescopic shock absorbers and anti-roll bar

Rear suspension: Live axle with four trailing links, coil springs and telescopic shock absorbers

Brakes: Discs (front), drums (rear)

Wheels: Alloy, 5.5 x 13.0 in.

Tires: 175/70 HR13

DIMENSIONS

Length: 162.2 in.　　**Width:** 62.5 in.

Height: 54.0 in.　　**Wheelbase:** 96.5 in.

Track: 53.4 in. (front), 50.4 in. (rear)

Weight: 2,300 lbs.

Triumph GT6 🇬🇧

It may look like a fastback version of the Spitfire, but the GT6 is much more than that. A smooth six-cylinder engine and luxurious interior turn it into a kind of mini E-Type.

Tight turning circle

Like other small Triumphs, the GT6 has an incredibly tight turning circumference of only 25 feet. It almost rotates around its rear wheels. In fact, it turns so tightly that there is severe wheel scrape on full lock.

Six-cylinder engine

Instead of the Spitfire's frail four-cylinder engine, the GT6 uses the six-cylinder unit from the Triumph Vitesse. It offers a more substantial amount of power and torque than the Spitfire's unit and is more refined.

Fastback roof

The racy fastback roof is grafted onto the same lower body panels as used by the Spitfire. The styling is similar to that of Spitfire Le Mans racers.

Backbone chassis

Although its main competitor, the MGB GT, used unitary construction, the GT6 stuck with a separate chassis. It is a steel-backbone design with a fork at either end to hold the engine, final drive and suspension.

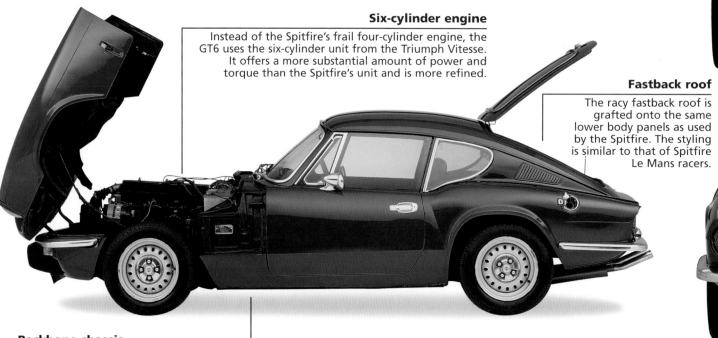

Revised rear suspension

The handling of the GT6 Mk I was much criticized, and so later cars gained a modified rear suspension with lower wishbones and double-jointed driveshafts.

Hood bulge

In order to clear the taller, longer engine, the Spitfire's hood had to be remodeled with a bulge. It was not only functional, but very agreeable with the car's performance image.

Specifications

1971 Triumph GT6 Mk III

ENGINE

Type: In-line six-cylinder

Construction: Cast-iron block and head

Valve gear: Two valves per cylinder operated by a single camshaft via pushrods and rockers

Bore and stroke: 2.94 in. x 2.99 in.

Displacement: 1,998 cc

Compression ratio: 8.0:1

Induction system: Twin Stromberg carburetors

Maximum power: 79 bhp at 4,900 rpm

Maximum torque: 97 lb-ft at 2,700 rpm

Top speed: 107 mph

0–60 mph: 12.3 sec.

TRANSMISSION

Four-speed manual with overdrive

BODY/CHASSIS

Steel chassis and two-door coupe body

SPECIAL FEATURES

Louvered vents on the C-pillar improve cabin ventilation.

The fold-forward, clamshell hood allows excellent access to the engine.

RUNNING GEAR

Steering: Rack-and-pinion

Front suspension: Double wishbones with coil springs and telescopic shock absorbers

Rear suspension: Swing axles with a transverse semi-elliptic leaf spring and telescopic shock absorbers

Brakes: Discs (front), drums (rear)

Wheels: Steel, 4.5 x 13 in.

Tires: Dunlop, 15SR-13

DIMENSIONS

Length: 149.0 in.   **Width:** 58.5 in.

Height: 47.5 in.   **Wheelbase:** 83.0 in.

Track: 49.0 in. (front), 51.0 in. (rear)

Weight: 2,013 lbs.

Triumph SPITFIRE

Compared to the cramped MG Midget, the Triumph Spitfire heralded a new beginning for sports car drivers. Nimble and agile, yet willing and exciting to drive, it became one of the best-selling sports cars of all time.

Swing-forward front end

All Spitfires feature a one-piece front end, encompassing the hood and front fenders. It swings forward for easy access to the engine and front suspension.

Improved soft-top

The Spitfire was conceived as a traditional-style British sports car with an open roof. The first Spitfires had a completely removable top. However, a much more practical soft-top arrived in 1967 on the Mk III. A detachable steel hardtop was optional.

Rack-and-pinion steering

The very light and direct steering derived from the Herald was remarkable for the tightness of its turning circle. At 23 feet, it was the tightest of any production car.

Overdrive option

No other small sports car offered optional overdrive. This Laycock device, operating on third and fourth gears, made highway cruising much more relaxed.

Michelotti styling

One of the main advantages of the Spitfire over the slab-sided MG Midget was its Italian styling by Michelotti. Michelotti was used again in 1970 to restyle the front and rear ends, notably adding a cut-off 'Kamm' tail.

Backbone chassis

The separate chassis is essentially that of a Herald but with the wheelbase shortened by 8 inches. It is a double-backbone channel-section, with outriggers to support the bodywork on each side.

Specifications
1967 Triumph Spitfire Mk III

ENGINE
Type: In-line four-cylinder

Construction: Cast-iron block and head

Valve gear: Two valves per cylinder operated by a single camshaft via pushrods and rockers

Bore and stroke: 2.90 in. x 2.99 in.

Displacement: 1,296 cc

Compression ratio: 8.0:1

Induction system: Twin carburetors

Maximum power: 75 bhp at 6,000 rpm

Maximum torque: 75 lb-ft at 4,000 rpm

Top speed: 97 mph

0–60 mph: 13.6 sec.

TRANSMISSION
Four-speed manual with optional overdrive

BODY/CHASSIS
Separate chassis with two-door open steel body

SPECIAL FEATURES

The Spitfire's wishbone suspension comes from the Herald sedan.

The bumper was raised on Mk III models to comply with U.S. safety legislation.

RUNNING GEAR
Steering: Rack-and-pinion

Front suspension: Wishbones with coil springs, shock absorbers and anti-roll bar

Rear suspension: Swing axles with transverse leaf springs and shock absorbers

Brakes: Discs (front), drums (rear)

Wheels: Spoked wires, 4.5 x 13 in.

Tires: 155/70 SR13

DIMENSIONS
Length: 149.0 in.   **Width:** 58.6 in.

Height: 44.3 in.   **Wheelbase:** 83.0 in.

Track: 49.0 in. (front), 50.0 in. (rear)

Weight: 1,680 lbs.

Triumph STAG

The Stag may have gained a reputation as being a fragile sports car—and an unreliable one at that—but its mix of good road manners, Italian styling, rarity and practicality make it an attractive classic today.

V8 power

Despite its refinement, the 145-bhp V8 was the Stag's Achilles' heel. The high mounted water pump often results in the engine overheating, a notorious Stag fault. Furthermore, the engine has a tendency to blow cylinder head gaskets and poor-quality control led to many warranty claims on blown engines.

BMW-like suspension

The Stag's suspension—MacPherson struts and lower wishbones up front and semi-trailing arms at the rear—is strongly reminiscent of contemporary BMW's.

Italian styling

The attractive final shape was a combination of Michelotti and Triumph ideas. Prototypes were shuttled between the Triumph factory and the Italian design house in Turin for modifications. The padded roll-over bar was a unique feature, as were the generously-sized rear seats.

Choice of tops

Customers could specify whether they wanted soft or hard tops (or both). The soft top worked very effectively with the T-bar, and the hard top. While it looked very attractive the top was often criticized for being heavy and cumbersome to fit.

Four-seater layout

The notion of a full four-seater convertible was very unusual in Europe. The Stag embodied a belief at the time that Leyland should be setting trends, not following them. It was thought that the Stag was the type of car that would sell well in the U.S., but this did not prove to be the case.

Unitary construction

Because the Stag used a much-modified version of the 2000 Sedan floorpan, it became the first Triumph sports car to use integral unitary construction. This improved handling and reduced chassis flex.

Specifications
1977 Triumph Stag

ENGINE
Type: V8

Construction: Cast-iron block and aluminum heads

Valve gear: Two valves per cylinder operated by a single overhead camshaft

Bore and stroke: 3.38 in. x 2.54 in.

Displacement: 2,997 cc

Compression ratio: 8.8:1

Induction system: Two Stromberg carburetors

Maximum power: 145 bhp at 5,500 rpm

Maximum torque: 170 lb-ft at 3,500 rpm

Top speed: 118 mph

0–60 mph: 9.3 sec.

TRANSMISSION
Four-speed manual plus overdrive or three-speed automatic

BODY/CHASSIS
Integral chassis with two-door steel convertible body

SPECIAL FEATURES

The four-speed overdrive transmission came from the 2000 sedan.

Stags are not true convertibles because they have a fixed B-pillar.

RUNNING GEAR
Steering: Rack-and-pinion

Front suspension: MacPherson struts with lower wishbones, coil springs, shock absorbers and anti-roll bar

Rear suspension: Semi-trailing arms with coil springs and shock absorbers

Brakes: Discs (front), drums (rear)

Wheels: Steel wire, 14-in. dia.

Tires: 185 x 14

DIMENSIONS
Length: 174.0 in. **Width:** 63.5 in.

Height: 49.5 in. **Wheelbase:** 100 in.

Track: 52.6 in.(front), 53.0 in. (rear)

Weight: 2,795 lbs.

Triumph **TR5/TR250**

The very short-lived TR5 was an interim model. It continued to use the slightly antiquated style of the 1961 TR4 but with a bigger, more powerful engine. After the TR5, Triumph continued to use the big six engine in the restyled TR6, until 1976.

Six-cylinder engine

There was more involved in stretching the 2.0-liter engine to 2.5 liters than lengthening the stroke. The crankshaft was strengthened, the bearing sizes were increased and the pistons and cylinder head were updated.

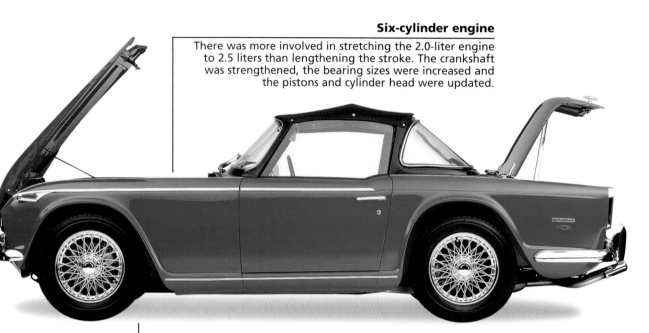

Separate chassis

The TR chassis has a steel box section frame which is narrow up front to carry the engine and then it widens out to almost the full width of the car. In the center section, there are two more box-sections forming a 'backbone.'

Optional tops

Apart from the full-fabric soft-top, the TR5/250 also came with a fixed rear window with either a steel targa top or fabric 'Surrey top.'

Carburetors or fuel injection

Unfortunately, the fuel injected engine could not meet U.S. emissions regulations and came equipped with twin Strombergs.

Center fuel filler

The TR5 has a race-style, quick-release fuel filler cap mounted in the center of the body just behind the rear window. This permits the car to be refilled from either side. It is a feature first seen on the TR2 and carried over to the TR6.

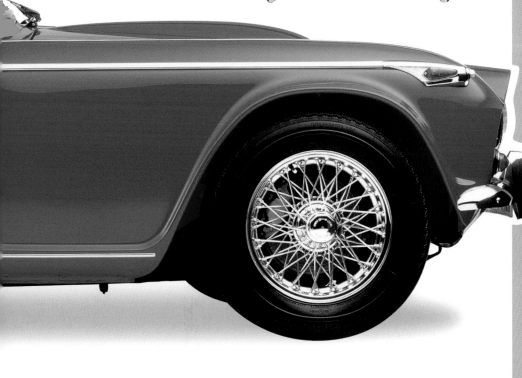

Specifications
1968 Triumph TR5

ENGINE

Type: In-line six-cylinder

Construction: Cast-iron block and head

Valve gear: Two valves per cylinder operated by single block-mounted camshaft via pushrods and rockers

Bore and stroke: 2.94 in. x 3.74 in.

Displacement: 2,498 cc

Compression ratio: 9.5:1

Induction system: Lucas mechanical fuel injection

Maximum power: 150 bhp at 5,500 rpm

Maximum torque: 164 lb-ft at 3,500 rpm

Top speed: 107 mph

0–60 mph: 10.6 sec.

TRANSMISSION

Four-speed manual with overdrive

BODY/CHASSIS

Separate chassis frame with steel two-door convertible body

SPECIAL FEATURES

Front marker lights are mounted in small pods on the top of the fenders.

The smooth six-cylinder engine is what gives the TR5 its impressive reputation.

RUNNING GEAR

Steering: Rack-and-pinion

Front suspension: Double wishbones with coil springs and telescopic shock absorbers

Rear suspension: Semi-trailing arms with coil springs and lever-arm shock absorbers

Brakes: Discs, 10.9-in. dia. (front), drums, 9.0-in. dia. (rear)

Wheels: Pressed steel discs, 4.5 x 15 in.

Tires: Radial, 165 HR15

DIMENSIONS

Length: 153.6 in.   **Width:** 58.0 in.

Height: 50.0 in.   **Wheelbase:** 88.0 in.

Track: 49.8 in. (front), 49.2 in. (rear)

Weight: 2,270 lbs.

Triumph TR6

Rugged and uncompromising, crude and old fashioned, the TR6 was one of the last of its breed and it had enough performance, style, and character to make up for all its shortcomings.

Rack-and-pinion steering

British manufacturers were the first to be convinced of the advantages of rack-and-pinion steering and the TR6 is so equipped.

Straight-six engine

The TR5 and TR6 were the only TRs to have a six-cylinder engine. The earlier cars had four-cylinders, as did the TR7. TR8s had V8s.

Foldaway top

The top is easy to put up and down. When stowed, it fits neatly away behind the seats and fits flush with the bodywork so it won't spoil the lines of the car.

Wishbone front suspension

In Britain, a sports car's front suspension was traditionally double wishbone. The TR6 is no exception.

Front disc brakes

The TR6 uses 10.9-inch Girling disc brakes in the front, while the rear brakes still use drums.

Semi-trailing arm suspension

The semi-trailing arm independent rear suspension was better than the old TR's live axle but it was not perfect, so Triumph gave it wide (for the time) rear tires along with stiff springs to limit its movement.

Overdrive transmission

Although the TR6 has a four-speed transmission, it's equipped with overdrive, operating on the top three ratios to effectively give seven gears.

Karmann styling

Karmann skillfully transformed the look of the TR with minimal changes. It added wraparound and squared tail lghts and redesigned the front end.

Dual exhaust

With a straight-six engine there was no need for twin exhaust tail pipes but this arrangement improves the rear styling.

Specifications
1970 Triumph TR6

ENGINE

Type: Straight-six
Construction: Cast-iron block and head
Valve gear: Two valves per cylinder operated by single block-mounted camshaft, pushrods and rockers
Bore and stroke: 2.95 in. x 3.74 in.
Displacement: 2,498 cc
Compression ratio: 9.5:1
Induction system: Lucas mechanical fuel injection
Maximum power: 150 bhp at 5,500 rpm
Maximum torque: 164 lb-ft at 3,500 rpm
Top speed: 119 mph
0–60 mph: 8.4 sec.

TRANSMISSION

Four-speed manual transmission with overdrive on top three ratios

BODY/CHASSIS

Box section perimeter chassis with steel two-door convertible body

SPECIAL FEATURES

Lucas mechanical fuel injection was intended to increase power, but it proved to be temperamental and unreliable at low speeds.

Karmann's restyle of the front and rear gave the TR6 a muscular look.

RUNNING GEAR

Steering: Rack-and-pinion
Front suspension: Double wishbones with coil springs, telescopic shocks and anti-roll bar
Rear suspension: Semi-trailing arms with coil springs and telescopic shocks
Brakes: Discs 10.9 in. dia. (front), drums (rear)
Wheels: Steel disc, 5.5 in. x 15 in.

DIMENSIONS

Length: 159 in.   **Width:** 58 in.
Height: 50 in.   **Wheelbase:** 88 in.
Track: 49.3 in. (front), 48.8 in. (rear)
Weight: 2,473 lbs.

Triagph **TR7**

Nothing looked anything like the TR7 when it arrived in 1975. Diehard Triumph fans had difficulty accepting it, but the new TR sold extremely well in the U.S., which was its main market.

Impact bumpers

The TR7 was designed during the height of the US Federal car safety programme. As such, it came with full-size rubberized safety bumpers, which it never lost in its six-year production run.

Four- to five-speed transmission

Early cars were fitted with tough four-speed manual transmissions from the Morris Marina. Triumph soon adopted the five-speed unit from the Rover 3500, initially as an option but later as standard equipment.

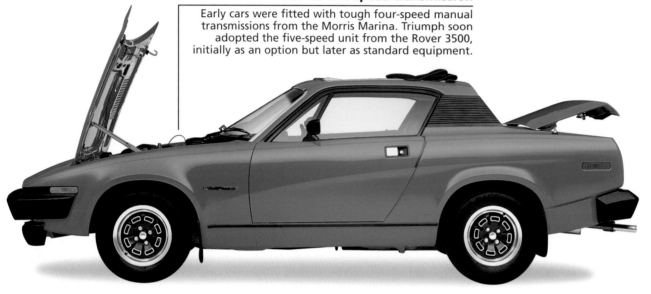

Coupe or convertible

Triumph's original plan had been to make a drop-top TR7 from the start, but concerns about a possible ban on open cars in the US led Triumph to launch the new sports car as a fixed-head only in 1975. The convertible did not arrive until 1979.

Specifications
1975 Triumph TR7

ENGINE

Type: In-line four-cylinder

Construction: Cast-iron cylinder block and aluminium cylinder head

Valve gear: Two valves per cylinder operated by single overhead camshaft

Bore and stroke: 3.55 in. x 3.07 in.

Displacement: 122 c.i.

Compression ratio: 8.0:1

Induction system: Two Stromberg carburetors

Maximum power: 90 bhp at 5000 rpm

Maximum torque: 106 lb-ft at 3000 rpm

Top Speed: 110 mph

0–60mph: 11.2 sec

TRANSMISSION

Four-speed manual or three-speed automatic (five-speed optional from 1976, standard from 1979)

BODY/CHASSIS

Unitary monocoque construction with steel two-door coupé body

SPECIAL FEATURES

Export versions, particularly U.S. cars, had different-pattern wheels.

Aerodynamics and U.S. lighting laws dictated pop-up headlights on the TR7.

RUNNING GEAR

Steering: Rack-and-pinion

Front suspension: MacPherson struts with lower lateral links, coil springs, shock absorbers and anti-roll bar

Rear suspension: Live axle with trailing arms, radius arms, coil springs, shock absorbers and anti-roll bar

Brakes: Discs (front), drums (rear)

Wheels: Steel 13 in. dia.

Tyres: 175/70 HR13

DIMENSIONS

Length: 164.5 in.

Width: 66.2 in.

Height: 49.9 in.

Wheelbase: 85.0 in.

Track: 55.5 in. (front), 55.3 in. (rear)

Weight: 2240 lbs.

Live rear axle

Triumph opted to use a simple live rear axle in the TR7. It is located by lower trailing arms and upper oblique radius arms and suspended by coil springs.

Controversial styling

Triumph described its new coupé as "the shape of things to come" and as "the bold wedge line of the great international sports racers." The bold wedge shape was penned by Harris Mann.

Tucker TORPEDO

Preston Tucker hired Alex Tremulis, one of the best car designers, to style the Torpedo. He had worked on the great pre-war Cords and produced an elegant and aerodynamic design years ahead of its rivals.

Flat-six engine

When his own engine proved impossible to develop, Tucker turned to a converted 5.5-liter, flat-six, water cooled, helicopter engine produced by Air Cooled Motors of Syracuse.

Rear radiator

The prototype Tucker was intended to have a front-mounted radiator connected to the rear engine by copper tubes. When the converted helicopter engine was fitted, the radiator moved behind the engine.

Wishbone suspension

Tucker wanted to use a double-wishbone suspension up front with rubber in torsion for springing. The rear was intended to have trailing links, again with rubber springs. This proved troublesome in the prototype because the alloy suspension arms were too fragile and had to be reengineered. Later cars had coil springs fitted both front and rear.

Safety features

Tucker was obsessed with safety so the Torpedo was years ahead of its time in making the interior safe. The dashboard rail is padded, the steering column is collapsible, and the passenger side footwell is large enough to act as a survival cell.

24-volt electrics

The prototype engine had hydraulic valve gear. The valves remained closed until the engine finally turned over during start ups. Therefore, a 24-volt starter was required.

ENGINE

Type: Air cooled flat six

Construction: Alloy block and heads

Valve gear: Two sidevalves per cylinder in an L-head operated by single block-mounted camshaft per bank of cylinders

Bore and stroke: 4.57 in. x 3.56 in.

Displacement: 334 c.i.

Compression ratio: 7.0:1

Induction system: Single Autolite carburetor

Maximum power: 166 bhp at 3,200 rpm

Maximum torque: Not quoted

TRANSMISSION

Four-speed manual preselector

BODY/CHASSIS

Separate steel-perimeter chassis with steel four-door sedan bodywork

SPECIAL FEATURES

The column-mounted gearshift is an unusual design, in keeping with the rest of the interior.

No fewer than six exhaust pipes stick out from the rear of the car, three for each bank of the flat-six engine.

RUNNING GEAR

Steering: Recirculating-ball

Front suspension: Double wishbones with coil springs and telescopic shock absorbers

Rear suspension: Twin wishbones with rubber springs and telescopic shock absorbers

Brakes: Drums (front and rear)

Wheels: Pressed steel disc, 15-in. dia.

Tires: 7.00 x 15

DIMENSIONS

Length: 219.0 in. **Width:** 79.0 in.

Height: 60.0 in. **Wheelbase:** 130.0 in.

Track: 64.0 in. (front), 65.0 in. (rear)

Weight: 4,235 lbs.

TVR 3000S

When many sports car manufacturers were giving up on open-roofed sports cars, TVR took a gamble and chopped the roof off the Taimar coupe to produce the outstanding 3000S.

Fiberglass body

Every TVR has been built with fiberglass bodywork. It is perfectly suited to small-volume production and means that styling changes can be made relatively easily and without vast expense.

Front-hinged hood

Engine access is at a premium because the car's nose tips forward and the engine is mounted well back.

Ford V6

TVR brought in the overhead-valve V6 engine that Ford used in its high-performance Capri in England. There was no competition as the cars covered different markets.

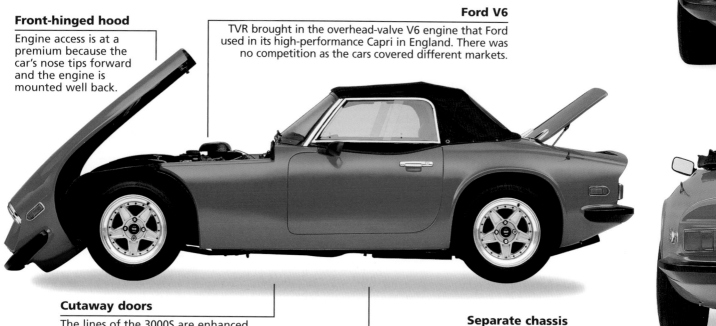

Cutaway doors

The lines of the 3000S are enhanced by a dip in the doors, an echo of narrow pre-war sports cars.

Separate chassis

In its early days, TVR decided that the main strength of its cars should come from a large, central backbone of tubular steel. The company has kept with that concept ever since.

Convertible roof

In the first version of the 3000S, the roof was a conventional fold-away type. From 1986, TVR used roof panels with a separate rear-window section.

Wishbone suspension

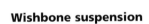

TVR gave the 3000S a double-wishbone suspension at the front, as usual, and it also uses double wishbones at the rear, with the bottom arms extremely wide-spaced to give the best possible wheel location.

Perfect weight distribution

TVR mounted the Ford V6 far back in the chassis, giving the car a near-perfect front-to-rear weight distribution.

Specifications
1978 TVR 3000S

ENGINE

Type: Ford V6

Construction: Cast-iron block and heads

Valve gear: Two valves per cylinder operated by a single centrally mounted camshaft with pushrods and rockers

Bore and stroke: 3.70 in. x 2.85 in.

Displacement: 2,994 cc

Compression ratio: 8.9:1

Induction system: Single downdraft carburetor

Maximum power: 142 bhp at 5,000 rpm

Maximum torque: 172 lb-ft at 3,000 rpm

Top speed: 124 mph

0–60 mph: 7.8 sec

TRANSMISSION

Four-speed manual

BODY/CHASSIS

Separate tubular-steel backbone chassis with fiberglass two-seat convertible body

SPECIAL FEATURES

A front-tilting hood gives good access to the Ford V6 engine.

Neat, five-spoke alloys give the 'S' its required sporty feel without looking too ostentatious.

RUNNING GEAR

Steering: Rack-and-pinion

Front suspension: Double unequal-length wishbones with coil springs and telescopic shock absorbers

Rear suspension: Double unequal-length wishbones with coil springs and telescopic shock absorbers

Brakes: Discs (front), drums (rear)

Wheels: Alloy, 14-in. dia.

Tires: Radial, 185/70 VR14

DIMENSIONS

Length: 155.0 in. **Width:** 64.0 in.

Height: 47.0 in. **Wheelbase:** 90.0 in.

Track: 53.8 in. (front and rear)

Weight: 2,340 lbs.

TVR **CHIMAERA**

Stunning looks as well as performance set the Chimaera apart. TVR styling is all carried out in-house in Blackpool, with traditional clay full-size models sculpted until the effect is just right.

V8 engine

There are now three versions of the all-alloy, GM-derived pushrod V8 engine available in the Chimaera: the base 240-bhp 4.0-liter, the 4.5-liter and the mighty 340-bhp 5.0-liter.

Carbon fiber roof

Instead of a conventional one-piece fold-down roof, the Chimaera's is in two sections: a rigid, lift-out carbon fiber center panel and a fold-down rear section.

Five-speed transmission

In place of the transmission from the Rover SD-1 sedan, TVR chose a Borg-Warner five-speed unit. Its overdrive-fifth gives a relaxed 27.5 mph per 1,000 revs in top.

Separate chassis

All TVRs have a separate chassis. It is an immensely strong construction of tubular steel that is so rigid there is virtually no cowl shake.

Rack-and-pinion steering

Rack-and-pinion steering is almost universal in sports cars, but what sets the TVR's apart is the extreme quickness of the rack. It is very high-geared, with only 1.9 turns lock to lock, making the car highly controllable in a slide.

Equal weight distribution

Mounting the engine well back in the chassis results in 50/50 weight distribution front and rear. This, plus short front and rear overhangs, give the Chimaera excellent handling.

Specifications

1998 TVR Chimaera

ENGINE

Type: V8

Construction: Alloy block and heads

Valve gear: Two valves per cylinder operated by a single camshaft with pushrods and rocker arms

Bore and stroke: 3.70 in. x 2.80 in.

Displacement: 3,950 cc

Compression ratio: 9.8:1

Induction system: Electronic fuel injection

Maximum power: 240 bhp at 5,250 rpm

Maximum torque: 270 lb-ft at 4,000 rpm

TRANSMISSION

Five-speed manual

BODY/CHASSIS

Separate tubular-steel backbone chassis with fiberglass two-seater convertible body

SPECIAL FEATURES

The rear of the roof folds into the trunk, where the center section can be stored.

All TVRs are styled in-house at the company's Blackpool base.

RUNNING GEAR

Steering: Rack-and-pinion

Front suspension: Double wishbones with coil springs, telescopic shock absorbers and anti-roll bar

Rear suspension: Double wishbones with coil springs, telescopic shock absorbers and anti-roll bar

Brakes: Vented discs, 10.2-in. dia. (front), 10.7-in. dia. (rear)

Wheels: Cast-alloy, 7 x 15 in. (front), 7 x 16 in. (rear)

Tires: Bridgestone S-02, 205/60 ZR15 (front), 225/55 ZR16 (rear)

DIMENSIONS

Length: 179.1 in.   **Width:** 76.2 in.

Height: 50.2 in.   **Wheelbase:** 98.4 in.

Track: 57.5 in. (front and rear)

Weight: 2,260 lbs.

Ultima SPYDER

The style and shape of the Ultima has evolved over the years, inspired by the mighty Group C endurance racers that run at the 24 Hours of Le Mans. It also has the performance to back up its racy appearance and image.

Choice of engine

The Ultima is able to use a variety of engines. The ones usually specified are the Rover V8 in 3.5-, 3.9- or over 4.0-liter form, or a Renault V6 in up to 3.0-liter or 2.5-liter turbo form. The Renault has the advantage that it can be used with its own five-speed transaxle. For ultimate performance, however, a 350-cubic inch Chevy V8 can be installed.

Separate chassis

The main members in the separate tubular-steel chassis are composed of 1.5-inch steel tube. The chassis is calculated to be stiff enough to take the force of a 1000-bhp engine without distorting.

Front radiator

A large four-row radiator is mounted at the front, with its water pipes running around the outside of the chassis rails. Cooling is assisted by two thermostatically-controlled electric fans, and cut-outs in the front bodywork channel the air.

Porsche transaxle

To cope with the power and torque of the Chevrolet V8, a very strong transaxle is required. The best choice is the Porsche 911 unit. A special adapter plate is needed to mate the Chevy engine to the Porsche transaxle.

Tuned exhaust

The Chevrolet V8 needs a purpose-built exhaust system to fit in the Ultima. It consists of equal-length tubular headers connected to dual mufflers and pipes, inclined at an angle to fit under the engine cover.

Quick-release wing

Different rear wings can be fitted depending on use. For racing, a full-width wing will generate up to 1,000 lbs. of downforce at speed. Both types connect to a chassis-mounted pylon with quick-release pins, which means they can be detached in seconds.

Specifications

1998 Ultima Spyder

ENGINE

Type: Chevrolet V8

Construction: Cast-iron block and heads

Valve gear: Two valves per cylinder operated by a single camshaft with pushrods and rockers

Bore and stroke: 4.0 in. x 3.8 in.

Displacement: 5,733 cc

Compression ratio: 10.2:1

Induction system: Single Holley four-barrel carburetor

Maximum power: 345 bhp at 5,600 rpm

Maximum torque: 379 lb-ft at 3,600 rpm

TRANSMISSION

Porsche five-speed transaxle

BODY/CHASSIS

Separate tubular-steel chassis with fiberglass or Kevlar/carbon fiber bodywork

SPECIAL FEATURES

A racing-style fuel filler cap reflects the Ultima's roots in competition.

Fiberglass or composite bodywork is offered on both the coupe and Spyder.

RUNNING GEAR

Steering: Rack-and-pinion

Front suspension: Double wishbones with coil springs and telescopic shock absorbers

Rear suspension: Double wishbones with lower toe control link, coil springs and telescopic shock absorbers

Brakes: AP Racing vented discs, 12-in. dia. (front and rear)

Wheels: Alloy, 8 x 15 in. (front), 12 x 17 in. (rear)

Tires: 225/50 ZR15 (front), 315/35 ZR17 (rear)

DIMENSIONS

Length: 152.7 in. **Width:** 72.8 in.

Height: 42.1 in. **Wheelbase:** 110.0 in.

Track: 60.1 in. (front), 63.0 in. (rear)

Weight: 2,180 lbs.

Vector **W8-M12**

Originally marketed as an all-American supercar using a Chevy-designed engine and a Toronado® transmission, the Vector W8 pulled the rug out from under both Lamborghini and Ferrari.

Advanced bodywork

Years before other manufacturers began using sophisticated composites in cars, the Vector's bodywork contained Kevlar, fiberglass and carbon fiber.

Aircraft-influenced design

As well as using aerospace materials and construction methods, the Vector's styling also recalls aircraft practice.

Turbocharged Chevy V8

In a bid to make this an all-American supercar, the engine was derived from a Corvette V8 unit. To produce enough power to make this the fastest car in the world, Vector used twin intercooled Garrett H3 turbochargers.

Honeycomb chassis

The advanced chassis is a semi-monocoque structure. Like an aircraft frame, it is constructed from tubular steel and bonded aluminum honeycomb, and is extremely light and incredibly strong.

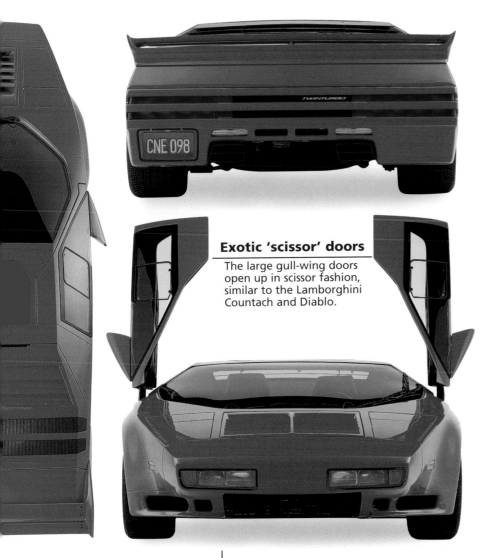

Exotic 'scissor' doors

The large gull-wing doors open up in scissor fashion, similar to the Lamborghini Countach and Diablo.

Oldsmobile® transmission

To transfer the immense power of the mid-mounted engine, Vector selected a suitably modified Toronado automatic transmission.

Powerful braking

With performance as breathtaking as the Vector's, brakes that can deal with speeds of up to 218 mph are required. The Vector has vented four-wheel discs measuring a massive 13 inches in diameter. Naturally, there is a sophisticated ABS system.

Specifications
1992 Vector W8

ENGINE

Type: V8

Construction: Cast-iron cylinder block and head

Valve gear: Two valves per cylinder operated by a single camshaft

Bore and stroke: 4.08 in. x 3.48 in.

Displacement: 5,973 cc

Compression ratio: 8.0:1

Induction system: Tuned port electronic fuel injection

Maximum power: 625 bhp at 5,700 rpm

Maximum torque: 630 lb-ft at 4,900 rpm

TRANSMISSION

Three-speed automatic

BODY/CHASSIS

Semi-monocoque honeycomb chassis with two-door coupe body in composite materials

SPECIAL FEATURES

Twin Garrett turbochargers can boost power up to 1100 bhp, a figure the Diablo engine could never match.

The radiator is mounted horizontally in the nose of the car, leaving little space for luggage up front.

RUNNING GEAR

Steering: Rack-and-pinion

Front suspension: Double wishbones with coil springs and shocks

Rear suspension: De Dion axle with longitudinal and transverse arms and coil spring/shock units

Brakes: Four-wheel discs

Wheels: Alloy, 16-in. dia.

Tires: 255/45 ZR16 front, 315/40 ZR16 rear

DIMENSIONS

Length: 172 in.   **Width:** 76 in.

Height: 42.5 in.   **Wheelbase:** 103 in.

Track: 63 in. (front), 65 in. (rear)

Weight: 3,572 lbs.

Venturi ATLANTIQUE

The Atlantique name evokes images of Bugattis. The lightweight car has many qualities, including 302-bhp, balanced handling and a luxurious interior. But best of all, perhaps, is its exclusivity—only 250 cars were built each year.

Twin-turbo V6

The transversely mounted, centrally positioned engine is a specially developed 3.0-liter V6. Made of aluminum alloy, it manages to achieve its mighty 302-bhp power output with help from twin Aerocharger Aerodyne Dallas turbochargers.

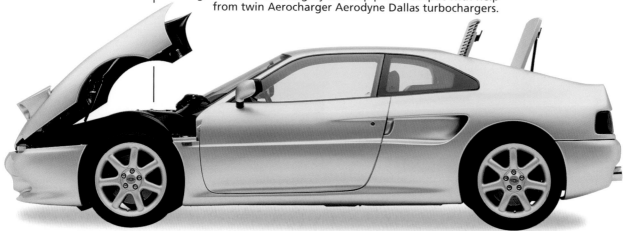

Renault transmission

The five-speed manual transmission is based on Renault's well-known transaxle. This unit has been fitted to innumerable mid-engined sports cars largely because of its compact dimensions and an ability to withstand high power outputs.

Vented disc brakes

The large-diameter disc brakes are vented in the front and rear. Anti-lock braking is standard, and the whole system is dual-circuit and servo-assisted.

Composite plastic body

The Venturi has lightweight composite bodywork. This provides the benefits of quick development times, lower production tooling costs and more affordable materials. Much of the bodywork is strengthened, and the Venturi rates as one of the most rigid plastic-bodied cars ever made.

Complex suspension

The Venturi's underpinnings were originally designed by race car driver Jean Rondeau, but after his death, they were redeveloped by racers Mauro Bianchi and Jean-Pierre Beltoise. There are double wishbones up front and a sophisticated multi-link rear end consisting of an upper arm/tie bar and twin parallel lower arms located by an adjustable tie bar.

Aerodynamic shape

The Venturi's simple and understated shape was created by Gerard Godfroy, one of the founders of the company and an ex-employee of Peugeot. Extensive wind-tunnel testing has produced a very slippery car, which boasts a drag coefficient figure of just 0.31.

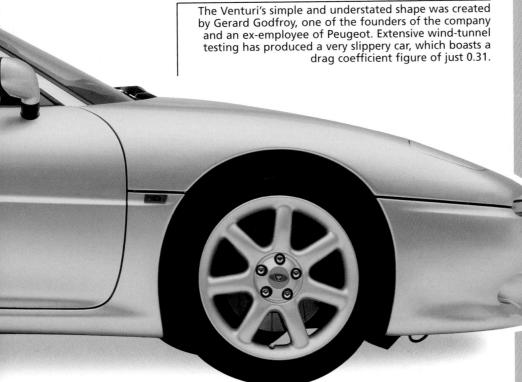

Specifications

1999 Venturi Atlantique 300

ENGINE

Type: V6

Construction: Aluminum block and heads

Valve gear: Four valves per cylinder operated by twin belt-driven overhead camshafts

Bore and stroke: 3.25 in. x 3.43 in.

Displacement: 2,946 cc

Compression ratio: 10.5:1

Induction system: Sequential fuel injection

Maximum power: 302 bhp at 5,500 rpm

Maximum torque: 298 lb-ft at 2,500 rpm

TRANSMISSION

Five-speed manual

BODY/CHASSIS

Separate backbone chassis with composite two-door coupe body

SPECIAL FEATURES

The Atlantique has four tailpipes; two on each side.

Engine-cooling vents are neatly incorporated into the styling.

RUNNING GEAR

Steering: Rack-and-pinion

Front suspension: Double wishbones with coil springs, telescopic shock absorbers and anti-roll bar

Rear suspension: Multi-link with coil springs and telescopic shock absorbers

Brakes: Vented discs (front and rear)

Wheels: Alloy, 17-in. dia.

Tires: 205/50 (front), 255/40 (rear)

DIMENSIONS

Length: 167.0 in.   **Width:** 72.5 in.

Height: 46.5 in.   **Wheelbase:** 98.5 in.

Track: 59.0 in. (front), 62.6 in (rear)

Weight: 2,750 lbs.

Volvo 120 SERIES

With handsome, full-width styling by Jan Wilsgaard, and continuing Volvo's astounding reputation for reliability, the 120-series was the car that really saw Volvo's sales take off in the U.S.

Strong engine
Volvo gained a reputation for reliability with its pushrod four-cylinder engines. This car has the 1.8-liter B18 engine with five main bearings. Twin SU carburetors take power to 90 bhp.

High build quality
High standards in the Volvo factory and the use of high-quality steel have ensured that most Amazons have stood the ravages of time remarkably well. Many unrestored cars are still in daily use.

All-coil springing
Unlike many sedans of its era, the Amazon is suspended with coil springs and telescopic shock absorbers.

Three body styles
Volvo offered the Amazon in three body styles. There were two- or four-door sedans and a five-door station wagon. Also, there was a handful of convertibles made by various coachbuilders.

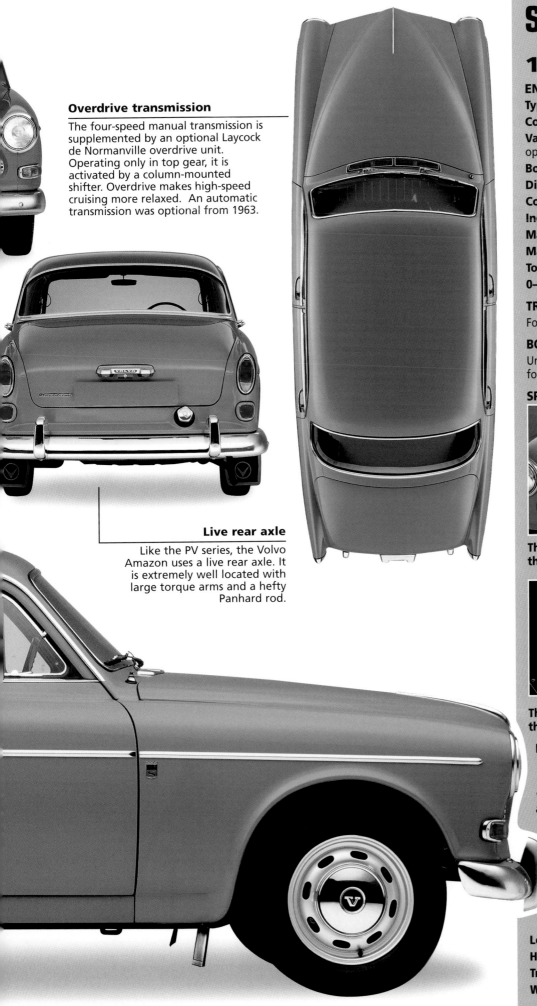

Overdrive transmission

The four-speed manual transmission is supplemented by an optional Laycock de Normanville overdrive unit. Operating only in top gear, it is activated by a column-mounted shifter. Overdrive makes high-speed cruising more relaxed. An automatic transmission was optional from 1963.

Live rear axle

Like the PV series, the Volvo Amazon uses a live rear axle. It is extremely well located with large torque arms and a hefty Panhard rod.

Specifications
1965 Volvo 122S

ENGINE

Type: In-line four-cylinder

Construction: Cast-iron block and head

Valve gear: Two valves per cylinder operated by a gear-driven camshaft

Bore and stroke: 3.31 in. x 3.15 in.

Displacement: 1,778 cc

Compression ratio: 8.5:1

Induction system: Two SU carburetors

Maximum power: 90 bhp at 5,000 rpm

Maximum torque: 105 lb-ft at 3,500 rpm

Top speed: 100 mph

0–60 mph: 14.9 sec.

TRANSMISSION

Four-speed manual; optional overdrive

BODY/CHASSIS

Unitary monocoque construction with steel four-door sedan body

SPECIAL FEATURES

The 1955 Chrysler Imperial influenced the styling, especially the grill.

The parking brake is mounted between the door and the seat.

RUNNING GEAR

Steering: Cam-and-roller

Front suspension: Independent with wishbones, coil springs, telescopic shock absorbers and anti-roll bar

Rear suspension: Live axle with coil springs, torque arms, Panhard rod and telescopic shock absorbers

Brakes: Discs (front), drums (rear)

Wheels: Steel, 6 x 15 in.

Tires: Radials, 5.9 x 15 in.

DIMENSIONS

Length: 175.2 in. **Width:** 64.0 in.

Height: 59.3 in. **Wheelbase:** 102.5 in.

Track: 51.5 in. (front and rear)

Weight: 2,380 lbs.

Volvo **P1800ES**

Volvo's 1800ES was part sports car, part station wagon and a real image breaker for the Swedish firm. The specification was hardly state-of-the-art, but it was in many ways a lively, charismatic car.

Fuel injection

Volvo's 1800 model switched to fuel injection from 1969, not only for the American market but for Europe too, which was unusual. The system chosen was Bosch's electronically controlled Jetronic, which enabled good emissions performance without serious loss of power.

Rear fins

Despite its rear-end makeover, the 1800ES retained the prominent rear fins of the 1800 coupe. This is one styling quirk that was well out of fashion by the 1970s.

Glass tailgate

A deep, glass rear hatch lifts up to access a neatly carpeted luggage area, usefully boosted in capacity over the regular coupe's. The station-wagon-style rear end also provides more headroom for rear-seat passengers and offers much better visibility.

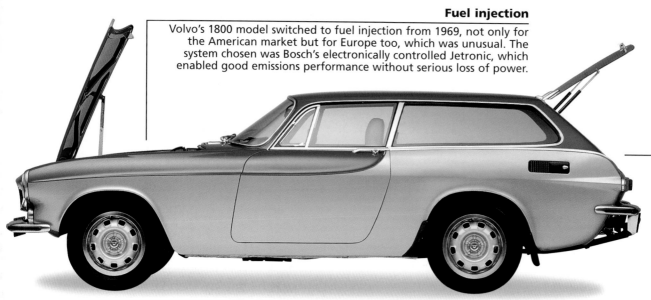

Four-wheel disc brakes

As part of Volvo's safety-first policy, it adopted all-around disc braking from 1969. That meant the 1971–1973 1800ES model always came with powered discs on each wheel.

Overdrive or auto

After experimenting with ZF transmission, Volvo fitted the 1800ES with its own four-speed, all-synchromesh manual unit with Laycock de Normanville overdrive. From 1972, there was also the option of a Borg-Warner three-speed automatic.

Specifications

1972 Volvo P1800ES

ENGINE

Type: Inline four

Construction: Cast-iron cylinder block and head

Valve gear: Two valves per cylinder operated by a single camshaft with pushrods and rockers

Bore and stroke: 3.55 in. x 3.2 in.

Displacement: 1,986 cc

Compression ratio: 8.7:1

Induction system: Bosch fuel injection

Maximum power: 112 bhp at 6,000 rpm

Maximum torque: 115 lb-ft at 3,500 rpm

Top speed: 116 mph

0-60 mph: 11.3 sec.

TRANSMISSION

Four-speed manual with overdrive

BODY/CHASSIS

Unitary monocoque construction with steel two-door station wagon body

SPECIAL FEATURES

Unlike earlier P1800 models, the ES has a black plastic grill.

Bosch fuel injection allowed the ES to meet strict U.S. emission tests.

RUNNING GEAR

Steering: Worm-and-roller

Front suspension: Wishbones with coil springs, shock absorbers and anti-roll bar

Rear suspension: Live axle with trailing arms, radius arms, Panhard rod, coil springs and shock absorbers

Brakes: Discs (front and rear)

Wheels: Steel or alloy, 15-in. dia.

Tires: 185/70 HR15

DIMENSIONS

Length: 172.6 in.   **Width:** 66.9 in.

Height: 50.6 in.   **Wheelbase:** 96.5 in.

Track: 51.6 in. (front and rear)

Weight: 2,570 lbs.

Volkswagen BEETLE

Simple, sturdy and robust: the Beetle was all of those things. It was practical and affordable too, and over the years its performance improved dramatically to keep it competitive for well over 30 years.

Flat-four engine

The flat-four engine was light, thanks to the use of alloy rather than cast iron, and the cylinder barrels could be detached for overhaul. Original power output was just 25 bhp.

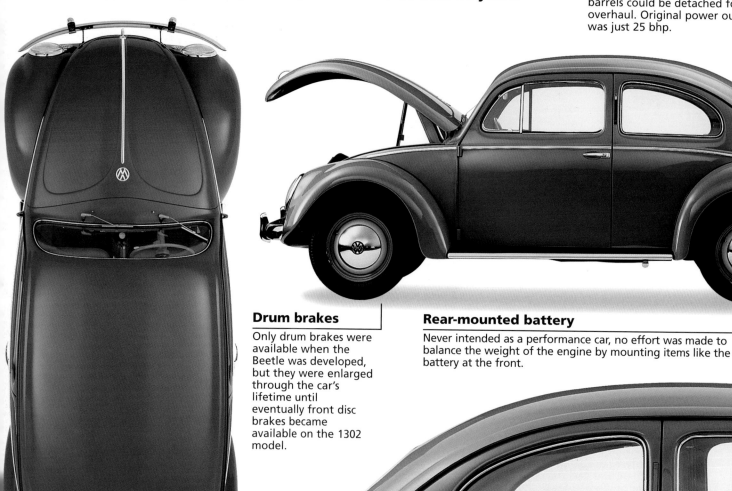

Drum brakes

Only drum brakes were available when the Beetle was developed, but they were enlarged through the car's lifetime until eventually front disc brakes became available on the 1302 model.

Rear-mounted battery

Never intended as a performance car, no effort was made to balance the weight of the engine by mounting items like the battery at the front.

Swinging arm rear suspension

Independent rear suspension was unusual when the Beetle was created, and although the swing axle system was simple, it worked well. It only became a problem when the Beetle acquired more power.

Hot air heater

With no water system a heater is hard to arrange. Early Beetles had a system which fed hot air through the sills into the passenger compartment to keep the rear window defrosted.

Flat windshield

Early Beetles had flat windshields. Later cars had more familiar curved windows that were less prone to annoying reflections.

Torsion bar front suspension

The Beetle has short trailing arms connected to torsion bars. This design was space efficient and more than adequate, even when its power was steadily increased.

Larger rear window

First designs for the Beetle showed no rear window at all. It entered production after the war with two small rear windows. The split rear window design was replaced with a single window in 1953 and was enlarged over the years.

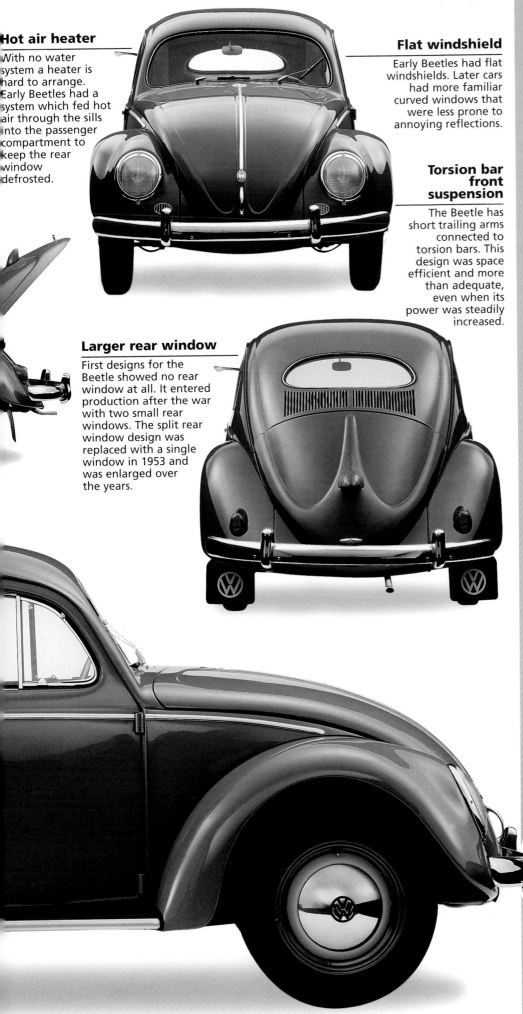

Specifications
1954 VW Beetle deluxe Sedan

ENGINE

Type: Air-cooled horizontally opposed flat-four

Construction: Aluminum cylinder barrels with cast-iron liners and alloy cylinder heads

Valve gear: Two valves per cylinder operated by pushrods from a single central camshaft

Bore and stroke: 3.03 in. x 2.52 in.

Displacement: 1,192 cc

Compression ratio: 6.1:1

Induction system: One solex downdraft single-choke carburetor

Maximum power: 30 bhp at 3,400 rpm

Maximum torque: 56 lb-ft at 2,000 rpm

Top speed: 78 mph

0-60 mph: 16.1 sec.

TRANSMISSION

Four-speed manual

BODY/CHASSIS

Separate steel body on pressed-steel backbone and floor-platform chassis

SPECIAL FEATURES

Early Beetles had semaphore indicators rather than flashing indicator lights.

Volkswagen's Wolfsburg factory was built on the land of Count Von Schulenberg. The Wolfsburg badge represents the Count's coat of arms.

RUNNING GEAR

Steering: Worm-and-nut

Front suspension: Double torsion bars with radius arms

Rear suspension: Swing axle with torsion bar and radius arms

Brakes: Drums, 9-in. dia. (front), 9-in. dia. (rear)

Wheels: Pressed steel 15-in. (front and rear)

DIMENSIONS

Length: 165 in.   **Width:** 61 in.

Height: 61 in.   **Wheelbase:** 94.5 in.

Track: 51.1 in. (front), 49.2 in. (rear)

Weight: 1,629 lbs.

Volkswagen KARMANN GHIA

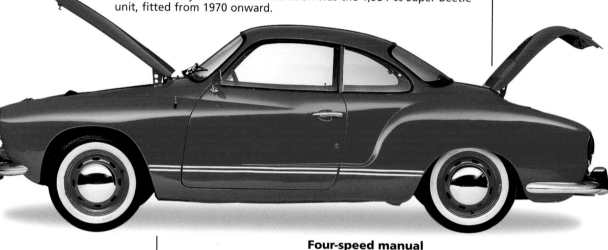

The Ghia's styling showed just what could be done with the standard Volkswagen Beetle. With a minimum of mechanical changes a new body transformed the car and it stayed in production for almost 20 years.

Flat-four engine

Although the Karmann Ghia started off with the 34-bhp, 1,190-cc version of the flat-four Beetle engine, many different versions were used over the years. The final iteration was the 1,584-cc Super Beetle unit, fitted from 1970 onward.

Rear-end heavy

Despite having a rear-mounted engine and 41:59 front/rear weight distribution, the Karmann Ghia handles quite nicely, especially once drivers have learned to master it.

Four-speed manual

The Beetle's four-speed manual was the only transmission choice until 1967, when a semi-automatic became available as an option.

Convertibles and coupes

The most popular version of the Karmann Ghia is the two-door coupe, with more than 360,000 being built by 1973. The convertible looks as attractive, although the top does not fold completely out of sight; only just over 80,000 were made, however.

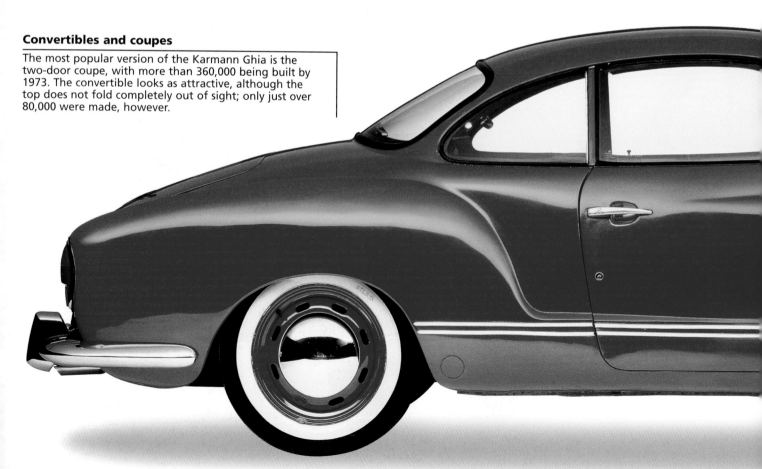

Front fuel tank

Like the Beetle, the Karmann Ghia has a front-mounted gas tank behind the luggage compartment. Total capacity is 11 gallons with a 1.3-gallon reserve, which could be switched through by moving a lever in the footwell.

Supercharged option

In the 1960s, the Judson Research and Manufacturing Co. of Conshohocken, Pennsylvania, offered a bolt-on supercharger for the engine, increasing power to 57 bhp.

Specifications

1961 Volkswagen Karmann Ghia

ENGINE

Type: Flat four

Construction: Alloy block and heads with separate finned cylinder barrels

Valve gear: Two valves per cylinder operated by a single block-mounted camshaft via pushrods and rockers

Bore and stroke: 3.03 in. x 2.52 in.

Displacement: 1,192 cc

Compression ratio: 7.0:1

Induction system: Single one-barrel carburetor

Maximum power: 40 bhp at 3,900 rpm

Maximum torque: 64 lb-ft at 2,400 rpm

Top speed: 78 mph

0-60 mph: 26.4 sec.

TRANSMISSION

Four-speed manual

BODY/CHASSIS

Modified VW Beetle floorpan with Karmann Ghia two-seater coupe or convertible body

SPECIAL FEATURES

This 1967 1500 model has been uprated with an open aircleaner.

Post-1958 cars are distinguished by their larger vents in the front panel.

RUNNING GEAR

Steering: Rack-and-pinion

Front suspension: Trailing arms with transverse torsion bars, telescopic shock absorbers and anti-roll bar

Rear suspension: Swing axles with torsion bars and telescopic shock absorbers

Brakes: Drums, 9.1-in. dia. (front and rear)

Wheels: Pressed steel discs, 5 x 15 in.

Tires: Bias-ply, 5.60 x 15 in.

DIMENSIONS

Length: 163.0 in. **Width:** 64.2 in.

Height: 59.2 in. **Wheelbase:** 94.5 in.

Track: 51.4 in. (front), 50.7 in. (rear)

Weight: 1,753 lbs.

Willys 65-KNIGHT

Some 1925 Willys cars, such as the coupe and roadster, were extremely attractive and stylish. The sedan, however, was built on upright lines designed to maximize interior space rather than look elegant.

Thermo-siphon cooling

There is no water pump for the engine. It relies on the thermo-siphon effect of the water moving around the engine and radiator as it heats and cools.

Wooden-spoke wheels

Standard equipment for the four-cylinder Willys were wooden spoke wheels. The smooth disc-type wheel could be ordered as an option and was more suited to the formal-looking sedan.

Engine vibration damper

To make the four-cylinder engine smoother, a Lanchester balancer was added. This uses two rotating cylinders geared together to rotate in different directions. As they rotate, they counteract the movement of the pistons, thereby giving the effect of a smoother engine with more cylinders.

Rear brakes

Four-cylinder Knights were not designed with high performance in mind, so they rely on mechanically operated brakes on the rear wheels only. These are the external-contracting type.

Sleeve-valve engine

One of the advantages of the sleeve-valve engine was that it improved with use. Carbon built up between the sliding sleeves after some miles, improving the sealing. As a result, the power output rose, as genuine independent tests proved.

Live rear axle

The standard form of rear suspension was used on the Willys 65-Knight, namely a live rear axle, which like the front beam axle, uses long, semi-elliptic leaf springs to locate and suspend it. The leaves are 2.25 inches wide and more than four feet long.

Specifications

1925 Willys 65-Knight

ENGINE

Type: Inline four sleeve valve

Construction: Cast-iron block, cylinders and sleeves

Valve gear: Inlet and exhaust ports cut in sliding sleeves

Bore and stroke: 3.63 in. x 4.50 in.

Displacement: 186 c.i.

Compression ratio: N/A

Induction system: Single MS2B carburetor

Maximum power: 40 bhp at 2,600 rpm

Maximum torque: N/A

TRANSMISSION

Three-speed manual

BODY/CHASSIS

Separate steel chassis frame with sedan bodywork

SPECIAL FEATURES

Brakes lights were a novel feature for the 1920s.

Rear opposite opening doors give access for the driver and passengers.

RUNNING GEAR

Steering: Worm-and-gear

Front suspension: Beam axle with semi-elliptic leaf springs

Rear suspension: Live axle with semi-elliptic leaf springs

Brakes: External contracting drums on rear

Wheels: Wooden spoke

Tires: 5.77 x 30

DIMENSIONS

Length: 183.8 in.   **Width:** 75.6 in.

Height: 77.0 in.   **Wheelbase:** 124.0 in.

Track: 55.5 in. (front), 56.5 in. (rear)

Weight: 3,060 lbs.

GLOSSARY OF TECHNICAL TERMS

A-pillar Angled roof supports each side of the front windscreen

ABS Anti-lock braking system

Acceleration Rate of change of velocity, usually expressed as a measure of time over a given distance such as a quarter of a mile, or from rest to a given speed, such as 0–60mph

Aerodynamic drag Wind resistance, expressed as a coefficient of drag (Cd); the more streamlined a vehicle, the lower the figure

Aeroscreen Small, usually individual, often semi-circular, windscreen fitted to early sportscars, sometimes hinged to enable them to lay flat

Aftermarket Accessory fitted to a vehicle after purchase, not always offered by the manufacturer

Airbag Secondary restraint device automatically inflated in the event of collision

Air cooled engine Where ambient air is used to cool the engine, by passing directly over fins on the cylinders and cylinder head

Air dam Device at the lower front of a car to reduce air flow underneath and thus prevent lift at higher speeds

Alternator Electrical generator using magnetism to convert mechanical energy into an electrical output (AC)

Aluminum block Engine cylinder block cast from aluminum, usually with cast iron sleeves or liners for the cylinder bores

Antique U.S. term for vehicles built before 1925

Anti-roll bar Transverse rod between left and right suspension at front or rear to reduce body roll

Atomizing carburetor Spray of fuel broken into a fine mist to aid combustion

Axle Rotating shafts or spindles forming the centerof rotation for one or more wheels

Axle tramp Bouncing when climbing a steep hill while exerting power in a low gear; usually only occurs with leaf-spring suspension

B-pillar the roof and door frame support behind the driver

Backbone chassis Chassis consisting of a single central structure, usually tubular

Badge engineering Selling of similar models with different manufacturer's name badges

Baffle Metal plates inside an exhaust system to absorb and reflect noise

Ball joint Ball and socket device used in suspension and steering mechanisms

Beam axle Axle that is rigid along its length, not having independent suspension

Bearing Device that transmits a load to a support with the minimum of friction between the moving parts

Belt drive Transmission of power from one shaft to another by means of a flexible belt

Bench seat Single, full-width seat at the front of the car for driver and passenger(s)

Bendix Helical gear and spring device that causes a starter motor pinion to be thrown into mesh with the starter ring

Bevel gear Conical-shaped gear wheel used to transmit power between shafts at 90 degrees to each other

bhp Brake horse power; 1 bhp = raising 550 foot-pounds per second or 745.7 watts; 1 bhp = torque x rpm/5252 with torque measured in foot-pounds

Big end Crankshaft end of the connecting rod

Birdcage chassis Chassis made from a complex arrangement of fine tubing, used on racing cars

Blown engine or 'blower' Engine fitted with a system of forced air induction such as a supercharger or turbocharger

Boat tail Styling where the rear of the car resembles the front of a boat

Bore The diameter of an engine's cylinder in which the piston travels

Bottom dead center (BDC) when the piston arrives at the bottom of its stroke

Bucket seat Seat with added support in leg and shoulder area to secure the driver while cornering, used in rally sport

Bulkhead Panel usually separating engine from cabin compartment

Bumper Rigid addition (usually) to bodywork front and rear to prevent panel damage in the event of collision, usually chrome-coated steel or plastic

C-pillar Side pillar to the rear of the rear seats supporting the roof

Cable operated Usually relating to brakes worked by a cable, not hydraulic pressure

Cabriolet Open-top car with a removable or folding roof; often abbreviated to 'cabrio'

Calliper Disc brake component in which hydraulic pistons move friction pads on and off the brake disc surface

Camshaft Engine component which controls the opening and closing of valves via lobes, either directly or indirectly

Capacity The volume displaced by every piston moving from BDC to TDC measured either in cubic centimetres (cc) or cubic inches (cu in); 1 cu in (CID) = 16.4cc

Carburetor Device for vaporizing fuel and mixing it with air in an exact ratio ready for combustion, via the inlet manifold

CC Cubic capacity, or cubic centimeters; the total volume of the displacement of the engine's pistons in all cylinders

Centrifugal clutch Clutch in which pressure is exerted on the drive plate only above a specific speed of rotation, so it engages and disengages according to engine speed

Chain drive Transmission of power via a chain passing between two sprockets

Chassis Component to which body, engine, gearbox and suspension are attached

Choke Narrowed section within a carburetor where airflow is accelerated, thus creating an increased vacuum and sucking in more fuel

CID Cubic Inch Displacement, U.S. measure of engine size

CIH Cam In Head, engine where the camshaft is in the cylinder head

Classic Specifically vehicles built after January 1, 1930 and more than 25 years old. In U.S., relates to vehicles made during the years 1925–1948 inclusive

Close ratio Gearbox with closely spaced ratios, used in competition

Clunker U.S. and Australian slang for an older car in poor condition

Clutch Device for controlling the transmission of power from the engine to the gearbox, usually by means of friction materials

Coachbuilt Vehicle body built by hand, usually by a specialist company

Coil spring Helical steel alloy rod used for vehicle suspension

Column change Gearchange lever mounted on the steering column

Compact U.S. term for small saloon car with 100–110 cu ft of passenger and luggage space

Compression ratio The ratio of maximum cylinder and combustion chamber volume with the piston at top dead center (TDC) to that at bottom dead center (BDC)

Concours d'élégance Competition judged on a car's condition and originality

Con rod Connecting rod that links the piston and the crankshaft, the little end connecting to the piston and the big end connecting to the crankshaft

Con rod bearings Bearings upon which the connecting rod runs

Coupé Two-door cross between saloon car and sports car (coupe in U.S.) often with token seats in the back (2+2)

Crash gearbox Constant mesh gearbox without synchro-nization, name taken from noise made when gears are selected

Crossflow A cylinder head which has inlet and exhaust manifolds on opposite sides

Custom Personalized paint, body or mechanical modifi-cations to a vehicle

Cylinder chamber in which piston travels, usually cylindrical in shape

Cylinder head Component which carries the sparkplugs, valves and sometimes camshafts

De Dion Axle/suspension system named after its inventor Count Albert de Dion, designed in 1894, where the driven axle is mounted on the chassis with universal joints at each end to keep the wheels vertical to improve handling, usually in conjunction with in-board disc brakes

DHC Drop-head coupé

Dickey seat Additional seat fitted to some vintage cars which folds into the trunk when not in use

Diesel engine Internal combustion engine which burns oil instead of petrol, without a spark ignition system, with the fuel/air mixture burning as result of high pressure

Differential Arrangement of gears in the drive axle which allows the drive wheel on the outside of a bend to travel faster than the one on the inside

Distributor Rotary switch which delivers the necessary charge to each of the sparkplugs at the correct interval

Disc brake System of braking by which friction pads are pressed against a flat, circular metal surface

Displacement Volume of the piston's swept area between BDC and TDC multiplied by the number of pistons

Dog clutch Simple method of engagement where one shaft has a square pin at the end, the other a square slot, requiring both shafts to be static or revolving at precisely the same speed

Dog leg first Gear selection layout where first and fourth gear are nearest the driver

DOHC Double overhead camshaft; where two camshafts are located in each cylinder head, one operating the inlet valves, the other the exhaust valves

Double wishbone Method of suspension where each wheel is supported by an upper and lower pivoting triangular framework, mainly used on sportscars

Downdraught carburetor Carburetor with a vertical barrel

Drag coefficient (Cd) Ratio demonstrating a vehicle's resistance while moving through the atmosphere divided by the flat area of an identical frontal silhouette with no axle length moving at the same speed

Driveshaft Shaft that transmits drive from the differential to the wheel, especially on front wheel drive cars with independent rear suspension

Drivetrain Entire power transmission system from the engine's pistons to its tires

Drophead Open top car with a removable or folding hood (DH). Also drophead coupé (DHC)

Drum brake Braking system whereby friction materials (shoes) are moved radially against the inside surface of a metal cylinder (drum)

Dry sump Where lubricating oil is contained in a separate reservoir rather than being held in the crankcase; often used in competition to prevent oil surge/starvation

Dual circuit braking Braking system which uses two separate hydraulic circuits to reduce risk of failure

EFI Electronic Fuel Injection

Elliot axle Front axle design where ends of the axle are forked to hold the kingpin

EOI Engine with exhaust Over Inlet

Epicyclic gear An internally toothed drum containing 'planetary' gears which revolve around the main shaft, which carries a 'sun' gear wheel with which they mesh

Ergonomic Layout of controls in an easy-to-use configuration

Exhaust Device, usually of metal pipe construction, to conduct spent combustion gases away from the engine

Fabric body Construction of bodywork where a lightweight waterproof fabric is stretched over a wooden frame; used on some veteran and vintage cars

Facia or fascia A car's dashboard or instrument panel

Fastback Body style of a car with a steeply sloping, aerodynamic rear end, similar to a coupé but usually with an opening hatch

Fender U.S. term for mudguard or wing

Fiberglass see glassfiber

Fin Styling element consisting of a angular 'fin' shape on the top of the rear wings

Fishtail When the rear of a rear-wheel drive car moves from side to side under power

Fixed head Hardtop version of a convertible car

Flathead Style of engine where the valves are mounted in the cylinder block, and the cylinder head has a flat surface

Flat-out At maximum speed, full throttle

Flat twin/flat four Boxer engine configuration where cylinders are horizontally opposed to each other, such as in the VW Beetle

Floorpan Structural floor to a car, part of the chassis

Fluid clutch Clutch using a fluid coupling, flywheel or torque converter

Fly-off handbrake Opposite operation to a conventional handbrake where a button is pressed to engage the ratchet; used for racing starts

Flywheel Rotating mass connected to the crankshaft assembly used to store energy and smooth power delivery

Four stroke Engine based on the Otto cycle (named after its inventor, Dr. Nicholas Otto) requiring four piston strokes for each power stroke

Forced induction Engine using a turbocharger or supercharger to pressurize the induction system to force air and hence more fuel, giving more power

Free-revving Used to describe an engine that responds quickly in terms of revs to accelerator pressure without a comparable increase in road speed at the wheels

Freewheel device Mechanism in the transmission to disengage the drive on the overrun

Freewheeling hubs Locked or free rotating front hubs on vehicles with selectable four-wheel drive, where the front transmission does not rotate when in two-wheel drive mode. Operated automatically via a traction control device, or manually by the driver

Fuel injection Direct metered injection of fuel into the combustion cycle by mechanical or electro-mechanical means, first devised in 1902

Glassfiber Strands of spun glass, either pressed or woven, set by a chemical process to form a rigid form. Used for bodywork construction, sometimes referred to as GRP (glass reinforced plastic) or fiberglass

Gearbox Component of the transmission system that houses a number of gears of different ratios that can be selected either automatically, or manually by the driver. Different gears are selected to suit a variety of road speeds throughout the engine's rev range

Gear ratio The revolutions of a driving gear required to turn the driven gear through one revolution, calculated by the number of teeth on the driven gear divided by the number of teeth on the driving gear

GP Grand Prix; race first run at Circuit de la Sarthe near Le Mans, France, in 1906

Grand Tourer Term originally used to describe an open top luxury car, now typically a high performance coupé

Grey import Vehicles imported privately, otherwise not available via an official manufacturer's source

Grille Metal or plastic protection for the radiator

Ground clearance Distance between the lowest point of a vehicle's underside and the ground when at its maximum kerb weight

GT Gran Turismo; Italian term used to describe a high performance luxury sports car or coupé

Gullwing Doors that open in a vertical arc, usually hinged along the center of the roofline

H-pattern Conventional gear selection layout where first and third gear are furthest from the driver and second and fourth are nearest

Half shaft Shaft that transmits drive from the differential to the wheel, commonly used on cars with a live rear axle

Handbrake Brake operated manually by the driver when a vehicle is static, usually operating on the rear wheels via a cable

Hardtop Removable car roof; a pillarless coupe in the U.S.

Hatchback Car with an opening rear panel that provides direct access to the passenger compartment

Helical gears Gear wheel with its teeth set oblique to the gear axis which mates with another shaft with its teeth at the same angle

Hemi engine An engine with a hemispherical combustion chamber

Hill climb Standing start uphill course timed against the clock

Hood Fabric covering on a convertible or open-top car, or U.S. term for engine cover

Hotrod A highly modified vehicle used for timed rest start acceleration races

Hubcap Decorative metal or plastic wheel cover, often with the car manufacturer's logo in the center

Hydractive suspension Suspension system where ride height is automatically lowered to aid stability at speed, and raised over rough surfaces to increase ground clearance, developed by Citroën

Hydraulic Mechanism by which the pressure of a fluid is used to control movement of other components, such as brakes and suspension dampers

Hydraulic lifters System of valve operation that uses pressurized lubrication oil

Hydrolastic suspension System of suspension where compressible fluids act as springs, with interconnections between wheels to aid levelling

Hypoid gear Type of gear design where drive is transmitted between non-parallel shafts, where the gears slide instead of roll against each other resulting in high pressure between gear teeth. Used on hypoid rear axle as well as many crownwheel and pinion gears, as well as worm and wheel

IFS Independent Front Suspension

Idler gear Gear interposed between two others to avoid

using overlarge working gears

Ignition Process by which fuel is ignited to produce an expansion of gases

In-board brakes Brake discs positioned towards the center of the vehicle at the inner end of each driveshaft to reduce unsprung weight, thus improving handling

Independent suspension System of suspension where all wheels move up and down independently of each other, thus having no effect on the other wheels and aiding stability

Intercooler Device to cool supercharged or turbocharged air before entering the engine to increase density and power

Internal combustion engine engine in which energy is transformed via the process of combustion in the engine cylinder and not in a separate chamber

IOE Inlet Over Exhaust; engine with overhead inlet valve and side exhaust valve

Kamm tail Type of rear body design developed by W. Kamm, where the rear end of the car tapers sharply over the rear window and is then cut vertically to improve aerodynamics

Kerb weight A vehicle's weight when unladen and without the driver but with tools and a full tank of fuel

Kickdown Shifts to a lower gear made to aid acceleration with automatic transmission when the accelerator pedal is pressed sharply to the floor

Kingpin Vertical post forming part of the front steering on older cars allowing the wheels to change in direction

Kit car Car supplied as a kit of (mainly body) components, with underpinnings often from a variety of different manufacturers. Introduced initially for those on a limited budget for construction at home, and not subject to VAT prior to 1973. Bodywork usually glassfiber

Ladder frame Tradition form of chassis with two constructional rails running front to rear with lateral members adding rigidity

Landau Large veteran car with a removable roof section over the front seats, a roof and window section in the center and a folding hood over the rearmost pair of seats; named after the town in Germany where it was first constructed

Landaulette Smaller version of a landau without the center-saloon section, having just a removable roof over the front seats and a folding rear hood behind

Leaf spring Method of suspension comprising one of more narrow strips of spring steel, typically semi-elliptic, fitted on mainly older vehicles

Le Mans Race circuit in northern France famous for its 24-hour endurance races, the first of which took place in 1923

Limited edition Made in a limited quantity, with a specification that is different to the normal production model; usually collectable

Limited slip differential Device to control the difference in speed between left and right driveshafts so both wheels turn at similar speeds. Fitted to reduce the likelihood of wheel spinning on slippery surfaces

Limousine Luxury car typically having a lengthened chassis and bodywork to provide greater interior space, often with a glass panel between the driver and passengers. Often abbreviated to 'limo'

Live axle Axle assembly patented by Louis Renault in 1899, where the axle contains shafts which drive the wheels

MacPherson strut System of suspension developed by Earle S. MacPherson in 1947, comprising a helical spring around a damper with a flexible upper mounting and a rigid mounting at the bottom, commonly used on the front though sometimes appearing at the rear

Magneto Type of electrical generator on some vintage and older cars

Manifold Pipe system used for gathering or dispersal of gas or liquids

Master cylinder Brake fluid reservoir and pump in a hydraulic braking system

Mid engine Vehicle with its engine mounted just behind the driver and significantly ahead of the rear axle to provide even weight distribution, thus giving the car better handling characteristics

Monobloc An engine with all its cylinders cast in one piece

Monocoque Body design where the bodyshell carries the structural strength without conventional chassis rails (see 'unitary construction')

Monte Carlo rally Famous rally named after the town in Monaco, France, which hosts the finish; first held in 1911

mpg Miles per gallon, measure of a car's fuel consumption

Mud-plugger Vehicle suited to off-road use

Multiplex Wiring system using a central processor and local processors to reduce the amount of vehicle wiring

Muscle car U.S. term to describe a high-powered car, usually over 400bhp

Normally-aspirated Engine charged by atmospheric pressure rather than by forced induction

Octane rating Measure of the anti-knock properties of fuel

Offset crankshaft Crankshaft layout where the crankshaft is not centrally below the cylinders, so that the con rod is more central to the piston during the power stroke to reduce wear

OHC Overhead Camshaft engine, where the camshaft is located in the cylinder head

OHV Overhead Valve engine, where the camshaft is located in the cylinder block, the valves are in the cylinder head operated by pushrods

Overheating A condition where the engine's coolant exceeds its maximum design temperature due to a fault or blockage in the cooling system or insufficient coolant/oil

Outrigger Extension to the chassis supporting the edge of the body or running boards

Overdrive Additional higher ratio gear(s), usually on the third or fourth gear selected automatically by the driver

Over-square Description of an engine in which the bore is greater than the stroke, as with most modern engines

Pagoda roof Car roof style that is concave in the middle and higher at the sides

Panhard rod Method of lateral location of a rigid axle to the chassis. Rod is mounted at one end of the axle and extends to the chassis near the other end of the axle

Phaeton U.S. term for a luxury convertible with a very large trunk

Pillarless coupé A coupé without a B-pillar where the door windows seal directly against the rear windows

Piston Moving plunger in a cylinder, accepting or delivering thrust

Planetary transmission See epicyclic gear

Poke Acceleration performance

Pop-up headlamps Headlamps that retract flush with the hood profile, used on sports cars to improve styling and aerodynamics

Power Rate of work, measured in horsepower

Pre-unit Description of a layout with separate engine and gearbox, opposite of 'in-unit'

Pre-selector transmission Gear selector system where a gear may be pre-selected before it is required, then later engaged by the driver by operation of a foot or hand control, common on buses

Prewar classic Term used for vehicles built between January 1, 1930 and September 2, 1939 inclusive

Prototype Full-size (usually) functional model of a new design

Pullman Luxury car or stretch limousine named after designer G.M. Pullman

Quarter light Small, often triangular window abutting an A or C pillar, usually opened by swivelling on its vertical axis

Rack and pinion System of gearing typically used in a steering box with a toothed rail driven laterally by a pinion on the end of the steering column

Radiator Device for dissipating heat, generally from the engine coolant

Reduction gearbox Gearbox positioned at the stub axles to reduce wheel speeds and increase torque, used to reduce weight and increase ground clearance

Retro design Styling which borrows design cues from an earlier model, typically with modern revisions

Rev counter (Tachometer) device for measuring rotational speed (revs per minute, rpm) of an engine

Rigid axle An axle or pair of stub axles where movement of one wheel has an effect on the other according to camber

Rocker arms Pivoting arm translating rotational movement of the camshaft into linear movement of the valves

Road car Vehicle meant for use on public roads as opposed to the racetrack

Roll bar Strong, usually curved bar either internally or externally across a vehicle's roof then secured to the floor or chassis to provide protection in the event of the car turning over. Used on some open-top sports cars

Rolling chassis Chassis

complete with suspension, brake components and steering – sometimes with an engine but never with a body

Rotary engine Internal combustion engine in which power is derived from a single rotor without reciprocating pistons, and very few moving parts. Pioneered by Felix Wankel in Germany, in 1956

rpm Revs per minute, measure of the crankshaft's rotational speed

Running gear General description of a vehicle's underbody mechanicals, including the suspension, steering, brakes and drivetrain

Saloon Traditional trunked vehicle with a fixed roof, two rows of seats and either two or four doors

Scissor engine Type of rotary engine typified by the Tschudi engine where the pistons travel in a circular motion

Scuttle shake Vibration, or horizontal movement especially noticeable in the dashboard on convertible cars where there has been a reduction in structural integrity

Sealed beam Light unit with lens, bulb and reflection as one sealed unit

Sedan U.S. term for a saloon car having four doors, or a two-door having a minimum of 33 cu ft of interior space

Sedanca Two-door coupé in which the front seats are open or have a removable top and the rear seats are covered by a fixed roof

Sedanca de Ville Typically a larger chauffeur-driven veteran car where the driver remains exposed to the elements and the passengers ride in a closed saloon body behind

Semi-elliptic spring Leaf spring suspension used on the rear axle of older cars in which the spring conforms to a specific mathematical shape

Semi-independent suspension System on a front-wheel drive car where the wheels are located by trailing links and a torsioned crossmember

Separate chassis Where the body and chassis are separate components which are bolted together. All pre-World War II vehicles had this configuration, but today it is used only on trucks

Sequential gearbox Gear selection layout in which the selection is made by a linear movement rather than in the conventional H-pattern, used on some sports cars and rally cars

Servo assisted Powered by a vacuum, air, hydraulics or electrically to aid the driver, giving a powerful output from minimal input. Typically used on brakes, steering and clutch

Shock absorber Hydraulic device, part of the suspension system, typically mounted between the wheel and the chassis to prevent unwanted movement, to increase safety and aid comfort. More correctly known as 'damper'

Short stroke Markedly oversquare engine

Sidevalve engine An engine where the camshaft is in the cylinder block and the valves are to one side below the cylinder head, mainly used on vehicles made prior to WWII

SOHC Single Overhead Camshaft Engine

Souped up Vehicle with an engine that has been tuned or increased in capacity to improve performance. Originally derived from 'suped', which referred to cars with a supercharger fitted

Spark plug Device for igniting combustion gases via the arcing of HT current between two electrodes

Spat Wheel arch extension commonly used to accommodate wider wheels

Spider Luxury open-top roadster, sometimes Spyder

'Split driveline' layout An extra set of epicyclic gears to provide a closer interval between the standard set of ratios, so an eight speed gearbox will actually have 16 gears

Spoiler Device fitted to the front of the car, low to the ground, to reduce air flow under the car and increase down-force, thus improving roadholding at higher speeds

Station wagon U.S. term for estate car

Straight 6, 8 An engine with six or eight cylinders in a single row

Suicide door A door hinged at its rearmost edge which opens to the front; fitted to some vintage and veteran cars, dangerous if opened while moving

Supercharger Mechanically-driven air pump used to force air into the combustion cycle, thus improving performance

SU Carburetors Type of carburetor pioneered by a company called Skinners Union in 1905

SV Sidevalve engine

Swept volume Volume covered by the travel of a piston, cylinder displacement

Swing axle Type of independent suspension of a drive axle which pivots near the center of the vehicle instead of at the wheel

Synchromesh Automatic synchronization using cone clutches to speed up or slow down the input shaft to smoothly engage gear, first introduced by Cadillac in 1928

Targa Removable roof panel and rigid roll bar, named after the Targa Florio race in Sicily

Tie bar Link or bar under tension or compression, used in the suspension and steering

Tonneau The rear seating area of a convertible, or a cover used to protect the passenger compartment of an open-top car against the elements

Torque The rotational twisting force exerted by the crankshaft, horsepower being the measure of torque over time

Torque steer Effect on the front wheels from the sudden delivery of power on powerful front-wheel drive cars

Touring car Luxury saloon car with a large luggage-carrying ability; also used for vintage models with a convertible body and two or four unglazed doors

Traction control Electronic system of controlling the amount of power to a given wheel to reduce wheelspin

Transmission General term for the final drive, clutch and gearbox. U.S. term for gearbox

Transverse engine Engine type where the crankshaft lies parallel to the axle

Transverse leaf spring Largely prewar suspension system in which a pair of leaf springs are mounted transversely, with one inverted, joined at their ends and mounted to the chassis and axle at their mid-points

Turbocharger Air pump for use in forced induction engines. Similar to a supercharger but driven at very high speed by exhaust gases, rather than mechanically to increase power output

Turbo lag Unwanted delay in response from the turbocharger when the accelerator is pressed

Two-stroke An engine cycle with a power impulse every other stroke. The fuel/air mixture is compressed beneath the piston before entering the combustion chamber v... the cylinder wall, hence ... valves or timing gear

Unibody Monocoque construction in which the floorpan, chassis and body are welded together to form one single structure

Unitary construction Monocoque bodyshell structurally rigid enough not to require a separate chassis

Unit construction Engine in which the powerplant and transmission are together as one, integrated unit

Unsprung weight The weight of components such as wheels, tires, brakes and suspension lying roadside of the car's springs

Valve Device used for regulating the flow of a liquid or gas

Venturi principle Basis upon which carburetors work: gas flowing through a narrow opening creates a partial vacuum

Veteran Specifically a vehicle built prior to December 31, 1918

Vintage Specifically any vehicle built between January 1, 1919 and December 31, 1939

Wankel Rotary engine invented by Felix Wankel in 1956, operating on a four-stroke cycle but without reciprocating parts

Weight distribution Ratio describing the amount of a vehicle's weight placed on the front and rear wheels respectively

Wet liner The lining of a cylinder which is in direct contact with its coolant

Whale tail Very large rear spoiler, initially developed by Porsche

Wheelbase Distance between front and rear wheel spindles

Yaw The turning motion of a car's body around a vertical axis, particularly prevalent while cornering